D1624961

MINDFUL
ECONOMICS

MINDFUL
ECONOMICS

HOW THE U.S. ECONOMY WORKS,
WHY IT MATTERS, AND HOW IT
COULD BE DIFFERENT

JOEL MAGNUSON

SEVEN STORIES PRESS
New York London Melbourne Toronto

Seven Stories Press
140 Watts Street
New York, NY 10013
www.sevenstories.com

In Canada: Publishers Group Canada, 559 College Street, Suite 402, Toronto, ON M6G 1A9

In the UK: Turnaround Publisher Services Ltd., Unit 3, Olympia Trading Estate, Coburg Road, Wood Green, London N22 6TZ

In Australia: Palgrave Macmillan, 15–19 Claremont Street, South Yarra, VIC 3141

College professors may order examination copies of Seven Stories Press titles for a free six-month trial period. To order, visit http://www.sevenstories.com/textbook or send a fax on school letterhead to (212) 226-1411.

Book design by Jon Gilbert

Library of Congress Cataloging-in-Publication Data

Magnuson, Joel.
  Mindful economics : how the U.S. economy works, why it matters, and how it could be different / Joel Magnuson.
    p. cm.
  Includes indexes.
  ISBN 978-1-58322-847-0 (pbk.)
  1. Finance--United States--History. 2. Capitalism--United States--History. 3. United States--Economic conditions--2001- I. Title.
  HG181.M283 2008
  330.973--dc22
                              2008018104

Printed in the USA.

9 8 7 6 5 4 3 2 1

I would like to thank the following people for their encouragement, editing and technical support, and for their wisdom, love, and friendship: Rebecca Casanova, Karen Deora, Samm Erickson, Christopher Flanagan, Herb French, Paul Halloran, Spencer Hinkle, Nikki Hurtado, Jim Johnstone, Melike Kayim, Chris Knight, Lynn McBeth, Steve Myers, Solomon Namala, Jordy Oakland, Anita Ramachandran, Amy Soucy, F. Robert Stuckey, Sydney Taylor, Kate Tosswill, Maya Trysil, Drake Wanless and a special thanks to Lisa Mann. I would also like to thank Amy Scholder, Dan Simon and the other people at Seven Stories Press for making this book come to life.

—Joel Magnuson

CONTENTS

Preface
A TIME OF DANGER AND OPPORTUNITY

The Eastern parable, Indra's Net, tells the story of a celestial net that extends infinitely in all directions. At each intersection, where the strands of the net cross, resides a sparkling jewel. Upon close inspection, however, the sparkle in each jewel is merely the light reflection of all the other jewels in the net. There is no single, ultimate source of light.

Like Indra's Net, economies are systems of interconnectedness. Each aspect is connected to all other aspects, and each problem is merely the reflection of all other problems. As economic and environmental problems in the U.S. become more severe, we can't blame one culprit or single cause. Rather, to grasp the situation and gain true understanding requires a holistic view and a clear knowledge of what the U.S. capitalist system really is.

Capitalism has now become a vast, Orwellian structure of power that spans the globe. For over a decade the World Trade Organization (WTO) has been at the center of this structure. It is telling that Pascal Lamy, the director general of the WTO, is admitting that "capitalism cannot satisfy us." The capitalist system is deeply troubled, and as it has a global profile, it transcends nations' abilities to deal effectively with the things that make it troubling. Many have expressed concern that this is rendering democratic sovereignty obsolete and communities helpless. But in fact, it is raising the importance of the sovereignty of local communities like never before. It is at the local level where people have the most democratic power and control that we see the seeds of lasting institutional and systemic change.

In November, 1999, the business and political ministry of the WTO convened in Seattle, Washington for its annual meeting. The goal of the meeting was to forge trade and investment policies that would assure the worldwide growth and expansion of capitalist institutions. Much to their surprise, the ministers were met with tens of thousands of anti-WTO protestors who were raising concerns that their trade policies undermine democracy and national sovereignty, provide little or no protection against exploitation and environmental destruction, and are unfair to developing countries. The confrontation between the protestors and the WTO ministry received significant media attention, which fostered public debate on trade issues and economics in general. Mountains of articles and books were written on the subject and "globalization" became a household word. The Seattle protests seemed to revitalize a sense of populism and grassroots empowerment. A sense of change was in the air. But as we close in on a decade later, very little substantive change has occurred. The U.S. and the global economy continue to follow the rules of capitalism as always.

If crisis is a catalyst for change, there has been no shortage of economic crises since the Seattle protests. Like a series of falling dominoes the size of bank towers, one large-scale crisis has slammed into another in a thunderous chain reaction. To begin with, the stock market crash that occurred between 2000 and 2002 wiped out about $7 trillion in financial wealth, constituting the worst financial crisis in history and many times greater than the Crash of 1929. This crisis was amplified by fraud-induced failures of corporate giants such as Enron, WorldCom, Adelphia, and Global Crossing, which themselves register as the largest bankruptcies in history. Within a few years, however, the stock markets rebounded with alacrity and the major indexes broke new records. The return of rising stock prices on Wall Street was in part due to record high oil prices and huge amounts of oil industry profits pouring into the U.S. financial system.

At the time of the Seattle protests, oil was trading in commodities markets at less than $20 per barrel; as of this writing the price is well over $100. Part of the reason for these high oil prices is that global oil production has finally reached its peak. This means that from this point on, oil will become an ever-more scarce, and ever-more expensive, commodity. Along with record oil prices come record profits for those who own this valuable resource. Exxon-Mobil Corporation is the largest oil company in the world, and as it boasts of $40 billion in profits in one year it is the most profitable company in America's history. Exxon's and other oil companies' profits are being pumped into the U.S. financial system with feverish intensity. As oil is largely bought and sold in global markets with U.S. dollars, these dollars naturally will find their way back to the U.S. This year alone, oil consumers have turned over $2 trillion into the bank accounts of oil companies and oil-producing nations. Like gold, oil has become one of the single most lucrative commodities in history. The U.S. financial system has become as dependent on oil money as the global economy is on oil. Knowing this, the U.S. government is waging and planning wars in order to gain control of lucrative oil fields, and more specifically, to gain control of the revenues generated from the sale of that oil. As oil money is pumped into the U.S., it serves to prop up stock values and gives banks huge deposits from which to make loans. In this way, oil money, combined with what former Fed Chairman Alan Greenspan referred to as a "global savings glut," is patching up an otherwise vulnerable and debt-ridden economy. Yet, in spite of peak production and high prices, oil is being consumed more voraciously than ever before. Looming on the horizon is what promises to be the most severe oil shortage in history.

Change is indeed in the air—climate change. Exxon is also at the center of public discourse on global warming, the most severe environmental crisis in history. Exxon has been criticized for its attempts to fog the issue of global warming by financing bogus scientific research. Coming to the company's defense at a press conference held at an annual shareholder's meeting, CEO Rex Tillerson asserted that, "We will continue to support groups that have good scientists involved and are thoughtful in what they write . . . Having a good debate on this is what is sorely needed." Among the scientific community outside those funded by Exxon, however, there is no debate—there is a consensus. The consensus is that global warming is a real-time event and its primary cause is the release of greenhouse gases largely caused by burning fossil fuels such as oil. When Exxon was criticized for not doing more to reduce greenhouse gas emissions, Tillerson responded by saying that, "Fundamentally though, we've got a business to run first, and we're going to do the things that are in the best interest of our shareholders over the long term." Though disingenuous on the issue of global warming, Tillerson speaks the truth about his company's legal responsibility to its shareholders. This reality then shifts the spotlight away from Exxon and back to the U.S. financial system where stock indexes are watched continuously as barometers of economic conditions. Riding on these stocks are not only the interests of wealthy investors, but also the trillions of dollars worth of assets held in pension funds, mutual funds, and even the foundations of nonprofits and educational institutions. Criticisms of a publicly traded corporation like Exxon for doing anything other than maximizing profits resonate oddly, like expressing indignation at a leopard who refuses to change its spots.

In any event, Exxon does not release greenhouse gasses into the atmosphere, consumers do. For over twenty years, American consumers have been obsessed with driving large, gas-guzzling sports utilities vehicles (SUVs), and at the center of the SUV industry is Ford Motor Company. With each new model, Ford's SUVs have become progressively larger and less fuel-efficient—the Explorer, the Expedition, the Excursion, and if followed to its logical conclusion, the last model would aptly be named Extinction as Ford is now hemorrhaging money in the billions. In 2007, Ford reported the worst annual loss in its history of $12.7 billion. These losses amount to the dollar equivalent of a Ford Mustang every minute throughout the entire year. The losses also resulted in the systematic elimination of about 75,000 union-scale, middle-income auto industry jobs. Yet, strangely, Ford's most profitable product line has been in its financial services. Ford has become more successful as a bank than as an auto manufacturer.

General Motors, once the flagship corporation of the United States, lost a staggering $38.7 billion in 2007. This is the biggest annual loss in the history of the auto industry and is the dollar equivalent of over two Cadillac CTSs every minute of the year. GM, Ford, and Chrysler are all making deals to buy-out their current employees' contracts to replace them with workers at half the pay scale.

Like Ford and GM, the rest of the manufacturing sector in the U.S. economy in general has been losing middle-income jobs steadily for decades. At the same time these middle-income jobs are disappearing, Wal-Mart has been spreading like a cancer as the new job market alternative. Wal-Mart is notoriously anti-union, and its employees fill the ranks of the working poor. Over the last two decades, Wal-Mart job growth increased nearly 5,000 percent to become the largest private-sector employer in the world. These trends, along with skyrocketing CEO compensation (Rex Tillerson's predecessor at Exxon-Mobil received a severance package of over $400 million upon retirement), show that income distribution in the U.S. is the most polarized it has been since the worst years of the Great Depression. Income and wealth inequality lead to a host of social problems as well as economic problems. Along with the deterioration of the socioeconomic middle class comes crime, domestic violence, community breakdown, and eventually political crisis.

The hallmark characteristic of the American middle class is home ownership. But as middle incomes continue to collapse, people can no longer make their mortgage payments. This brings us to another crisis—the subprime loan disaster and housing market crash of 2007. With very few exceptions, housing prices across the United States have been falling, and the result is the most severe housing market crisis in over two decades. As people are defaulting on their loan payments, banks are saddled with trillions of dollars worth of "non-performing" loans—loans that are not being paid back. Part of this stems from the fact that banks have been flush with oil money and other sources. For banks, these deposits are liabilities on which they must pay returns. Banks cannot shove these deposits under their mattresses; rather they are compelled to turn those liabilities into interest-earning assets. The easiest way to do that in large volume has been to make mortgages, even if it means making loans to people who are not able to afford the monthly payments.

Addressing many of these problems with insight are writers such as David Korten, Marjorie Kelly, William Greider, Joel Bakan, Naomi Klein, and others. The common theme of their work is that corporate America is out of control. These critics envision American corporations as sociopathic entities with tremendous political power, and with executives who rule over the global economy with the arrogance of a privileged aristocracy. Though the authors provide much important information, they fail to show that every crisis is systematically linked to every other crisis.

In *Mindful Economics*, I propose that we identify this pattern of interconnectedness. American corporations may very well be out of control, but they are only a part of a much bigger system that is experiencing a historically momentous crisis. Companies like ExxonMobil and Ford play a role in global warming, for example, but so do American drivers. As people commute and travel in their cars and trucks—usually one person per vehicle—they are adding to the millions of tons of carbon dioxide released into the atmosphere. Atmospheric carbon dioxide is the leading cause of global warming, which is causing rising seawater levels, flooding of coastal regions, creating severe and erratic weather patterns, drying trends, declining crop yields, and drought. Given that global warming is real and its effects are beginning to show, people are naturally looking for someone to blame. We might start by blaming the auto industry for not making environmentally cleaner vehicles. But these were hugely profitable businesses and have been so for decades. Wall Street investors were cheering corporate profits, governments were happy to collect tax revenues on those profits, mutual funds were happy to see growth in their equity, and people were pleased to live away from their workplaces and commute in large SUVs just as much as auto-industry workers were pleased to have stable livelihoods. Banks were happy to take the oil and auto industry profits as deposits and families were happy to borrow those deposits to mortgage homes, especially ones that they could not afford.

Every sector of the economy is playing a role in the problems of every other sector. The core issue here is that these problems are systemic. Pithy stabs at corporate America can ease our sense of frustration with cathartic venting, but do not lead to long-term solutions. If we listen carefully to those in positions of power—CEOs, bankers and other leaders in the corporate world—we'll hear the same mantra repeated over and over: their primary task is to provide returns to investors. In other words, these problems are directly rooted in the core logic of the capitalist system.

In America, most critics are not willing to take this issue head on. To the extent that capitalism is discussed at all, it is usually softened with qualifiers such as "corporate capitalism," "global capitalism," "market capitalism," or "disaster capitalism." The message is that capitalism has lost its way in the world. Corrupted by corporate institutions, it has lost touch with its soul. If we could only reform it with controls on these institutions and find ways to mitigate the disasters, capitalism would somehow return to its original and benign purpose.

I understand this reluctance and fear of being branded by a hostile audience. I do much public speaking about the consequences of capitalism, and rarely do I have the luxury of preaching to the choir. All too familiar are angry faces loading their rhetorical weapons with bullets inscribed with words like "communist," "utopian," "idealist."

But we do not have to be communist, utopian, or idealist to see the true nature of our economic and environmental realities. We simply need awareness, the ability to see things systemically, and to have an understanding of the logic of capitalism that drives this system. Capitalism has not lost its way in the world, and it has never wavered from it original purpose of profit maximization for an investor class. Since its inception over 400 years ago, capitalism has relentlessly followed this purpose, and it has always been corporate, global, market-oriented, and disastrous.

I'm reminded of the Chinese word for crisis, *weiji*, which is a composite of two words: "danger" and "opportunity." As these historically momentous crises are crashing all around us, the opportunity to start building new alternatives presents itself. The first step in this process of change is for people to learn about their economy, its history, and its most powerful institutions. In *Mindful Economics*, I lay out the groundwork that I hope will help people move economic activity in a new direction. As people change the economic institutions in their communities, they will begin to change their culture. And as they change their culture, they will also change their economic system. Positive change must be firmly grounded on a foundation of knowledge and insight. With this knowledge and insight comes the power to work toward a better future. My hope is that as you journey through this book you will realize this empowerment, you will develop the insight to penetrate the mythology that surrounds capitalism in America, and you will look critically at American economic institutions with openness, directness, and without delusion.

Joel Magnuson
Spring 2008

INTRODUCTION

America's first president, George Washington, died in his home at Mount Vernon in 1799. At the age of sixty-seven, he was suffering from what was probably a severe bronchial infection or pneumonia, but the disease itself was not fatal. The former president died because his physician bled him to death. As part of his treatment, Washington's doctor, James Craik, drained over five pints of blood from his body. Bloodletting, or "phlebotomy" as it was then called, was practiced for thousands of years though there has never been the slightest evidence of any curative powers. Nonetheless, the practice remained widely accepted throughout the eighteenth and nineteenth centuries as a treatment for virtually every ailment imaginable. Blind faith in the superstition of bloodletting prevented doctors from seeing that their "cure" was not only failing to make people well, it was actually causing their deaths.

Standard textbook economics also holds steadfast to an irrational belief in the magically curative powers of unregulated markets and private enterprise—the cornerstone institutions of capitalism. Like the one-cure-fits-all dogma of the phlebotomists, mainstream economists profess that market-based incentives and the profit motive stand as remedies for nearly every economic problem. Standard economic theory is also grounded in a superstitious belief that there exists an "invisible hand" that manifests in unregulated markets and guides economic activity toward balance, stability, and prosperity.

Today many policymakers are profoundly influenced by this superstition. Political leaders consistently follow the recommendations of economists who profess the benefits promised by a free and unregulated capitalist economy. For example, economists assured the federal government that the airline industry would be made more stable and efficient with free-market deregulation. Economists also promised that wholesale energy shortages would be corrected with deregulated electricity markets. And with profit incentives and free markets to trade pollution permits, economists promised that environmental destruction would be curtailed. The same economists preached to the world that developing countries could prosper if they opened their economies to a global system of free enterprise and markets.

Yet, like bloodletting, there has been no evidence of such curative powers of free-market capitalism, and the promises of mainstream economists did not come to pass. After two decades of market deregulation the airline industry is now fraught with heavy losses and bankruptcies. Wholesale energy markets have suffered wild instabilities after market deregulation, and this resulted in rolling blackouts, skyrocketing electricity prices, and historic bankruptcies. Environmental destruction and resource depletion continue unabated, and the disparity between rich lands and poor is wider than ever.

The practice of bloodletting has been abandoned for well over a hundred years, yet the eighteenth-century superstition of the "invisible hand" of free markets is still actively taught in colleges and universities across the United States. Just as bloodletting made no contribution to curing diseases, textbook economics contributes little to people's understanding of how economic systems actually function. On occasion, this fact is admitted by professional economists. According to Nobel Prize-winning economist, Robert Merton, he was surprised ". . . to discover that this highly mathematical and abstract theory that [he] played with for the sheer enjoyment of it actually had a practical use."[1] Nobel Laureate economist, William Vickrey, also confessed that his research was of "minor significance in terms of human welfare."[2] David Kreps of the Graduate School of Business at Stanford University laments the view that academic economists are engaged in "high mathematics making ridiculous assumptions."[3] He seeks to defend the discipline by asserting that economists are actively engaged in real-world applications. But such projects are generally attempts to try to find ways to make economic issues conform to theory, otherwise they must stand far outside standard university curriculum. From both within the discipline and without, academic economics is widely criticized for its detachment from reality and irrelevance to real world issues.

If educating people about the economy is not the purpose of academic economics, what is? According to scholar and critic, E. K. Hunt:

". . . economists did succeed in erecting an impressive intellectual defense of the classical liberal policy of laissez faire [free-market capitalism]. They did it by creating a giant chasm between economic theory and economic reality, however. From the 1870s until today, many economists in the neoclassical tradition have abandoned any real concerns with existing economic institutions and problems. Instead, many of them have retired to the rarefied stratosphere of mathematical model building, constructing endless variations on esoteric trivia."[4]

According to another critic, standard economic theory functions as "an ideological shield against intelligent introspection and civic responsibility."[5] In other words, these critics contend that the primary function of academic economics is not to contribute to real-world understanding, but to provide an ideological defense of capitalism.

In virtually every college textbook on the subject, economics is discussed in a way that suggests that capitalism is as natural and eternal as the sun. Look at any standard economics text and somewhere near the beginning you will find a description of what are called "factors of production," the basic resources used to produce goods and services. These factors are invariably listed as "Land," "Labor," "Capital," and "Entrepreneurship." Entrepreneurship, economists teach us, is a fundamental resource for production. To someone new to economics, this description would suggest that without the capitalist entrepreneur, or business investor, economic production could not take place. This description ignores and nullifies any production that is not carried out by private-sector entrepreneurs such as in the public sector or by households, nonprofits or community-based institutions. The subtle message presented in standard textbooks is that there is really only one approach to production—the capitalist approach—and serious criticism of this approach is virtually nonexistent. As they ignore serious alternatives and criticisms, textbooks function to indoctrinate rather than educate.

Not surprisingly, criticisms of capitalism are met with much resistance in the economics profession. Libraries and bookstores are well-stocked with books and articles about problems associated with capitalism's core institutions: market instability, excessive power of large corporations, deceptive accounting practices and the list goes on. In the economics profession, however, it is acceptable to treat such problems as only "bad apples" or anomalies, and it is generally not acceptable to suggest that these problems might be systemic, or related to the capitalist system itself. To question the capitalist system is to commit heresy before the pantheon of the economics profession.

Questioning capitalism also goes against the grain of American culture in general. A belief in the curative powers of capitalist markets and enterprise—real or imagined—runs deep in the American psyche. Most Americans live out their entire lives without ever considering that there might be long-term, systemic problems associated with their economy. Naturally, therefore, most Americans tend to be skeptical of any such suggestions. It is our contention that such skepticism is derived from both a lack of understanding of capitalism and from a heavy dose of pro-capitalist indoctrination by education institutions and commercial media. It is also our contention that taking a critical view of capitalism is not anti-American. It is our view that the United States has proven its resilience and can stand up under such critical observations.

In the fall of 2000, Public Broadcasting Service aired a documentary titled *Commanding Heights*. The film was based on the book titled *The Commanding Heights: The Battle Between Government and the Marketplace That Is Remaking the Modern World* (1998) by Daniel Yergin and Joseph Stanislaw. This so-called "battle between government and markets" is presented by the authors as an extension of the Cold War between the United States and the Soviet Union. In the context of the Cold War, people are said to be faced with only two choices for organizing their economies: a "free-market capitalist system" or a "centrally planned state socialist system." From this presentation it would follow that if a person has only those two choices and were to criticize capitalism, he or she must necessarily be an advocate for centrally-planned state socialism. Therefore, any criticism of capitalism would suggest a belief in an enemy system that collapsed in the early 1990s with the dismantling of the Soviet Republics. The conclusion that follows is that criticisms of capitalism must necessarily stem from a belief in a system that not only failed, but no longer even exists. By this logic, there cannot be any viable alternative to capitalism in the U.S., and any suggestion to that effect is likely to be summarily dismissed as nonsense.

What is most misleading about the way Yergin and Stanislaw frame the economic debate as "a battle between government and markets" is the fact that governments and markets are not antagonistic institutions. They have always existed simultaneously in both the Soviet Union and the United States. In fact, capitalism is a system that is as much the creation of governments as it is of entrepreneurs. Every economy is a mixture of both capitalist and socialist systems and people have never had to choose between governments or markets.

In spite of such academic and cultural resistance, we aim to introduce a fresh, critical perspective on capitalism. The state socialist economies of the former Soviet Republics collapsed over sixteen years ago, and so did the Cold War between the United States and the Soviet Union. We seek to educate people about the nature of American capitalism and to present a critical perspective that is not filtered through a black and white, Cold-War-era, lens.

The critical perspective offered here is not based on the idea that capitalism is flawed in some way. In our view, capitalism is a system that functions exceptionally well. For centuries capitalism has been a powerful, dynamic, and growing system that has dutifully served its intended purpose. It is also a system from which millions of people around the world have benefitted. Our criticism, rather, is that capitalist systems have consequences. These consequences are both immediate and long-term, and are potentially dire.

Mindful Economics is intended to be an educational resource for people who are concerned about these consequences of capitalism. In particular, we look at three problem areas: environmental degradation and resource depletion, inequality, and financial market instability, and we treat each problem area as systemic. That is, we see these consequences as inherent and inseparable aspects of the capitalist system itself. Solutions, therefore, require systemic change brought about by a gradual development of alternative institutions. Contrary to the arguments of those who claim that there is no viable alternative to capitalism, alternatives are not only viable, they can be found all across the United States. Through a network of alternative institutions, people can begin building local alternatives to capitalism, and these alternatives can naturally evolve out of the system that is currently in place. However, this also means that before people can pursue alternatives, or even understand the consequences of capitalism, they must first do the hard work of understanding the nature of the current economic system.

Mindful Economics is therefore organized into three parts. The first (Chapters One through Eight) is a description of the American capitalist system and its key institutions, the second (Chapters Nine through Eleven) covers the most important consequences of the system, and the third (Chapters Twelve through Fourteen) covers alternatives.

Chapter One introduces the economic system of the United States by exploring the basics of economic systems and basic economic processes. In this chapter, we establish a systems-institutional framework for studying economics. We view economies as systems, and see that the most significant economic problems are systemic in nature. We also outline the basic processes and elements that are common to all systems, as well as the essential characteristics of specific systems, namely capitalism, socialism, and pluralism—the mixture of capitalism and socialism.

Some of the most important institutions of American capitalism are households, private businesses, and the market system. In Chapter Two, these institutions are explored in some detail. The market system, or "cash nexus" is a network of markets that hold households and businesses together in a mutually antagonistic, but interdependent, relationship. More specifically, it is a system mainly dominated by large corporate enterprises. In this chapter, we also narrate the history of how these large corporations grew into the dominant positions they hold today, and frame this history as part of the broader history of capitalism.

The conflicts inherent in the market system have led to institutional complexity in the U.S. economy. In Chapter Three, we examine how businesses strive to make product markets less competitive by merging into giant corporate monopolies or associations of businesses. Historically people have reacted to these monopolies and pushed for government legislation to break them down. Workers also joined together to form labor unions in an attempt to control conditions in labor markets. Both business associations and labor unions formed federations, or umbrella organizations, that are now nationwide and politically very powerful. Conflicts between people and businesses have also played out in the political arena. Chapter Four explores the role of government institutions and key legislation as part of the institutional fabric of the U.S. economy.

Chapters Five and Six go to the heart of the economy—the financial system. Chapter Five explores the various types of money and banking institutions that have come and gone in American history. We also take a close look at the current and most important monetary institutions in operation in the economy today, including various types of depository institutions and the Federal Reserve System. These institutions are complex and serve multiple purposes including the war-making powers of the federal government, but their paramount pupose is to provide a stable monetary system for the capitalist economy. Although these constitute the heart of the U.S. economy, none are directly democratic. The most powerful financial institution in the U.S. economy is the Federal Reserve System, and it is deliberately insulated from political pressure; this also means insulated from democratic accountability. In Chapter Six, we take a close look at Wall Street institutions and at the stocks and bonds traded by these institutions. The original purpose of these institutions was to aggregate funds from a wide base in order to finance large-scale investment projects. Today, however, most of the trading activity on Wall Street has little to do with real investment and much to do with casino-style speculation.

In Chapters Seven and Eight, we complete our picture of the U.S. economic system. Chapter Seven outlines the economic connections the U.S. economy has with the rest of the world. At one time the U.S. economy was an unparalleled economic superpower and was able to sell its goods and services to countries around the world. Over the last thirty years or so this has changed. The U.S. is finding it increasingly difficult to export goods to off-shore markets, yet its imports continue to soar. The result is growing trade deficits and mounting debt. The U.S. has become financially dependent on foreign creditors to keep its domestic economy from experiencing a crisis and this dependency relationship cannot be sustained over the long run.

Chapter Eight ties all the institutions together into a single ensemble—the "capitalist machine." Like a machine the U.S. economy relentlessly pursues economic growth. Yet growth is unsteady and the machine often misfires and slides into recessions and depressions. Chapter Eight examines the boom and bust patterns that ensue as the machine accelerates and decelerates. We also question whether ongoing growth is a positive contribution to human well-being.

Chapters Nine, Ten, and Eleven survey three problem areas, or consequences, of American capitalism. Chapter Nine covers environmental problems such as global warming and resource depletion. In this chapter, we link these problems directly to the growth imperative inherent in capitalism. Capitalism must grow and therefore cannot be sustained, nor can it be environmentally friendly even if the majority of people in a capitalist society want it to be. Chapter Ten explores the problem of inequality. Here we also see this problem as a consequence of capitalism, although not exclusively. Capitalism is a system that revolves around business property, and business property ownership is not something that is accessible to a broad base of the population. In American capitalism, it is something that is overwhelmingly owned by a very small percentage of the most affluent members of society. This ownership gap between the rich and poor contributes much to income inequality. In this chapter, we discuss not only the problems of income and wealth inequality, we also extend this to political inequality, and to the inequality of access to information in the media. In Chapter Eleven, we examine a pattern of financial market instability that has occurred throughout history in places where capitalist institutions prevail. From the early capitalist institutions in Holland in the seventeenth century up to the current stock market and housing market bubbles, we identify a clear and discernable pattern. This pattern is rooted in the capitalist practice of buying and selling in markets in order to make profits.

In the last three chapters, we introduce the elements of a mindful economy as an alternative to capitalism and its consequences. Chapter Twelve lays the groundwork for institutional and systemic change toward non-capitalist alternatives. We introduce a set of core values and principles on which all economic institutions are to be built and maintained. The core values of a mindful economy are environmental sustainability, social justice, and stability. With these values in mind, people can begin the process of building a network of institutions that are compatible with each other, but are non-capitalist institutions. Composed of this network of institutions, a new economic system can begin to take root. Chapter Thirteen explores these institutions in specific detail. We take a close look at cooperatives, small businesses, public enterprises, and financial cooperatives that are all part of a locally based, non-capitalist, democratic economic system. We contend that these institutions can be developed in such a way as to eliminate the long-standing inequalities, antagonisms, and instabilities associated with capitalism. Finally, in Chapter Fourteen, we explore ecologically sustainable practices of consumption and production, and how basic economic institutions can be structured to incorporate sustainable practices. We emphasize that sustainability and capitalism are not compatible. The primary reason for this is that a sustainable system is, by definition, a steady-state system and capitalism cannot survive in a steady state because it is programmed to grow.

Capitalism is a system that relies almost exclusively on the institutions of private property, money, and the market system; a system that needs to grow in defiance of our dwindling resource base and the limited carrying capacity of our planet; and a system in which the majority have little or no say in what, how, or for whom production takes place. It is a system in which the power and freedom to choose or make demands in the marketplace is held only by those with money and excludes those who are without it. In our view, the long-term consequences of such a system are profound and the need for change is becoming increasingly exigent. Just as phlebotomy bled the sick, the planet and its inhabitants are being bled of their vitality by pathological economic systems.

A mindful economy, by contrast, is a system in which economic activity is rooted in democratic institutions, socially controlled by an active citizenry, and shaped by the values of people in their communities. Democracy is a central feature of a mindful economy as a path toward directly meeting the needs of people and communities. As it is rooted in the core values of environmental sustainability, economic justice, and stability, a mindful economy is necessarily set apart from capitalism. As the mindful economy breaks away from its capitalist heritage to become a truly democratic system, citizens must play a central role as agents for institutional change.

The path toward a mindful economy is not an easy one. Redirecting institutional change is extraordinarily difficult. Part of the difficulty lies in the fact that institutions are bound to specific ideologies or worldviews. This means that not only do we need to change our institutions, but we also need to change our way of seeing the world. This challenge is eloquently summed up by Daniel Quinn:

> If there are still people here in 200 years, they won't be living the way we do. I can make that prediction with confidence, because if people go on living the way we do, there won't be any people here in 200 years. I can make another prediction with confidence. If there are still people here in 200 years, they won't be thinking the way we do. I can make that prediction with equal confidence, because if people go on thinking the way we do, they'll go on living the way we do—and there won't be any people here in 200 years.[6]

Bringing about institutional and systemic change is difficult but not impossible. In fact, it is inevitable. Ongoing institutional change is the historical rule and not the exception. Slavery was the prevailing institution of Ancient Greece and Rome, and the ideas of Aristotle that justified slavery with a belief that it was a natural part of human life also prevailed. By the middle ages, feudal institutions evolved from Roman slavery and the naturalistic ideas of Aristotle evolved into the theistic ideology of the Catholic Church. And when capitalist institutions replaced feudal institutions, secular ideas of the classical economists became the new authority.

The lesson learned from history is that change is inevitable. This also means that capitalism will eventually come to an end, economies will evolve in a new direction, and they will be accompanied by new belief systems. Our hope is to be a part of this evolutionary change, and to help guide it in a mindful way toward a desirable future rooted in democratic principles, stability, social justice, and environmental sustainability.

1

ECONOMIC SYSTEMS

Like every other economy in the world, the economy of the United States is a system. It is a social system in which about $11 trillion worth of goods and services are produced, distributed, and consumed every year. The amounts and prices of these goods, how they get produced, who does the work, and how the goods are distributed among the population are all determined within this immense social configuration—the economic system.

Once we come to understand that the economy is a system, we also see that social and environmental problems that have economic causes are systemic and that solutions to these problems require a systems approach. When we take a systems approach, we see that every economic event that occurs has an impact on the overall system, and at the same time, these events are shaped by the system. A systems approach holds that specific problems can be remedied, but not solved by treating them in isolation. Solutions require examining problems as extensions from the broader whole of the economic system in its entirety. For example, environmental degradation caused by excess production and consumption cannot be solved by a specific fossil tax here or green energy subsidy there, nor can problems of wealth and income inequality be solved with a minimum-wage law here or a living-wage ordinance there. These policies and laws can remedy environmental and inequity problems to some extent, but they cannot solve them as long as these problems stem from the structure of the economic system itself. Real and lasting solutions to these problems require a systems approach that will bring about systemic change.

To develop a systems view, imagine a mobile suspended delicately on a string. If one touches any part of this mobile, the entire structure begins to move because all the pieces are linked together in some way. Similar things happen in an economy. If one part changes, everything in the economic system begins to change. A rise in oil prices, for example, will cause fuel and chemical prices to rise, which will directly affect all transportation, agriculture, and manufacturing industries. Price inflation will soon follow which, in turn, will cause banks to raise interest rates and this will affect bond prices, consumer credit, and so on. Every part of the economy is connected to every other part.

The fact that our economic activities of production and distribution are organized within a system is not an accident; it is a human necessity. This necessity stems from the fact that humans are far more likely to survive when they are connected socially in groups rather than acting in isolation. Certain animals such as bears, hawks, or owls are naturally endowed with survival instincts and abilities. With their physical strength and powerful sense of smell, bears have an easier time finding food and surviving alone in the wilderness than would a human being. A hawk or an owl has the ability to fly and is endowed with superior visual acuity. Humans, however, are not highly impressive as physical beings and are not likely to survive for long if they are socially disconnected from other humans. What sets humans apart from other animals is an unparalleled ability to coordinate themselves socially. People— as well as other species such as some insects, canines, and most primates—have learned to survive by socially organizing and coordinating their work. By learning how to divide and systematically coordinate work tasks, humans became more effective hunters, gatherers, farmers; and eventually manufacturers, engineers, and scientists. The capacity to organize socially, and to create culture and civilization, is a salient characteristic of the human species. It is also the key to our ability to adapt and thrive in vastly different areas with vastly different climates and natural resources.

The social and systematic organization of production and distribution is necessary not only for our survival, but also because of the complexity of coordinating these processes. Imagine something relatively ordinary like a bakery. What goes into the process of baking bread? A baker would need flour, water, yeast, salt, labor, at least one oven, baking pans, mixers, and some energy source. The baker somehow must acquire all these ingredients, equipment and resources, but how is all this made available to the baker? The baker must also know what size to make the loaves, the type of flour to use, and the proper texture of bread that the consumers want. Also, the companies that make the ovens and pans must also know the size, quantities, and specifications of these goods. And what goes into the production of an oven? How do the equipment manufacturers of these goods know the size, quantities, and specifications of the steel, wires, electrical components, paint, and glass to make the ovens? And what about the chemical properties of minerals that must be taken into account when considering the production of metal baking pans so they do not melt or warp or change the flavor of the bread during baking? The list of things that must be orchestrated just to make a loaf of bread is endless, and the fact that any of it is effectively coordinated amidst this complexity is evidence of the highly evolved social nature of the human species.

There are no guarantees, however, that economic processes will always be adequately coordinated. If we do not carefully and purposefully coordinate production and distribution, economic and social breakdown can quickly follow. Badly coordinated economic activity can result in crises such as mass unemployment, poverty and destitution, ecological breakdown and crop failures, financial market crises, hyperinflation, bankruptcies, and business failures. Economic crises can also lead to a much broader unraveling of society resulting in crime, political unrest, and even revolutions and wars.

Even when economies are well coordinated, there is still no guarantee that production and distribution will bring about well-being for all members of society or even the majority. Over the span of the history of civilization, humans have trudged through innumerable systems for determining how productive work is to be organized. Some have been more successful than others in serving the needs of people. The healthier and more functional economic systems have generally been those that were responsive to the needs of people to have decent and secure livelihoods and were rooted in the values of their communities. But more often than not, human labor has been put to work in order to serve the enrichment of small but powerful social classes at the expense of slaves, serfs, indentured servants, or impoverished sweatshop labor—a characteristic of the labor conditions for much of the world today.

All systems, including social systems, are comprised of a network of integrated components that when brought together into a coherent whole serve a broader purpose. Understanding the components of a system, however, is not sufficient for understanding how the system functions. A systems approach requires understanding *both* the essential components of a system *and* how these components cohere into an organized whole. For example, a computer is a system that consists of various essential components such as a microprocessor, a hard drive, a monitor, and a keyboard. Each of these components is brought together into a specific configuration. None of the components has any real functional relevance by itself. It is only when all the components are integrated into a specific configuration that they serve the higher function of information processing. An automobile is also a system consisting of a motor, tires, transmission, chassis, and so forth. By themselves, these parts serve no meaningful function. Only when they are integrated do these parts serve the higher function of transportation. In the same way, economic systems are comprised of certain essential components that facilitate the production, distribution, and consumption of goods and services.

The essential components of an economic system and how they function are best understood when they are seen not in isolation, but rather as they are connected to a larger social and cultural milieu. Money is an essential component of any economy, but it serves no purpose by itself unless there is something produced by businesses that one could buy with it. Businesses also play a key role, but they cannot make profits unless there are households willing and able to buy their goods, and there are markets in which the goods can be bought and sold. Households cannot be consumers in the U.S. economic system without a source of income to earn money to spend in the marketplace. It is only when money, markets, businesses, and households are brought coherently together into a specific configuration that they facilitate economic production, distribution, and consumption. Together they comprise a system and that system serves a broader purpose that transcends the specific purposes of the components themselves.

The broader purpose served by an economic system depends on the characteristics of the system itself. Every economic system that has ever existed in the world is unique and therefore has served a unique purpose. One purpose could be to secure the well-being of all members of its society; another could be to enrich a small and privileged class of slave owners, lords, monarchs or business magnates. The question of the broader purpose of an economic system is at the very core of a systems approach to economics. We not only strive to understand the purpose of systems, but also that systemic change can alter the direction and the purpose of the system—perhaps even for the better. Systemic change involves redefining the character of the economic system by restructuring its essential components and building it in such a way that those components can function together and move toward a new purpose.

So what do we call these essential components of an economic system? The renowned institutionalist economist, Clarence Ayres, observed it best in *The Theory of Economic Progress*:

> Some sort of division of the social whole into parts is inevitable, and
> for this the familiar 'institutions' stand ready to hand.[7]

In other words, the systems approach to economics begins by analyzing the social whole to get to the essential components—institutions. Then, by integrating these institutions together into the social whole, we get a coherent picture of both the components of an economic system and how it orchestrates (or fails to orchestrate) the production, distribution, and consumption of goods.

INSTITUTIONS

A social institution is an established social practice or structure that is characteristic of a particular society and exists to direct or control human social behavior. It is a mode of social organization that brings about ordered human behavior and meaning to that behavior. An institution is, as Ayres teaches us, a division of the broader whole of society. An institution is a human creation but its origins cannot be traced to the invention of a single person; rather, it has roots in social customs, conventions, and the daily lives of people.

Much of the daily lives of most people consists of institutionalized behavior even though many of us may be not aware of it. A typical greeting at the family breakfast table is structured by the norms of family institutions. A commute on the freeway is an exercise in following laws established by state institutions. And when people are at work their actions are largely directed by corporate or other business institutions. An afternoon of shopping is organized within various types of commercial or market institutions, and the day ends with a return home to the family institution once again. These institutions and the rules they impose on our behavior determine societal norms; what is considered socially normal. The choices that we make and how we make them are largely determined by the institutions that surround us and they guide our social behavior. As such, institutions become deeply embedded in our cultural fabric and our ways of thinking and are scarcely called into question.

Social institutions have both structural and functional significance. As a social structure, an institution determines the nature of certain social relationships. Inherent in each of these institutional relationships is a structure of power in which some are in a position of authority to direct and command behavior while others are being controlled. For example, the institutions of the family and marriage determine the relationships between parent and child, or between husband and wife. There exists a power relationship between parent and child within the institution of the family such that the parent is usually the controller of social behavior and the child is controlled. The familiar rebellious adolescent behavior occurs when children begin to grow out of these norms of control and seek to control their own behavior. In some cultures, there are also power relationships between husband and wife in which one commands and the other obeys.

A church institution determines the relationship between a pastor and congregation. Here again there is generally a power relationship in which priests or pastors direct the social behavior of the members of their congregations. There are also power relationships between state authorities and citizens where state authorities make and enforce laws that citizens are meant to obey.

As a social function, an institution directs human social behavior to achieve a specific purpose. The purpose of the family institution is, among other things, to care for and educate children, and perhaps to care for the elderly. The function of the church is largely seen as an institution for moral and spiritual guidance. The state's traditional function is largely to maintain law, order and justice.

Like social institutions, economic institutions also have both structural and functional significance. In every economic institution there are social relationships and structures of power. As social structures, economic institutions direct and control human work by empowering some with the authority to direct and control the work of others. The legal institution of the right to private property in business enterprises ultimately defines the relationship between the employers (owners) and employees. Employers are the bosses and have the power to direct employees to follow their orders. The employer regularly commands to the employee what work to do, when to do it, and how much to do, and very little is left to choice by the employee. Markets are also economic institutions in which there is a structure of control. Whether by powerful businesses or business associations, investor pools, governments or labor unions, markets are typically controlled in some way or another. The idea of a marketplace that is free from any sort of institutional control is a libertarian "free market" myth and largely nonexistent.

In their functional role, economic institutions serve specific purposes. The purpose of business enterprises is to facilitate production of goods and services. Markets facilitate distribution and the exchange of money, products, and information. These and other institutions work collectively as a system, and that system serves a larger economic purpose.

As we come to understand the primary institutions of our economy and how those institutions work together systemically, we begin to understand the economic system itself. Once we understand the economic system, we can see more clearly the broader purpose it serves, and whether or not this purpose extends to the well-being of the population. Whether the institutions are democratic or authoritarian, whether they direct people to build shelters or nuclear weapons, to produce food and clothing or pyramids, to build prisons or foster child nutrition—the basic underlying pattern is always the same. Human labor is directed by institutional forces to carry out the basic economic process of production, distribution, and consumption. Let us now turn our attention to these basic economic processes, as they have remained central aspects of human life and culture over several millennia of human civilization.

BASIC ECONOMIC PROCESSES: PRODUCTION, DISTRIBUTION, AND CONSUMPTION

Getting a sense of how our lives are affected by the economy swirling around us is difficult because of its enormous complexity. An eagle's-eye view of the U.S. economy would see a labor force of about 140 million people, factories, machines, trucks, computers, banks, office buildings, farms, hydroelectric dams and millions of other things teeming with activity within a massive spider's web of complexity that churns out almost $11.6 trillion worth of goods and services every year. Although the complexity is staggering, economic activity nevertheless fits neatly into a simple pattern: the production, distribution, and consumption of goods and services. Every moment of economic activity is anchored to these three basic processes.

With a systems view, we can also see that these processes are interdependent and that one cannot exist without the other. If we begin with production, we can see that production is predicated on consumption, for in order for people to be producers they must also be consumers—they must be fed and clothed. But in order to be consumers, something has to be produced and distributed for consumption. Thus, consumption leads to more production, which leads to more distribution, which, again leads to more consumption, and so on in a never-ending cycle integral to the human life process.

PRODUCTION

Unlike wildflowers or seahorses, most goods that humans need for living do not occur naturally and have to be produced by human labor. Nature is not directly amenable to human consumption and has to be transformed. This is the essence of economic production. Defined in the broadest sense of the term, economic production is a process in which people create things that did not exist before by transforming energy and resources contained in the crust of the earth into goods or services.

Economic production is both a creative and transformative process. Production is creative in the sense that after the production process is complete something new is created that did not exist before. If you buy a new car, it may be very similar to other cars on the road of the same model but it is unique in its own way—it is your car with its own quirks and characteristics. When a car or any other product is built, something individually distinctive is created that did not exist prior to its manufacture. Production is also transformative in the sense that finished products are always made by transforming pre-existing things such as raw materials and natural resources. For example, a wooden table and chair were produced by transforming wood from trees into the finished product. Raw materials have to be transformed—cut, pounded, melted, reshaped, and reconfigured into a final product. Production transforms hops and water into beer, clay into ceramic pots, steel into bridges, and cotton or hemp into clothing.

In addition to being a creative and transformative process, economic production can also be seen as an "input-output" process. Resources are drawn into the *input* side of the production process and then transformed into finished goods and services that are created and emerge from the *output* side (see Figure 1).

Every good or service that has ever been consumed in the world was produced from resource *inputs* or "factors of production." These inputs are drawn from people and our environment and brought into the process of making finished goods and services. Inputs are the natural resources, human effort and creativity, tools, raw materials, machinery, and energy combined in a way that results in goods and services for human consumption. Generally, economic inputs fall into four broad categories: land, natural resources, and natural production; labor; human-made resources and technology; and organizational ability.

Land, Natural Resources, and Natural Production. This category includes land itself as well as any resource taken from nature that can be used as an input in production. These would include vegetation and other living organisms, fossil fuels, minerals, water and oxygen, and topsoil. But our planet is not a warehouse that stores these resources like inert substances passively waiting to be used in production. They are themselves the result of natural production processes. Just as people make things with their labor, the planet also performs productive work—natural production. Human life on this planet would be impossible without natural production processes such as photosynthesis; the hydrologic cycle of evaporation, condensation, and precipitation; or biological processes such as transforming carbon dioxide into oxygen or composting organic matter into nutrients. These processes provide humans with most of our energy resources, a food chain, fresh water to drink, and fresh air to breathe.

Future generations' ability to produce things will depend on how thoughtfully we currently harness natural production and use natural resources. A fair and intelligent use of resources requires a systems view with a critical examination of our current economic system's demands on these limited resources.

Labor. Although natural resources and natural production are vitally important, economic production could not exist without human labor. This is human work defined in a broad sense of the term. Labor used in the production of goods comes from both the mind and the body, and can be either skilled or unskilled. Labor involves the intellectual work of a writer or an analyst, and the creative work of an artist, designer, or engineer, as well as the physical work of farmers and manual laborers.

Human-made Resources and Technology. These resources themselves are outputs which are subsequently used as inputs for further production of final goods and services and are not produced by nature or are naturally-occurring. The list of human-made resources includes tools, machines, buildings, mills and factories, training facilities, warehouses, transportation systems, and much more.

Some of the earliest artifacts of human civilization are these human-made resources such as hammers, axes, spears, and other tools fashioned from stone, wood, and bone. The ability to make and use tools became a key characteristic of *Homo habilis,* the earliest known species heading along the evolutionary path leading directly to modern humans. With their ability to make and use tools, *Homo habilis* distinguished themselves from other primates and established the beginning of a two-million-year historical continuity of economic production and material culture.

Current economic production is linked both to the past and the future through the rich material culture of human-made resources. Once the wheel was invented in Mesopotamia, it would never have to be reinvented. Each generation uses the tools and technology developed by their ancestors, improves upon them and passes these improvements on to future generations. Economic production exists in a continuum of technological development in which one generation's creativity builds on the creativity of all preceding generations. Technology is thus continually evolving and as it evolves, so does our ability to produce goods and services.

Technology, however, does not develop in a vacuum. Again, with a systems view, we can see that technology develops in the context of the specific demands of an economic system. The appropriateness of technology should be assessed thoughtfully, and with a critical understanding of how our current system fosters its development. If "necessity is the mother of invention," as the saying goes, then we should be asking ourselves what technology our economic system necessitates and to what purpose. We should also consider that alternative economic systems can foster new and yet-to-be imagined technologies—possibly for alternative and better purposes.

Organizational Ability. For humans, economic production is social and must be socially organized. Even with the mobilization of human labor, the harnessing of nature's productive processes, and the use of human-made resources, the production process could still not effectively work without some planning and social organization. The planner brings together resources in the right quantities, with the right specifications, and into the right production mix so that economic production is successful in bringing about its intended results. Like the conductor of a symphony orchestra or the director of a film, organizational management, planning, and leadership in economic production are crucial. Without this resource, the productive effort would be chaotic and wasted.

One of history's most famous economists and social critics, Thorstein Veblen, asserted that the creative and transformative work of economic production derives in part from a parental instinct to see that our offspring have a fair chance at a better life. Driven by this instinct, Veblen argues that each generation seeks to make its material standard of living better than the last by seeking higher and higher levels of production for a given community of people. But, if Veblen's assertions are true, this productive instinct is limited to the extent that it can be sustained only by the carrying capacity of the natural environment. If production systems grow beyond this capacity, then, ironically, the productive capacity of our children's and grandchildren's generations will be jeopardized and our duty as a parent is compromised. Very

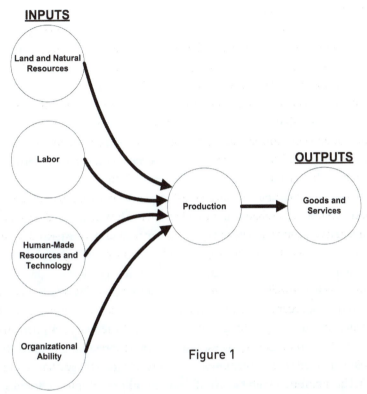

Figure 1

few individuals would argue that advances in technology and productivity have not brought about substantial improvements in people's lives, but as our economic system demands more and more from our planet, these same advances could eventually bring about a speedy decline in human welfare.

One principal aim of this book is to elevate an awareness of the effects that economic production is having on our planet, as well as what impact it will have on our future generations. Another is to question whether our need for ongoing growth is truly driven by Veblen's notion of parental instincts, or whether it now is driven by the internal demands of the economic system itself.

DISTRIBUTION

Distribution follows production. Production is the creative process that transforms resource inputs into finished goods and services. Once the finished goods and services are successfully produced, the next step is to successfully distribute them among the population. With a systems view we see that our economic system and its prevailing institutions determine the specific distribution of goods and services.

The nineteenth-century philosopher John Stuart Mill asserted that whereas economic *production* is based in part on technology and certain scientific principles, economic *distribution* is based on purely institutional forces. That is, once goods are produced, it is ultimately up to the social and political rules that govern society to determine how those goods will be distributed. Mill writes:

> Whatever mankind *produce*, must be produced in the modes, and under the conditions, imposed by the constitution of external things . . . It is not so with the *Distribution of Wealth.* That is a matter of human institution solely. The things once there, mankind individually or collectively can do with them as they like. They can place them at the disposal of whomsoever they please, and on whatever terms.[8]

Finished goods flow from producer to consumer according to the socially determined principles of predominant institutions. Historically many societies distributed goods according to principles established by non-democratic, authoritarian institutions in which the slave owner or feudal lord received the majority of wealth produced by a mass of slaves or peasants who received very little. In other cases, distribution is structured according to principles of universal access for all members of the community, principles of fairness or equity, or a principle based on the proportionality of individuals' contributions to production. As we develop a clearer picture of the U.S. economy as a system, we will see that distribution takes place largely according to an ability-to-pay principle such that goods are allocated according to those who have the money to pay for them.

As we will see shortly, the U.S. economy is primarily capitalist. This means that goods and services are sold and distributed mainly in the marketplace. This also means that one's share in the distribution of the overall output of production is mainly determined by the amount of money one has to bring to the market. Markets are economic institutions created to facilitate the exchange of goods, and the foremost role of money is to be a medium of this exchange. If one lacks sufficient money, then one has nothing to exchange and is therefore automatically rationed out of the distribution loop. Markets ration goods away from those who cannot afford to pay and toward those who can.

If society decides that there are certain goods or services that are simply too important to leave to this rationing function of the markets, it can change its economy into a more socialistic system. Under socialism, government insti-

tutions play a more significant role in providing alternative systems of distribution. For example, governments can tax incomes of one group—typically
the more wealthy—and transfer this income to another—typically the poor,
and thereby alter a distribution pattern that would otherwise be set by the
market.

There are few, if any, real-world examples of purely capitalist or purely
socialist economies. Most are hybrids of more than one type of system, but
can lean more heavily in one direction or another. Whether an economy is
more socialistic or more capitalistic will have a significant bearing on distribution patterns. In more socialistic economies, government tax-and-transfer
programs have had a significant impact on making certain essential goods and
services more evenly distributed among the population. For example, with a
progressive tax structure (the more income the higher the percentage of taxes
paid) governments can draw financial resources away from the more affluent
sectors of the population to subsidize housing, food, healthcare, and other
social needs of the less affluent or disabled or elderly. Education, once considered the domain of the affluent, is now generally provided through
government tax-and-transfer programs as are most other public services such
as police and fire protection, port facilities, transportation infrastructure, airports, national defense, consumer food and drug protection, and so forth. In
most modern industrial economies outside the U.S., healthcare is considered
an essential service that is too important to leave to market forces and is distributed as a public service to a broad base of the population through
government programs.

In capitalistic economies, it is generally believed that the more effort one
exerts in production, the more income one can earn, and therefore the larger
share of distribution one can enjoy. That is, distribution is supposed to be
based on a principle of contribution to production. Those who enjoy high
material standards of living are able to do so because they have worked
harder or because they have greater skills in production. One of the popular
myths of the American economy is that it is the "land of opportunity," and
that one's standard of living is a direct reflection of how hard one has worked.
Upon close inspection, however, it becomes clear that the equality or inequality of distribution in the U.S. has only a small relation to the work or
productive contributions of the population. At a very simple level it is obvious that if people make no effort to be productive, they would not expect to
also enjoy a high material standard of living. But in fact, wealth ownership
seems much more related to the wealth and social status of one's parents,

ethnicity, gender, and other factors that have little to do with productive effort or skill level.

CONSUMPTION

Once goods and services have been produced and distributed among members of society, people can then consume them to satisfy their biological and social needs—real or imagined. In an economic sense, consumption means being able to inhabit a dwelling place, transporting oneself from one place to another, eating food and drinking water, wearing clothes, communicating, reading a book or newspaper, watching a film, and a thousand other things that people do when they are using (or using up) the things produced in the economy.

The word "consumption" often implies something negative. It can suggest that by consuming, people are using something to the point of depletion. In earlier times, "consumption" was used to refer to tuberculosis, and was associated with alcoholism and drug addiction. Today it also can carry a negative connotation, as it is often associated with "consumerism." For clarification, therefore, it is necessary to make the distinction between healthy and fulfilling consumption and pathological or excessive consumption.

Healthy consumption is that which is necessary to sustain both physical and psychological well-being. According to psychologist Abraham Maslow, people are motivated in their actions by needs that are yet to be satisfied. Such needs are arranged by Maslow in a hierarchy or ladder beginning with basic physiological needs such as food, clothing, and shelter, then to higher needs of safety, love, and esteem, and then to the loftiest need of self-actualization. As such, healthy levels of consumption of goods and services are those that satisfy the basic needs for food, clothing, shelter, self-esteem, and so on up the ladder.

Consumerism, on the other hand, is a pathological phenomenon deeply rooted in American culture. It grows out of an irrational notion that by accumulating ever-larger amounts of consumer goods, one will achieve proportionally higher amounts of fulfillment and esteem.

A mindful approach would encourage healthy forms of consumption and discourage the pathological kind. This, again, requires us to take a systems view. Consumerism is a product of our economic system's need to grow continuously. It emerged at the beginning of the twentieth century at a time when the production of consumer goods being pumped out of the factories created a need for mass consumption and businesses had to find ways to get people to buy and spend in ever-increasing quantities. Modern marketing strategies and media imagery spin sophisticated illusions that deliberately suggest that through pathological consumption one can achieve higher social status and dreamlike self-aggrandizement.

As the U.S. economic system continues to create an ever-larger consumer base for its output, most of the people in the world are still far from meeting even their most basic needs such as food, clothing, shelter, and education for their children; adequate healthcare; and safe neighborhoods. If allowed to continue unchecked, this asymmetry between the hedonistic "good life" of American-style consumerism and grinding poverty for a majority of the world's population will at some point very likely lead to a political crisis.

To understand how economies coordinate and control the basic economic processes of production, distribution, and consumption and for what purpose requires a systems approach. An economic system has an integrated set of institutions that direct production, facilitate distribution, and pattern consumption in specific ways in order to achieve a specific purpose. Depending on the overall purpose of the system, certain institutions will be more dominant than others. Capitalism and socialism are the most important economic systems in the world today. Each has its own specific economic institutions and each has its own ultimate purpose. As mentioned earlier, virtually every economy in the world is a hybrid of both capitalism and socialism, and some lean more heavily on capitalistic institutions and others lean more heavily on socialistic institutions. Here we turn to more specific definitions of these two systems as well as the hybrid of the two—economic pluralism.

CAPITALISM

Capitalism has been the dominant economic system in Western civilization for the past four centuries. Today it is the dominant economic system for the world. Although the specific form it has taken has changed dramatically over the span of its existence, its defining features and purpose remain the same. The overall purpose of capitalism is to make and accumulate profits for an investor class who own and control the property of private businesses, i.e., capital. Hence the name "capitalism," for it is a system that endows the owners of capital with sovereign control over economic production.

Deeply integrated in the system of capitalism is a specific process of accumulation that begins and ends with money. The investor class accumulates monetary or financial wealth by investing money in private businesses that produce goods or services. These investments can be made directly by purchasing business property such as buildings, tools, and equipment, or indirectly in the form of corporate stocks. However the investments are made, capitalists take ownership of the businesses and direct the production of goods and services that are sold in markets for, the capitalist hopes, a profit. The money from these profits is subsequently reinvested for another round of investments and profit making. The monetary wealth of the capitalist investor class can thus grow and accumulate into perpetuity, without limitation, and even without the capitalists themselves ever being required to set foot on a factory floor.

In order for the capitalist system to accumulate money for investors in this way and thus be a truly capitalist system, it must include the following essential characteristics:

1. Private property rights and the private ownership of business enterprise.
2. The market system.
3. The social separation of ownership and work.
4. The profit motive.
5. The growth imperative.

The first and perhaps most important characteristic of capitalism is the institution of private property and the private ownership of business enterprise. A capitalist must have a legal right to own the property of a business in order to have full command over how this property is to be used. *Property*, in the sense that it is used here, refers to business assets such as the raw materials, tools and equipment, buildings, resources, etc.—the capital that is used in the production of goods and services. In the United States such legal right is an institution that is legally guaranteed by the Fourteenth Amendment of the U.S. Constitution which says, ". . . nor shall any State deprive any person of life, liberty, or property, without due process of law."[9]

In a capitalist system, there must be widespread acceptance in society of the notion that individuals not only have the right to privately own capital, but also have the right to all of the profits generated with that capital. If people were not assured that their business assets and profits were protected as private property, there would be no such private investments—and without private investments there would be no such thing as capitalism.

It is through the specific right to personally own capital that production is controlled. The legal right to property and profits allows the owner full sovereignty over how property is to be used in production. When someone buys a consumer good such as a pair of shoes, those shoes become their property, and they have the right to do with it what they wish. In the same way, the owners of capital have the right to do what they wish with the business assets they own. This sovereign control over business property effectively gives the investor class control over all production processes in the economy. This control extends to labor as well. By controlling production, the owner has full power to determine who is or is not hired to work in management or production. The owners of capital are the bosses, and they wield power to command to employees how to produce, what to produce, for what purpose, and so on.

Without the right to privately own and control business property, a capitalist system, like a human without a head, could not function.

The second defining characteristic of capitalism is the institution of the *market system*. A capitalist system must have a well-developed system of markets that employs the use of money and facilitates the exchange of goods, resources, and information. The central aim of a capitalist system is the accumulation of money for the investor class—a process that begins and ends with money. To accomplish this, labor and other resources used as inputs in the production process must be attainable with money. The finished goods, or outputs, must be sold for money as well. This requires a system of markets that allows for a fluid exchange of these inputs and outputs for money. A well-developed system of markets ties together production inputs and outputs in such a way that allows capitalists to make and accumulate money profits simply through buying and selling.

Markets for goods and services have existed for thousands of years, but what led to the development of capitalism was the modern creation of this system of integrated markets. Capitalism came into being as something historically unique with the creation of labor markets, markets for land and natural resources, and capital markets. In the capitalist market system human labor is hired in labor markets for money, natural resources and capital equipment are acquired in markets for money, land is rented or purchased with money, and the final goods and services are sold for money in markets. In this way a capitalist makes money purely through buying on the input side and selling on the output side—buying low and selling high in the market system. Prior to the ascent of capitalism in the sixteenth century, such a system was not possible. Land and its resources were then considered the domain of God and were not ordinarily thought of as commodities to be bought and sold for money in markets. Nor was labor hired for wages in labor markets. Human labor was embedded in a system of hierarchy of servile relationships that revolved around the control of land, not money. There were few or no institutions created for raising finance capital, and human-made resources such as the equipment and tools used in production were not so much privately owned as they were used collectively in peasant communities or controlled by guild masters. Eminent economic historian Karl Polanyi described the process of transforming land, labor, and capital into marketable commodities as a historical sea change leading to modern capitalist development in the eighteenth and nineteenth centuries. Polanyi refers to this sea change as "The Great Transformation."[10]

The capitalist market system came to be seen as the arena in which a competitive "Darwinistic" struggle for survival of businesses is carried out. Greedy or inefficient producers are to be weeded out in a kind of free-market natural selection in which only the producers of the best quality and lowest costs survive. It came to be widely believed that this model of "survival of the fittest" best serves the public interest. A strong dose of competition in the marketplace would by itself keep greed or shoddiness in check, and would assure that the public interest would be protected by allowing only the fittest producers to remain in business.

Distribution is also carried out through the capitalist market system. In a purely competitive market system in which the markets are unfettered by outside institutions, inputs and outputs are allocated according to conditions set by the forces of supply and demand in the marketplace. If a particular good is in high demand, the prices will begin to rise. Higher prices tend to earn higher profit margins that will attract capitalists to the market, and the supply of these goods will increase to meet the higher demand. If an output is in low demand, the prices will begin to fall and the lower prices mean lower profits, causing the capitalists to pull out of the market and the supply of the goods to fall to meet the lower demand. In this way the market forces of supply and demand distribute goods or outputs in the direction of highest demand and away from lowest demand.

Inputs are similarly distributed to businesses in the market system. If a particular job skill is in high or low demand, employers will bid the wage or salary upward or downward, and this will either attract or repel employees. Equipment or raw materials will also be distributed to the businesses according to the conditions set by their respective markets; where they are in highest demand, prices will be higher and the resources will be automatically channeled in the direction where they are most wanted.

In a purely capitalist economy, the coordination of the distribution of goods, services, and productive inputs is carried out in a system of markets by virtue of the forces of supply, demand, and prices. With this exclusive reliance on markets, the capitalist system revolves around money. This reinforces the power and control of those in society that have money—namely the wealthy investor class. People without money are essentially powerless in a market system. Capitalism thus created a class separation based on monetary wealth.

The third defining characteristic of capitalism is the social or class *separation of ownership and work*. By definition, the owners of capital, or the investor class, do not make money by their own work in production. Their income derives from owning capital, and from buying and selling in the marketplace. Capitalists are people whose primary source of income is derived from owning business property. They may or may not perform actual work in production, but such work is not necessary for them to make profits. Profits are paid to owners not to workers. Conversely, workers do not earn their income from owning but from performing actual work. They may or may not earn some income from a share of ownership of business property, but their primary source of income comes from their labor as they work for a wage or salary.

Although most small businesses and partnerships are privately owned, they are typically not what we would call "capitalist." In these small enterprises there is little or no real separation of ownership and work. Most owners of small businesses have to work in those businesses in order to keep them going and to continue earning their income. Long before capitalism came into being there existed small, privately owned businesses such as handicraft shops, farms and bakeries that operated much like small businesses today. The owners of these small businesses derive their livelihoods from working in their businesses, not from making financial investments. In other words, for small business people there is no separation of ownership and work and small business owners typically are not considered members of the investor class.

It should be added that a capitalist investor class must also be a relatively small percentage of the population. To have an economic system that fully integrated private ownership and work, and the income it generated from ownership were widely shared among the population, such an economy would be the dream of utopian socialists, but it would not be capitalist. In fact, it is hard to derive a definition for such a system because it has never existed.

The fourth defining characteristic of capitalism is the *profit motive*. Recall that the purpose of capitalism is to make and accumulate profits. Without non-capitalist institutions operating outside of those that make up a purely capitalist system, the only goods and services that would be produced in the economy would be those that are the most profitable. If high-quality household appliances were more profitable to produce than low-quality ones, people would have the higher quality goods. And if cocaine production were more profitable to produce than antibiotics, then the profit motive of capitalism would assure that cocaine would be produced in abundance and there would be a shortage of antibiotics. A product's real usefulness or its contribution to people's well-being are of secondary importance in a capitalist system. What determines whether something is or is not produced is its profitability.

The fifth defining characteristic of capitalism is the *growth imperative*. The earnings that flow to capitalist investors take the form of percentage rates of return. Mathematically, this works the same as compound interest in a savings account in which the principal investment grows at some percentage rate. Anything that grows at a constant percentage growth rate is growing exponentially. For the capitalist class to continue to accumulate monetary wealth at an exponential rate, the production process from which the profits are generated must also grow exponentially—increasing at an accelerating rate. The implications of this are profound, for it means that the drive for the accumulation of ever-larger amounts of money for the investor class also drives growth in production of goods and services. Without this growth, the capitalist system will slide into a recessionary crisis or even a depression, which is widespread systemic failure. To serve the interests of the investor class and to prevent a systemic crisis, it is imperative that economic production experience continuous growth.

An economic system that lacks any of these characteristics is not, by definition, a functioning capitalist economy. Although there is no system that is purely capitalist in existence today, capitalism is still the dominant force in the U.S. economy.

SOCIALISM AND PLURALISM

Socialism emerged within the context of revolutionary political and economic events in eighteenth and nineteenth century Europe. To many astute observers and critics at this time such as Karl Marx, John Stuart Mill,

Thorstein Veblen, and others, some form of socialism would develop as a response to problems and conflicts that had become an inherent feature of the industrial capitalist system.

The Industrial Revolution had promised that everyone would enjoy the progress, wealth creation, and new prosperity and opportunity wrought by technological advancement ushered in by the capitalist entrepreneur. The French Revolution promised "Liberty, Equality, and Fraternity" for all. Not only were these revolutionary promises not ushered in, in the eyes of working people the capitalist class intentionally betrayed them. For many within the ranks of the working class, capitalism became a system with tremendous disparities of income and wealth distribution and severely limited access to opportunity. Although tremendous wealth was created within the capitalist system, it was disproportionately concentrated in the hands of a small class of industrialists, merchants, bankers, and professionals. The institution of private property became the privilege of the wealthy classes to privately own coal mines and textile factories in which working people toiled long hours under miserable working conditions. Property came to be seen as a privilege similar to land ownership of the traditional aristocracy—the political class that was to be overthrown in the revolution. The experience of capitalism for working people in the nineteenth century was not prosperity and opportunity, but rather chronic poverty, tenement slums, low wages and long hours, uncertainty, and deplorable working conditions. In their desire to find a path out of the slums of capitalism, people began clamoring for socialist reforms, joined socialist political parties, and built socialist institutions. As such, socialism emerged as a backlash to unfettered capitalism of the nineteenth century.

As an economic system, socialism is founded on a principle that the people, through the auspices of government institutions, can democratically control economic activity. In its early stages of development, socialism hoped to expand the role of democratic government to occupy a central place within the economy.

The first and perhaps most important defining characteristic of socialism is the institution of public property and the public ownership of business enterprise. Socialism is built on the democratic principle that by extending political power to a broad base of the population and thereby empowering people with the control of the state, economic control would be in the hands of the people. The people, using their political power, could direct economic production and distribution of goods and services in ways that would benefit themselves and not a wealthy minority. In a true democracy, the majority of the people obtain control over government policies, and in a socialist system people sustain control over the machinery of the economy through state-run institutions. In this way, the public ownership of businesses became a central and defining feature of a socialist economy. The extent of actual government ownership in the economy varies from country to country, but it now exists virtually everywhere on the planet.

Modern socialist economies typically have state or municipal ownership and control of larger, basic industries such as agriculture and forestry, mining, transportation, utilities, telecommunications, and banking. Socialism also maintains state-run agencies to provide key public services such as education, police and fire protection, and healthcare.

Another defining characteristic of socialism is the existence of economic planning by government institutions. Under a capitalist system, planning is carried out by the business owners and their managers. Under a socialist system, state agencies make decisions about how to allocate productive resources according to certain criteria determined by public policy. Whereas planning and key decisions in capitalism are made for profit maximization, in a socialist system decisions are based on broader political goals. For example, if a public policy is to make primary and secondary education universally available to all citizens, then state agencies will work toward bringing together the resources needed to build and staff public schools. Alternatively, a public policy might be to achieve fairness or stability in the basic industries or services. To achieve this goal, the state would assume ownership and control of these enterprises. This is typically found in large-scale and vital industries such as postal services, energy, telecommunications, and transportation.

Another central aspect of a socialist economic system is the existence of government agencies geared toward wealth and income redistribution designed to benefit the working class and the poor. A wide variety of social programs were created as an attempt to redress disparities between the wealthy and the poor inherent in capitalist systems, and further as an attempt to try to engineer a politically stable middle class. Governments carry out what are commonly referred to as tax-and-transfer programs in which one sector—often upper-income groups, but not always—is taxed and these financial resources are then channeled to another sector of the population either as cash payments or in the form of public services. Perhaps the most common such tax-and-transfer programs would be public education, socialized healthcare, public housing or housing subsidies, social retirement, disability benefits, and welfare programs financed through progressive tax structures in which the wealthy pay higher tax percentages.

Where socialist tax/transfer programs are prevalent, there are also relatively high tax burdens as a percentage of overall income. Sweden is one of the more socialistic of European economies and it ranks as one of the highest taxed nations. In 1999, tax receipts in Sweden were 61.5 percent of its national output. Other countries that lean more in a more socialist direction such as Denmark or France have tax burdens of 58.1 percent and 48.6 percent respectively. On the other hand, more capitalist-leaning countries such as Australia and the United States sustain tax burdens of 35.4 percent and 31.4 percent of their national incomes.[11]

The main differences between capitalist and socialist systems are to be found in the types of institutions that are used for carrying out most of the basic processes of production, distribution, and consumption. Capitalist systems rely more heavily on the institutions of private property and markets, whereas socialist systems rely more heavily on public institutions. But as has been noted above, there are no purely capitalist or socialist systems—including that of the United States. All modern economic systems exist as hybrids of both capitalist and socialist institutions, and the only real difference is one of magnitude or emphasis. Such hybrid systems are known as pluralist or mixed economies.

The distinctions between post Cold-War economic systems started to blur as socialist economies embarked on a transition process in which they began assimilating capitalistic institutions, and as capitalist systems retained socialistic institutions. Perhaps nineteenth-century socialist economists like Karl Marx and others who foresaw socialism entirely replacing capitalism failed to imagine a blending of the two—the current reality for all industrial economies.

CONCLUSION

One of our goals in this book is to get a complete understanding of capitalism in America and its key institutions. Much of what follows in the next several chapters is a detailed description of the U.S. capitalist system, and a critical assessment of its consequences, which are severe and are growing in severity. We look critically at the workings of the capitalist system in its entirety and at its overall purpose, and we question whether this is the best system for people and our planet.

In our view, we see capitalism as a system that is non-democratic and whose primary purpose is financial wealth accumulation for a relatively small percentage of the population. Moreover, it would take a tremendous leap of the imagination to make the claim that the widespread separation of ownership and work—a salient feature of capitalism—is somehow democratic. Capitalism is a specific kind of system that is grounded in the institutions of private property, money, and the market system. It is a system that will always grow even though the resource base of the planet cannot accommodate this growth. It is also a system in which few people have control over what, how, or for whom production takes place. It is a system that favors money over all else and makes life difficult for those who do not have much of it. The implications for such a system are far-reaching and the need for change is becoming clearer each day.

In our critical assessment of capitalism, we do not argue that it is failing, or flawed in some fundamental way. Capitalism has proven for centuries to be a stunning success in achieving its own stated purpose of wealth accumulation for the investor class. Rather than arguing that capitalism is flawed or failing, we argue that it has consequences, and we suggest mindful alternatives to avoid these consequences.

A mindful economy is built on a foundation of democratic institutions which is governed by people who are active in their communities. This kind of grassroots democracy is a central characteristic of a mindful economy as the main path toward directly meeting the needs of people. Unlike capitalism, a mindful economy is always firmly situated in the core values of environmental sustainability, economic justice, and stability. Such a system requires that citizens play a key role in community building and institutional development. Organizing our economic activity mindfully and purposefully to bring about the well-being of people sustainably within their environment is the central idea and central purpose of mindful economics. At the same time, such mindfulness requires a systems view of economics because economies themselves are complex systems.

2

THE CASH NEXUS

Households, Corporations, and the

Market System

Recall that the ultimate purpose of any capitalist system is to generate and accumulate business profits for investors. This purpose is achieved through the workings of a system of input and output markets (see Chapter One, Figure 1) where the investors/entrepreneurs "buy low" in input markets and "sell high" in output markets. Buying, selling, and taking profits is the essence of capitalism, and market transactions have come to be the mediators of virtually all economic relationships in the capitalist world. Money and markets tie consumers to producers, households to businesses, and employees to employers. It should not come as a surprise, therefore, to know that money is elevated to a level of paramount importance in a capitalist economy.

Money is what we need to acquire in our jobs. We need money to pay for our housing, food, and clothing. With money, we are contenders in the marketplace and if we are without money in a capitalist society, we become stranded on an island amidst a sea of money-for-product exchanges. In the U.S., people without money are alienated both from other people and from things. Without money, people cannot share in the consumer culture that has become the American norm, are shut out of a chance for "the good life," and find it difficult to live with a sense of dignity or self-respect. Money-making in America has risen to a supreme virtue and a supreme measure of personal worth. Virtually everything under the sun is valued in monetary terms; everything takes on a marketable value and is transformed into that which can be bought and sold for money. Conversely, everything that cannot be converted into money is viewed as having no value. Such a money-based culture was referred to as the "cash nexus" by the nineteenth-century historian, Thomas Carlyle, who lamented that "cash payment has become the sole nexus of man to man."[12] In such a money-based culture, money-for-product exchanges are everywhere and these exchanges take place in the *market system*.

THE MARKET SYSTEM

Specific markets are embedded in this cash nexus. They bind the households and businesses into a mutually dependent but antagonistic system (see Figure 1). The antagonism stems from the fact that households and businesses have diverging interests in the marketplace. Households generally prefer to pay lower prices in the goods-and-services markets, and businesses try to get the highest price the markets can bear. Businesses prefer to pay lower wages and salaries in labor markets, and working people try to get the highest wage or salary the labor markets can bear. The result is a continuous tug-of-war between buyers and sellers, producers and consumers, and employers and employees. As we will see in the next chapter, this antagonism has a long and sometimes even bloody history.

The vast majority of Americans are not capitalists or members of the investor class, but are working people who rely on their wages and salaries for their livelihoods. The terms of their employment such as pay, benefits, and working conditions are strongly influenced by the forces of supply and demand in the labor markets. If some people have particular job skills that are in high demand by businesses and are also in short supply, they tend to get favorable wages and salaries and working conditions as they have the leverage to bargain in a "seller's" labor market. Nevertheless, there is no guarantee that being highly skilled or a hard worker will result in high pay. If these skills are not wanted by businesses, or if there is an overabundance of people with these skills, businesses can easily force wages or salaries downward by pitting workers against workers in a "buyer's" labor market.

Working people buy their food, transportation, housing, and other goods and services with the income they earn from their labor. Just as the forces of supply and demand in labor markets influence wage and salary levels, the prices people pay for these goods and services are also influenced by the forces of supply and demand. If goods and services are relatively abundant in supply and there is not excessively high demand, then they will be priced inexpensively in a "buyer's" goods-and-services market. If there is scarcity and high demand, then there will also be higher prices in a "seller's" market. Households and businesses are thus locked in a struggle in which each is trying to gain enough leverage to protect their interests in both labor and goods-and-services markets. With enough leverage, for example, supply could be deliberately limited by sellers to create a high-priced seller's market either for labor or products. Buyers on the other hand, could limit their demand, or boycott, and create a low-priced buyer's market. The struggle for this kind of advantage between households and business, however, is not balanced as businesses have grown into giant multi-national corporations and have the ability to dominate both sides of the market system. Far from a balanced "equilibrium" as the classical economists had envisioned, the scales of market power are tipped in favor of big business.

In the nineteenth century, Thomas Carlyle saw that an unbalanced market system created an unfortunate impasse for the mass of poor people living in Great Britain where the market system first came to full development. The working poor were trapped because, although they were willing to work hard, unfavorable labor market conditions kept their pay so low as to keep them in a chronic state of poverty. At the same time their plight was worsened by the fact that monopoly businesses maintained high fixed prices in goods-and-services markets. Although Carlyle was observing the economic conditions in Britain, the same conditions also came to prevail in North America in the nineteenth century.

Working conditions generally improved throughout the nineteenth and twentieth centuries as working people in Britain and the U.S. began to exert greater political influence through collective union action and at the ballot box, and society moved further away from an exclusive reliance on markets. Economic pluralism emerged with the creation of labor unions and government institutions that lessened the harshness of the purely capitalist market system. Nevertheless, the system of interlocking labor and goods-and-services markets remains the dominant structure that binds together the core economic institutions—households and businesses—in the U.S. economy.

HOUSEHOLDS

Several millennia before the existence of Microsoft, General Motors, or the Federal Reserve System, there was the household. It is in the household—the most primal of all economic institutions—that economic activity originates. In fact, the word "economics" originates with the classical Greek word *oeconomia* meaning "householding." In ancient Greece, agriculture constituted the bulk of production and work was primarily carried out by the small *oecos*, meaning the household estate or family farm. The Greeks were independently minded and held a well-run, self-sufficient family estate in high regard. The proper management of the household estate was so important to the Greeks that the famous general, teacher, and historian Xenophon (434–355 B.C.) wrote a treatise on the subject titled, *Oekonomikos*, arguably the first text on economics in the history of Western civilization.

Two-and-a-half millennia later the household remains as a core economic institution and a locus of economic activity. The processes of production, distribution, and consumption could not exist without the vitality of the household. In standard economics textbooks, the household is regarded as merely a place in the cash nexus into which wage income flows and from which consumer spending originates. Certainly households perform an essential function in the U.S. economy by earning and spending dollars, but households also play a much more extensive role. Households are the progenitors of the labor force sending about 151 million people out to work in the U.S. economy each day. They are also the centers for early childhood education and socialization, the wellsprings of productivity, and a source of finance capital and creativity. Although it is seldom recognized as such, a good deal of economic production takes place in households as well.

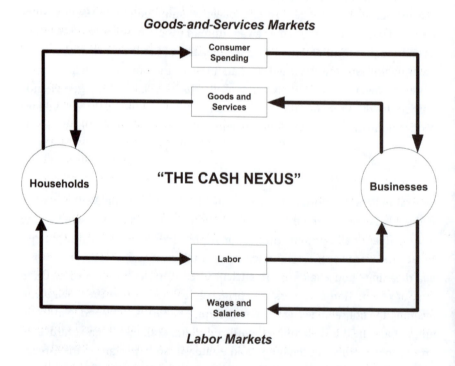

Goods-and-Services Markets

Consumer Spending

Goods and Services

Households   **"THE CASH NEXUS"**   **Businesses**

Labor

Wages and Salaries

Labor Markets

Figure 1

Within the U.S. economic system, the household's principal function is to bring in money from earned labor and spend it on goods and services. American households are expected to be consuming machines, for without mass consumer spending on mass-produced goods and services, capitalist businesses would not be able to make profits. Dutifully fulfilling this expectation, most Americans spend nearly all of their after-tax income on consumer goods and maintain the lowest savings rate of all so-called developed economies.[13] But before spending money on consumer goods, households must first obtain it as income or borrow it.

In a general sense, households have the ultimate claim to all income generated in the U.S. economy. It is to individuals and families in households that income ultimately flows in the form of wages, salaries, corporate dividend payments, interest income, farm income, rent payments, profits from small businesses, and government subsidies such as social security benefits or pensions. But within these different forms of income, the vast majority of households earn their income by working for a wage or salary. According to the Bureau of Labor Statistics (BLS) data for 2006, the median household income[14] for America's labor force is about $48,201 and the average hourly earnings rate is between $16 and $17 per hour, or between $9 and $10 per hour if adjusted for inflation.[15]

BLS data also shows that workers earning $16 to $17 per hour are also producing about $136 worth of goods per hour.[16] This disproportionality between what workers get paid and the value of what they produce stems directly from the goal of capitalism—to maximize profits for investors, not wages or salaries for working people. Moreover, according to *Business Week*, wages and salaries paid to working people as a share of national income has been on a steep decline over the last few years.[17] So if working people are getting paid only a fraction of the market value of their output, how do goods get purchased? In other words, where do workers get the money to purchase all these goods and services they produce? The answer is *debt*.

Not only do American households have the lowest savings rate compared to countries with similar economies, they also have the highest debt. The trendsetters in American consumer culture are not the middle class, but the wealthy. As the top-income-earning sector of the population rises in financial wealth and earnings, it also raises the standard for what is considered to be "the good life." In an attempt to emulate the living standards of those financially above them, middle-income households borrow with credit cards and home-equity loans. Lower-income households continuously spend more than they bring in income and thus continuously borrow. Total household debt as a percentage of after-tax income rose from about 55 percent in the early 1990s to about 80 percent in the mid-1990s, and during those same years the ratio of household assets to debt declined from about 8 percent to about 6 percent.[18] Although credit card debt and other forms of consumer installment debt have risen, the bulk of this increase is in long-term mortgage debt and home equity refinancing. According to *Business Week*:

> [T]he growing reach and efficiency of financial markets makes it far easier to take money out of a formerly illiquid [not easily converted to cash] asset, such as a home, without actually selling it. Refinancing a mortgage used to be a complicated and expensive process, limiting how often it could be done. Now, low-cost deals have enabled many to refinance repeatedly as rates have dropped. Similarly, it's far easier to get home equity loans, which now total over a trillion dollars.[19]

Household debt has increased at a much faster rate than the increase in household income. This spreading of indebtedness raises warning flags about the overall vitality and security of the household sector—a centrally important part of any functioning economic system.

Secure households are also important as the wellspring of productive labor. Households are where people rest, sleep and eat their meals so as to be able to return to work the next day. Households are where people prepare for work, wind down from work, and do all the other things that are important for maintaining and rejuvenating a productive labor force. Moreover, households are where most people raise their children so that they can become socialized as productive members of a community, and eventually enter the labor force to sustain continuity in the economic process.

Households also carry out significant economic production in addition to being centers for consumption and the regeneration of the labor force. Hundreds of billions of dollars worth of production takes place within households, though practically none of it gets recognized in the official Gross Domestic Product (GDP) statistics. When people fix their cars, make their own furniture, tend vegetable gardens, and care for children and the elderly, they are creating value that is economically useful, but not officially recognized as part of national output. If people were to instead pay businesses for these things, even though it is the same work, it would be counted and recognized in government statistics. The failure to account for these contributions is not arbitrary. It is evidence of a societal bias against any mode of production that stands outside the capitalist money economy or the cash nexus. If household production were to be counted as part of GDP, it could potentially add as much as 20 percent to the $11 trillion U.S. economy.

As we have seen, the market system evolved to achieve the ultimate purpose of capitalist profit-making. Only production that is carried out within this cash nexus is seen as legitimate. And as the capitalist market system evolved, it increasingly ensnared households into a web of market relationships with businesses. Households have, of course, existed for thousands of years, but over the history of modern capitalism they have become less self-reliant and more dependent on the system of money and market exchanges. This is particularly true in the United States. Americans make fewer goods and services for themselves and acquire more and more from markets than ever before. People come to rely less and less on non-money interactions in their communities and more and more on the job markets for their livelihoods. From a systems view, we see this trend not as a result of individual choices, but as a necessary result of the profit-centered system of capitalism.

BUSINESSES

At the core of any capitalist economic system is the institution of private property—specifically private ownership of business enterprise. Currently there are somewhere between twenty and thirty million for-profit businesses operating in the U.S. economy. Most of these are operating as capitalist institutions and share a common drive to maximize profits. But within the institution of private enterprise there is an amazing variety of different forms of business ownership, size, organizational or managerial structures, business cultures, and policies. Business enterprises are in a constant state of flux and transformation with corporate mergers, buyouts, new businesses starting up, and hundreds of thousands dissolving or moving off shore every year. The consequences of such instability are often unsettling for people and sometimes disastrous for entire communities. Instability, however, is not necessarily inevitable. If they choose to do the hard work, people can direct the development of business institutions such that they are stable and accountable to the people and communities where they do business.

The most common classifications of business ownership are *sole proprietorships, partnerships, corporations,* and *state-owned or government-owned enterprises.* Since only about 10 percent of measured economic production in the U.S. is carried out by state-owned businesses, our focus for now will be mainly on the prevailing forms of private business ownership. Less common, but growing in popularity are *S corporations* and *limited liability companies* (LLC).

The *sole proprietorship* is a form of business ownership in which only one individual owns the business. Given the institution of private property rights, the sole owner or proprietor has sovereign control over virtually all aspects of the business. Sole proprietorships are typically small, locally owned businesses and are relatively easy to establish. These are the businesses that we are likely to come in contact with on a daily basis such as a family-owned restaurant, dry cleaners, a hair salon, or an independent plumbing contractor. As a single individual, the owner's ability to capitalize is limited and so the scope of operations is also constrained. The owners of sole proprietorships assume the full legal liabilities of the debts of their businesses. This means that if someone invests $100,000 to start a business and that business amasses $500,000 in debt, the responsibility for paying the full $500,000 rests with the owner even though he or she personally only invested a fifth of that amount. The status of unlimited liability of sole proprietors is a key characteristic distinguishing it from a corporation.

Sole proprietorships are many in number, but they carry a small percentage of overall output. Of all the firms operating in the U.S. economy, roughly 72 percent are sole proprietorships but these firms contribute to only about 5 percent of the total private-sector output. Their small share of output stems from the fact that most sole proprietorships are so small compared to the few but gigantic Fortune 500 corporations.

The ability of small, independent sole proprietorships to survive is being challenged. One market after another is becoming dominated by large corporate chains that are systematically driving family farms, independent coffee shops, clothing merchants, music stores, and hardware stores out of communities where many have played an integral role for generations. The health of the local small business sector is a fundamental component of the overall economic vibrancy of any community, urban or rural. Small, locally owned sole proprietorships contribute to the economic vitality of a community by keeping and reinvesting their profits with other small businesses and households in the local community. The large transnational corporations, on the other hand, drain profits from local communities and redistribute them as dividends to investors located far from the sources of these profits.

Another form of business ownership is the *partnership* in which there are two or more owners. Partnerships amount to about 8 percent of all the firms operating in the U.S. economy and produce about 9 percent of the private-sector output. As with sole proprietorships, the owners of a partnership have unlimited liability for the debts of the business. Partnerships in the U.S. economy are more likely to be organized in skilled professions such as health clinics, law offices, accounting services, or engineering firms. Some investors in a partnership may have limited liability status, however, with their potential liability limited to the amount of their investment. The distinction between a sole proprietorship and a partnership can be blurred when the business is family-owned. As with a sole proprietorship, the owners of a partnership have the rights to all the profits generated by their business.

The *limited liability company* (LLC) attempts to merge the advantages of a corporation and partnerships. It is not taxed as an entity separate from its owners as is a corporation, but like a corporation it has limited liabilities for its owners. Similarly, the *S corporation* can elect to not be taxed as a distinct legal entity separated from its owners. Federal income taxes are levied on the income of the shareholders. This "flow through" tax provision in the Internal Revenue Code allows the S corporation to pass its tax liabilities on profits to shareholders, and allows shareholders to deduct losses from their personal income tax. These tax advantages may or may not exist at the state level.

Although sole proprietorships and partnerships are grounded in the institution of private property, they do not necessarily fit well within the modern capitalist economic system. The main reason for this is that in these smaller businesses, there is no separation of ownership and work. Small business owners and professionals in partnerships earn their income through work, unlike capitalists who derive income from owning business property. On the other hand, the form of business ownership that does fit seamlessly into the modern capitalist system is the publicly traded, limited liability *corporation*. Potentially more powerful than any household, government agency, or other institution in the U.S. economy, the corporation is a specific form of private business that has unique characteristics that set it apart from other forms of business ownership.

THE CORPORATION

Without question the dominant economic, political, and cultural institution in the United States is the large, publicly traded transnational corporation.

Though the corporate world is diverse, what we describe here are the for-profit, capitalist enterprises that account for about 86 percent of all private-sector sales in the U.S. economy, and the largest of these—the Fortune 500 corporations—account for about 42 percent of national output.[20] With sales revenues often greater than the economic output of entire states or even entire countries, large corporations wield tremendous power and influence in American society and culture. Auto industry executives, for example, have the power to determine not only what cars and trucks people can buy, but they also decide the standards for auto safety. Executives at commercial banks that have merged with insurance companies have the ability to decide what is, or is not, appropriate healthcare. Executives in the corporate telecommunications and media empires determine what films, music, and books define American culture. Ironically, these giant corporations that dominate the political and cultural landscape of the United States—a country that prides itself on being the vanguard for democratic movements around the world—are fundamentally non-democratic institutions.

Corporations are protected by law as though they were human beings. Like people, corporations can own property, file lawsuits, sue and be sued by other people or other corporations, and enter into binding contractual relations with others. Like people, corporations are protected by constitutional rights of privacy and freedom of speech. As corporations are seen as people in the eyes of the law, they are also treated as special and privileged individuals; for a corporation has its own income tax structure that differs (it is typically lower) from state and federal income taxes placed on real people. But unlike a person, a corporation cannot be incarcerated or subjected to capital punishment.

Corporations are specific institutions that come into being only when they are recognized and licensed by state governments. A key characteristic of corporations is that they are not created by entrepreneurs or investors; they are, in fact, insulated from them. Investors who buy stocks are providing corporations with financing, and are otherwise legally separate from the company. Corporate executives or managers are also legally separate from the corporations in which they work, and while they are responsible for their own actions, they are not liable for those of the corporate entity. In other words, corporations stand as distinct entities that are legally separate from those who create, own shares in, work for, or manage them.

The most distinguishing characteristic of a corporation—the limited liability of shareholders—stems from this legal separation of the corporation and its investors. Shareholders are the owners of a corporation, but they are not liable for the debts or other legal liabilities of the companies in which they invest. As opposed to the individual proprietor or partner in a business who are fully liable for the debts of their firms, the only liability for corporate shareholders is the dollar amount of their original investments in stocks.

Imagine, for example, a corporation that is initially financed with $10 million, of which shareholders purchased $4 million in stocks, and the remainder is raised by issuing corporate bonds or taking out bank loans. If the corporation were to go bankrupt, the investors stand to lose the only $4 million they originally invested, and they would not be responsible for the $6 million owed to creditors. If a sole proprietorship, on the other hand, is capitalized by $4 million by the entrepreneur's investment, and $6 million in bonds or loans, in bankruptcy the entrepreneur could lose not only the original $4 million, but also would be responsible for paying the other $6 million to creditors as well.

Since its inception centuries ago, the publicly traded corporation proved to be an expedient way to amass investment funds from a widely dispersed group of investors. Investors are drawn to corporate ventures by the allure of potentially limitless profits, yet with liabilities that are limited only to the amount of their original investments. As money can be attracted from a multitude of investors, it becomes possible to finance large-scale businesses such as shipbuilding companies, railroads, or mining companies that require much more capital than could be raised by an individual proprietor.

A corporation capitalizes, or initially finances, its business operations by issuing securities such as stocks and bonds to investors, or by taking out bank loans. Stocks, both "common" and "preferred," are certificates that document shares of ownership for the shareholder. Preferred stocks typically have fixed dividend payments. Dividends are shares of the net earnings of the company paid to shareholders on a per-share basis. Issuing preferred stock obligates the corporation to regularly pay the owners a predetermined share of the profits. The vast majority of corporations are capitalized by means of issuing common stock. Common stocks have no such fixed dividends and since most corporations would opt to not have to make fixed dividend payments, common stocks are more prevalent. Another important distinction between common and preferred stock is that common stocks come with voting power, a key element in corporate governance (see explanation below) while preferred stocks do not.

Whereas a stock represents a share of the ownership of a corporation, a bond represents debt. A bond is a kind of IOU to bondholders with a promise to pay the sum of the credited amount plus interest. Unlike shareholders, bondholders are not owners of a corporation, but rather are its creditors. Being a creditor has an advantage for bondholders as they are first in line to get paid in the event of the bankruptcy or liquidation of a corporation.

The process of creating a corporation typically begins with legal documentation filed with a state government. The process is actually quite simple. The first step is to have an attorney draft what is known as *articles of incorporation*, or sometimes referred to as a *certificate of incorporation*. This is a legal description of the corporation to be filed with the secretary of state office in the state where the company is being formed. The articles include the name and address of the corporate headquarters, a description of its business activities as consistent with the laws of the state including its purpose, the number and type of shares issued, and the designation of the board of directors. Listing the purpose of the corporation is centrally important and in states where government control of corporate charters are the lease strict such as Delaware, the purpose can be as generally stated as, "engaging in any lawful activity." For a capitalist enterprise, this means engaging in any activity that will maximize profits. We will return to this issue in a later chapter as we explore alternatives to capitalism and see that these alternatives can be legally defined to serve other purposes that are based on the needs of people and their communities.

State governments usually list the public and social responsibilities that corporations must include in their articles of incorporation. Once these responsibilities are included, the state issues a corporate charter—the permission to be a corporation and an agreement by the corporation to follow the state guidelines. From that point on, the corporation exists as a distinct legal entity that is contractually obligated to its shareholders, and also is obliged to follow the rules and guidelines set out by the state in the articles and charter. Corporate bylaws—also part of the legal documentation—provide legal and managerial guidelines directing the day-to-day business activities along the lines set out by the articles of incorporation and the corporate charter.

Once the corporation is created as a distinct institution, its operations still have to be governed in some way. Like all other forms of business enterprise within capitalism, sovereign control over a business rests with the ownership. As such, control or governance of a corporation ultimately lies with shareholders. To achieve a coherent management structure from a diffusion of independent shareholders, corporations typically employ an electoral process in which owners of common stock are endowed with one voting right for each share owned. Common shareholders are sent a ballot on which they cast votes for board of director nominees and other election items that have a bearing on the status of their ownership. They will elect members of the board of directors with the expectation that the directors will then oversee the governance of the corporation to their benefit and satisfaction. Shareholders can also vote on the designation of independent auditors, and vote on corporate resolutions related to social and ethical aspects of the corporation's business activities. This process should not, however, be confused with democratic governance. Unlike the electoral process in a true democracy where each citizen has one vote, voting rights in a corporation are allocated on the basis of "one share, one vote." This means that a single person who owns a majority of shares can control an election outcome. In fact, for large corporations with widely diffused shareholders, a simple 5 percent or 10 percent ownership could be enough to sway the outcome of an election.

Through the election process, the torch of corporate governance and control is passed from the common shareholders to the board of directors. The board is the governing authority of a corporation and acts as a custodian looking after shareholders' interests. The board of directors typically is not involved in the day-to-day running of the company itself, for that is the job of the top management personnel. The directors hire the top management team or officers, oversee the management team's decisions including executive compensation, decide the amount of dividends (if any) to issue common stock shareholders, periodically review the business's finances, approve or reject mergers with other corporations and establish other policies and goals. The prime goal of any corporation's board of directors is to see that the shareholders realize the maximum returns on their investments.

The unique status of a corporation as a distinct and separate entity means that the question of control and governance plays a major role in the ultimate success or failure of the company. The typical structure of corporate governance in its most basic form is shown in The Corporate Hierarchy. In a top-down authoritarian structure, the typical corporation in a capitalist economy is governed by very highly paid top executives whose incomes are often several hundred times that of their front-line employees.

The top management or officers of a corporation are the executive personnel hired to run the corporation. These top executives such as chief executive officers (CEOs), chief financial officers (CFOs), presidents, and vice presidents make the key decisions that are passed down to various mid-level managers who, in turn, pass them down to the rank-and-file employees.

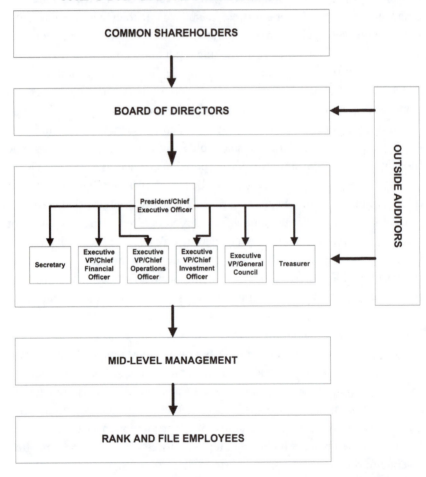

Figure 2

High-level executives are theoretically accountable to the board of directors, but that accountability is often nullified by the fact that the chairman of the board of directors frequently also holds a key position in the top management. The distinction between the board of directors and top executives, many of whom have come to be principal shareholders, has blurred. As the supreme governing authority, the board is expected to hold independent judgment over the decisions made by top management. More likely, however, boards are "rubber stamp" bodies rather than watchdog authorities—submitting without question to the aspirations of top management. This murkiness of ownership and management responsibility is also often extended to the supposedly independent "outside" auditing firms.

Outside auditors are accounting services firms that are hired on an annual basis to review the financial records of corporations and provide them with accurate and lawful documentation of the financial status of the businesses. Their job is to make sure that the corporations' accountants are following the appropriate accounting procedures as stipulated by Generally Accepted Accounting Principles (GAAP). This documentation is then made available to investors as key information regarding the financial health of the business. Many auditing companies, like the boards of directors, have become rubber stamp bodies and all too often comply with the wishes of the corporate executives. This pattern is often facilitated by complex financial incentives for the accounting agencies to provide unrealistically positive reports.

Beginning with the bankruptcy of Enron in 2001, the corporate sector experienced a wave of record-breaking bankruptcies. Much of these were brought about by widespread corporate fraud, conspiracies, and other white-collar crimes. As a result, the U.S. economy experienced the greatest wave of corporate scandals and the largest loss of shareholder equity in the history of the planet, not to mention the loss of billions of dollars in pension funds, and the sacking of millions of employees. In many cases, these laid-off workers also lost substantial investments in the company's shares, pensions, and other benefits. At the center of these scandals are conflicts of interest between the top executives and shareholders, employees and other stakeholders. In the wake of these scandals, the question of proper corporate governance became a high-profile political issue. In an attempt to deal with these problems, Congress passed the Sarbanes-Oxley bill in 2002. Under Sarbanes-Oxley, corporations are required to create a corporate governance committee whose members are independent of the company. The committee is also required to have a charter that specifies the purpose, responsibilities, and evaluation procedures of the committee. Lacking any real punitive enforcement powers, the Sarbanes-Oxley bill was largely a symbolic attempt to deal with corporate conflicts of interest, rather than providing a real solution to the problem.

By 2004, the evidence was overwhelming that conflicts of interest within corporate governance remained widespread. In 2004, *Business Week* published a report analyzing the compensation of the highest-paid executives for some 350 to 400 of the biggest corporations covering 35 major industries. From this list approximately 80 percent of the executives listed held dual titles of board member—usually chairman—and a position within top management—usually chief executive.[21]

The problem of whether boards of directors are truly independent oversight bodies within corporate governance remains largely unaddressed, leaving the broader economy vulnerable to still more fraud-induced instabilities. Taking a systems view, this should not come as a surprise. Capitalism has never been, nor was it ever intended to be, a system designed to bring economic benefit to a wide sector of society. Its overriding purpose has always been to make profits and accumulate wealth for investors.

As it is structured in the U.S. economy, the corporation is an authoritarian, non-democratic institution. As such, it is a fitting component of modern capitalism. Recall that an institution is a social structure of power that can control and direct human social behavior. As an institution, the corporation has a life of its own that transcends the lives and actions of its employees, even including its top managers. The personnel within the top management or board of directors are transitory, but as the institution remains in existence, it continues to carry out its mandate of profit maximization. Corporations are owned and controlled by their principal shareholders and have virtually no legal accountability to the people who work for them or the communities in which they carry out business, except that which is externally imposed on them by government legislation.

In the current system, corporations are institutions specifically created to serve the interests of their investors. However, corporations are also created under the authority of state governments. This means that legal and political machinery could be used to change the fundamental process and assumptions that bear on chartering corporations. In a mindful economy, with a politically active population and a true democracy, the corporation could be redefined as an institution that is created not to serve the interests of a small investor class, but to serve the broader interests of people and communities. We will explore these possibilities in later chapters.

THE HISTORY OF THE CORPORATION IS THE
HISTORY OF CAPITALISM

Recall that capitalism is a system that works according to a specific logic that begins and ends with money. In this system, investors put money into a business enterprise that produces goods or services to be sold in the marketplace for a larger amount of money and thereby create profits. The profits are, in turn, reinvested for another round of money making—and so the monetary wealth of the capitalist accumulates into perpetuity, without limitation and without ever having to participate in the actual work of the enterprise. In fact, the actual production and distribution of goods and services is incidental to the capitalist's goal of accumulating profits. For centuries making profits may have been the goal of the small craft brewer, furniture maker, merchant or family farmer, but these people have always had to work for their livelihoods and are not considered as capitalists in the true sense. Capitalism emerged historically as an economic system when it separated ownership from work, and this form of business ownership was perfected with the creation of the modern corporation.

In 1923, Thorstein Veblen described the separation of ownership and work inherent in the corporate institution as a system of "absentee ownership." He described a business arrangement in which a person can own and enjoy the profits of a business by owning stocks without working for or even seeing the business one owns. Veblen's absentee owner is a capitalist who receives money income from owning and not from working. Veblen writes, "Safe and sane business men would go in for incorporation only on a good prospect of getting a little something for nothing . . ."[22]

There has never been a more expedient form of capitalist absentee ownership than the creation of a corporation. The corporation, with its emphasis on money, buying and selling, and the separation of ownership and work is the perfect embodiment of the logic of capitalism. In this sense, the history of the corporation is inseparable from the history of capitalism.

The prototype for the modern corporation—the joint-stock company—emerged in the sixteenth century as an adjunct to the power of monarchs who were building modernized and militaristic nation-states. As the land-based feudal systems were left behind, European monarchs began to see the political advantages of having stockpiles of gold and silver. With gold and silver, the premier international currencies of that time, a king or queen could hire mercenaries, build warships, buy weapons, and construct spectacular monuments for their self-aggrandizement.

The monarchs sought gold and silver by undertaking large overseas ventures to acquire land, cheap labor, and raw materials, as well as gold and silver itself, and to seize profitable trading opportunities. The earliest joint-stock ventures were high-risk overseas voyages of discovery, plunder, and trade that required considerable capital investment in ships, shipbuilding, and cargo. To meet this demand for capital, they enlisted the help of merchants and bankers who were experienced in creating new methods of finance. It was here that the joint-stock company first came to full development.

These early corporations were able to become large-scale business enterprises by selling shares to a broader section of the population—virtually anyone with some money and the willingness to risk it in such a venture. The principal advantage of the joint-stock company was that wealth could be gathered and centralized, yet at the same time the financial risk was decentralized as it was diffused among a multitude of investors. To centralize capital in this way, new market institutions needed to be developed. Indeed, markets of all kinds were springing up in the cities throughout Europe: stock markets, bond markets, commodities markets, and trading entrepots. Stock exchanges in Lyons, Amsterdam, and London became the new centralized markets in which shares in joint-stock companies could be bought or sold on a regular basis.

The joint-stock companies of the sixteenth and seventeenth centuries were private businesses, but the charters were created and controlled by the monarchs. Typically, they were created when a king or queen would grant special charters that gave companies the exclusive rights to trade in spices, tea, textiles and other commodities in a particular area. As the monarchs retained ultimate control of the corporation, they could determine whether the company would live or die just as they could with the human subjects of their realm.

In Britain by the end of the seventeenth century, the number of corporations was growing exponentially as charters were being granted for large-scale business operations such as mining, domestic and overseas trade, waterworks, and other public utilities.

Perhaps the most famous of the chartered companies was the British East India Company, founded by Queen Elizabeth I in 1600. The British East India Company was notorious for its aggressive expansion into India where it effectively controlled, both economically and politically, the entire subcontinent for hundreds of years. By the eighteenth century, the British East India Company became the largest and most powerful corporation in the world. At the same time, other well-known charter companies were making inroads into North America that would establish the foundation for major transformations of the continent. The Hudson Bay Company was instrumental in establishing Canada as a British colony, and the Virginia and Mayflower Companies—subsidiaries of the British East India Company—were powerful forces in colonizing the United States.

The early corporation, with its limited liability for investors and separation of ownership and work, quickly became the paramount institution for private business. At the same time, it co-evolved with market institutions. These institutional developments, in fact, ushered in the creation of the modern capitalist system. Yet built into this arrangement was an inherent source of conflict. The monarchs who created the corporations and controlled their charters were often at cross-purposes with the members of the entrepreneurial class who financed them. The monarchs were less interested in capitalism and more interested in building nation-states and augmenting their political power, but the investor class was interested in private wealth accumulation. With the ascent of capitalism came the belief that investors should rightfully accumulate money, profits, and wealth for themselves and not for the monarch. This conflict was ultimately resolved in bloody violence.

The conflict between the *ancien régime* of the sovereigns and the emerging class of capitalist entrepreneurs was at the very heart of the American and French Revolutions that began in the late eighteenth century. The capitalists emerged triumphant, and as the power of Europe's ruling monarchies began to decline, so did their ability to maintain control over the corporate charters. The purpose of the corporation as an institution soon shifted from serving the aggrandizement of kings and queens to the capitalist agenda of profit maximization for its shareholders.

Nowhere did this development occur with as much force and rapidity than in the United States. After the American Revolution, the institutional map of the United States economy was redrawn. New forms of governmental institutions were created, and the corporation became a powerful independent institution relentlessly pursuing its goal of accumulating financial wealth for the owners of capital. As modern American capitalism was being forged in the bloody cauldron of war, the state, which was once the creator of the corporation, became its dutiful servant.

For many historians the American Civil War (1861-1865) is seen as the last of a series of capitalist revolutions that spanned nearly 350 years. The Civil

War brought the quasi-feudal slave system in the American South to an end, and this allowed capitalism to expand and consolidate throughout a broader, unified nation. The United States became a kind of testing ground for a pure form of capitalism with giant corporate monopolies in a central position. With the passing of a series of business-friendly legislations and other institutional developments during and after the war, an economic environment was created that allowed large corporations to ascend to unprecedented levels of wealth and power.

One such institutional development was the National Banking Act of 1863. The Banking Act created a unified monetary system that helped commerce expand into a nationwide system. Another development was the passage of The Pacific Railway Acts of 1862 and 1864 which granted enormous subsidies and loans to large and powerful railroad corporations that competed with each other to construct large interstate lines. The legislation authorized the federal government to grant over 179 million acres of public land as right-of-way for building railroads to railroad companies. The government also gave additional subsidies to railroads for laying track in difficult or mountainous terrain. These grants and subsidies created enormous wealth for the railroads and their principal shareholders, but also facilitated the nationwide expansion of industry. The United States economy eventually became a massive market system in which a handful of the largest and most powerful corporations flourished.

As corporations grew in wealth and power, they ascended to dominate all major industries as corporate monopolies. That is, the nationwide market system became increasingly controlled by powerful corporations and not by competitive forces. The gladiatorial combat for market share, in which each business is pitted against every other for survival, concludes with only one left standing—monopoly. As these surviving monopoly corporations grew, one industry after another fell under their control such as railroads, banking, chemicals, steel, meatpacking, sugar, biscuits, oil, and many others. Once their competitors in the marketplace were eliminated, the final battle of the corporate monopoly was to liberate itself from its creator—the state governments that still maintained control over the corporate charter.

As long as state governments control the corporate charter, they also have the power to require the corporation to use part of its earnings in the public interest to finance, for example, infrastructure and schools. State control could also extend to seizing control of an entire industry for public health or security reasons. Such power of the state stands at cross-purposes with the drive for profit maximization. Large corporations grew to become more powerful than many state governments and used that power to challenge states' control over their charters in the courts. Corporations began filing lawsuits arguing that state control was arbitrary and a violation of their constitutional rights. To have such constitutional rights, however, corporations had to be recognized as a kind of person in the eyes of the law. This status of legal "personhood," and the constitutional rights that came with it was the ultimate political and legal achievement of corporate strategists at this time, and may be the single most significant institutional development in the history of American capitalism. By winning corporate personhood, corporations were granted the legal sanctity of free speech, peaceable assembly, liberty, and property that could not be taken from them by the state without due process. Capitalism in the United States was thus liberated from government control as it had been nowhere else in the world, and it got there in the vehicle of corporate personhood.

The corporate personhood movement was spearheaded by Supreme Court Justice Stephen J. Field (1816-1899) who was appointed by Abraham Lincoln in 1863, and served for more than thirty years. Under the guidance of Justice Field, constitutional amendments at the end of the Civil War were reinterpreted in a way that was quite different from their original intention. Though the amendments were directed at eliminating slavery and protecting the rights of individuals, they were twisted by corporate attorneys to imply protection of property rights and business interests. So interpreted, corporations gained a legal basis from which they could liberate themselves from state legislation and state control of their charters.

The Thirteenth and Fourteenth Amendments to the U.S. Constitution, ratified in 1865 and 1868, were explicitly directed toward the abolition of slavery and securing political rights of former black slaves in America. Amendment 13 provides that "neither slavery nor involuntary servitude, except as a punishment for crime whereof the party shall be duly convicted, shall exist within the United States, or any place subject to their jurisdiction."[23] Amendment 14, Section 1, provides that, "No State shall make or enforce any law which shall abridge the privileges or immunities of citizens of the United States; nor shall any State deprive any person of life, liberty or property, without due process of law; nor deny to any person within its jurisdiction the equal protection of the laws."[24] Incidentally, this Amendment represents the first time the U.S. Constitution gives the Federal government specific authority over the state governments.

Although these Amendments were directed toward the freeing of black slaves, Justice Field interpreted them in a much broader sense, asserting forcefully that they should be applied to corporations. Corporations, Justice Field argued, should be seen as no different from human beings in the eyes of the law. The deeper implications of Field's interpretation would be that state governments could not regulate the corporate charter without due process, nor could they maintain control over the corporate charter any more than they could directly control the lives of human U.S. citizens without specific legal justification. Corporate personhood—the recognition of a corporation as a person in the eyes of the law—was thus becoming institutionalized.

Established under dubious circumstances, corporate personhood was finally achieved as a result of a landmark Supreme Court case, *Santa Clara County v. Southern Pacific Railway (1886)*. From the proceedings of *Santa Clara*, the justices implied that corporations are held by law to have the same legal standing as people, though they made no actual ruling. Yet from this implication, subsequent rulings were made in favor of corporate personhood citing *Santa Clara*, and these subsequent rulings stand as Supreme Court precedents. Corporate personhood became institutionalized as a result of a series of otherwise minor Court decisions that followed.

So armed with the constitutional protection of persons, corporations began their legacy of power and dominance decades before women won the right to vote. Liberated from meddlesome state authorities, the corporate "person" was free to maximize returns for shareholders, take control of markets, buy out competitors, and attain monopoly control of entire industries without regard or responsibility for the interests of real people affected by their actions. Between 1898 and 1904, about 1,800 formerly independent corporations were consolidated into 157 giant companies—many of which were illegal monopolies.[25] By the beginning of the twentieth century, corporations rose to account for about 70 percent of all non-agricultural employment, and shortly after the end of World War I in 1918, the number had risen to 87 percent.[26]

Today, of the some 30 million businesses operating in the U.S. economy, only about 5 million are corporations, yet they account for the majority of all economic production. And within this group, a super team of the largest 1 percent claims more than two thirds of all corporate income in the U.S. economy. The large publicly traded corporation is unquestionably the dominant economic institution in the United States economy. Emboldened by federal government subsidies, patent protections, the effective removal of state controls of corporate charters, and the constitutional protections provided by corporate personhood, the corporation now towers over American society. The corporation continues to defy most attempts to bring it under democratic control or regulate it in the public interest. And although it routinely defies accountability to democratically elected government, the corporation is nonetheless able to exert enormous influence on local and national government. Thorstein Veblen observed that the state, once the progenitor and overseer of the corporation, came to be its servant:

> . . . the chief concern of the constituted authorities in all the civilized nations [is] to safeguard the security and gainfulness of absentee ownership. This state of things is now plain to be seen, and it is therefore beginning to cloud the sentiments of the underlying population at whose cost its security and gainfulness are maintained.[27]

The current buzzword for placing corporate interests above that of democratic governance is "deregulation." Deregulation has been sold to the American public as a process in which businesses would be disciplined by competitive market forces rather than public agencies. By virtue of this market discipline, businesses would be forced to serve the public interest. Historically, however, the most frequent outcome of deregulated markets is a corporate monopoly that has driven its rivals out of the market and has effectively eliminated the discipline of market competition. The primary duty of these corporate monopolies is to serve the interests of shareholders, not the public.

From here a deeper irony follows—serving the public interest is exactly what a corporation cannot do if it wants to prevail in a competitive market environment. A corporation that is cut loose from state controls does not have a place for social responsibility in its internal structure. In fact, it was precisely the social responsibilities that were written into the corporate charters by the states that the corporations fought against in their quest for personhood. As a capitalist institution, a corporation has only one mandate: to maximize profits for its shareholders, not to be responsible for the general benefit of the broader community or for sustaining the health of our natural environment. This mandate is a contractual obligation, and the managers of a corporation have a legal, fiduciary responsibility to their shareholders to carry it out. It is the law.

Social and environmental responsibility typically runs counter to profit-making. Strip-mining and clear-cut logging, for example, reap more short-term profits than environmentally sustainable methods of mining or forestry, and sweatshops are more profitable than paying union scale or living wages. Price-gouging, market manipulation, deceptive advertising, aggressive market campaigns aimed at children, and even money-laundering as a way to turn profits from illicit transactions into legitimate assets are all practices that bring in more profits for shareholders. Moreover, the managers or boards of directors cannot be held responsible or accountable for any social or environmental destructiveness that results from their business decisions, for they are merely following the orders of their shareholders. The shareholders also cannot be held accountable, for they have limited liability status. As such the corporation has become the pristine and ideal embodiment of capitalist logic—profitability without accountability.

Here is one example. The global pharmaceutical industry, controlled by a few dozen mega-corporations, is often criticized for notorious price-gouging of its customers and maintaining monopoly controls over drug patents. Hank McKinnel, CEO of drug giant Pfizer, confessed that he would prefer to make his company more socially responsible, but is constrained by the fact that his duty to shareholders comes first.[28] *Business Week* recently published a review of a new book titled, *The $800 Million Pill*, by Merrill Goozner. The book exposes profiteering by the pharmaceutical industry and its public relations cover-up. Goozner charges that the relentless claim by the industry that tremendous profits are needed for research and development is only partially true at best. *Business Week*, however, defends the pharmaceutical industry:

> What he [Goozner] has actually discovered is that the pharmaceutical industry is a business, with all the good and bad that capitalism brings. Of course, drug makers charge the highest prices the market will bear for their products, just as other manufacturers do. Anything less, and they're not doing their duty to shareholders . . . In fact, there often is an inherent conflict between doing well financially and doing what's best for medicine. At the same time, there are plenty of public-spirited industry scientists and executives who are horrified at the shenanigans some companies use to maximize profits. The author tells some of the disturbing stories but fails to recognize the demands of business.[29]

Business Week provides a glimpse of the systemic nature of economic problems of capitalism. The pharmaceutical industry cannot be blamed for profiteering; this is the overriding demand of the capitalist system itself.

This is not to deny that corporations can, and often do, engage in business in a moral or responsible manner, but most show no real inclination to do so unless such practices can also improve upon, or not negatively affect, their bottom line. Destructiveness, venality, greed, and moral turpitude do not necessarily define all corporations or businesses in our economy. But these qualities do exist, nevertheless, in abundance largely as a consequence of the demands for profit-maximization. Corporations do not hesitate to claim credit when they actually do make decisions that help protect the environment or human rights, and in some cases they actually do such things. But these decisions can only be sustained as long as they do not detract from the corporation's institutionalized mandate to maximize profits. Even when socially responsible practices are the result of popular pressures or government regulation, the industry will often advertise its compliance as good citizenship.

In the same way that ownership and work are separated in the capitalist system, ownership and moral or ethical principles are also separated. As shareholders, boards of directors, and executives are all insulated from financial liability, so are they insulated from the moral consequences of their businesses. Shareholders as absentee owners are not required to be concerned about how their profits are made. In such a system, otherwise morally centered individuals work for a corporation that carries out activities that are contrary to their values. Shareholders may also lead exemplary personal lives while the companies they own carry out reprehensible policies on their behalf. Likewise, consumers routinely make purchasing decisions that result in practices they would otherwise condemn. Corporations that successfully oppose government regulations designed to protect people from price-gouging or toxic-waste dumping often employ these same people the regulations were designed to protect. Thus the victims of corporate irresponsibility are themselves compelled, as dependents of these companies, to applaud the resulting higher corporate profits. In the end, many people are compelled to collectively work toward purposes that would otherwise be seen as destructive and pathological if undertaken by individuals. With the publicly traded, limited liability corporation as the dominant institution, predatory business practices become institutionalized.

CONCLUSION

The cash nexus is a market system that locks together households and businesses in a mutually dependent and mutually antagonistic relationship. The dominant institution in this relationship is the large, Fortune 500 transnational corporation. The corporation rose to its position of supremacy because it, more than any other institution, is the embodiment of the capitalist system's drive for profits and wealth accumulation for an absentee class of investors. Because of its drive for profits, social, community, and other concerns that are important to people are subordinated. Perhaps more importantly, these large institutions defy democratic accountability and the ability for people to control the outcome and consequences of economic activity.

It is our contention that in a mindful economy, people can take back control of the business side of the market system by taking an active role in their local economy. People, if sufficiently organized, can take control of businesses in their communities by creating their own corporations with their own corporate charters and their own bylaws. It is not necessary for people to be dependent on businesses that are primarily designed to enrich a small class of investors and are indifferent to the needs of communities. Creating business alternatives for a more mindful future is something we will explore in detail in later chapters.

In a mindful economy we take a broader systems view. When taking a systems view we see that the historical antagonism between households and businesses in the market system has given rise to a higher level of institutional complexity in the U.S. economy. As businesses began to form monopolies, pools, cartels, and business associations to gain control of product markets and combat unionization in labor markets, people began seeking government legislation to protect their interests in both product and labor markets, and labor unions began organizing to protect the interests of workers. These attempts to transcend the crude forces of supply and demand in the market system led to the creation of new economic and political institutions that are now an integral part of the U.S. economic system. It is to these institutions—business associations, labor unions, and government agencies—that we will turn our attention to in the next two chapters.

3

CONFLICT IN THE CASH NEXUS
Labor Unions and Business Associations

Systems abound in nature. Complex structures of relationships exist among living organisms in arid deserts, tropical rainforests, or in the depths of the oceans. Conflict also abounds in nature, and this conflict plays an important role in driving natural systems to evolve toward higher and higher levels of complexity. The most obvious source of conflict in nature is that between a predator and its prey. As a species falls under attack by a predator, it will adapt strategies to elude its predator and survive. The predator, in turn, develops new predatory strategies to which the prey must again adapt a survival counter-strategy. In each move, both the predator and prey evolve to higher levels of sophistication and complexity. Similarly, if swarms of insects repeatedly attack a plant, it can evolve to produce a natural pesticide in its leaves. The pesticide is a new feature of the plant's biology making the plant a more complex organism. The insects, however, will evolve to become more resistant to the pesticide and by doing so they also develop into organisms that are more complex. The plant must, in turn, adapt again and so the overall natural system evolves to higher orders of complexity.

Just as predator/prey relationships in nature lead to complexity, conflicts in the market system have also led to a more complex economic system. The conflicts over prices between buyers and sellers or over wages between employers and employees have resulted in attempts by each to gain market power and control. By growing into giant corporations and forming monopolies or cartels, businesses can gain control over the supply side of product markets and control prices. Consumers respond by pressing for government legislation to break down this corporate power. In labor markets, workers organize into labor unions also with the intention of gaining control of the supply side of labor markets. Businesses respond by forming associations to counteract union power, promote anti-union government legislation, or support anti-union electoral candidates. As the drama of this conflict between businesses and consumers or workers unfolds, the institutional fabric of the U.S. economy evolves to higher and higher levels of complexity. In the last

150 years of U.S. economic history, the capitalist system has been evolving into a more complex, pluralist system in which labor unions, business associations, and government agencies have transcended the market-based system to become key institutions in the economy.

THE MYTH OF LAISSEZ FAIRE

The idea that the U.S. economy is based on a free-market system is largely a myth. It is a myth rooted in eighteenth and early nineteenth-century ideology commonly referred to as *laissez faire*. *Laissez faire*, a French term that literally means "let [people] do [as they please]," gained widespread popularity in Britain and America along with the contributions of classical economists and philosophers including Francois Quesnay, Adam Smith, David Hume, Thomas Jefferson, and others who sought to liberate economic activity from the arbitrary control of monarchs and other members of the privileged aristocracy. Jefferson stated the *laissez faire* belief succinctly: "That government is best which governs the least . . ."[30] Adam Smith and other proponents of *laissez faire* accused the monarchs of Britain and Europe of using government institutions to control economic activity for their own aggrandizement and not for the economic well-being of people. Smith, wielding his path-breaking treatise, *An Inquiry Into the Nature and Causes of the Wealth of Nations* (1776), led the *laissez faire* charge with a sophisticated vision of a free-market economy. In Smith's view, a market economy has the ability to self-regulate for the maximum benefit of people and increase the wealth of nations as long as it is left free from the heavy-handed use of government authority.

The idea of a self-regulating market economy is based on an assumption that freely moving prices will always adjust to changing market conditions and will automatically bring about balance, order, and prosperity. In the *laissez faire* view, if imbalances such as long-term shortages, surpluses, or widespread unemployment were to emerge, these imbalances are assumed to be temporary anomalies that will be corrected by price adjustments in the market system. For example, if a food shortage were to occur, food prices would automatically rise; with rising prices, farmers would have an incentive to produce more food for the market and the shortage would eventually be eliminated. Or, if unemployment were to rise in labor markets, this would naturally push down wages or salaries, and lower wages would give private employers an incentive to hire more workers, thus eliminating the unemployment problem. Central to the *laissez faire* argument is the belief that markets will always self-regulate to achieve the best possible balance in which both buyers and sellers are satisfied and potential conflict between them is eliminated.

Like all myths, the myth of a perfectly balanced, self-regulating system of markets serves a social purpose. It sustains a belief in the inherent goodness and fairness of a pure model of capitalism in which the prevailing institutions are unregulated private business and markets. The myth also sustains a belief that government agencies or union institutions are unwanted fetters that prevent self-regulation in the marketplace and result in imbalances and inefficiencies. By perpetuating the myth of a self-regulating market system, business interests are able to weaken public support for union organizing or government regulation. Free-market ideology has served to mold public opinion in ways that favor business interests over organized labor, and markets over government regulation. It has also served to create a climate of opinion that is more accepting of large corporations' ascent to commanding heights of wealth and power.

One of the great ironies of the *laissez faire* myth is that a free and unregulated market is probably the last thing that most well established businesses actually want. For most businesses, a free market is an undesirable environment in which new competitors are free to challenge existing businesses, where prices are uncertain, and there is a constant threat of losing market share and profits. No businesses actually want to see their product markets openly flooded by competitors who threaten to drive prices and profits into the ground. In the several hundred years of capitalism, businesses have embraced the interventions of government so long as those interventions protect their profitability from the wild uncertainties of unregulated competition. The subtext of the free-market myth is to build support for a capitalist system that is free, but only in the sense of being free from institutional controls that could threaten the primary purpose of profit maximization, namely government regulatory agencies or "red tape" and labor unions. Once liberated from these burdensome institutions, big businesses become free to assert their control and dominance in the market system.

Although this myth does contain fragments of truth and represents an important ideology that has guided the operation of the U.S. economy, it is a poor representation of the economic reality. The U.S. economy is more accurately described as a "controlled market" system than a "free-market" system. Certainly labor and product markets in the cash nexus are influenced by the forces of supply and demand, but they have never been completely free from influence and control on the part of powerful interests. Domination of product markets, particularly by large businesses, has historically been the rule rather than the exception. Throughout the nineteenth and early twentieth centuries, virtually every basic industry was dominated by powerful corporate trusts and monopolies. Today, the picture is very much the same. In the pharmaceutical industry, for example, a handful of large companies—in collaboration with government agencies—controls drug patents and therefore controls the supply of prescription drugs. The markets for heating oil and gasoline are controlled by a few large oil companies that control refinery output, media access is dominated by giant telecommunications conglomerates, and retailing is rapidly falling under the control of the world's largest corporation, Wal-Mart.

Labor markets also cannot be considered as free markets. Although the forces of supply and demand for job skills do play a role in determining salaries and working conditions, these markets are not free from cultural or political influences such as race and gender discrimination, cultural biases, and outsourcing, or from unionization and government legislation such as minimum-wage laws or living-wage ordinances. Control, power, influence, and domination are not exceptions in the market system, they are the rules, and attempts to gain such control have led to much conflict.

For the most part, large corporate enterprises have prevailed in the struggle between people (workers and consumers) and businesses for control of markets. The principal reason for their success is that they represent high concentrations of wealth and ownership of business assets. In a capitalist system, advantage always lies with those who own and control these assets, which are the principal means of producing wealth. By forming monopolies, trusts, and business associations, or by their absolute size, large corporations continue to hold dominant power in the U.S. economy and have never deviated from their ultimate goal to maximize profits.

In the pages that follow is an examination of these struggles in the market system with labor on one side and business on the other. The historical record shows that businesses used every method available to outdo their competitors, to seize monopoly control in product markets, and to crush attempts by labor unions to organize. The record also shows that unions sought to control labor markets and protect workers from what they saw as the abuses of their employers, as well as from competition from a seemingly endless supply of cheap labor migrating from one area to another. Both sought political power in government, and both took political action against the other. Tensions and conflicts grew between labor and business and this resulted in some of the worst violence in American history. Out of this conflict emerged an institutionally diverse system that has transcended the basic market forces of supply and demand despite the popular mythology of *laissez faire*.

MONOPOLIES, TRUSTS, AND BUSINESS ASSOCIATIONS

We can see from names like Standard Oil Co., General Electric, and General Motors that the aims of the founders of these corporations were not modest. As evident in both their names and their actions, corporate giants in America set out to create monopolies, monopsonies, trusts, and other structures of economic power. The methods these businesses employed varied, but their aims were always the same—to control and dominate the market system.

The most direct way to control a product market is to monopolize. A monopoly occurs when one firm either has control of the market on the output side of the market system, or is in a position to dominate its competitors single-handedly. With monopoly power, a business can restrain market trade by keeping a certain amount of production off the market, and create artificial shortages and a seller's market. By creating artificial shortages, a business is in a position to leverage higher prices than a truly competitive market would allow and to sustain higher profits. Moreover, as a business firm establishes a monopoly in product markets, it can also gain monopsony power. Similar to a monopoly, a monopsony occurs when there is only one employer or buyer in labor and other input markets. With monopsony power a firm can force down employees' wages and prices paid to suppliers as they are left with little or no options to work or sell elsewhere. By driving up prices in product markets and driving down labor and resource prices in input markets, corporate giants become highly profitable. With these high profits, they shine as models of highly successful capitalist enterprises.

Monopoly capitalism reached its high point in the hundred years spanning the mid-nineteenth to mid-twentieth centuries. During this period, most of the basic industries such as steel, oil, tobacco, sugar, and others were monopolized by companies such as U.S. Steel Corporation, Standard Oil Co., American Tobacco, and the American Sugar Refining Company. However, it is difficult to gain monopoly control of a market by the brute force of price competition alone, and perhaps impossible to sustain for any prolonged length of time. These businesses therefore used other more sophisticated methods to gain market control by organizing entire industries into complex financial structures known as *trusts*. The creation of the corporate trust was perhaps the most significant contribution to the development of monopoly capitalism, and was largely masterminded by investment banker J.P. Morgan.

The son of a wealthy banker, John Pierpont Morgan used his inheritance to begin his own investment banking business. Established in 1895, J.P. Morgan & Company specialized in brokering large quantities of gold and underwriting stocks for the railroad industry. Early in his banking career, Morgan made a fortune selling gold to the U.S. government through a syndicate of commercial banks. The U.S. Treasury Department was teetering on a major crisis as it was about to deplete its reserves of gold—the principal commodity backing the value of the dollar at that time. Under the leadership of Morgan, a group of commercial banks combined into a syndicate and entered into an agreement with the Treasury Department to exchange gold for government bonds. The bonds were then immediately resold by the banks to investors for a substantial profit. In these financial deals, Morgan and other bankers came to realize that collusion rather than market competition was a far more lucrative mode of profit making. Morgan stated explicitly that, "We do not want financial convulsions and have one thing one day and another thing another day . . . I like a little competition, but I like a combination better."[31]

With combination and collusion as his guiding principles, Morgan began organizing steel and other industries into powerful financial arrangements that came to be called trusts. At the center of these trusts were holding companies that were financed by the deposits held by commercial banks. These holding companies were shell companies—corporations that existed on paper but did not produce goods or services. Typically, a holding company would buy controlling shares—at least 50 percent—in all or most of the companies within a particular industry such as oil or sugar refineries. By owning enough shares in formerly independent firms, the holding company would eventually gain control of the entire industry and thereby could control the output of that industry as a single monopoly. By controlling production, the trust could then restrain trade, control prices, and reap huge profits. Companies participating in the trust arrangement were freed from the risks and discipline that real price competition would otherwise impose on them.

In the decades surrounding the turn of the nineteenth to the twentieth century, Morgan's trust enterprises played a central role in combining formerly competitive firms into corporate empires including U.S. Steel Corporation, Standard Oil Co., and American Telephone and Telegraph (AT&T). With Morgan's financial assistance, Andrew Carnegie succeeded in combining all the major steel producers into a single trust. The steel trust encompassed over 150 factories and controlled about two-thirds of the entire U.S. steel market in nearly every category from ore extraction to finished products such as wire, steel tubing, and railroad iron. From its earliest beginnings, modern steel production in the United States was organized not by the forces of supply and demand of the free market, but by the monopoly control of a corporate trust.

Another famous example of a corporate trust at the turn of the twentieth century was Standard Oil Company founded by John D. Rockefeller. Also with Morgan's assistance, Standard Oil Co. stitched together a trust that held a controlling interest in virtually every oil-producing firm in the United States. At its peak, Standard Oil controlled 90 percent of America's oil industry. Under similar trust arrangements, American Telephone and Telegraph gained monopoly control over the entire country's telephone system and International Harvester controlled over 85 percent of all farm machinery production in the U.S. Nonetheless, each trust was a flagrant violation of the Sherman Act, the first anti-trust law designed to limit corporate power and such dominance in the marketplace.

The U.S. Senate conducted an investigation into these violations and produced a report that disclosed that at one time J.P. Morgan sat on the board of forty-eight corporations and John D. Rockefeller on thirty-seven.[32] Morgan and Rockefeller, who were once rivals in the trust-building business, eventually combined their resources to form the ultimate corporate colossus known as the Northern Securities Corporation. This was an amalgamation of corporate directorates of some 112 companies combining over $22.2 billion in assets.[33] In one sector after the next, the pattern of trust building was the same, and a handful of corporate barons stood astride over entire industries.

The myth of free-market capitalism provided cover for the reality of monopoly capitalism ruled by these giant corporate trusts. Dispelling this myth, writer and social critic, Matthew Josephson, revealed that business enterprise in America more resembled the estates of feudal lords, or barons, than modern business enterprise. In his famous book, *The Robber Barons*, Josephson writes:

[We live in] an America in which the citizen was born to drink the milk furnished by the milk Trust, eat the beef of the beef Trust, illuminate his home by the grace of the oil Trust, and die and be carried off by the coffin Trust.[34]

Far from admitting their reliance on these anti-competitive structures, however, corporate barons of the late nineteenth and early twentieth centuries concealed their monopoly power behind bold proclamations of the virtues of free-market capitalism. In the *North American Review* Andrew Carnegie immodestly credited the free market for his business success, and reassured his audience that all is for the best:

> The price which society pays for the law of competition . . . is also great; but the advantages of this law are also greater still, for it is to this law that we owe our wonderful material development, brings improved conditions in its train . . . The laws of accumulation will be left free; the laws of distribution free. Individualism will continue, but the millionaire will be but a trustee for the poor; entrusted for a season with a great part of the increased wealth of the community, but administering it for the community far better than it could or would have done for itself.[35]

Carnegie could not have truly believed that the laws of competitive markets should be left free, for Carnegie gained his original position of advantage in the steel industry from government tariffs (import taxes) on imported steel. Beginning with the Morrill Tariff (1861) and other high-tariff legislation passed after the Civil War (1861-1865), the U.S. steel industry was protected from foreign competition, particularly from the British who had developed a new, technologically superior process for producing steel. Carnegie saw an opportunity to make a fortune by bringing this new technology into the U.S. and seizing a position of advantage in the steel markets while taking cover under government tariffs. Without worrisome offshore competition, and by taking advantage of the early adoption of technology copied from the British, Carnegie Steel was able to dominate the steel industry in the United States for many decades.

It would also take a long stretch of the imagination to see Carnegie as a benevolent trustee for the poor. He became one of the richest men of his era, not by his charitable works, but by paying his own steel workers bare subsistence wages for twelve-hour workdays, and by aggressively and even violently crushing union-organizing at his steel plants. All the while, he sustained monopoly control of steel prices and high profits. With those monopoly profits, Carnegie pushed potential competitors out of the market; competitors who often offered better pay and conditions for their workers.

It was rare to find a corporate magnate who seriously played the role of a public-spirited administrator of community welfare. J.P. Morgan famously proclaimed outright contempt for public responsibility when he angrily asserted, "I owe the public nothing."[36] Railroad baron Billy Vanderbilt expressed his sentiments on the public responsibilities of the corporation, "The public be damned. I am working for my stockholders."[37] Proclamations of "free enterprise" seemed to be interpreted by the corporate giants to mean the freedom to dominate entire industries and the freedom to use their wealth as they pleased without the meddlesome concerns of the well-being of people.

POPULAR OPPOSITION

A groundswell of opposition rose to challenge this arrogance of the barons of industry and the concentrated power of corporate monopolies. At the same time that Morgan, Carnegie, and Rockefeller were building their corporate empires, workers were joining forces to take direct, and sometimes violent, action against what they perceived to be economic injustice. Membership in labor unions was increasing exponentially despite the risks of job loss, legal persecutions, and even violent intimidation. Alongside these unionized workers, farmers' associations and progressive citizen groups were also organizing, agitating, boycotting, and putting pressure on their elected legislators for political reform directed at breaking down the excesses of corporate power. Bending to forceful grass-roots pressure that came to be known as "populism," legislators began drafting new laws designed to curb the power of the corporate monopolies.

The first major piece of such legislation was the Sherman Anti-Trust Act of 1890. Named after Senator John Sherman of Ohio, the Sherman Act states that "every contract, combination in the form of trust or otherwise, in restraint of commerce among the several states, or with foreign nations, is hereby declared illegal." Sherman saw a need for the federal government to respond to widespread popular demands for reforms and to use the power of their votes to return a share of economic power to ordinary people. He suggested that if the government failed to do so within the regular political channels, the country would be facing a more dreadful and radical uprising. In a speech before the U.S. Senate Sherman warned that, "You must heed their appeal or be ready for the socialist, the communist, the nihilist. Society is now disturbed by forces never felt before . . ."[38]

Although Congress can pass reform legislation, such laws can only be effective if the judicial branch properly interprets their intentions, and if the executive branch properly enforces them. Neither of the other two branches of federal government showed the political will to do so, at least not in the years immediately after the passage of the Sherman Act. The Supreme Court narrowly interpreted the Sherman Act to apply to commerce (buying and selling) and not to manufacturing or production. As trusts in steel, oil, and sugar controlled production and refining, they were allowed to form and to continue to abuse their monopoly power unchallenged in the courts.

Not content with merely neutralizing the intent of the Sherman Act, big businesses sought to use the law to crush labor unions. Unions were becoming more active in pursuing workers' interests by organizing workers and orchestrating strikes and boycotts. Invoking the Sherman Act, business attorneys labeled these tactics as unlawful conspiracies to restrain trade in labor markets.

Nonetheless, popular opposition to the undemocratic power wielded by corporate monopolies continued unabated. Over time, the political winds began to shift slowly against the monopolies and in favor of organized labor and the populist movement. In addition to the pressures coming from the ballot box, American political leaders seemed to be genuinely concerned that a radical, working-class rebellion in the United States could actually happen if the political system failed to respond as John Sherman had warned.

Riding this wave of populism into the White House was the "trustbusting" president, Theodore Roosevelt. Roosevelt, following the assassination of President McKinley in 1901, pushed for more assertive government enforcement of anti-trust legislation, including the famous breakup of the Morgan/Rockefeller Northern Securities Company. In 1908, Roosevelt's former vice-president Robert Taft was elected president. Taft continued Roosevelt's stand against corporate monopolies and pursued the dissolution of the Standard Oil and the American Tobacco trusts in 1911. Standard Oil was broken up into smaller companies that are now familiar names in the oil business: Mobil Oil, Exxon (now Exxon/Mobil), ARCO, and Chevron. American Tobacco was also segmented into the American Tobacco Company, Liggett & Myers, and P. Lorillard.

The movement to draft and enforce anti-trust legislation did not end in 1911. In 1912, Woodrow Wilson became president and the White House moved from Republican to Democratic control. Wilson continued the earlier administrations' efforts at anti-trust reforms, and in 1914, his administration pushed through the Clayton Act and the Federal Trade Commission Act (see

Chapter Four for the details). These laws were specifically designed to bolster the Sherman Act and punish businesses for predatory practices, including a provision in the Clayton Act prohibiting the use of the Sherman Act to get court injunctions for breaking union strikes and boycotts. The act explicitly declared that "the labor of a human being is not a commodity or article of commerce" and not subject to the provision prohibiting restraint of trade in the Sherman Act.[39]

Since that time, anti-trust legislation and enforcement has waxed and waned depending on the political ideology of those in power. During the 1920s, the Republican administrations of Harding, Coolidge, and Hoover were more business-friendly and ignored corporate combinations and price-fixing, particularly in financial markets. Collusion among finance companies came to be one of the key factors that led to financial market collapse and the subsequent Great Depression of the 1930s.

By the Depression years, Democrat Franklin D. Roosevelt's administration once again raised the profile of pro-labor and anti-trust legislation. Under the leadership of the new Roosevelt administration, much progressive legislation that collectively came to be called the "New Deal" was passed. Part of the New Deal was the passage of the most important piece of pro-labor legislation in American history—The National Labor Relations Act of 1935 (see in the next section on Labor Unions). Roosevelt also drove through the Robinson Patman Act of 1936 to strengthen the Clayton Act, particularly outlawing predatory pricing as a means to dominate markets.

Since the New Deal era, the federal government has periodically brought suits against corporate monopolies forcing their breakup into smaller companies or other significant changes. In 1975, for example, Xerox had nearly 100 percent market share in paper copiers until Nixon administration officials forced it to license patents of its machines to competitors, after which its market share fell below 50 percent. The American Telephone and Telegraph (AT&T) monopoly was broken up into twenty-two local companies in the early 1980s. The current trend, however, is similar to that of the 1920s in that the federal government is less concerned about the ascent of gigantic corporate empires that are allowed to climb to unprecedented levels of control and power.

Competitive markets, the *laissez faire* myth tells us, are mechanisms for disciplining greedy or inefficient producers in a struggle for the consumers' dollars in which only the fittest companies survive. What is concealed by this myth, however, is that after the process of natural selection in the marketplace is complete, the resulting "winner" is left alone to establish a monopoly. Ironically, once these monopolistic winners gain unchallenged control of their markets, they seek cover under the myth of a self-regulating competitive market system that they themselves have destroyed. Whether they are monopolies in the strict sense of the term, or corporate giants wielding much power, the result is the same—control and domination rather than true competition.

The Fortune 500 corporations that reside at the center of the U.S. economy today continue to dominate basic industries like oil, auto manufacturing, retailing, insurance, and telecommunications. With massive amounts of cash at their disposal, these businesses not only hold a controlling position in the market system, but also dominate much of the policy-making and government regulation in the political arena as well. We will turn to this topic once again in a later chapter.

BUSINESS ASSOCIATIONS

Gaining monopoly power over markets was only one of the methods employed by businesses to assure their steady flow of profit making. Businesses with common interests organized themselves into formal associations largely as a political counter-measure to populism and union organizing. As they currently stand, business associations have brought together local or industry-specific companies such as The National Food Processors Association, The American Brass Association, The American Iron Association, and The Mine Owners Association. They have also created national "umbrella" associations such as the National Association of Manufacturers and the United States Chamber of Commerce that represent a broad spectrum of business and industry interests.

Some business association activity is directed toward achieving relatively benign goals that benefit its members. Such activities include gathering industry or market information that members would not have the resources to gather individually, setting industry standards for product specifications and quality, engaging in promotional activities that would collectively benefit the constituent businesses, and hosting conferences. Business associations also advise certifying boards and licensing agencies, and determine product-testing standards in conjunction with government regulatory agencies. They also may provide support services such as credit, insurance, and consultation for member businesses.

There are currently about 8,000 registered business associations actively operating in the United States. Washington D.C., the political nerve center, has the highest concentration of business associations with about 1,200 headquartered there, compared to about 700 in the state of New York and fewer than 500 in California.[40] The National Association of Manufacturers and The United States Chamber of Commerce are among the most powerful lobbying operations in American politics.

When business associations first came into being around the turn of the twentieth century, however, their purposes were less benign. They combined the resources of individual businesses to influence government legislation and pressure public officials, to collaborate in their efforts to weaken the power of unions by bringing immigrants and children to work as strikebreakers, to gain court injunctions to stop boycotts organized by labor unions, and to promote pro-business propaganda by controlling and influencing newspapers. Although the specific industries represented by business associations differ and their immediate purposes are multifaceted, their ultimate goals have always been the same—to control markets and to maximize investor profits. These associations still flex their sizable political muscles as an integral component in their strategies aimed at achieving these goals for their constituent businesses.

The National Association of Manufacturers (NAM) was formed in 1895, and its principal goal at the time was to fight against any recognition of the legitimacy of trade unionism. One of its first major goals under the leadership of David M. Parry was to organize local business associations to campaign against the "closed shop" model of union contracts. A closed shop is one in which every employee of the business is required by contract to join a particular union. The campaign was successful in consolidating employers and giving them a common cause as the champions of "individual freedom." Their ultimate aim, however, was to encourage the employers to hire immigrant laborers; many whose native language was not English, and who experienced difficulties reading labor contracts and, therefore, were not inclined to sign closed shop agreements. In the early 1900s, Parry successfully raised the anti-closed shop propaganda campaign to the national level and public opinion began to stir against unions in the name of "freedom." NAM was also politically aggressive and organized a sophisticated lobbying machine that was geared to defeat any candidate who appeared friendly to labor unions.

Currently the National Association of Manufacturers is more concerned with influencing public policy through political action than fighting labor unions directly. One of its principal aims has been to forge a consensus among its membership companies on trade relations with foreign countries. It also works on specific issues such as reducing employees' healthcare benefits for employees or gaining government subsidies.[41]

A much larger and comprehensive umbrella business association is the United States Chamber of Commerce. The U.S. Chamber was founded in 1912 with the intention of creating a unified federation of businesses that would approach labor organizing and other issues with a single voice. It is the largest umbrella organization in the world representing the interests of over three million business enterprises. The U.S. Chamber has over 3,000 state and local chambers, which contain over 830 affiliated business associations and 90 international chambers.[42] Its members include large multinational corporations as well as small businesses, but the governing structure tends to favor the interests of large corporations as most of the directors who sit on the board of the Chamber are also executives of Fortune 500 corporations.

The Chamber is mainly focused on using its size and vast financial resources to lobby federal and state governments on legislative issues that affect the business interests of its members. In the mid-1970s, under the leadership of President Richard Lesher, the Chamber became a powerful lobbying machine and successfully influenced federal government legislation for cutting corporate taxes, deregulating industries, and busting powerful labor unions.

The U.S. Chamber and local Chambers boast that their full-time lobbying teams work around the clock to influence legislators and regulators to write laws and administer them in business-friendly directions. The Chambers keep their members informed of proposed legislation and regulatory or judiciary issues in their newsletters and their magazine, *Nation's Business.* The Chamber typically marshals its forces on key legislative issues with direct mail campaigns, phone banks, campaign contributions through its political action committee, and direct communication to members of Congress. It also assists legislators and their staffs by drafting proposed language that is sometimes voted into pro-business laws just as they were written by lobbyists, without amendments or even in some cases without a close reading on the part of the elected representatives who vote for them.

In 2004, Chamber of Commerce President and CEO Tom Donohue boasted their success as a lobbying militia for businesses:

> To briefly recap, the Chamber put 215 people on the ground in 31 states; sent 3.7 million pieces of mail and more than 30 million e-

mails; made 5.6 million phone calls; and enlisted hundreds of associations and companies in our web-based 'VoteForBusiness.com' program to educate and mobilize voters. Combining these activities with ILR's [Institute for Legal Reform] voter education efforts in 16 state Supreme Court and Attorney General contests, as well as our targeted campaign to make so-called tort reform a factor in the presidential race, the Chamber invested up to $30 million in the November 2 elections.[43]

And at its website the Chamber advises businesses on how to undermine minimum-wage laws:

> Whether you need to know how to comply with the new minimum wage law or how to manage your liability risk, we're here to help. Our publications, *Nation's Business* and *The Business Advocate,* provide regular legislative updates and in-depth analyses on issues affecting your business.[44]

The Chamber's "tort reform" project has been a crusade to undermine laws which are written to compensate victims of accidents or illnesses that are caused by dangerous or illegal business practices. In the late 1980s, the Chamber created the Institute for Legal Reform (ILR) as an agency guiding corporations on how to undermine or avoid these laws. The ILR has also pursued the more aggressive tactic of launching attack ad campaigns against judges who ruled in favor of victims in tort cases. The ILR has also funneled campaign dollars that are used to affect election outcomes.[45]

In the election year of 2008, Donohue vowed to wage an aggressive campaign to punish any political candidate who was not aligned with business interests. Donohue promised to, "build a grass-roots business organization so strong that when it bites you in the butt, you bleed."[46] He also vowed to spend more than the $60 million they spent in the last presidential election.

Although the Chamber has targeted politicians and judges who are viewed as less sympathetic to business interests, its chief antagonist is organized labor. Historically, the U.S. Chamber joined the NAM on anti-closed shop campaigns, and has been determined wherever possible to keep local labor markets "free" of labor-union organizing. Thus far in the twenty-first century, the Chamber has been more focused on specific issues such as supporting presidential orders prohibiting mandatory labor agreements such as "living wage" rules on federally funded projects, and challenging pro-union legislation in the courts.

Like NAM, the Chamber also stands in opposition to government regulation of business. Most notable is its antagonistic relationship with the U.S. Occupational Safety and Health Administration (OSHA). In a lawsuit filed in 1998, the U.S. Chamber of Commerce along with the National Association of Manufacturers won a court injunction to stop OSHA's Cooperative Compliance Programs (CCP). The CCP plan set out to reduce job-related injuries and illnesses and attempted to approach over twelve thousand employers that had a documented track record of workplace hazards. The plan was to require employers to cooperate with on-site inspectors in exchange for technical assistance in correcting workplace hazards and lighter penalties for future violations. Over ten thousand companies that were targeted by OSHA agreed to participate, but then backed out of the agreement when the Chamber/NAM suit was filed. The OSHA program remains dormant and focuses on reviewing claims dealing with unsafe working conditions.

Another high-profile umbrella business association is the Business Roundtable (BRT). Sensing that the Chamber and NAM were both too generic in that they appealed to the lowest common denominator of large and small businesses, the executives of the largest Fortune 500 corporations formed their own elite association in 1972. Whereas the Chamber and NAM were focused on fighting labor unions and promoting business-friendly legislation at the local and national levels, the BRT set its sights on the global interests of America's largest industrial, banking, insurance, retailing, transportation, and utilities corporations. Supposedly competing firms in these sectors sit, side by side, formulating a consensus on how to direct American and international economic policy toward their profit-maximization goals. In a manner similar to the proclamations of Carnegie in which the "millionaire is to be the trustee of the poor," the BRT demonstrates its own and perhaps more sophisticated version of corporate paternalism:

> [The BRT] is committed to advocating public policies that foster vigorous economic growth, a dynamic global economy [verb] . . . that basic interests of business closely parallel the interests of the American people, who are directly involved as consumers, employees, shareholders and suppliers. Thus, CEOs, although they speak as individuals, have responsibilities that relate to many factors . . . that affect the well-being of all Americans.[47]

In other words, what is good for highly compensated CEOs and the large corporations they manage, is necessarily good for all. This has been a common sentiment among business leaders since former General Motors Chairman Charles E. Wilson testified to the U.S. Senate in 1955 that, "What is good for General Motors is good for America." However, it is a sentiment that has not been shared by millions of working people who oppose the concentration of wealth and power into the hands of a few giant corporations. The principal force in this opposition is organized labor.

LABOR UNIONS

Labor unions are well-established institutions in the U.S. economy. Unionization is based on the principle that working people can act collectively to gain some influence over the markets for their labor, and ultimately protect their livelihoods from their employers as well as from excessive competition among themselves. Modern labor unions developed at a time in the late nineteenth century when the barons of industry were building their monopoly empires. As businesses grew and became more powerful, it became clear to many working people that they would become increasingly powerless to negotiate with their employers as individuals, and so they turned to organized labor unions. Collectively workers gained formidable power in labor markets. Just as businesses achieved monopoly power by controlling the supply of goods in product markets, workers saw that they could gain power by limiting the supply of labor that enters labor markets. By doing so, workers could exert some control over the prevailing wage and other conditions in their line of work. Part of the ability to control the supply of labor stems from an underlying ability to limit the number of people who have access to training. By controlling the training of workers, organized labor can limit the number of skilled workers entering the markets. Thus, the hallmarks of unionization—organized control over skills and collective action—became part of the institutional fabric of the U.S. economy.

The earliest labor unions in America developed in the eighteenth and nineteenth centuries as associations of skilled artisans and craftsmen that had their roots in the guilds of medieval Europe. The medieval guilds were authoritarian and hierarchical craft or trade associations that controlled every aspect of pre-modern industrial production. Guild institutions organized the work of weavers, metalworkers, masons, cobblers, carpenters, shoemakers, bakers, and others in skilled trades. Workers were ranked within their guilds according to their skills and experience, beginning with the apprentice and moving up to the journeyman through master status. The sovereigns of the guilds were the guild masters. Under the paternalistic guidance of guild masters, guilds set strict rules on production processes, payment and working conditions, and the prices of goods as they were sold in the town markets. The most important function of the guilds, however, was to control apprentice training programs. By controlling worker training and skills, the guilds maintained monopoly control over the workers' trade—a function that carried over into modern labor unions long after the medieval guilds faded from memory.

Skilled labor unions in America first developed in the New England states and along the Atlantic seaboard where the supply of skilled labor was relatively scarce. Labor unions were virtually nonexistent in the southern states as the economies there were mainly agricultural and slavery was the dominant economic institution. New England city officials believed that the skills of iron and glass workers, tool makers, bakers, carpenters, and others needed protection as "licensed trades" because these workers and their skills were necessary for maintaining the well-being of the general public. They also believed that well-organized and licensed labor markets would prevent chronic labor shortages and this would prevent inflation caused by rising wages. When negotiating pay and working conditions with their employers and officials, workers in licensed trades banded together in unions and acted collectively.

The labor movement in the United States gained momentum in the mid-nineteenth century as industrial capitalism came into full swing. Industrialization and the factory system brought substantial increases in output and productivity, which created tremendous wealth for the factory owners. At the same time, steam-powered machines were displacing many skilled workers out of their jobs, and masses fell into a grinding poverty never before seen in history. Writers such as William Blake, Charles Dickens, Émile Zola, and others witnessed the dark side of industrialization and the slum conditions that came with it: long and dangerous hours, child labor and generally miserable living conditions. The dirty and overcrowded slums of British industrial cities that were lamented by British poet William Blake as "satanic mills" were recreated in American cities, and became breeding grounds of militant forms of organized labor—particularly among the less skilled laborers. Historian Howard Zinn describes the condition for working people in Philadelphia and New York:

In Philadelphia, working-class families lived fifty-five to a tenement, usually one room per family, with no garbage removal, no toilets, no fresh air or water. There was fresh water newly pumped from the Schuylkill River, but it was going to the homes of the rich. . . . In New York you could see the poor lying in the streets with the garbage. There were no sewers in the slums, and filthy water drained into yards and alleys, into the cellars where the poorest of the poor lived, bringing with it a typhoid epidemic in 1837, typhus in 1842. In the cholera epidemic of 1832, the rich fled the city; the poor stayed and died.[48]

It was not uncommon for working people to labor twelve-hour days, seven days a week resting only one day of the year—on Christmas. Textile, steel, and food processing plant workers would, after a twelve-hour shift, walk to their crowded tenement homes that were freezing cold in the winters and suffocating with heat in the summers, and their children suffered from lice and a multitude of infectious diseases. Many of the working people who had no choice but to live in these industrial cities fetched their drinking water from outdoor taps that drew water from underground wells contaminated with raw sewage. People did not have gardens in which they could grow food and relied on local, unregulated merchants who sold spoiled food at high prices, and peddled milk that was adulterated with formaldehyde as a kind of crude and highly toxic preservative.

To make matters worse for working people, the capitalist system, with its heavy reliance on the market system, was proving to be highly unstable. Changing market conditions brought about business cycles in which a boom period of rapid growth and inflation would be followed by deep recessions and depressions. Business cycles brought excessively high prices one year and unemployment the next. These economic instabilities were frequently followed by food riots and urban unrest as angry mobs clashed with local police who were often acting as hired agents on behalf of wealthy business owners.

Zinn chronicles the working-class rebellions in the United States as spontaneous outbreaks of collective rage in which mobs of angry workers stormed into affluent neighborhoods throwing bricks and torching buildings. Such rebellions against the rich were swiftly crushed by the local police and militia. Yet often the collective rage would take the form of hostilities between different groups within the working classes such as religious hatred between Protestants and Catholics, distrust of immigrants, or racial hatred of black workers or any other group that was seen as a threat to already flooded labor markets. Workers were beginning to see that protection of their labor markets from an influx of newly arrived immigrant laborers was just as important as conflict with their employers, and both became key forces driving unionization.

Between 1877 and 1890, six million immigrants arrived in the U.S., and between 1860 and 1900 there were fourteen million new arrivals.[49] Immigration from abroad and higher levels of worker mobility within the U.S. was making it easier for business to pit worker against worker in increasingly competitive labor markets. Businesses associations pressured government officials to increase the inflow of labor from abroad. If workers in one area or industry organized a strike, companies employed new immigrants or black workers who were largely excluded from unions, and sometimes women and children as strikebreakers. As the U.S. economy expanded and the market system extended westward and southward, labor migrated from region to region. These patterns of labor migrations allowed employers to bring workers in from one geographical area to another in order to crush localized labor activism. At the same time, businesses were expanding their scope of operations to dominate their markets throughout the nation. It eventually became clear to union organizers that workers needed to act collectively and on a much larger geographical scale to counter the power of these nationwide business monopolies and powerful associations.

Localized workers' associations began to evolve into citywide associations, and citywide associations evolved into national organizations. Local trade unions began combining with other local unions to form federations, and federations combined into national unions. Larger unions were also more effective in centralizing funds that could be used to support workers and their families during protracted strikes or lockouts. By the second half of the nineteenth century, national labor unions had become a formidable opposing force to the umbrella business associations.

One of the first labor organizations to manage a nationwide union was a guild-like association of skilled shoemakers known as the Knights of St. Crispin. Like other unions comprised of skilled workers, the Crispins had skills that were not so easily replaced by unskilled labor. Beginning in the early 1860s, they patterned their organization after the centuries-old masons' guild and preserved the tradition of both organizing skilled labor and maintaining the quasi-religious rites and rituals of the medieval guilds. The masters of the medieval guilds were just as much concerned with Judgment Day and saving souls as they were with maintaining control of their trades. Guild members were required to behave according to strict moral standards and sustain devout religious practices. The Crispins carried on this tradition.

At its peak in the 1870s and 1880s, the Knights of St. Crispin had hundreds of lodges located across the country and successfully organized strikes for better pay and working conditions, especially in the shoe-making industry. A central problem facing organizations of skilled workers was that their skills were increasingly being rendered obsolete with the introduction of mechanized production processes that could be operated with unskilled or semi-skilled labor. With mechanization of shoe production and the development of shoe factories, the Crispins lost much of their bargaining power and the union eventually collapsed.

In the early years after the American Civil War, national unions represented a small percentage of overall membership as most labor unions were still mainly organized at the local level. Nonetheless, nationals were growing and becoming more powerful. The most successful were craft unions. Craft unions are unions that are organized along the lines of occupation such as carpenters, iron workers, or machinists. Industrial unions are unions that seek to organize along the lines of a particular industry such as mining, railroads, or meatpacking. In industrial unions, workers in an industry were collectively organized into the same union regardless of their occupation—skilled or unskilled. Given the large number of unskilled workers in industrial unions, strikebreaking was easier for owners and managers because it was not difficult to find plenty of nonunion, unskilled workers to replace those who were unionized and striking. Both craft and industrial unions built national organizations, but crafts were more successful in achieving their aims.

In 1866, a convention of various local craft unions was held in Baltimore, Maryland in which some 200,000 to 400,000 unionized workers convened to combine their locals into a national federation. This federation came to be known as the National Labor Union (NLU). One of the most significant achievements of the NLU was a successful strike of 100,000 workers in New York for a mandatory 8-hour work day.

The NLU's first president, William Sylvis, an ironworker and organizer of the first national craft union, had long been committed to the idea of building worker-owned cooperatives and putting an end to the wage labor system. In the 1860s and 1870s, Sylvis was challenging capitalism in the United States at a time when Karl Marx and other critics of capitalism had not yet become well-known. A blow to the NLU came in 1873 during a deep depression that caused massive increases in unemployment for both skilled and unskilled workers. The surplus of unemployed and hungry workers made strikebreaking and other anti-union activities easier for businesses to carry out, and the NLU quickly began to disintegrate. Fearful and distrusting of outsiders, many local craft unions began to withdraw from the national organization and returned to their local roots. Craft unions became increasingly conservative and sought to collaborate with businesses and to share in the wealth created by the capitalist system. On the other hand, many industrial unions became more radical and wanted to see capitalism come to an end. These two approaches to capitalism caused a deep schism in the labor movement that got deeper with each downswing in a business cycle.

The economic hard times of the 1870s started a militant phase among the more radical branches of the labor movement. Mass demonstrations, strikes, and food riots were taking place all over the country and this was exemplified in the great railroad strikes of that decade. Emboldened by weakening national unions and a growing surplus in labor markets, the Baltimore and Ohio (B&O) Railroad was the first of a series of railroads to announce cuts in wages that were already at a bare subsistence level. This resulted in a spontaneous strike at the B&O station in Martinsburg, West Virginia during which workers stopped trains from moving by disconnecting the locomotives and holding them ransom in the roundhouses until the wage cut was removed. The strike at Martinsburg ended with the intervention of federal troops, but had already begun to spread to the Pennsylvania railroad and included violent conflict in Pittsburg. A mob of railroad workers joined forces with sympathetic factory workers to stop all the trains from moving in or out of Pittsburg. The Pennsylvania railroad company succeeded in bringing in a militia of troops from Philadelphia to clear the tracks. Gunfire was exchanged between some of the workers in the crowd and the troops, and depots and grain elevators were set on fire. About two dozen—mostly workers—were killed in the skirmish that ultimately ended with the arrival of several thousand Pennsylvania National Guardsmen.

The railroad strikes and riots spread to other railroad cities such as Harrisburg, Reading, St. Louis, and Chicago. Invariably, the strikes were easily broken. In the aftermath of the railroad strikes, workers gained very little by way of concessions from the powerful railroad companies. Unions were largely crushed, and over one hundred workers were killed and thousands imprisoned under charges including conspiracy in restraint of trade.

The railroad strikes and violence of the 1870s galvanized a sense of class consciousness among working people in America. That is, people began to develop an awareness that the difficulties they experienced shared by all members of the working class. The Social Labor Party was formed in the United States in 1877, and the development of revolutionary socialist ideology became a palpable threat to the capitalist system. Within a few years, political leaders began to fear the country was heading toward a widespread working class revolution just as the Ohio Senator, John Sherman, warned when sponsoring anti-trust legislation.

Another direct result of the railroad strikes and riots of the 1870s was the growth and development of the Knights of Labor. Like the Knights of St. Crispin, the Knights of Labor also used a medieval title that reveals their roots in the guild tradition. The founder, Uriah Stephens, was both a brother of the Freemasons and was trained for the ministry. Like the Crispins, the Knights not only were concerned with organization of labor, but also taught its members to be honest, to stay away from alcohol, and to glorify God. Originating in Philadelphia in 1869, the Knights seized the opportunity provided by the railroad strikes and working class consciousness to organize virtually all the local labor unions in the area into a single body. At its peak in 1886, it evolved into a well-organized association of over 80 skilled trades and some 700,000 workers.[50]

The Knights sought to open their ranks to a "greater brotherhood" of blacks, women, and unskilled workers. Once the organization was made more accessible, its membership began to expand rapidly. However, this openness also created a backlash within the movement, as the openly racist membership requirements of many earlier unions had become a tradition that many members and locals felt driven to maintain, even at the expense of worker solidarity. There was also discord among members on how to achieve their goals. Their leader, Terence Powderly, was a strong believer in peaceful cooperation rather than conflict to resolve differences, and he was opposed to strikes as a means to achieve the union's goals. Yet despite Powderly's disapproval, unions organized within the Knights continued striking and some were quite successful in obtaining their goals.

The Knights of Labor had another inherent weakness that ultimately contributed to its demise—it was unable to resolve the perennial conflicts between skilled members of craft unions and the ranks of unskilled workers in industrial unions. A gap between skilled and unskilled workers in the labor force was widening. The skilled unions were jealously seen by the unskilled as privileged and were resented by many of the growing masses of unskilled workers that filled the ranks of the organization. At the same time, skilled unions were having more success in striking and felt the unskilled workers were a drag in their movement. In addition, with mechanization of production, skilled jobs were rapidly being eliminated and replaced by unskilled or semi-skilled workers. Growing more distrustful of unskilled workers, skilled unions began to splinter away from the Knights to build their own exclusive umbrella federation of skilled unions. Skilled unions were making gains as they were more effective in maintaining tighter controls on the supply of labor through limiting apprenticeships and worker training. Unskilled workers, however, were experiencing the brunt of the hard times brought about by recessions. Their unions responded by becoming more radical and militant, but the skilled labor unions wanted to distance themselves from extremist factions in the labor movement. Theirs was a more elite approach to unionism that came to be known somewhat derisively as the "aristocrats of labor." Many of the radical groups sought to overthrow the capitalist system and what they perceived as brutal exploitation of workers, whereas the elite skilled unions sought to collaborate with their employers as partners in the capitalist system.

The conflicts between the elites of labor and the unskilled workers were heightened by the racial divides within much of the movement. Exclusionary practices by many skilled unions forced black workers into the ranks of the unskilled and non-organized, even when they had the required skills and experience. Shut out of most unions, many black workers were recruited as strikebreakers, which in turn aggravated the resentment felt toward them by white workers. This divide and conquer system worked very well to the advantage of businesses.

Already weakened by conflict and dissention within its ranks, the Knights of Labor began to disintegrate after it was unfairly blamed for acts of violence that occurred at Haymarket Square in Chicago in 1886. The events of Haymarket had a deep impact on the labor movement.

Chicago in the late nineteenth century was a gathering point for radical labor activists. To the great concern of the barons of monopoly capitalism, many anarchist and communist groups were organizing in Chicago and openly advocating the use of violence to end the capitalist system. At the same time labor unions and federations of unions, including the Knights of Labor, began pressing for a mandatory eight-hour workday and for union recognition in collective bargaining. Thousands of workers and their sympathizers at the McCormick Harvester Works—one of the giant monopolies—went on strike. The company brought in strikebreakers to cross the picket line, violence and rioting broke out, and the local police fired guns into the riotous mob killing a few workers and wounding many. A local group of anarchists and other radicals called for revenge.

A meeting was called May 4th, 1886, at Haymarket Square at which several thousand workers assembled to listen to speakers address the events surrounding the strike. After some time had passed, many of the workers had gone home and the police arrived to disperse the remainder of the crowd. A bomb suddenly exploded killing seven policemen, and during the pandemonium that ensued, 68 police officers wounded each other with their own panick-driven crossfire. At the behest of a "citizens committee" comprised of Chicago businessmen, police arrested eight anarchist leaders that the committee wanted to be blamed for the violence. After a perfunctory trial and futile appeals, the anarchists were convicted of murder. Four were hanged and one committed suicide in prison though none of them were in Chicago on the day of the explosion.

The hangings served only to intensify conflict. A kind of hysteria of violent conflict ensued between organized labor and powerful businesses and their associations. Businesses used the outbreak of violence to bring down the Knights of Labor. Blamed for the violence in the business-friendly press, public opinion turned against the Knights. As they were already weakened by internal conflicts, the blame for the Haymarket riots sounded their death knell. The Knights of Labor disbanded in 1886. During that same year in Chicago, however, a new and more powerful national federation of labor union came into being—The American Federation of Labor (AFL).

The AFL was comprised of the skilled craft unions that splintered off from the Knights of Labor. Under the leadership of Samuel Gompers and Adolph Strasser of the national Cigar Makers Union, the AFL became the largest federation of unions the labor movement had ever seen. Although the skilled craft unions wanted to distance themselves from what seemed to be the more volatile and militant elements of the labor movement, they nonetheless considered the Knights of Labor not aggressive enough due to Powderly's disdain for organized labor strikes. The AFL unions set their sights on achieving more practical and tangible results such as shorter work hours, better pay, improved working conditions, and collective bargaining. They used strikes effectively as their primary weapon against recalcitrant employers. The AFL was a kind of centrist institution within the labor movement and its leaders were openly critical of socialists and others who advocated the overthrow of capitalism.

On the more radical side of this growing schism in the labor movement was the American Railway Union (ARU), founded in 1893. Organized by socialist Eugene Debs, the ARU was the largest group of organized labor outside of the AFL umbrella. Just as the railroad strikes in the 1870s were precipitated by a deep recession, a recession hit in 1893 throwing millions of workers into unemployment and much labor unrest followed. During this recession, Debs formed the ARU as a national organization to bring solidarity to all railway workers in the United States.

In June of 1894, ARU workers at the Pullman Palace Car Company went on strike after deep pay cuts and called for a nationwide boycott of the Pullman passenger cars. Pullman, like many businesses of those years, had monopoly control over production of passenger cars used in rail transportation. This meant that all trains that carried passengers had Pullman cars, and so a boycott of Pullman amounted to a boycott of all passenger trains. In Chicago, all passenger train movement in or out of Chicago was stopped. Despite the efforts of the General Managers Association (a business association representing railroad owners) to break the boycott and the strike, it continued. Eventually President Grover Cleveland answered a call from the General Managers and sent in federal troops to break the strike at which point the strike turned violent. Pullman cars were set on fire and an angry mob of some five thousand strikers and sympathizers gathered to confront the federal troops as well as the local police and state militia who were brought in to break the strike.

The Pullman strike was crushed by sheer force of arms. Dozens of workers were killed or wounded in a single day of rioting, and hundreds of workers were arrested. Eugene Debs was sentenced to six months in prison and the American Railway Union disintegrated. Nonetheless, the rhetoric of the socialist overthrow of capitalism and labor militancy continued to intensify.

Even in areas controlled by moderate AFL unions, pitched battles were breaking out between workers and their employers. Most exemplary was the Homestead Strike at the Carnegie Steel mill at Homestead, Pennsylvania in 1892. The AFL had a very strong and well-organized local of about 800 workers in the national Amalgamated Associations of Iron and Steel Workers. Carnegie decided to break the union and cut their wages. They closed down the plant, fired the steel workers, and replaced them with non-union strikebreakers.

Carnegie hired private militias through the Pinkerton Detective Agency to break strikes and force picketing workers away from the plant. Contracting a private militia was a familiar tactic used by other corporate giants to break labor unions. Striking workers were prepared to take up arms to defend their jobs and engage the Pinkertons in a pitched battle. The Pinkertons were driven away from the Homestead plant, but were soon replaced by a contingent of Pennsylvania National Guardsmen who seized control by overwhelming force. In the end, the Iron and Steel Workers were utterly defeated at Homestead as the strike finally ended and 1,300 of the original 3,800 workers who went on strike returned to work with severe pay cuts and a return to the 12-hour workday. This defeat was a major setback for the AFL.

Similar struggles between organized labor and businesses and their associations nonetheless continued well into the twentieth century. Thousands of urban industrial workers were organizing, striking, and shutting down operations on the railway lines, in the bakeries, stockyards, factories, and shipyards in all the major cities from San Francisco and Seattle to Chicago, Detroit, and New York. Miners across the country were organizing strikes and often engaged in armed battles with the company militias and strikebreakers. The results were most always the same—guardsmen brought in to crush strikes and escort strikebreakers until one after the other, the strikes and the unions that organized them were broken.

Even though they were losing every battle, it seemed that workers were winning the long-range war over workers' rights. Hard times for millions of workers and their families around the country engendered more sympathy for the workers than for the wealthy barons of industry of the gilded age for whom they worked and with whom they fought. Politically, the climate of public opinion was shifting in favor of labor and populism, and workers were seeing pro-labor candidates nominated and elected into office at the local, state, and federal level.

One of the first signs of victory for labor was the executive action taken by Republican President Theodore Roosevelt. As mentioned above, political leaders were increasingly responding to popular pressure to break down the power of corporate monopolies. Under the leadership of Roosevelt, not only were corporate trusts being dismantled but also labor unions were, for the first time, seen by the executive branch of government as legitimate economic institutions. In 1902, Theodore Roosevelt intervened in a United Mine Workers strike involving over 100,000 workers in the anthracite coal mines in northeastern Pennsylvania. After appointing a commission to mediate the labor dispute, the Roosevelt administration delivered a clear message to the business community that the means and ends of organized labor are legitimate. This represented a substantial shift away from a half-century of government troops being used to assist businesses in breaking strikes.

Popular and political support for organized labor was further solidified as the nation became horrified when it learned of two gruesome events signifying a kind of bloody callousness with which capitalist business enterprises pursued their profit maximization: the Triangle Shirtwaist Fire of 1911 and the Ludlow Massacre of 1914.

In the spring of 1911, a fire broke out at the Triangle Shirtwaist Company, one of hundreds of sweatshop garment factories in New York City that employed exclusively women workers, most of them recent immigrants from Southern and Eastern Europe. In the years leading up to the fire, women workers were organizing themselves into the International Ladies Garment Workers Union. The union organized strikes, marches, and achieved a modicum of success. Yet working conditions for the most part remained miserable and they worked twelve-hour days under crowded, dirty, and dangerous conditions. When the fire began, the women, mostly teenage girls and young women in their twenties, were trapped inside because Triangle had locked the doors from the outside to prevent them from taking fresh air breaks and shirking. 146 people were either burned to death or died leaping out of windows or down elevator shafts. The entire city of New York was appalled and over 100,000 people marched down Broadway in protest. Responding to popular pressure, the state of New York formed a commission charged with the responsibility of investigating hazardous working conditions and spearheading reforms in industrial safety. Although there were worker safety rules on the books, lax administration and even outright bribery had made them ineffective.

A few years after the Triangle fire in 1911, a coal miners strike was organized by the United Mine Workers at the Colorado Fuel and Iron (CF&I) mine in Ludlow, Colorado. CF&I was a subsidiary of the Rockefeller empire and literally owned the town of Ludlow. Like many mining and lumber towns in the west, the company not only owned the mine, but also the shacks where the mine workers and their families lived, and the stores where they bought their food at excessively high prices. Workers were paid in a scrip or local currency issued by the mining company, which was redeemable only in the establishments owned by the company. The miners went on strike for better pay and working conditions, and in retaliation CF&I evicted the striking workers from their homes and were forced to move into tent encampments in the hills outside the town. CF&I hired a private militia—the Baldwin-Felts Detective Agency—to use machine guns and rifles to break up the strike and attack the tent encampments. At the same time, the company was bringing in trainloads of strikebreakers from outside of Ludlow to work in the mine. The miners fought back and the Baldwin militia killed many, but the strikers held on.

The governor of Colorado called in the Colorado National Guard. The guardsmen were mercenaries paid by the Rockefellers. On behalf of CF&I, the guardsmen brought in strikebreakers and proceeded to fire bullets into the tent encampments in which men, women, and children were trying to live out the strike. The miners began to fire back with their own guns. Many fled the encampments with their children and some dug pits inside their tents below ground level to escape the bullets that tore through the tent canvas. In their final assault the guardsmen rode in on horses and set the tents ablaze with torches and the entire encampment was burned to the ground. Thirteen women and children were found burned to death. These deaths stirred outrage that swept across Colorado. Miners left their jobs and took up arms against the guardsmen. Many of the guardsmen themselves disobeyed orders and refused to fight the miners. Thousands demonstrated at the State Capitol in Denver and the protests spread across the country. In the end, however, dozens of miners and their families were killed, the strike was broken, and the union failed to achieve their aims.

As the intensity of working-class rebellions grew, so grew the fears of a full-scale revolution. Many disaffected workers who were shunned by the more elite craft unions in the AFL joined more radical labor organizations and organized strikes, boycotts, and other actions. Collective bargaining was rapidly disintegrating into a cycle of open workplace sabotage and violence countered by harassment, dismissals, and more violence. Conflict in the cash nexus was reaching its boiling point.

Political leaders feared an all-out working-class revolution. They began pushing for reforms that would redress the imbalances between a handful of corporate giants and the masses of poor workers and their families. Anti-trust laws were ratified along with a major breakthrough with the passage of the Railway Labor Act in 1926. The Railway Labor Act made it legally necessary to resolve labor disputes by creating a system of advisory boards and commissions to assist in mediation and arbitration. This act paved the way for much stronger and more comprehensive labor legislation written after the onset of the Great Depression of the 1930s.

In the deepest phase of the depression, the unemployment rate rose to nearly 25 percent. For unemployed workers there were no unemployment insurance, social security, welfare programs or any other social safety net that would keep laid-off workers from falling directly into poverty. In 1934 millions of teamsters, textile workers, longshoremen, railroad workers, and others from a host of different industries went on strike. That same year hundreds of thousands of workers who were still excluded from the AFL and disillusioned with radical socialist and anarchist groups began to form yet another umbrella organization. In November of 1935, a committee within the AFL known as the Committee for Industrial Organization began the process of organizing industrial unions under a new umbrella. The move to create strong industrial unions that organized all the workers in an industry whether they were skilled or unskilled seemed to be a logical opposition to the deskilling process of automation and the advent of the assembly line with the indignities of so-called "scientific management."[51] This new umbrella organization came to be called the Congress of Industrial Organizations (CIO).

The CIO was stitched together under the leadership of John L. Lewis of the United Mine Workers. Lewis introduced an effective technique of striking in which the workers would organize "sit down" strikes where they would stay on the job but would refuse to work. This form of strike was particularly effective in assembly-line factories. Rather than walking off the job, which would make room for strikebreakers, the sit-down strike allowed workers to take direct control of the production process by physically blocking strikebreakers' access to assembly-line workstations. Many workers literally would sit down in front of their machines and refuse to work unless their demands were met. Keeping with the tradition of industrial unions, the CIO was much more militant and aggressive than the AFL, but the CIO directed worker rebelliousness toward constructive solutions and encouraged union meetings, contract negotiations, and the use of a strike or sit-down as a last resort. Membership in the CIO soared to over six million by the onset of World War II, a number matched only by the AFL. With these two nationwide umbrella organizations, the AFL and the CIO, organized labor became a deeply rooted and powerful part of the institutional fabric of the U.S. economy.

In 1935, the most far-reaching and important piece of pro-labor legislation ever passed was signed into law: The National Labor Relations Act, also known as the Wagner Act named after its sponsor, Senator Robert Wagner of New York. Section 7 of the act grants workers ". . . the right to self-organization, to form, join, or assist labor organizations, to bargain collectively through representatives of their own choosing, and to engage in concerted activities, for the purpose of collective bargaining or other mutual aid or protection."[52] To ensure this right the act also contained the following key provisions:

Section 8(1) outlaws employer interference with the Section 7 rights of employees.

Section 8(2) makes employer domination or support of a labor organization illegal.

Section 8(3) prohibits employer retaliation either through discharge or other reprisal against those engaged in union activity.

Section 8(5) required an employer to bargain with the representatives chosen by his employees.[53]

To administer these provisions the Wagner Act created the National Labor Relations Board (NLRB). As a government agency, the NLRB manages elections in which union members determine which union will represent them in their contract negotiations and is intended to ensure that the employers bargain with the legitimately elected union representatives in good faith. Thus, from 1935 onward, labor unions were legally established as legitimate economic institutions. This did not come, however, without challenges from big business and business associations. The conflict in the cash nexus took another turn as businesses and business associations began pushing for legislation and anti-labor candidates as a counter move to the Wagner Act.

The most significant backlash to the labor movement came shortly after WWII with the passage of the Labor Management Relations Act of 1947, also known as the Taft-Hartley Act—pressed into legislation by the Chamber of Commerce and the National Association of Manufacturers. The Chamber of Commerce and National Association of Manufacturers focused not on trying to repeal the Wagner Act but rather on reducing the power of big labor unions by successfully supporting conservative, anti-union republican legislators in the congressional elections of 1946. Once the business community got their candidates into office, they quickly moved to pass the Taft-Hartley Act. The act amended the Wagner Act with three main provisions: (1) it forbids "closed shop" agreements in which unions by way of contract require employers to hire union members, (2) establishes presidential power to limit strikes and call for an eighty-day cooling off period under national emergency situations and (3) allows for individual states to pass "right to work" legislation banning closed-shop contracts in which employers can only hire workers who are members of a local union, or union shop contracts in which all employees working for a particular company are required join a union within thirty days after they are hired. The eighty-day cooling off provision was a blow to unions because it gave almost complete power to an anti-labor president to stop a strike and allow a business to have eighty days to stockpile inventory and make other preparations for when the strike would resume. After the passage of Taft-Hartley, labor union membership and influence steadily declined. The NAM and Chamber of Commerce have since kept up their aggressive anti-union political work and gained the upper hand in keeping businesses in America union-free.

As yet another countermove to businesses in this conflict between business and labor, the AFL and CIO began to forge an alliance. The two mammoth labor organizations began to overlook the perennial differences between the elite cooperative, business-oriented unions under the AFL umbrella and the more militant, conflict oriented unions under the CIO umbrella. Both unions focused their energies on organizing workers in areas or industries where labor representation did not exist, rather than competing with each other over the same workers in unionized shops. They wanted to expand their ranks and consolidate their power so as to present a more formidable countervailing political and economic force to the business interests under the umbrellas of the NAM and Chamber of Commerce. The result of this consolidation came in 1955 with the merger of the AFL and CIO into a single umbrella, the AFL-CIO.

Conflict in the cash nexus currently takes place largely in the political arena and the days of pitched gun battles between workers and the hired guns of business have faded into history in the U.S. Yet history seems to be repeating. The large corporate monopolies of the nineteenth century have returned to assert control over not only markets but the levers of government as well.

Effective anti-union efforts have succeeded in driving down union membership and power. Part of this has been due to hard-hitting foreign competition that began in the mid-1970s. Unions were largely blamed for American businesses' inability to compete by maintaining an "inflexible" labor force that was unable to adapt to a rapidly changing global economy. Their emphasis on flexibility, of course, meant that businesses sought to push down wages and labor costs so as to be price competitive in global markets. Many U.S. manufacturers have chosen simply to shift their manufacturing operations offshore where labor is cheaper. The decline in manufacturing in the United States is probably the single most important reason for the overall decline in union membership. Business associations nonetheless have consistently kept up their anti-union activities.

Today businesses and their associations clearly have the upper hand in the conflict in the cash nexus. The constant threat of outsourcing jobs to "right-to-work" states and to offshore operations allows them to keep union efforts at bay and to maintain leverage in labor markets. At the same time, businesses are becoming increasingly large and product markets are once again falling under the control of dominant corporations as they did in the late nineteenth and early twentieth centuries. The largest and most powerful corporation today is Wal-Mart. Wal-Mart is also the largest private-sector employer in America and is aggressively anti-union. Fraught with employee grievances, sub-standard wages and class-action lawsuits, Wal-Mart has recently been in the spotlight of independent media and labor organizers. Following an election by its employees at a store in Jonquiere, Canada to be represented by the United Food and Commercial Workers, Wal-Mart announced that the store will shut down and fired two hundred workers. Wal-Mart's action put a chill over labor activism and unionization efforts at other Wal-Mart stores came to an abrupt end.[54]

   If labor succeeds in its uphill battle to organize Wal-Mart and other businesses of that scale, it could mark a turning point in the labor movement in the U.S. and would be a major success in the conflict in the cash nexus. Some state and local governments are using political resources attempting to require Wal-Mart and similar large retailers to increase wages and/or benefits to the point where their workers are not relying on taxpayer-supported social programs such as food stamps, Medicaid, and subsidized school lunches.

CONCLUSION

What remains at the core of the conflict in the cash nexus is not the aggressive anti-union activities of businesses or the militant organizing activities of labor unions. At the core of the conflict are the rules governing the capitalist system itself. The cash nexus is the market system in which capitalist profit making is carried out. The expectation of the investor class is that business will take whatever measures it deems necessary to maximize their returns. This would entail controlling prices in product markets and putting the hammer to wages and salaries in labor markets. To this end, companies like Wal-Mart are playing by the rules set under the rubric of American capitalism. Any true and lasting resolution to this conflict must address these rules, not the actions of businesses that play by those rules.

In a mindful economy, we seek to change the rules by which business decisions are made. As we will see in later chapters, the conflict between businesses and consumers, employers and employees, can be largely mitigated by eliminating the separation of production and consumption, and the separation of ownership and work—key features of the capitalist system. By building new institutions based on cooperative models in which consumers and employees are also owners and stakeholders, antagonisms in the market system will begin to evaporate.

Such a mindful system must evolve from the system that exists now. The current system, like the predatory/prey relationship between pests and plants, has evolved to higher levels of complexity as a result of two centuries of conflict. Part of this complexity derives from the growth and development of large corporations and their business associations on one side, and large unions and their umbrella organizations on the other. In the middle of this conflict is government. Each side has attempted to exert political influence on candidates and impact legislation that will help its cause. To expand our vision of the U.S. economy, we will now turn our attention to the role played by government and how government institutions have added to its institutional complexity.

4

GOVERNMENT AND THE ASCENT OF CAPITALISM

In the early 1980s when the U. S. economy was in a deep recession, American President Ronald Reagan frequently asserted that, "government is the problem, not the solution." President Reagan was attempting to reinforce a belief among Americans that the role government institutions play in the economy ought to be kept to an absolute minimum. In this view, government should be prevented from overstepping its bounds and kept from hindering the operations of the capitalist market system. Government should be limited to a supporting role such as constructing and maintaining infrastructure, training the work force, protecting business property, and providing security. Yet government institutions should provide these services only if it is not profitable for the private sector to provide them. Government intervention in the market system should be limited to something like a referee who only steps in to assure that all are playing by the capitalist rules. When government is relegated to a sideline position, the core institutions of private property and markets can maintain their central place in the capitalist economy. As described in the last chapter, this anti-government view has its roots in the *laissez faire* ideology of Adam Smith, Thomas Jefferson and other influential philosophers of the eighteenth century. As we also saw in the previous chapter, however, *laissez faire* ideology is based largely on myth.

Capitalism has never required a self-regulating market system that is free from government intervention in order to succeed in making profits for investors. In fact, businesses generally find unbridled, Darwinistic competition in markets to be intolerably self-destructive, and have sought to create a controlled market system rather than a free-market system.

In practice, the anti-government rhetoric of *laissez faire* was not used to create smaller government, or to reduce the profile of government in economic activity. The rhetoric of *laissez faire* was used to strip the capitalist economy of regulatory aspects of government that interfere with profit making such as state controls of corporate charters, corporate income taxes or taxes on wealthy investors, pro-labor legislation, or environmental laws.

Government has always played a central role in building capitalist systems, and capitalism could not have come into existence without it. In the pages that follow we will see that, *laissez faire* ideology aside, it was not the class of capitalist entrepreneurs, but governments that created the key institutions that shaped the development of the modern capitalist system. We will also see that government has played another important role: as a forum for democracy through which people sought to create new institutions in order to protect themselves from what they perceived as injustices and damage wrought by the single-mindedness of capitalist profit-making.

GOVERNMENT AND THE CONSTRUCTION OF THE CAPITALIST SYSTEM

Throughout the history of capitalism, both in Europe and in the United States, governments fostered an environment in which capitalism could grow and flourish. Governments unified their national monetary systems, established standardized systems of weights and measures, and took other measures to facilitate the growth and expansion of commerce. Governments chartered corporations and granted monopoly trading rights to corporations, and the principal investors of these companies amassed huge fortunes from their government-protected trade. Governments also fashioned property right protections, acquired colonies, and created many other institutions that together gave rise to the profit-oriented, money-based system of capitalism. Most significantly, governments created the market system itself.

Recall from Chapter Two that the market system is a key institution of any capitalist system. Labor and other resources are hired or purchased with money on the input side of the market system, and finished goods and services are sold for money on the output side of the system. Although output markets for goods and services have existed since the beginning of human civilization, markets for wage labor and land had to be continued. Only then could capitalists make their profits from buying low in input markets and selling high in output markets.

According to economic historian, Karl Polanyi, land, labor, and other resource inputs had to be forcibly made into commodities in order to suit the needs of capitalism. The challenge for capitalist development, however, was that people in pre-capitalist societies did not view land and labor as things to be bought and sold with money, with the notable exception of slavery. People's work and the land on which they lived were embedded in broader cultures that were not market- or money-oriented. Although markets have always existed, capitalism created a need to turn society into "One Big Market"[55] in which everything, particularly land and labor, is unnaturally, or fictitiously, transformed into commodities. Polanyi writes:

> The crucial point is this: labor, land, and money [finance capital] are essential elements of industry; they also must be organized in markets; in fact, the markets form an absolutely vital part of the economic system [of capitalism]. But labor, land, and money are obviously *not* commodities; the postulate that anything that is bought and sold must have been produced for sale is emphatically untrue in regard to them. . . . the commodity description of labor, land, and money is entirely fictitious.[56]

For Polanyi, the great transformation was completed in Britain and other countries by the nineteenth century, when the market system came to full development. This unnatural condition was, according to Polanyi, forcefully imposed on society not by members of the capitalist class, but by governments. In other words, blazing the trail for building a capitalist market system were the governing classes and the institutions they created.

GOVERNMENT AND THE COMMODIFICATION OF LAND

In the European Middle Ages, land was the principal source of wealth and power, but was not generally viewed as something that could be bought and sold as a commodity. All land was considered the domain of God. Monarchs were granted the "Divine Right to Rule" over the land by God and they, in turn, granted high-ranking nobles (princes, counts, or dukes) sovereignty over a subdivision of the kingdom in exchange for political or military allegiance. Nobles similarly subdivided their domains, and granted land to lesser nobles (knights and barons), also for political allegiance or military service. Land was thus an integral part of a complex system of hierarchical relationships among the ranks of the nobility. Land could no more be considered a sellable commodity than the mayor of New York City today could consider selling the island of Manhattan.

This view of land began to change as European economies began the transition away from the land-based system of feudalism to the money-based system of capitalism. In the 1530s, King Henry VIII of England broke ties with the Roman Catholic Church, seized the land holdings of the church, and began selling them for money. Henry closed down hundreds of monasteries in England and exchanged the monastery land for cash with merchants and other entrepreneurs. In doing so, the monarchical government of England set a high-level precedent by allowing land to be exchanged for money—land was being commodified, but not by entrepreneurs, rather by government institutions.

This process of commodifying land was further accelerated by the plague. Plague epidemics had ravaged Europe on and off for centuries wiping out huge swaths of the working populations and throwing many feudal lords into poverty. As peasants were dying off, the lords had no means with which to extract wealth from the land. By the sixteenth century, gold was flowing into Europe from government-owned colonies in the New World, and in an effort to stop the slide into deeper poverty, feudal lords began selling parcels of land for newly-minted gold coins. The ruling classes of European governments—monarchs and nobles—began accelerating the process of systematically transforming land into a saleable commodity. Once the birthright of the aristocracy, land was now something that could be sold for gold, and with this gold, nobles joined the entrepreneurial class engaging in trade, commerce, and profit-making.

GOVERNMENT AND THE COMMODIFICATION OF LABOR

Just as land was being commodified, so was labor. Prior to the development of capitalism, labor was traditionally seen as a natural part of human life and work was the duty of the individual to the rest of feudal society. This did not fit well within a capitalist economy, and a system of wage labor had to be invented. Although guild workers in pre-capitalist systems were paid in money, they did not offer their labor to employers in open labor markets. Peasant labor also was not seen as something that could be sold to the highest bidder. Guild workers and peasant farmers were bound to their masters and lords, and generally could not offer their services to others. The invention of a wage-based labor market allowed capitalists to freely hire labor or lay off workers as they needed. But the institutional developments that led to a wage labor system came not from capitalist entrepreneurs, but from governments. The most significant of these developments began in Britain with the "enclosure" movement and the Poor Law Amendment Act in the nineteenth century—both were the result of government legislation.

The enclosure movement took place over many centuries. It was a process of converting land that was traditionally granted to peasant farmers as "commons" for growing food, into fenced (enclosed) pastureland for sheep grazing. By 1801, the enclosure process was formally sanctioned and codified into law by the British Parliament. Parliament was dominated by the wealthy members of society who were increasingly interested in private property rights and commercial agriculture, and who wanted to buy farmland in order to convert it to sheep pasture. Lamb's wool was becoming a lucrative commodity in the wool trade and a principal raw material in the burgeoning textile industry. Enclosures uprooted farmers from what had been their most natural occupation and turned them into dispossessed vagrants or paupers sent adrift to the growing industrial towns of Manchester, Leeds, Bradford, Birmingham and, of course, London. With the enclosures, the British government created an open labor market in which peasants had no choice but to sell their labor to whomever would hire them for a money wage. Workers shifted from being subjected to the paternalistic authority of lords and guild masters, to being subjected to the forces of supply and demand of labor markets.

To assure a steady supply of labor into these markets, Parliament amended the Poor Laws which constituted a kind of early welfare system. The Poor Law Amendment Act of 1834 was intended to remove a growing number of paupers from public assistance. Supporters of the act argued that it was passed as a measure to improve the "moral character" of Britain's burgeoning population of poor people. The amendment was based on a cynical assumption that poverty derived from laziness and immorality, and that poor people were undeserving of any form of public assistance. Workers were expected to earn their living by working for a wage and government authorities refused any form of public assistance to the poor unless they left their homes and went to grueling workhouses. These workhouses were established by government, but were often used by private businesses. The conditions were deliberately harsh and demoralizing so that poor people would have little choice but to turn, cap in hand, back to the wage labor market. Impoverished workers rebelled as their conditions of poverty worsened. The British government reacted violently by killing hundreds, incarcerating hundreds more, and suspending the Habeas Corpus Act—a law protecting individuals from arbitrary detention by government.

In this way the wage-based labor market, not something that naturally springs forward from the human spirit, was coercively imposed on working people by government. The result of the amendment was that the wages capitalists had to pay to workers were kept as low as possible as workers were desperately pitted against one another in a Darwinistic struggle for survival in labor markets. Far from a *laissez faire* system of limited government, the administration of these legal reforms became increasingly complicated and difficult to enforce, which actually required an even greater role played by government. Polanyi writes:

> Even those who wished most ardently to free the state from all unnecessary duties, and whose whole philosophy demanded the restriction of state activities, could not but entrust the self-same state with the new powers, organs, and instruments required for the establishment of laissez-faire.[57]

Wrenched loose from the constraints of tradition, culture, and government relief, labor was mobilized into labor markets. Government legislation created a new institution in which an entire class of people was transformed into a mass of individuals forced to sell their labor to the highest bidder in the marketplace. Out of the horrors of the government workhouses, which were operated more like concentration camps, working people of Britain were, according to Polanyi, "rushed blindly for the shelter of a utopia market economy."[58] By force of government power, the cash nexus was given its labor market.

Governments of Britain, Prussia under Bismarck, France under the Third Republic, and eventually the United States were aggressively engineering a market system in which, as Polanyi notes, ". . . nothing must be allowed to inhibit the formation of market nor must incomes be permitted to be formed otherwise than through sales."[59] At every turn, governments of Europe and North America were building the institutions that would allow capitalism to grow and develop.

As we saw in Chapter Two, corporations have always been created by governments, and have now become the dominant economic institutions in American capitalism. In the U.S., government institutions also granted mining rights, railroad subsidies, trading rights, and a host of other opportunities for profit-making. Today high tech, defense, and pharmaceutical companies receive free research, development, and technology from government institutions. Capitalist profits have been protected by government-imposed tariffs and patent-protected markets. Opportunities for international market expansion have been cleared by the government creation of global institutions such as the International Monetary Fund, the World Bank, and the World Trade Organization. Virtually every major industry, particularly in the manufacturing sector, has been at the receiving end of government assistance and financial support. In short, government and big business have always been partners in the game of profit-making.

Yet it is to government that working people have turned for restitution when they began to feel that the rules of the game are weighed against them. Another significant function of government, therefore, is to provide a forum within which people can exercise their democratic rights.

GOVERNMENT AS A FORUM FOR DEMOCRACY

Although government institutions have played a major role in the historical development of capitalism, this role is complex and often contradictory. On the one hand, government in the United States has always been a force working on behalf of capitalism and on the other it has passed and enforced legislation that undermines business profits. This contradiction arises from the fact that government has not only served to create capitalist institutions and to subsidize profit-making, it has also served as a forum for popular democracy. Using the power of elections, initiatives, and referendums, people have put grass-roots pressure on their political leaders for legislation aimed at protecting them from the potential destructiveness and many injustices inherent in capitalism.

This popular pressure has gone beyond organizing labor unions or attempting to break up powerful corporate monopolies as we saw in the last chapter. People also mobilized politically in opposition to child labor, unsafe working conditions, environmental destruction and a myriad of other byproducts of relentless profit maximization. Again, Polanyi writes:

> . . . the trading classes [capitalists] had no organ to sense the dangers involved in the exploitation of the physical strength of the worker, the destruction of family life, the devastation of neighborhoods, the denudation of forests, the pollution of rivers, the deterioration of craft standards, the disruption of folkways, and the general degradation of existence including housing and arts, as well as the innumerable forms of private and public that do not affect profits.[60]

As masses of working people mobilized for protection, they turned to government as a forum in which they could express their democratic rights and demand institutional reform.

Part of capitalism's destructiveness derives from the instabilities of the market system. An innate feature of markets, particularly financial markets, is that they have a tendency to self-destruct rather than self-regulate as in the utopian fantasies of *laissez faire* ideology. Evidence of the inherent instability of the market system is plentiful: price inflation followed by price collapse, stock market bubbles followed by widespread panic and crashes, business cycle booms followed by busts, and labor market growth followed by recessions and widespread unemployment.

After decades of a career in making his fortune in financial market speculation, multibillionaire capitalist and financier George Soros reflects on the dangers of attempting to construct a market system free from government control:

> This idea was called *laissez faire* in the nineteenth century . . . I have found a better name for it: market fundamentalism. The open societies of the world—commonly referred to as the West—exhibited considerable cohesion in the face of a common enemy. But after the collapse of the Soviet system, open society, with its emphasis on freedom, democracy, and the rule of law, lost much of its appeal as an organizing principle and global capitalism emerged triumphant. Capitalism, with its exclusive reliance on market forces, poses a different kind of danger to open society. The central contention of this book [*The Crisis of Global Capitalism*] is that market fundamentalism is today a greater threat to open society than any totalitarian ideology.[61]

In this passage Soros not only warns of the dangers of attempting to build an economy exclusively on market forces, he also identifies a fundamental conflict between pure capitalism or "market fundamentalism" and democracy and the rule of law. Capitalism, which primarily serves the financial interests of a small investor class, and democracy, which serves the rights of a broad base of the population, coexist within the structures of government in a mutually antagonistic relationship.

Without government as a forum for democracy, the U.S. economy would look much different than it does today. It would perhaps have remained much as it was in the nineteenth century when it was controlled by the arbitrary rule of slave owners and corporate monopolies, and the vast majority of American workers would be laboring in a state of servitude and illiteracy. Yet this critical role of government is largely ignored in virtually every economics text-book used in American classrooms.

A truly democratic government is one that provides rules and procedures through which people can freely and openly confront economic problems that have a substantive effect on their lives. A true democracy must therefore have two essential elements: procedural democracy and substantive democracy.

Procedural democracy establishes the rules and procedures of the machin-ery of government. Procedural democracy includes the right to file petitions, rights to civil liberties, the right to vote or hold office, and the right to exercise freedom of speech, majority rules, minority rights, and other elements that establish the rules of democracy. Universal suffrage and the right to hold office are extended to a broad base of the population and not to a small priv-ileged few. In a legitimate democracy, these rules, rights, and procedures are extended to the population without arbitrariness or discrimination.

Substantive democracy is the fruit of procedural democracy. People par-ticipate in the political process not for the intrinsic joy it brings, but for substantive reasons. Citizens participate in democratic government because by doing so they can make improvements in their lives. The direct material gains people make by participating in a democratic political process is sub-stantive democracy. Social justice, safe working conditions, equal pay, fair access to opportunity, safety, education, healthcare, and income security are the things that substantively affect people's lives.

People in their roles as consumers or workers are stakeholders in the econ-omy. By participating in the procedures and in setting the rules on how the economy is governed, they can affect their chances of getting a fair share. An active citizenry expressing itself through legitimate democratic processes can build economic institutions that are inherently democratic and accountable to people and communities. Such accountability is not something that is intrinsic to capitalist institutions.

Without procedural democracy, there is no peaceful process through which people can demand material improvements in their lives. Without sub-stantive democracy, there is no purpose for procedural democracy and the procedures are merely symbolic. For generations, groups and individuals in America have used democratic government as an instrument to bring about both procedural and substantive reforms such as suffrage for blacks and women, federal government regulations of interstate commerce, the expan-sion of available credit, the building of public schools and the institution of a progressive income tax structure necessary to finance them. Procedural and substantive democracy are what stand between people and child labor practices, starvation wages, corporate control of markets, and a host of other practices that would otherwise be constantly present in the capitalist system. Moreover, these practices are present in many non-democratic societies around the world where capitalism is flourishing.

Below are some examples from the historical record of government legislation gained by an active citizenry. By using government as a forum for democracy, people were able to achieve economic justice and make general improvements in their lives. As much as Americans believe in the myth of *laissez faire*, there nonetheless remains a long-standing tradition of political action and the use of government institutions to counter the harshness of the capitalist system.

THE INTERSTATE COMMERCE ACT (1887)

The Interstate Commerce Act was the first significant piece of legislation that created a federal government regulatory agency. The government was authorized to put limitations on the freight rates charged by the railroads. Its intention was to protect family farms from price gouging by the large and powerful railroad corporations. Its enforcement was difficult and fraught with legal battles and controversy, but the legislation would become the model for much more regulatory legislation that followed. One example was the Elkins Act (1903) which prohibited a common tactic used by the railroads of granting rebates for big and powerful corporate customers such as Rockefeller's Standard Oil Company.

THE SHERMAN ACT (1890)

(See Chapter Three)

THE PURE FOOD AND DRUG ACT (1906)

The Pure Food and Drug Act was the first legislation that sought to protect consumers' food and medicine from dangerous or deceitful business practices. Investigative journalists and writers like Charles Edward Russell, Upton Sinclair, and Thomas Lawson helped consumers become aware of the safety hazards of their food and medicines. Beef, for example, was often unsafe to eat as it was adulterated with toxins, and processed in highly unsanitary slaughterhouses. Moreover, it was sold at excessively high prices as the powerful beef trust controlled nearly the entire U.S. market. In another instance, pharmaceutical companies were acting more like narcotics traffickers selling patented medicines that were compounds of highly addictive drugs and alcohol, creating epidemics of addictions, and taking huge profits. In addition to popular outrage in general, civic organizations and government agencies began pressing government for legislation to regulate how food, particularly beef, and drugs were produced and marketed to the population. Congress, however, was reluctant to respond at first due to political ties with the beef industry.

With the political will and leadership of Harvey Wiley from the Department of Agriculture and the "trustbusting" President Theodore Roosevelt, the Pure Food and Drug Act was eventually pushed through in 1906. This legislation, among other things, created the Food and Drug Administration (FDA) that, along with the Department of Agriculture, is empowered to carry out inspections and tests of all food and drug products to determine their safety for human consumption. The FDA was among the first of a long line of new federal government "watchdog" agencies created to stand guard against abuses wrought by businesses that pursue profit-making over public interest. In that same year another piece of legislation was passed, The Meat Inspection Act, which focused particularly on overseeing the meatpacking industry.

THE CLAYTON ACT (1914)

The Clayton Act was the second and perhaps more potent piece of anti-trust legislation. The original anti-trust law, the Sherman Act, was largely ineffective in bringing the giant trusts to justice for their abuses of market power. Written by Alabama Congressman Henry Clayton, the Clayton Act sought to strengthen the Sherman Act with more precise language and provisions. Among other things, the Clayton Act prohibits exclusive sales contracts in which a wholesaler pressures a retailer to carry its product exclusively. The act also prohibits discriminatory or cutthroat pricing aimed at driving a particular competitor out of business. A number of other provisions made it much more difficult for businesses to engage in predatory practices, and it substantially decreased their ability to establish monopolies and to control markets. Incidentally, the Clayton Act also made it unlawful for businesses to use the Sherman Act to get court injunctions to break up strikes organized by labor unions.

THE FEDERAL TRADE COMMISSION ACT (1914)

The Federal Trade Commission Act established the Federal Trade Commission (FTC), another watchdog agency within the federal government that is empowered to enforce the provisions in the Sherman and Clayton Acts. The commission consists of a board of five members appointed by the U.S. president for seven-year terms. The FTC is responsible for maintaining standards for determining what is considered unfair competition and for investigating and taking legal action against businesses that violate antitrust laws.

THE SOCIAL SECURITY ACT (1935)

The Social Security Act is unquestionably the most far-reaching product of substantive democracy in American economic history. The act was passed during the depths of the Great Depression. It became clear to most observers that America's millionaires were not going to serve as the trustees of the poor as Andrew Carnegie asserted, and millions of Americans were thrown into poverty during the Depression and they stayed in poverty. Part of President Franklin D. Roosevelt's New Deal, The Social Security Act was passed on August 14, 1935 as a government anti-poverty program. In a broad sense, the act authorized the federal government to institute a new tax and transfer the revenues through a series of programs designed to fight poverty, particularly among the aged, disabled, or unemployed. Funding for these programs was secured by the Federal Insurance Contributions Act (FICA) which authorized compulsory payroll tax—a tax paid by both employees and employers as a flat percentage of an employee's income.

The Social Security Act contained three broad provisions referred to as "Charts." The first Chart provided old age insurance and a very modest benefit to be paid upon a legally stipulated time of retirement. Before this legislation, workers would have to work until they were physically unable, at which point many having lost their incomes would fall directly into poverty. With the first Chart, the fear of old-age poverty was substantially reduced as the Federal government instituted benefits for all retired workers.

The second Chart authorized the federal government to use its powers of taxation and spending to provide compensation to unemployed workers. Like retired workers, many unemployed workers who lost their incomes during recessions would fall into poverty until they were able to find another job. The Social Security Act made provisions, under certain restrictions, to provide benefits for workers while they sought new employment.

The third Chart provided federal government grants to states as public assistance for the blind, the disabled, the elderly, and dependent children, child healthcare, and many other public health programs. The third Chart was later amended in the 1960s with additional public assistance programs such as Medicare, Medicaid, Food Stamps, and others of the so-called welfare programs.

Despite staunch opposition by businesses that did not want to pay the tax, the Social Security Act brought the first major, federally mandated socialistic institution into the U.S. economy. The Social Security Act was a direct challenge to capitalism, which at the time, was experiencing a severe crisis. For decades Social Security has contributed to substantive improvements in people's lives by reducing poverty and providing a small but important safety net during economic hard times—hard times being a recurring theme in the market system.

THE SECURITIES EXCHANGE ACT (1934)

The Securities Exchange Act created another federal government watchdog agency, the Securities and Exchange Commission (SEC). The SEC oversees the entire stock-and-bond trading industry and its market transactions. The SEC consists of five commissioners, appointed by the U.S. president and confirmed by the Senate, each serving staggered five-year terms. The agency is also charged with the responsibility of ensuring that financial markets are free from fraud, market manipulation, investor pools, and other unfair trading activities. Financial market fraud and manipulation were among the leading causes of the dramatic stock market boom in the 1920s and the tremendous crash of 1929, which precipitated the Great Depression. The hope was that by eliminating these dubious stock-and-bond market dealings, financial markets would become more stable, which would lead to a more secure and stable economy.

THE NATIONAL LABOR RELATIONS ACT (1935)

The National Labor Relations Act is considered to be one of the most significant pieces of Roosevelt's New Deal legislation, and was often referred to as the Magna Carta of labor. Like the Social Security Act, it was a challenge to the capitalist market system. Empowered with this new legislation, unions intensified their organizing activities and membership spread rapidly in nearly all of the major industries including automobile, steel, electrical, and other manufacturing sectors. Millions of workers who gained legitimate union representation experienced real, material improvements in their living standards. (See Chapter Three)

THE FAIR LABOR STANDARDS ACT (1938)

The Fair Labor Standards Act was another tremendous benefit for working people. The act requires that all employers pay their hourly workers a federally mandated minimum wage, as well as an "overtime" entitlement for work performed over forty hours per week. Perhaps even more important, however, was that the legislation abolished the centuries-old practice of exploiting child labor. The Fair Labor Standards Act explicitly prohibited "oppressive child labor" which meant employing children under the age of sixteen, or between sixteen and eighteen in an environment that could be detrimental to the health of a child of that age.

THE CIVIL RIGHTS ACT (1964)

The Civil Rights Act was signed into law in the summer of 1964 as part of President Lyndon B. Johnson's "Great Society" social programs. The act specifically addresses the problem of racism and sexism in America, and contains provisions that have had a positive economic impact on the lives of racial minorities and women. The act prohibits discrimination by hotel or restaurant owners, trade unions, schools, or employers based on gender or race. This legislation unlocked the door to social and economic opportunity that, up to that point, had been locked to women, blacks, and other minorities. To enforce the anti-discrimination laws the Civil Rights Act established another federal watchdog agency: the Equal Employment Opportunity Commission (EEOC) comprised of five members and a general counsel appointed by the U.S. president and confirmed by the Senate.

THE OCCUPATIONAL SAFETY AND HEALTH ACT (1970)

The Occupational Safety and Health Act is a comprehensive law that focused on worker health and safety and jobsite hazards. In a general sense, the act provides that businesses must maintain a workplace that is free from health hazards or physical dangers such as exposure to dangerous chemicals, lack of proper ventilation or respiration equipment, inadequate first aid or protective gear, and exposure to fire or excessive temperatures. Health and safety standards are established by the Occupation Safety and Health Administration (OSHA), another federal watchdog empowered to enforce those standards and impose fines and other legal action if businesses are in violation. OSHA performs tens of thousands of workplace inspections every year, as well as conducts worker safety workshops and seminars. Since its inception, jobsite accidents, injuries, and deaths were reduced significantly, and the overall health and safety of workers improved as well.

THE CONSUMER PRODUCTS SAFETY ACT (1973)

The Consumer Products Safety Act establishes mandatory consumer product safety standards. The act created the Consumer Products Safety Commission (CPSC), a federal watchdog that, like many others, consists of five commissioners and a general counsel. The CPSC began operations in 1973 with the intention of overseeing tens of thousands of consumer products and protecting consumers from hazards or injuries, particularly those to children. Since its inception, it has decreased the rate of injury and death associated with consumer goods by 30 percent. The CPSC also conducts research and publishes information about product-related injuries.

THE AMERICANS WITH DISABILITIES ACT (1990)

The Americans with Disabilities Act extends the civil rights act to include people with disabilities. The act covers a spectrum of disabilities from physical disabilities to emotional illness and learning disabilities. Like the Civil Rights Act, the ADA attempts to increase access to the structure of opportunities for people with disabilities.

The above is but a small sample of the legislation that people won, through legitimate democratic processes, despite the fierce opposition by businesses. Through these government programs people made substantive gains in their lives, but these gains came at the cost of capitalist profits. By breaking down monopoly control over markets and forcing businesses to charge fair prices, to clean up their factories, to pay fair wages, to end the practice of employing children, to recall dangerous products from the markets and so on, capitalism came to be less profitable than it was in the *laissez faire* days of the nineteenth century.

Not surprisingly, business associations like the Chamber of Commerce consistently challenged such legislation by framing it as excessive, whimsical "big government." The business associations' condemnation of excessive government is typically combined with laudatory narratives of the benign private sector and self-regulating power of free markets. Yet it was precisely the abusive practices of powerful businesses in the private sector and instabilities in the market system that gave rise to so-called "big government" in the first place.

The condemnation, nonetheless, is loud and powerful and has a significant influence on the climate of public opinion. The federal government, under pressure from corporate lobbyists, is rolling back and repealing much of the progressive legislation that consumers, citizens, and workers fought hard to gain. Taken to its logical conclusion, such deregulation would mean returning to the days of poisonous food, child labor, racism, and sexism at the workplace; dangerous working conditions; and monopoly control of markets. If this comes to pass, capitalism will emerge triumphant and will restore its profit-making imperative at the peril of substantive democracy.

The economic role of government goes beyond providing a forum for democracy and substantive legislation. Government also plays a direct role as an economic agent by using its powers of taxation and spending to provide services directly to the population.

GOVERNMENT AND PUBLIC SERVICES

One of the substantive achievements gained by people in democratic societies is universal access to publicly provided services. Basic services such as education, police and fire protection, transportation infrastructure, national defense, and public parks are generally provided to people in democratic societies on a principle of universal access. Universal access means that any resident living where public services are provided has free and open access to these services. Public services obviously cost money to provide and are paid for by taxpayers, but under the principle of universal access, people do not have to have paid taxes in order to be provided with these services. Everyone in the United States is universally protected by national defense provided by the federal government regardless of whether or not one has paid taxes. The same is generally true for local police and fire protection and, though to a lesser extent, education.

The provision of public services under the principle of universal access is a relatively recent development in American history. Up to the mid-twentieth century, education was largely only available to those who had the money to pay for private schools or the responsibility of church organizations. In many cases, defense, justice, and other government protections were often available only to the wealthy. American society was characterized by widespread illiteracy and insecurity, conditions that are not conducive to building a modern democracy.

In *laissez faire* capitalism, government is only to be a producer of goods and services in the event of a "market failure." That is, if private business fails to succeed at making adequate profits and the service is nonetheless considered necessary, then it becomes the responsibility of government agencies. Such a system could succeed only insofar as society accepts that these services will be rationed according to an ability-to-pay principle, not universal access. Public safety and fire protection, schools, infrastructure, port facilities, and sewage treatment plants can be operated in the private sector for a profit as long as their market segment is limited to a sector of the population that has the money to pay high enough prices to sustain capitalist profits. Moreover, what is considered a high enough price is determined by investors, not democratically by citizens.

A key distinction between countries with democratic institutions and those without is the relative degree to which the governments extend public services to their populations. There exists a strong correlation between the strength of a society's democratic institutions and the well-being of its population. A common characteristic of so-called "third world" countries are stark inequalities of wealth and income distribution, poverty, and the lack of well-funded public services. Another is a general absence of procedural and substantive democracy. As George Soros indicated, countries in Western Europe and North America moved away from capitalism and moved toward democracy, rule of law and more pluralistic economies—particularly in the latter half of the twentieth century. Capitalism, on the other hand, is flourishing in non-democratic, underdeveloped countries where private businesses do not have to recognize the rights of people, and where the wealthy are not burdened with meddlesome government taxation and programs for basic services.

There is a deeper reason for the incompatibility of capitalism and the provision of public services. Defining characteristics of capitalism include the institutions of private ownership of property, property rights, and the market system. In this system, when a good is provided for sale in the market, the buyer becomes the owner of that good and retains the full and exclusive rights to the benefits of that good. When one buys a pair of shoes, one retains the exclusive right to the benefits of wearing those shoes and does not have to share the benefits with others. Yet there are certain goods or services that cannot have benefits transferred as such. For example, street lights and traffic signals are provided with the purpose of providing public safety. If the lights and signals were to be provided through the private sector, then only those who paid for them would have the property rights to enjoy the safety benefits. The same would be true of national defense, traffic patrol, public parks, and education. But the benefits accrue not only to those who directly pay for them, but also spill out into society in the form of general functionality or livability. There is no practical way to exclude others from enjoying these social benefits, and given this non-excludability, a purely capitalist economy would simply not offer the services. Under capitalism, public safety and general livability would have to be sacrificed in the name of property right exclusion. Such a sacrifice stands in direct opposition to substantive democracy.

Thus, an important role of government is to provide public services to the population as a function of substantive democracy. How far the government should go and how many services it should provide is, of course, subject to much debate. What is considered necessary and therefore placed into the public sector differs from one country to the next. Some countries find that basic healthcare, housing, and a four-year college education are too important to be left to the market's "ability-to-pay" principle and are made universally accessible, just as K-12 education is provided in the U.S.

Regardless of the extent, public services must be financed in some way. To understand the mechanism for raising public financing and spending on public services we turn our attention to another role of government—carrying out fiscal policy.

GOVERNMENT FISCAL POLICY

Fiscal policy refers to government policy with respect to taxation and the expenditures of public funds. The most important function of fiscal policy is to secure funds and carry out the appropriate spending to provide government services to the general population. About one-third of the national income generated in the U.S. economy annually is channeled toward government for public programs. As a result of this magnitude, the policies government officials make regarding how to tax, who to tax, how much to tax, and on what programs to spend those tax dollars can have a significant impact on the pattern of spending in the economy. Fiscal policy, therefore, is not only a means to fund public services, it is also a means by which government can influence overall economic activity. That is, like households and businesses, government is also an important economic agent.

With government as an economic agent, fiscal policy is often used as a kind of economic steering mechanism. Governments can deliberately influence the pace of economic growth by either increasing or decreasing spending on goods and services produced in the economy, or by increasing or decreasing the amount of taxes they collect. The origins of this view of government fiscal policy as a steering mechanism can be traced back to the work of renowned Depression-era economist, John M. Keynes.

Writing in the 1930s, Keynes saw that government could use its powers of spending and taxation to achieve stability and to lower unemployment. If the national economy is sliding into a recession in which overall economic activity is slowing down and unemployment is beginning to increase, governments can "turn the wheel" and steer the economy toward growth by spending larger amounts of money on goods and services. Keynes asserted that the principal cause of recessions or depressions was insufficient buying power, or "effective demand," which results in gluts or chronic oversupplies of inventories. In other words, supply and demand are out of balance in the marketplace. Government can then step in and play the role of a spending agent to bring demand into balance with supply. By doing so, businesses have new customers to whom they can sell their goods, and in turn start producing more—the economy grows and unemployment falls.

Altering patterns of spending in the market economy is only part of the story of fiscal policy. The other is taxation. For Keynes, government spending should be financed by a progressive tax structure in which the higher income earners pay higher taxes as a percentage of their income than those with lower incomes. Keynes's reasoning for advocating a progressive tax structure was based on the need to increase spending. Lower income households spend virtually all of their income, and upper income individuals save much of theirs. Savings, for Keynes, is not what the economy needs to pull itself out of a recession or depression; spending is. With lower tax liabilities for low incomes, more spending money would remain in the hands of a broader sector of the working population and this would lead to the creation of a larger market. Tax revenue can also be skimmed off the upper income groups and channeled to government agencies for more spending in the goods-and-services markets.

Keynes was one of the first economists of note who advocated that government could play an activist role in economic affairs in this way. The Keynesian approach to fiscal policy became generally accepted and was codified into law with the Employment Act of 1946 despite the lingering tradition of *laissez faire*. The Employment Act gave Congress the legal responsibility to use its power to carry out large volume spending to stimulate economic growth and eliminate unwanted unemployment. During the thirty years that followed the passage of the Employment Act, Keynesian economics remained orthodox fiscal policy, but that began to change when the U.S. economy began to experience the unusual condition of simultaneous high inflation and recession in the 1970s.

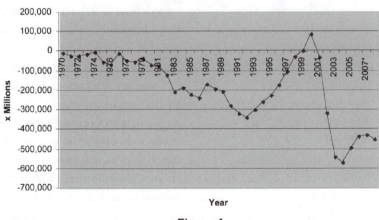

Figure 1

Source: "The Budget For Fiscal Year 2008," Historical Tables, Table 1-1

The Keynesian progressive income tax structure was rolled back when upper-income households began receiving huge tax cuts in the 1980s under the leadership of President Ronald Reagan. In his famous, "Government is not the solution to our problems government is the problem," speeches, Ronald Reagan set about an agenda to aggressively cut the tax liability for the wealthy. In his first year as president in 1981, Reagan attempted to restore anti-government *laissez faire* rhetoric to political discourse, and pushed through the largest tax cut in American history. And although his vision for smaller government was put into practice with tax policy, Reagan actually increased government spending—mainly by ramping up spending on military procurements. During the Reagan years of the 1980s, the United States government plunged deep into spending deficits and the U.S. economy reversed itself from being the world's largest creditor nation to the world's largest debtor. The data in Figure 1 shows that prior to Reagan taking office, the federal government deficit was approximately $73 billion and by the end of his first administration deficits soared to $212 billion.

Reagan's successor, George H. W. Bush drove budget deficits even higher to hit a world record of $290 billion in 1992. President Bill Clinton pushed through a modest tax increase for upper income households and in the last three years of his administration, the federal government began to experience budget surpluses. For the first time in forty years, government tax receipts were exceeding expenditures. But the Reagan/Bush tax cuts for the rich were restored when George W. Bush became president in 2001. The new tax cuts caused budget deficits to soar and surpass the records set by his father's administration.

The logic behind the Reagan/Bush/Bush tax cuts is based on an approach to fiscal policy known as "supply-side economics." This approach to fiscal policy holds that economic growth is stimulated by investments on the supply side and not from consumer spending on the demand side as Keynes contended. By cutting taxes particularly for the wealthy and super wealthy, more money would be saved and these savings would be channeled into financial investments such as corporate stocks and bonds. Corporations could then use these invested funds to increase overall capital formation—machines, factories, and equipment used in production. With more capital, the economy would grow and so would employment. The benefits of this growth would subsequently "trickle down" to the middle and low-income population in the form of newly created jobs with paychecks.

Fiscal policy and the role of government in the economy are continuously changing. Each presidential administration pursues a set of policy goals that are different from the last. What remains constant, however, is an ongoing commitment to preserving the capitalist system. Both Keynesians and supply-siders, although they differ on policy, share a steadfast commitment to capitalist growth. The lesson they all have learned from the Great Depression was that without growth, capitalism would begin a process of disintegration and this means political disintegration as well.

Government has the power to make and enforce laws and to tax, borrow, and spend to substantively improve people's lives. But what the U.S. government has always kept as its highest priority is the preservation of capitalism, and the wealth accumulation of the investor class. Nonetheless, people have been able to exact concessions in the form of progressive legislation despite their government's marriage with capitalism. In the U.S. capitalist system, government institutions such as social security and agencies that provide public services are tolerated only in the Keynesian sense that they are ultimately good for spending, which is good for capitalist growth.

CONCLUSION

One of our purposes of this and the previous chapter is to dispel the myth that the U.S. economy is based on a "free-market" system. In general, the word "free" in this context signifies a system in which government control or intervention in the economy is largely absent. Capitalism has never been free from government control and, in fact, could not have come into being without the work of government. *Laissez faire* ideology is mythology directed toward molding public opinion against government policies or regulations that might interfere with capitalist profit-making. Despite the fact that the U.S. is predominantly a capitalist system, people have, for over a century, pushed for legislation to give government more power to watch over, regulate, and have an impact on the direction of production and distribution within the capitalist system. In other words, people have used both substantive and procedural democracy as a means to fight against injustices, inequalities, and instabilities that are the direct consequences of the capitalist system.

A mindful economy is a system that is firmly rooted in procedural and substantive democracy. Democratically accountable government is naturally a necessary part of this system, particularly at the local level. But in a mindful economy we see democracy extending far beyond the electoral processes and lawmaking. We envision a system in which people rely less on acts of legislation to get concessions from an otherwise non-democratic system. As we will see in Part Three, a mindful economy builds procedural and substantive democracy into all economic institutions. In other words, a mindful economy is one that is intrinsically democratic and is therefore fundamentally non-capitalist, self-reliant, and places people and communities—and not only investors—at the center of basic economic process, and renders people less dependent on government legislation to achieve fairness or equity.

5

THE U.S. FINANCIAL SYSTEM PART I
Money and Banks

Capitalism is a money-based system. It is a system in which money has risen to supreme importance, and a system that places much emphasis on market exchanges, taking money profits, and accumulating financial wealth. Access to money and the accumulation of money have been principles around which the financial system of the United States has developed. Like the natural fauna and flora that evolve in an ecosystem surrounding a particular stream, the financial system of the U.S. economy has evolved around the main stream of capital accumulation. Money is the liquid that keeps the stream flowing.

In this chapter we will take a close look at money and will see how money is created within the banking system and controlled by the central bank of the U.S.—the Federal Reserve System. Here and in the next chapter, we will also explore how financial institutions such as commercial banks, organized stock exchanges, and bond markets have evolved to devise new ways to pull together and concentrate ever-larger sums of money. We will also see that the function and purposes of the U.S. financial system are inextricably bound to the function and purpose of capitalism.

THE FINANCIAL SYSTEM'S SOURCES AND USES OF MONEY

The U.S. financial system serves two broad purposes. The first is to create and maintain a stable supply of money, and the second is to assemble and concentrate large amounts of money from widely dispersed sources, and redirect them toward various uses. As shown in Figure 1 below, money is collected on one side of the system from household savings, retained business profits, and other sources of funds, then it is channeled out the other side to be used for investments in business capital, government spending, consumer spending, and speculation. If someone deposits some of his or her paycheck into a savings account with a commercial bank, this money is a *source* for the financial system. Banks will then lend a portion of that money to borrowers who *use* the money to buy things such as cars or homes. Or, someone may save money for retirement by pooling it with others into a mutual fund. As that money flows into a mutual fund, it is a *source* that can then be used to buy corporate stocks and bonds, and the stocks and bonds themselves are the means by which a corporation can access cash to *use* for capital investments. In a thousand more ways, the U.S. financial system brings together sources and uses of money.

By performing its function of collecting, concentrating, and redirecting money, the U.S. financial system also serves the deeper purpose of capitalist profit-making and accumulation. Loans from commercial banks, for example, facilitate consumers' purchases of more expensive goods on which business profits are made. Access to consumer credit serves as a supercharger for business sales. The financial system also facilitates stock and bond sales as a way to gather funds for corporations to make the necessary investments that will augment the growth and expansion of the capitalist system. And the stocks and bonds themselves are instruments with which market players can take profits through speculative buying and selling. As we saw in the last chapter, financial markets have been used to build trusts and corporate monopolies that dominate entire industries.

Capitalism created the impetus for inventing and reinventing new financial instruments that allow for ongoing capital accumulation. As businesses grow in size, the mass of their capitalization or initial money investments grow proportionally. Economic expansion has been the principal driving force behind the creation and recreation of new financial instruments—stocks, bonds, loans or mortgages, certificates of deposit, money market accounts, mutual funds, and derivatives. These instruments help to aggregate and concentrate money to be used as fuel for the acceleration of the capitalist machine. This acceleration, more than anything else, has shaped the development of U.S. financial institutions over the last two hundred years.

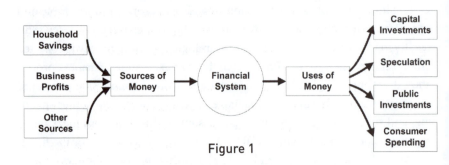

Figure 1

As new financial instruments surface, new institutions are also developed in order to create markets for these instruments. Stock exchanges, electronic stock quoting systems, investment banks, commercial banks, bond markets, and mortgage companies are examples of institutions that develop, buy, and sell financial instruments. Together the instruments and the institutions that create and trade them have evolved as new technologies that more effectively draw money from sources and redirect it toward uses. The paramount use is always to enhance capitalist growth and wealth accumulation. Other purposes of the U.S. financial system such as raising money to serve the needs of individuals and communities have been more incidental and are of secondary importance.

People have always needed to have a place where they could store money for safekeeping. Farmers have always relied on regular flows of credit during the long seasonal cycles between agricultural production and the payments from that production. College students need access to loans for their education. Communities need financing for infrastructure, schools, security in old age, and for building homes. Yet these financial needs, though met to some degree in American society, rank lowest on the list of priorities of U.S. financial institutions. In a mindful economy, we reverse this order and seek to redirect and redefine our financial instruments and institutions in ways that make the needs of people the primary function of the financial system. We will turn again to this purpose in a later chapter.

THE FINANCIAL ECONOMY AND THE REAL ECONOMY

Aside from seeing how money is collected from its sources and redistributed to its uses, there is another dimension to understanding the financial system in the U.S. economy—its relation to the "real" economy. Like two sides of a coin, there exists the financial economy of money, stocks, bonds, and loans, and the real economy of the production and distribution of goods and services. The financial economy revolves around money and the real economy revolves around what people can buy with that money. These two facets of economic activity are profoundly inseparable and are tied together by the institution of money.

As we will see, the main function of money is to act as a medium through which real goods and services are exchanged in markets. In every market transaction, money turns into real goods and services for the buyer, and real goods and services turn into money for the seller. For these market exchanges to be functional and reliable, a stable relationship between money and the real production of goods and services must be maintained. In addition, as investors put money into the bank or the stock market with the hope of earning interest or some rate of return, the value of these financial investments grows in monetary terms. The real economy of goods and services must also grow proportionally in order to provide a stable balance between the financial growth of money and the real goods and services people can buy with that money.

If a stable proportionality between the financial and real is not maintained, this can lead to extreme economic instability such as rapid price inflation, recession or depression, and even collapse. One of the most vivid examples of such instability occurred in Germany in the years between World Wars I and II. Germany's money supply was allowed to increase so rapidly that its value in terms of purchasing power of the currency collapsed to practically nothing. With a collapse in the value of money, market exchanges became impossible and the real economy of production and distribution came grinding to a standstill. Germany's economy was ruined, and this ruination was the source of political instability and the ascent of fascism.

The importance of the real economy is material, whereas the importance of the financial economy is institutional. Real food, clothing, and shelter have importance because their physical properties satisfy wants or needs of people, but the physical properties of money, stocks, or bonds are practically irrelevant. The physical properties of dollar bills, in other words, are less important than the institutionalized power they contain, without which they would be worthless paper. People cannot eat, wear, or live in dollar bills, yet if the bills are part of a stable monetary system, they contain the power to command food, clothing, and shelter from the real economy. So an important first step toward understanding our financial system and its relation to the real economy is to understand its most elementary part—money.

MONEY

Money is a social convention that has existed in a variety of forms for thousands of years in virtually every culture on the planet. People socially determine what particular things will be their money, as well as what other things such as slices of cheese or pieces of wood will not be their money. If people in a society establish a practice or convention to accept a certain thing as money, then that thing becomes the currency of that society. In its physical form, money can be practically any token or artifact: cowhides, salt bricks, shells, stones, pieces of metal, paper bills, magnetic strips, or numbers on electronic ledgers. If society does not have the social convention to accept such things as their money, then no matter what it is made of or what it looks like, the thing will not be money. In other words, money is not a particular thing it is an institution.

Regardless of its physical form, what is important is that society sustains faith in its money. If people do not have faith that the thing will perform its functions as money, it will fail. For instance, if a buyer attempts to give a handful of seashells in exchange for some product and the seller does not accept the shells as payment for the product because he lacks faith in them, then the shells will not function as money and will remain only as shells. But if the seller does have faith and accepts the shells with the idea that he can use the shells to buy something else like firewood, and the firewood vendor accepts shells in order to buy bread and vegetables, and the bakers and farmers also accept the shells, then there is sufficient faith in the community and the shells become an established institution as money. It is said that money does not grow on trees, but it would as long as enough people had faith that a particular kind of leaf was money.

Although money has shown remarkable resilience as it has transformed itself to adapt to new social and political climates, there remains a tendency for instability. The potential instability of money stems from the fact that faith can be elusive and difficult to establish. There is a long historical record of populations losing faith in their particular form of money. It is not unusual for a country's currency to swing from being part of a reliable monetary institution one year to worthless paper the next. When this happens, a breakdown between the financial and the real economies occurs, which is usually followed by a severe crisis.

Once it is established as a reliable institution, money can serve various economic and political purposes. Money can effectively coordinate production and distribution and has improved the lives of people and communities by liberating them from cumbersome barter (direct good-for-good) exchanges. Money can help commerce and trade flourish which also contributes to a general rise in people's living standards. But at the same time, money has also facilitated murderous religious crusades, governments' ability to wage war, and has fostered pathological greed and speculative manias. As economic systems evolve, money and monetary institutions also evolve. As a social institution, money is something that people can shape and evolve toward the healthy purposes of serving the needs of people and away from destruction, greed, and pathology.

As an institution that is both positive and useful to people, money performs three primary functions. Money is the medium of market exchanges between buyers and sellers, it is also a way to store value over time, and it is a unit of account or standardized way of measuring value. As a medium of exchange, money facilitates market transactions between buyers and sellers. This is the most important function of money, for without money a modern economic system could not exist. This is particularly true for capitalism. Capitalism, with its heavy reliance on buying and selling in markets, necessarily creates a heavy dependence on money for the production and distribution of goods and services. Production depends on the producer being able to buy energy and other resources with money and hire labor for a money wage or salary. Distribution relies on market exchanges in which buyers with money receive goods and services by paying the market price, and those without money receive nothing. Without money as a medium of exchange, labor could not be hired, raw materials could not be bought, finished goods could not be sold to consumers, and production and distribution as we know it would be sent back to the Stone Age.

As a medium of exchange, money has facilitated one of the most significant developments in economic history: the division of labor based on specialization. Specialization means that each person or community can become more productive by limiting their work to what they do best and leaving other people or communities to do what they do best. With money as an accepted institution, the fruits of each person's labor can be exchanged with every other person's. The productivity and efficiency gains from division of labor and specialization are tremendous, but this is only possible with money as a widely accepted medium of exchange. If one community does not accept something as a medium of exchange from another, the two communities cannot trade and will be forced either to be self-sufficient or to exchange on the basis of barter. Although barter does not preclude exchange, it does make it far more difficult.

Under a barter system, people must exchange goods directly for other goods. Healthcare would have to be traded directly for furniture, vegetables for cloth, grain for shoes, and so on. Also, inputs like labor and energy would have to be exchanged directly for outputs or finished products. In order for such barter exchanges to successfully take place, both parties must simultaneously want what the other has to trade, a circumstance that economists refer to as a "double coincidence of wants." For example, if a person who specializes in cloth production is seeking vegetables for dinner, she must seek out a vegetable farmer who also just happens to be seeking cloth for making clothes. It is unlikely that such people can find such double coincidences and far more likely they will be forced to become self-sufficient, and all the efficiency gains from division of labor would be lost. With a well-established institution of money, the need for a double coincidence of wants is eliminated and virtually every good, service, or resource can be exchanged for every other good, service, or resource.

The second function of money is that it is a store of value. Money can be saved, and when people save money they are actually storing purchasing power over time. As such, money must be such that it does not deteriorate and significantly diminish in value while being stored for use at a later date. Gemstones and gold or silver coins have performed this function well for thousands of years as they retain their value and can be stored over long periods of time. Perishable things or things that degrade quickly would function poorly as money because they would quickly lose their value and money would always have to be quickly spent or its value would be lost.

If money functions well as a store of value, it also functions well as a medium of exchange. If people fear that the thing being used as money will not be a reliable store of value, it is unlikely that they would accept it as a medium of exchange and faith in money would be lost. As we will see, paper currency proved to be difficult to establish as money. People did not have faith that paper would retain its purchasing power over time and refused to hold on to it as a store of value.

The third important function of money is that it serves as a unit of account. As a unit of account, money becomes a yardstick by which the value of things is measured. A modern economy cannot function without a well-established convention of using money as a unit of account any more than a house can be built by carpenters who all use different systems of measurement. As we saw in an earlier chapter, when nations began the process of modernization, weights and sizes came to be measured in nationally standardized units and this greatly facilitated the expansion of trade and the development of the capitalist market system. Similarly, as money became nationally standardized, price tags, accounting ledgers, and balance sheets all used the same measurement of value.

Through the process of trial and error, societies discovered that certain things naturally worked better than others as mediums of exchange, stores of value, and units of accounts. The combination of metal coins and paper currency seemed to be an expedient formula and established the monetary foundation upon which modern economic systems were built.

COINS AND PAPER CURRENCY

The practice of coinage was first developed in the ancient Greek city-state of Lydia in the seventh century B.C., and quickly spread to virtually every city-state in the eastern Mediterranean. Economic life of ancient Greece was transformed from a primitive barter system during the Greek Dark Ages (1150–800 B.C.) to a flourishing system within which goods could be traded throughout the Aegean and Eastern Mediterranean seas. With their official emblem stamped on each coin, each city-state could assure purity and weight of each coin thus sustaining the faith of merchants and tradesmen.

Gold, silver, and bronze coins proved to be exceptional mediums of exchange. Coins became the principal medium of exchange throughout the Roman and Medieval civilizations and commerce steadily advanced. As trade expanded, however, the disadvantages of metal coins could no longer be ignored. Perhaps the greatest problem with coinage is that the money supply would be limited to the availability of precious metals from which coins are minted, and these metals seemed to be always in short supply. In the face of chronic shortages, a common practice employed to increase the supply of coins was to debase the coins by shaving a margin of the edges off the coins and using the shavings to make more coins.[62] As the quality of coins steadily deteriorated, so did people's faith. Another disadvantage of metal coins is that they are heavy and burdensome to carry over long distances, and they could easily be stolen by roving bandits and pirates who preyed on merchants traveling along predictable trade routes. Moreover, as the merchants' trade routes expanded and the quality of coins became increasingly uncertain, converting from one local coin to another became increasingly unpredictable. Hauling their coins and merchandise over long distances, merchants would have to find a currency converter at each destination and the fees charged for these services were unpredictable. Such unpredictability and uncertainty can be serious obstacles to long-distance trade.

To help deal with these problems associated with coins as mediums of exchange, Italian merchant bankers invented the bill of exchange in the thirteenth and fourteenth centuries. The bill of exchange became the prototype of modern paper money such as the dollar bill.

By the end of twelfth century up to the seventeenth century, merchant banking in Europe came to be dominated by powerful Italian families. As merchant bankers, they were engaged in both trade and finance. From the Asti and Lucca families in the twelfth and thirteenth centuries, to the Bardi and Peruzzi in the fourteenth century, and to the enormously powerful Medici bank from the fifteenth century on, these dynasties made their fortunes in long-distance trade and went on to use their fortunes to develop a thriving banking business. Their banking practices were directed toward financing and expediting long-distance trade by creating new financial instruments and by establishing a vast international network of branch banks throughout Western Europe.

The earliest Italian merchants began at medieval trade fairs where they would arrive with wooden tables (called *banco* in Italian, which is the origin of the word "bank") and offer to convert currencies, insure cargo, and provide other financial services. Their most significant contribution, however, was their use of the bill of exchange as a method of sidestepping the Roman Catholic Church's ban on usury (charging interest on loans).

The bill of exchange was a paper IOU drafted by a merchant bank that specified that the bank would pay a certain sum of money in gold or silver in a certain location, at a certain time on behalf of a merchant. For example, say a merchant from Paris buys a load of spices in Venice and transports the cargo to Paris for resale. Instead of carrying coins all the way from Paris to Venice to pay for the spices, the merchant could have the Paris branch of the Italian merchant bank draft a bill of exchange promising to pay a certain amount of money in the local Venetian coin, the *ducat,* to the Italian spice dealer. The French merchant, upon arrival, would pay for the spices with the bill of exchange whereupon the spice dealer could present the bill to the branch of the same banking house in Venice for payment in coins.

Trade, however, was more often two-directional. The French merchant would probably bring a load of French grain to be sold in Italian markets, and again a bill of exchange would be issued promising to pay the grain grower in France payment in French coins, the *ecus.* The French merchant is thus freed from having to carry gold or silver coins from Italy back to France. Having branches in both cities, the accounts of the merchants would be settled, and after collecting a fee, the bank would pay the French merchant profits in coin or simply credit his account.

As a promissory note to pay a sum at a future date, the bill of exchange was not seen as a loan—although in essence it was because it was a means of financing long-distance trade—and so the fees charged for their services were not prohibited by the Church's ban on usury. The Italian bankers were in the best position to provide these services because they had extended their operations into a multitude of branches throughout Europe. Moreover, they charged lower fees, were trusted, and their practice of currency conversion was reliable, so they easily ascended to dominate the financial services industry.

Backed by gold and silver coins, the bill of exchange instilled faith in people as something of real value and not just a mere paper document. As more and more bills of exchange circulated, it eventually became an established practice for people to begin accepting the bills as a form of currency—a medium of exchange as well as a store of value and a unit of account. Thus, the prototype for paper money was established and, combined with metal coins, the foundation for money, so critically important to the capitalist system, was constructed.

Paper money as a medium of exchange became more widespread when commercial banks began issuing "bank notes" in the eighteenth and nineteenth centuries. The merchant banks evolved into depository institutions in which people would deposit their gold and silver coins, or "specie" as the coins came to be called, for safekeeping. Once deposits were made, banks would issue notes as deposit receipts. The bank's name and a promise to redeem in gold and silver specie were printed on each note. As they were backed by the promise to redeem in coins, the notes were seen as having real value, were accepted by merchants as money and began to circulate as currency.

Bank notes were a great convenience, as were the bills of exchange, because buyers and sellers were freed from having to produce gold and silver to cover every transaction. For this convenience, banks charged fees and made profits. For merchants, the advantages of not having to always use gold or silver money for every transaction outweighed the costs of paying the fees to the banks.

The next stage of evolution of paper money came when notes began to be backed by something infinitely more expandable than gold and silver—debt.

Paper money evolved from bills of exchange to bank notes as the banking industry evolved from merchant banking to depository institutions. Bankers began to realize that they did not have to hold on reserve all of the gold and silver specie for potential redemption. They realized that it was unlikely that all of their depositors would demand to redeem their notes in specie at the same time. Operating on that realization, banks began producing more and more notes, the value of which exceeded the actual amount of specie available for redemption. These notes were then used to make loans on which the banks could charge interest.

For banks, gold and silver deposits were liabilities because the banks did not own the coins and would have to return them to the owners upon demand. At the same time, the deposits were used to produce income-earning assets such as farm loans or mortgages. The more notes the banks could issue, the more assets they could produce and the more interest they could collect. In this way, banks created a sort of inverted financial pyramid. At the narrow base of the pyramid were the gold and silver specie deposits that widened into a much broader quantity of paper money and debt at the top. An inverted pyramid is not a stable structure. As banks created more paper money and debt, they exposed themselves to greater risks and hastened banking instability by issuing more notes than what could be immediately redeemed in gold and silver. The larger the top side of the pyramid of money expanded, the riskier the practice of banking became. Banks became increasingly exposed to the possibility that a mass of people would rush to the bank and demand to redeem the notes. When this happened, and it did frequently, people would quickly lose faith in the bank notes and this would lead to a monetary collapse.

This pattern of over-extending paper money and debt followed by monetary collapse was a common occurrence during the first century of money and banking in America.

THE TORTURED HISTORY OF AMERICAN MONEY

Despite its risks and potential for instability, commercial banking continued to expand over the first hundred years of American history and became a key component of the U.S. capitalist system. A close look at the long struggle for a stable monetary system reveals two important themes. The first is the political need of the federal government to create money in order to finance war. The second is the economic need of commercial banks to create a monetary system to serve the needs of market transactions. As mentioned above, the extent to which U.S. monetary institutions historically served the needs of people and the economic needs of communities was more of a side effect, and was subordinate to the dominant themes of warfare and capitalist expansion.

During the first hundred years of its history, the monetary system of the United States was based primarily on a mishmash of gold and silver coins, paper bank notes issued by unstable private banks, and various attempts by the U.S. Treasury Department to create a national currency. It was a century or more of trial-and-error attempts at creating something that today seems commonplace: a stable dollar.

The word "dollar" is derived from the sixteenth century coin known as the *talergroschen*, or the *taler* for short, that was current throughout much of the

Holy Roman Empire. After the disintegration of the Empire, the *taler* settled to become one of a number of local forms of money circulating in various locations including England and Scotland. To distinguish their coins from the English version, the Scots began calling the coin the "dollar." The name migrated from Scotland to the American colonies where it took root.

During the early colonial period in America, English monarchs were hoarding gold and silver coins. The monarchs would not allow the coins to flow out of country or into the American colonies, nor would they allow the colonies to mint their own coins. As an alternative, Americans used Spanish coins that were being minted on location at the mining colonies in Mexico and Peru. With expanding trade among the colonies, these coins became current throughout much of the western hemisphere. Depending on where they were being used, the Spanish coins would be given different names—in the Spanish and Portuguese colonies the coins came to be known as the *peso* or the *real*, and in the American colonies it was the dollar.

From its earliest beginnings, the American federal government's attempt to create a basic monetary system based on gold and silver coins was fraught with trouble. The first dollars minted by the U.S. Treasury Department under the direction of Alexander Hamilton were patterned after the Spanish coins. The Spanish coins sustained a gold-to-silver value ratio of 15-to-1, which means that it would take 15 silver coins to buy 1 gold coin. In order to sustain this ratio, there would have to be a similar ratio of gold and silver prices on the open market for precious metals. This was seldom the case, however, due to dramatically fluctuating prices for precious metals as quantities produced by mines waxed and waned. As the ratio of gold to silver values on the market shifted from, say, 15-to-1, 25-to-1, or 30-to-1, the monetary system with a fixed 15-to-1 gold to silver coin ratio could not be maintained, and the coins would become an unreliable medium of exchange. In this way, the U.S. Treasury created an unstable monetary institution. Without stable money, setting prices, writing contracts, negotiating wages in labor markets, and all the other aspects of money/market transactions also become unstable.

Paper dollars proved to be even less stable than coins. Paper money in the United States prior to the 1860s came principally from private wildcat banks operating under state charters. These banks were referred to as "wildcat" banks because they were poorly regulated by the states and were left free to brazenly expand bank notes and loans with practically nothing of tangible value to support the notes. As described earlier, banks collected deposits of gold and silver specie and proceeded to construct a ballooning pyramid of loans made in the form of paper bank notes or paper dollars. These dollars, though promising to be redeemed in gold or silver specie, were largely worthless because far too many more were issued than what was realistically redeemable.

In 1857, all the state-chartered banks in America simultaneously stopped redeeming dollar bills in silver coins. A widespread banking panic ensued as people began to lose faith in dollar bills as a medium of exchange and a huge swath of financial ruin was left in its wake. Nonetheless, this wildcat system of money and banking continued to grow throughout most of the nineteenth century. Before 1790, there were only three banks operating under state charters, by 1800 there were twenty-eight, and by 1811 the number had grown to eighty-eight.[63]

In an attempt to make the banks more stable, state governments began regulating banks under a fractional reserve model. This meant that the banks were required to keep a certain fraction or percentage of specie on reserve that was proportional to the amount of bank notes that were issued by the banks. The problem was that there were always shortages of gold and silver coins which, given a fixed fraction or proportion to bills, made money excessively scarce. In order to widen the base on which bank notes were secured, states began requiring that notes issued by state-chartered banks be partially redeemable in state government bonds. The bearers of bank notes could then redeem their notes in interest bearing government bonds, rather than the chronically scarce gold and silver specie. The bonds, however, were only as good as the state governments' ability to honor them, which, in most cases, was dubious. More instability was created as states began defaulting on their bond payments and attempting to roll over their debts into more bond issues. In the years leading to the Civil War, nearly all the wildcat state banks in America had failed and left behind them a trail of worthless paper and a general public victimized by financial ruin as their wealth, savings, and purchasing power disintegrated.

The early attempts to create a national paper currency issued by the federal government also met with dismal failure. The first attempt at issuing a national currency came when the colonies formed the Continental Congress and began their struggle for independence. In 1775, Congress authorized the issuance of a paper currency to help finance the Revolutionary War. By Congressional decree the bills, or "Continentals" as they came to be known, were to be legal tender, which meant they were to be used for discharging all debts. The bills were also "fiat" currency meaning that they were not backed by gold, silver, or anything else of tangible value. Instead, the bills were secured by an anticipation of gold and silver tax revenues collected from tariffs. As the

Continentals were based on a government promise that seemed highly uncertain to many, the currencies did not succeed in gaining the faith of the population as a secure medium of exchange, and they eventually failed. The lack of faith in the Continentals created a climate of distrust of any currency created by the federal government. People were naturally suspicious of a government policy that imposes a paper currency on its population for the purpose of raising money for war. It would not be until several decades later that the U.S. Treasury Department would once again attempt to issue a national currency, and the reason again was war—the American Civil War.

Money became a much more centralized institution in the United States with the onset of the American Civil War. Just as the Revolutionary War led to the creation of the Continentals, the Civil War gave rise to new U.S. Treasury Department notes known as Greenbacks. Although there was popular pressure to expand the money supply from farmers in the western states who sought more available credit and higher prices for their agricultural products, the greatest momentum behind the creation of the Greenbacks was the need to finance the war. The National Banking Act, passed by Congress and signed into law by Abraham Lincoln in 1863, authorized the Treasury Department to issue a fiat currency that, like the Continental before it, was not backed by gold, silver, or any other commodity. Like the Continental, the Greenback was declared to be legal tender for all payments of debts owed. Also like the Continental, people did not have faith in the Greenback and it quickly lost its value and prices soared. People ended up paying higher prices in the same way they did when a national sales tax was imposed. Nonetheless, the U.S. Treasury continued to print its currency for decades.

With the National Banking Act, the federal government also established federal charters for national banks. Under the act, large national banks under a federal government charter could issue notes just as state banks. Unlike the state bank notes, the national bank notes were to be a uniform national currency and were backed by U.S. Government bonds. A 10 percent tax was also placed on notes issued by state banks with the intention of pressuring state banks out of the business of issuing notes. The dollars created by state banks were thus systematically phased out and replaced by a national currency. In addition, the U.S. Treasury began to issue gold and silver certificates that were currencies redeemable in gold or silver at fluctuating prices.

In the fifty-year period between 1863 and the establishment of the Federal Reserve System (the "Fed") in 1913, money and banking were becoming more centralized. The U.S. currency consisted mainly of the Treasury Department's notes and certificates, notes issued by national banks that were backed by U.S. government bonds, and a smaller percentage of metal coins. The localized state bank notes were quickly disappearing. At the same time, the federal government was asserting more and more control over monetary institutions and banking became more centralized. Large national banks rose to dominance in the banking industry in the same way that corporate monopolies rose to dominate the steel, oil, and railroad industries.

The simultaneous rise of large corporate monopolies and large national banks was not a coincidence. During the Civil War, the process of concentrating and redistributing money to finance the war effort was a top priority of the U.S. financial system. After the Civil War, its priorities shifted toward building a highly concentrated and centralized capitalist economy. National banks stitched together a system of branch banking that spanned state lines and linked together rural and urban branches. With this system, national banks could concentrate money deposited by people all across the nation and redirect the money to finance urban industrial growth, as well as to finance corporate takeovers, to form trusts, and for casino-style financial market speculation.

As capitalist development became the paramount goal of the U.S. financial system, a dilemma surfaced. On the one hand, the economic system requires a stable monetary system in order to facilitate money-for-commodity transactions in markets. On the other hand, building a stable monetary system can create rigidity or inflexibility. Capitalism must always grow in order to provide steady returns to investors, and this necessitates a flexible money supply. Too much flexibility, however, can lead to severe instabilities and the kind of monetary collapse that stemmed from the wildcat state banking system or from the Treasury Department's worthless fiat currency. Yet rigidity can lead to money shortages that will choke off capitalist growth, and possibly cause recessions or depressions. Facing this dilemma, and observing a series of severe depressions that followed monetary instabilities in 1873, 1882, and 1893, government authorities attempted to create monetary stability and erred on the side of rigidity. After several attempts at stabilizing currencies with a "bimetallic" standard in which notes were backed by a combination of gold and silver, in 1900, the U.S. government adopted the most rigid of all methods to stabilize a currency—the fixed gold standard.

The international gold standard began with the Bank of England in 1816. As a monetary institution, the gold standard was an international system of payments in which all participating currencies were to be fixed to some quantity of gold as a common denominator. Prior to adopting the gold standard, U.S. Treasury notes were backed by government bonds and by gold and silver—a bimetallic standard. Since it was first attempted by Alexander Hamilton, however, the bimetallic monetary standard has always been plagued by an unstable ratio of gold and silver prices on the open market. With the ratification of the Currency Act of 1900, the U.S. government officially ended bimetallism and allowed the U.S. Treasury to issue notes that were to be fixed and redeemable at about $25 per ounce of gold. To secure the standard, the Treasury Department reserved a fund of $150 million in gold coins and bullion.

The gold standard seemed like a sensible way to achieve monetary stability, but stability came at the cost of rigidity. The gold standard required that Treasury notes be maintained at a fixed proportionality to the amount of gold it held on reserve. Luckily, new gold reserves were being discovered, and with the expansion of gold, the money supply could expand. With more money, credit became more plentiful and farmers and others could borrow at reasonable interest rates. For a time, it seemed the gold standard had solved the problem of banking instability.

Below the surface, however, weaknesses in the banking system persisted. National banks continued to siphon bank reserves from across the national landscape and concentrated them on trust building and speculation rather than on the more legitimate purposes of financing agriculture and industry. In the summer of 1907, a number of speculative ventures in the stock market failed and a rash of bankruptcies spread through Wall Street brokerage firms. At that time there was no insurance for depositors, so when the bankers lost money in speculation, so did depositors. The news of trouble in Wall Street spread and this precipitated a run on the banks, and wealthier depositors demanded their money in the form of gold. As with all other such panics, there was not enough gold to pay off all depositors and banks became insolvent.

To make matters worse, people began to fear another banking collapse and began hoarding gold. At the same time, a sense of panic became widespread and people demanded to redeem their Treasury notes in gold. The supply of gold held by the Treasury declined, causing an even greater shortage of money precisely at a time when it needed to expand. The panic was followed by a deep depression and the "invisible hand" of *laissez faire* was trembling violently. More and more people were financially at the end of their tethers, including members of the wealthier classes.

The U.S. capitalist system was hurt by the panic of 1907 in another way. Banks began selling off bonds in order to obtain cash or liquidity during the bank panic and bond prices fell rapidly. For the bondholders, falling bond prices caused a steep decline in the value of their wealth holdings. It seemed obvious to most observers that the monetary institutions of the U.S. were not serving the central purpose of capitalism, and this more than anything else created the push for monetary reform. Although for decades people had been striking, boycotting, forming unions and political parties, and pushing for monetary reforms, the call for thoroughgoing banking reform began only when the violent booms and busts brought ruin to the wealthy. Exercising their political power, wealthy individuals started pressuring the federal government to make permanent reforms to the money and banking system.

After the panic of 1907, Congress soon passed the Aldrich-Vreeland Act (1908). The act established a National Monetary Commission that would investigate strategies for monetary and banking reform. Their recommendation was to charter a new central bank. The main obstacle to creating this central bank, however, was the deeply entrenched ideology of *laissez faire* and the widely felt distrust of "big government." For a period of over seven decades, the United States was the only capitalist economy of significance without a central bank. In 1913, that changed with the creation of the Federal Reserve System.

President Woodrow Wilson signed into law a permanent charter for the Federal Reserve System on December 23rd, 1913. The Federal Reserve Act resolved to modernize the system of revenue collections and disbursements for the Treasury Department, to stabilize and make flexible the money supply, to stabilize the check-clearing process, and to make the financial system safer for profit-making. To appease those who were distrustful, the act called for a somewhat "decentralized" central bank. That is, not to create a single-government-owned and controlled bank, but to create a system of twelve regionally based Federal Reserve Banks, each owned by private banks, not the federal government. The Federal Reserve System came into being as a unique privately owned institution with a public mandate.

The Fed was to create monetary stability by acting as a lender of last resort. That is, the Fed would hold a portion of the deposits of banks throughout the economy as reserves and use those reserves as an emergency source of money from which commercial banks could borrow when they were facing panics or money shortages. However, the problem of rigidity remained as the U.S. dollar was still fixed to the gold standard.

The great stock market boom and bust of the 1920s and 1930s proved that the creation of the Fed alone was not sufficient to achieve the kind of financial stability government officials and members of the business community were seeking. As the dollar was still anchored to the gold standard, the Fed's ability to stabilize the financial system was severely limited. The creation of the Fed also generated a false sense of security among bankers and brokers who were making questionable loans for speculation. Speculators believed that if something went wrong, the Fed would now be there to fix it. When the stock market began its crash in October 1929, the harsh truth was revealed that the Fed simply did not have the resources to stem the general financial market meltdown and the Great Depression that followed.

One of the principal causes of the financial crisis was the collapse of the international gold standard centered at the Bank of England. World War I created a severe financial problem for Great Britain and other European countries that were torn asunder by warfare. To pay for the war effort the Bank of England temporarily suspended its commitment to the gold standard and began printing pounds beyond the limitations set by the standard. After a few unsuccessful attempts to re-fix the pound to a measure of gold, the Bank of England permanently abandoned the international gold standard in 1931. In a series of chain reactions, the gold standard began to collapse. The U.S. devalued the dollar to $35 per ounce of gold in international payments and suspended gold redemption of Treasury notes domestically. France abandoned the gold standard in 1934, and Germany was in the midst of one of the worst currency devaluations in the history of the planet. The international gold standard finally disintegrated and international trade fell dramatically. Crises and instability were not unusual in capitalist economies, but by the 1930s, capitalism was experiencing its worst crisis in its history and it was on a global scale.

In response to the Depression, the federal government pushed through economic reform legislation including new laws for controlling banking and stock market activity. In 1934, President Franklin D. Roosevelt nationalized the domestic gold supply. This meant that the federal government set out to confiscate gold as it became officially a controlled substance and gold coins were withdrawn from circulation. Those who surrendered their gold coins voluntarily received about $20 per ounce, and those who tried hoarding risked having their gold taken by the government without compensation. The government melted the gold coins and bullion into bars and stored them in a depository built at Fort Knox Kentucky. In 1934, all national bank notes were withdrawn from circulation as well, and control of the supply of money depended exclusively on policies of the U.S. Treasury Department and the Federal Reserve System. From that point on, private banks were no longer in the business of producing paper money.

The financial crises of the 1920s and 1930s, and the long, painful depression that followed delivered a fierce blow to the capitalist system. Government officials, scholars, and leaders in the business community began to see that these crises were not only avoidable, but also were among the primary causes of World War II. To address these problems, a conference of over seven hundred representatives from forty-four nations was organized at Bretton Woods, New Hampshire in June of 1944. The goal of the conference was to begin the process of creating new international financial institutions including a new institution for stabilizing international currency exchanges: the gold exchange standard.

The Bretton Woods gold exchange standard sought to create international financial stability by pegging all currencies to a common denominator. Unlike the gold standard, it was the U.S. dollar that served as the common denominator. However, the dollar itself retained the gold backing. The U.S. was the only major economy that did not permanently suspend the earlier gold standard in the 1930s, and maintained a fixed rate of $35 per ounce of gold. Other countries agreed to fix their currencies to the dollar with a range of flexibility in their exchange rates to the dollar of about 10 percent. In other words, the gold exchange standard was a system in which the U.S. dollar was pegged to gold, and other participating currencies were pegged to the dollar.

After the creation of the Bretton Woods system, the U.S. dollar took on two important characteristics. First, the dollar became a global currency just like the Spanish coins had in the seventeenth and eighteenth centuries, and gold had in the nineteenth century. As a global currency, many commodities such as oil and sugar were bought and sold in international markets for dollars and some countries, when experiencing instability of their own currencies, adopted the dollar as their preferred medium of exchange. The other important characteristic was that the dollar could be redeemed at $35 for one ounce of gold bullion in the settlement of international payments resulting from trade. As it turned out, for many of the same reasons as in the past, these two characteristics of the dollar would bring about yet another crisis, and ultimately hastened the end of the international gold exchange standard.

Under the gold exchange standard, the U.S. dollar achieved stability and surpassed the British pound as the world's premier currency. But as an international currency, dollars were being circulated around the world in ever-larger amounts and eventually the U.S. Treasury and the Fed began to lose track of the amount of dollars that were in global circulation. This problem worsened during the Cold War when the U.S. government built a network of military bases that spanned the globe. To sustain these bases, the U.S. government had sent dollars outside the country. By the mid-1960s, the U.S. became deeply entrenched in a war in Vietnam that was increasingly unpopular and expensive and lasted for about a decade. The unpopularity of the war prevented Congress from approving new taxes needed to pay for the war, so it borrowed heavily. The borrowed funds flowing into the U.S. Treasury allowed the government to increase the money supply relative to its supply of gold. By doing so, the Treasury was recreating the unstable pyramids that brought down the wildcat banks in the nineteenth century. The U.S. government, preoccupied with the Cold War and its own imperial ambition, allowed its currency to balloon out far and away above its real value in gold. To anyone who was paying attention, it was becoming clear that the government would soon not have enough gold reserves to maintain its gold backing in international payments.

Central banks of foreign governments that were holding large amounts of dollars began to suspect that the U.S. might not be able to redeem the dollars in gold at the fixed rate of $35 per ounce. France and other countries began showing up at the "gold window" demanding to exchange their dollars for gold and the U.S. Treasury was forced to send large amounts of gold out of the country at a time when it needed as much gold as possible to support the dollar. Fearing an exhaustion of the supplies of gold at Fort Knox, President Nixon ordered the end of the gold exchange standard in 1971. The dollar quickly depreciated and the international system of fixed exchange rates came to an end.

In order to place a firewall between the government's will to wage war and its ability to finance war by printing money, the U.S. government ended the Treasury Department's authority to print money. 1971 was the last year Treasury notes were put into circulation and from then on controlling the money supply became the exclusive job of the Federal Reserve System.

Today the U.S. dollar is a fiat currency controlled by the Fed. There are no international systems of fixed exchange rates, gold is no longer a controlled substance, and there is no gold or any other commodity backing the dollar. So what sustains the dollar's value and prevents it from being worthless paper? The easiest answer to that question is to say that the dollar's value derives from its purchasing power, or what a person can buy with it. This means also that the dollar is backed, in a sense, by the nation's gross domestic product (GDP). How much of the nation's GDP people can buy with their dollars depends largely on Federal Reserve System policy. If the Fed creates too much money, then dollars increase proportionally to GDP and begin to lose value resulting in price inflation. If the Fed keeps money too tight then money becomes scarce and expensive which chokes off growth and could cause an economic slowdown. How the Fed accomplishes this is a complex process that we will explore in the next section.

When reflecting on this tortured history of American money, it appears that the legitimate needs of ordinary people were placed below war, speculation, and profit-making on the list of priorities. The economic health of rural and urban communities was weakened, and the livelihoods of people suffered real economic damage as bank panics and speculative pyramids crashed leaving behind a trail of economic wreckage. With each financial crisis, however, monetary institutions in the U.S. have evolved and have become stable, though not necessarily because stable money was needed by people, but because it was needed by the capitalist system. Yet as of this writing, the federal government's skyrocketing war budget is scoring record federal budget deficits. At the same time, the U.S. economy is also hitting new records in its trade deficits with the rest of the world. As these deficits and debts mount, it becomes increasingly likely that the U.S. monetary system will once again contort with instability, and once again it will be ordinary people who pay the price with skyrocketing prices, widespread unemployment, or both.

Ironically, the U.S. often pronounces itself as the vanguard of democratic movements around the world, yet its own monetary system—the lifeblood of the economy—is dominated by non-democratic institutions: corporate banks and the Federal Reserve System. It is to these institutions that we now direct our focus.

AMERICAN DEPOSITORY INSTITUTIONS

As we stated earlier, the purpose of the financial sector of the U.S. economy is to pull together funds from widely dispersed sources and direct them toward specific uses. Financial institutions, including depository institutions, are the intermediaries in this process. Depository institutions are what people normally think of when they think of "banks." Private sector depository institutions are capitalist enterprises, and like any other capitalist enterprise, they exist to maximize profits. Standing as intermediaries between the depositors (sources) and borrowers (uses), banks mainly make their profits on the difference in interest rates paid to depositors and the rates charged on loans.

The economic significance of depository institutions goes beyond providing financial services such as holding deposits and making loans. Depository institutions also have the capacity to create money. Although private sector banks no longer issue bank notes or paper currency as they did in the nineteenth century, they still can create money in the process of pyramiding loans from a fraction of deposits. The more money banks lend out, the more money they add to the overall money supply. Banks can also destroy money and reduce the money supply by making fewer loans.

As banks can influence the money supply in this way, they are tightly regulated by the central bank, the Federal Reserve System. In the pages that follow, we will examine the different types of banks that operate in the U.S. economy. We will also see how the Fed controls the amount of cash reserves held by banks, and thereby holds a grip on the amount of loans these banks can make from their deposits. Relaxing or loosening this grip is the key to how the Federal Reserve System controls the money supply of the United States. We will also see that depository institutions and the Federal Reserve together form a complex structure that works to keep the capitalist money machine running around the clock.

State and federal governments control the number of depository institutions operating in the U.S. economy by controlling bank charters. Charters are essentially the contracts that allow businesses to operate as banks and follow banking regulations. National banks are chartered by the office of the Comptroller of the Currency within the U.S. Treasury Department. The banking or treasury departments of state governments charter state banks. Federal law requires that all nationally chartered banks become members of the Federal Reserve System, though membership is optional for state banks and the majority of state banks opt not to be members. Whether or not they are Fed members, all depository institutions are required to hold a percentage of deposits (reserves) on account with the Fed. These banks are also required to pay premiums to, and be insured by, the Federal Deposit Insurance Corporation (FDIC).

Depository institutions fall into four general categories: commercial banks, savings and loans associations, savings banks, and credit unions. The most prevalent are *commercial banks*. There are roughly eight thousand commercial banks in the U.S. operating under either national or state charters and controlling over $7 billion in assets. Commercial banks hold the majority of standard checking and savings account deposits and typically offer a full spectrum of financial services: making consumer, business, and real estate loans; underwriting letters of credit; and investing in government or corporate bonds (more on these in the next chapter). Commercial banks also issue certificates of deposits, or CDs, which are special accounts that pay a specified rate of interest over a specified period on deposits over a certain minimum amount. Commercial banks also create money market accounts for depositors that typically pay higher rates than savings accounts and require higher initial deposits.

Savings and loans associations (S & Ls) were originally established as financial cooperatives in the nineteenth century by builders' associations to help wage earners to become home owners—something that traditionally was the privilege of the wealthy. As cooperatives, the shareholders are also the depositors who receive dividends as shares of the bank's profits. Because of changes in federal banking regulations in the 1980s, S & Ls have expanded the financial services they offer far beyond their original purpose and have come to resemble commercial banks. Most are no longer cooperatives, but they are still primarily mortgage lenders.

At their peak in the 1960s—during an era of dramatic home ownership expansion—there were well over four thousand savings and loans associations providing financial services in the U.S. As part of the Reagan Administration's *laissez faire* ideology in the 1980s, regulatory control of S & Ls began to evaporate. Poor regulation and lax government oversight opened the door to fraud, corruption, and the practice of placing customer deposits into highly risky loans and junk bonds. The result was one of the worst banking crises in American history in which about 75 percent of all savings and loans associations in the U.S. fell into bankruptcy. As the now-defunct Federal Savings and Loans Insurance Corporation insured the deposits, the costs to the federal government were staggering. Today there are scarcely one thousand savings and loans banks in operation, only a shadow of what the industry was in the past.

Savings banks, also known as mutual savings banks, have a small niche in the financial services industry. They were originally established in the nineteenth century as locally based alternatives to the wildcat state banks and national banks that frequently destroyed the savings of millions of families. Savings banks typically operated in communities where they encouraged working people to save what they could and, at the same time, provided small personal loans. Savings banks were seen as a relatively safe and secure place for people to put their money that was destined to be used locally. Public-spirited leaders who were interested in providing financial assistance to the low-wage working class founded savings banks. The first of such banks was established by Reverend Henry Duncan of Rothwell, Scotland known as the "Savings and Friendly Society" for the people in his parish. Today there are about 1,400 savings banks in operation in the U.S. and they are evolving into more full service banks that offer checking and savings accounts, CDs, and other financial services. Many are expanding into chains, losing their local character, and with changes in banking regulations they are becoming more like small-scale commercial banks.

Credit unions, like saving and loan associations, were originally established as cooperatives in which the depositors were also shareholders and operated primarily as nonprofits. German farmers established the prototype for credit unions in the mid-nineteenth century. The farmers would buy shares in an agricultural financial cooperative that would make low interest loans available to the farming community. Now credit unions are typically organized within various self-defined communities of people: members of the same profession, people who work in the same industry or people who belong to the same labor union. Credit unions provide a full range of financial services, but focus mainly on checking, savings deposits, and small personal or short-term loans. As nonprofits, credit unions do not have to pay investors a rate of return and this allows them to pay higher interest rates to depositors and to charge borrowers lower rates. There are thousands of credit unions scattered across the United States, but because they are relatively small, they constitute only about 5 percent of overall banking assets.

Regardless of the category, the core business of depository institutions is to take deposits, make loans, and profit from the differences or "spread" in interest rates. Banking as such fits well within the capitalist program of buying low, selling high, and taking profits. Over the last forty years, the amount of credit extended by depository institutions has expanded dramatically as banks formed bankcard associations and began issuing credit cards. Prior to the creation of credit cards, bank loans—no matter how small—had to be made in person as face-to-face transactions between the borrower and the bank. With cards, loans are made with the stroke of a pen.

The first major credit card began in 1965 when Bank of America in San Francisco formed licensing agreements with other banks to process transactions with borrowed funds through a centralized system. The system was based on the concept that consumers, once approved, were authorized access to credit at various banks by issuing plastic cards called the BankAmericard. These agreements among banks solidified into a bankcard association in which the participating banks shared the costs of administering the inter-bank system and extended the bankcard program to smaller banks. In this way, banks had established a single network using a standardized plastic card to extend lending capacity and ability to earn interest income from a much broader sector of the population. In 1977, BankAmericard was renamed Visa.

Another bankcard association was formed in 1966 to compete with BankAmericard and operated under a similar arrangement with a standardized card known as MasterCharge; in 1979, it changed its name to MasterCard. With the development of these and other major credit cards, the banking industry experienced the most dramatic expansion of consumer credit, and debt, the world has ever known. Perhaps more importantly, credit cards allowed the capitalist system to continue to grow and expand, as it was no longer limited to the purchasing power of consumer incomes. Consumer spending, a critical component of capitalist profit-making, could be charged.

As banks drive to make more profits for their investors, they are driven to lend to an ever-widening sector of the population and thereby earn more interest income. By doing so, however, the banking industry becomes riskier as it extends credit to borrowers who are less likely to pay back their loans. With increasing risk comes the greater likelihood that banks will lose depositors' money and raise the possibility of bank panics and instability.

After nearly a century of such panics, monetary collapses, and general instability in the real economy, the banking industry has been covered with a thick blanket of regulatory and institutional controls to combat instability. Arguably the two most significant regulatory developments that have served to stabilize the banking industry have been the creation of the Federal Deposit Insurance Corporation (FDIC) and the empowerment of the Federal Reserve System to control the reserves of all depository institutions.

The Federal Deposit Insurance Corporation was created in 1933 during the depths of the Great Depression. Prior to the 1930s, a clear pattern had been established in which recurring crises in the financial economy would lead to recurring crises in the real economy of production and employment. Reform was badly needed, but most of the attempts at reform were ineffective as the policy makers were still guided by *laissez faire* ideology and thus would exclude federal government programs as part of the reform package. This changed with Franklin D. Roosevelt's New Deal administration. The FDIC was created to reduce the occurrence of panics or runs on banks. The goal of creating the FDIC was to instill confidence among depositors that their life savings would not disappear if banks were becoming insolvent. With such assurances, people were less likely to rush to pull their money out of the bank at the first sign of trouble. The federal government created the FDIC to insure deposits up to a certain limited amount (originally $5,000). Today the FDIC insures bank accounts up to $100,000 per institution. After the creation of the FDIC, bank panics became far less frequent and banking industry became far more stable.

Insuring deposits alone is not sufficient to create a stable banking industry. In addition to panics, another source of instability is the process of pyramiding too many loans over a narrow base of reserve. Thus, to achieve more stability the Federal Reserve System was created in 1913 as an institution that can, among other things, control that base or the fraction of cash reserves held by depository institutions. By doing so, the Fed can control lending volume and the overall supply of money in the U.S. economy.

THE FEDERAL RESERVE SYSTEM "THE FED"

The Federal Reserve System was chartered by Congress as the central bank for the United States in 1913 and has become a centrally important economic institution in the United States. The Fed was primarily chartered to build a reliable system of revenue collections and disbursements for the federal government, to create an efficient check-clearing process, and, most importantly, to create a stable yet flexible money and banking system. To understand how the Fed sustains this control we must first explore its institutional structure. We will then examine how it controls money and credit in the United States within this institutional structure. With its control over money and credit, the Fed has tremendous influence on economic activity overall.

Figure 2 on the next page shows the overall institutional structure of the Federal Reserve System. Executive control over the Fed system lies with the Board of Governors based in Washington D.C. The Board of Governors holds broad decision-making powers and sets banking guidelines, but the day-to-day operations of carrying out policy actions, supervision, and providing services for banks is handled by the twelve district banks. Sitting on the Board are seven members, each of whom is appointed by the President of the United States and confirmed by the U.S. Senate in a manner similar to the appointments of Supreme Court justices. Within the seven members there is a chairman and vice chairman whose positions are subject to four-year reappointments.

Though the President makes the appointment decisions, Board of Governor decisions are deliberately insulated from the political influence of the federal government. Each member serves a fourteen-year term and the terms are staggered to prevent a single presidential administration from appointing a majority on the Board and thereby influencing Fed policy. Once a board member is appointed, he or she cannot be reappointed once the fourteen-year term has expired. Policy decisions do not have to be ratified by Congress and the Fed is self-funded such that it does not depend on Congressional appropriations to finance its operations. The Fed runs on an annual budget between $3 and $4 billion, financed by fees and interest payments charged to member banks, and from the interest income on a portfolio of between $400 and $500 billion in U. S. Treasury Department bonds.

The Fed is a unique institution that has both private and public characteristics. It is privately owned (explained below), but at the same time is the creation of Congress with a federal government charter. Although the Fed is

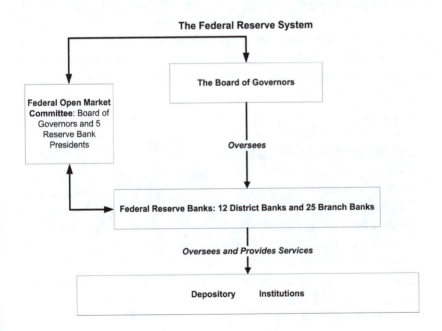

Figure 2

privately owned, it is not a capitalist institution in the sense that it is not allowed to keep and accumulate profits. By law, the Fed is required to turn over any net earnings after covering its operating expenses back to the U.S. Treasury.

By structuring the Board of Governors in this way, and by having an independent funding base, the Fed has gained much freedom from pressures coming from Washington politics. Such political insulation of the central bank is ominous; for the Fed's autonomy from the war-making powers of government has also made it immune to democratic accountability. None of the Federal Reserve policies requires voter approval, nor are any of the members of the Board of Governors democratically elected officials.

Under the watchful eye of the Board of Governors are the twelve Federal Reserve Banks and twenty-five branches that carry out all of the day-to-day operations of the Fed (see Figure 3 below). Each Reserve Bank is a separate corporate entity with a nine-member board of directors comprised of executives from large banks or large corporations. The owners of the shares of the Reserve Banks are member commercial banks in their districts and each share receives a fixed dividend. As privately owned corporations, the directors are elected by member banks. Unlike most private corporations, however, the shares cannot be bought and sold in stock markets, and ownership does not endow owners with control over policy-making decisions.

At the foundation of the Fed structure is the relationship between the Reserve Banks and the depository institutions in their districts. In this rela-

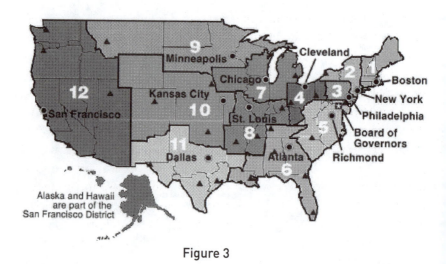

Figure 3

tionship, the Fed both supervises and controls the lending practices of banks, but also provides important services for its member banks. Bank membership binds depository institutions to the Fed financially as well. Depository institutions can apply to become members if they meet the membership requirements that are set and approved by the Board of Governors. Once the application for membership is approved, a bank must "subscribe" stocks to the district Reserve Bank.

Subscription as such means turning 6 percent of the capitalization (generally meaning stocks) of the bank over to the district Reserve Bank in exchange for a fixed 6 percent annual dividend, and for check-clearing and other services provided by the Fed. The steep subscription requirements are largely what prevent most state-chartered banks from becoming members. It must be emphasized, however, that even if a bank does not apply for membership it is still legally required to follow monetary policies established by the Fed. In other words, not being a member does not mean that a state bank will be free from Fed supervision and control.

The Fed has thirty areas of supervision and control of state-chartered depository institutions noted as "Regulations A through EE."[64] These areas include placing limits on the credit depository institutions extended to borrowers, regulating the use of debt for investments in the stock market, and monitoring state banks to assure that they comply with federal and state banking laws. Whereas it is the job of the Federal Reserve to supervise state banks, the U. S. Treasury Department supervises national banks.

In addition to supervising state banks, the Fed also provides services to member banks. One such service is that each Reserve Bank and their local branches maintain adequate quantities of coins and paper currency to meet the needs of banks in their district. Although the Fed issues the currency to banks, it does not print money. The actual printing of money is done by the Treasury Department's Bureau of Engraving and Printing that contracts with the Fed to provide currency at the cost of printing only.

Another service the Fed provides is check-clearing. Check-clearing is the process of settling accounts between banks as checks are written to draw down the balances of accounts in one bank and increase the balances in another. All Fed Reserve Banks and branches are equipped with the facilities to provide fast, highly automated, and centralized check-clearing services to depository institutions. The Fed also provides electronic funds transfer services, maintains vaults for safekeeping of valuable assets, provides research, and publishes data on economic activities in each district.

The Fed is also a banker to both member banks and to the U.S. Treasury Department. Depository institutions that need to borrow funds on a relatively short basis can borrow from the Fed at interest rates significantly below those charged by commercial banks. The rate banks pay to the Fed is called the "discount rate" and, as we will see, the discount rate is part of what the Fed uses to set monetary policy.

The Federal Reserve System is the banker to the federal government's Treasury Department. The U.S. Treasury, through the Internal Revenue Service, collects between $2 and $3 trillion in tax revenue from individuals and businesses annually. As the taxes are paid, the money flows into special interest-earning accounts known as Treasury Tax and Loan Accounts (TTLs), maintained in thousands of commercial banks across the nation. The TTL account balances are reported by the commercial banks to the Fed. The Fed, based on the needs of the Treasury, will direct the funds held in the TTL accounts to Treasury Department accounts held at Reserve Banks. From these Reserve Bank accounts, the cash managers at the Treasury Department write checks to pay for the federal government's operating expenses. The Fed also functions as an investment bank to the U.S. government (see Chapter Six on Investment Banks). At any given time, the U.S. government is likely to spend more money than what it brings into its TTL accounts, and so to cover its expenditures the government must borrow by selling government bonds at auctions held by Fed Reserve Banks.

Although the services the Fed provides to the banking industry and the U.S. government are important, its most important function is to carry out monetary policy. Recall that part of the original intention of creating the Federal Reserve System was to sustain a flexible yet stable monetary system by centralizing control over the nation's money supply. Monetary policy is a set of policies determined by the Fed to control the cash reserves that lie at the base of the money pyramid built up by bank lending. By controlling the availability of cash reserves in the banking system, the Fed can also control the availability of credit and the cost of credit—interest rates. In other words, the Fed controls the entire inverted pyramid of cash, by controlling the cash reserves at the narrow base.

To understand how the Fed controls the inverted pyramid of money, it is first necessary to understand how depository institutions create and destroy money. As described earlier in this chapter, banks have always been able to create money by pyramiding interest earning credit (assets) over a much narrower base of deposits (liabilities); that is, by lending out more than what they retain in cash money "reserves" in their accounts. In short, depository institutions do not print money, but they create money by making loans.

Say, for example, someone makes a deposit of $10,000 into a bank account. By the rules set by Fed policy, the bank must hold about 3 percent of that deposit as a cash reserve. This means that the 3 percent of the $10,000, which amounts to $300, must be set aside as a cash reserve, but the other $9,700 of that deposit can be lent to borrowers. If the bank does not hold "excess reserves," that is, reserves above what is required by the Fed, and lends out the entire $9,700, that $9,700 is newly created money that did not exist before. The money supply can continue to expand as the borrowers either deposit their $9,700 in loans back into the bank and thus create new deposits, or they spend the money and the sellers deposit the money back into the banking system. Either way, the $9,700 becomes a new deposit of which 3 percent ($291) must be held on reserve and the remaining $9,409 is subsequently lent out, and the process of pyramiding money starts all over again. So, the more money banks lend, the more money they create. By the same reasoning, as banks lend less money and loans are paid back, money is actually destroyed. Thus, money can expand or contract exponentially as banks lend more or less. As one can imagine, unless this process is tightly regulated, it can very quickly become unstable.

To maintain stability the Fed centrally controls the amount of cash reserves held by banks at the narrow base of the money pyramid. The Fed has three "levers" it can push and pull to control these bank reserves. The pushing and pulling of these levers is collectively referred to as *monetary policy*. By adjusting monetary policy, the Fed can control the narrow base of the pyramid of bank credit, and by controlling the base it controls the entire pyramid—the money supply and interest rates for the overall financial system.

One such lever is to directly control the base of the inverted pyramid of money by controlling the percentage of each deposit that banks must hold as cash reserves on account with the Fed. This percentage is referred to as the *reserve requirement ratio* and the ratio varies between 0 and 10 percent depending on the size and type of deposit—the larger the deposit, the larger the reserve requirement ratio.

By altering the percentage of required cash reserves, the Fed can increase or decrease the availability of loanable funds. For example, if the reserve requirement ratio on a deposit of $50 million is 10 percent, this means that the bank must hold $5 million of that deposit on reserve and can lend out the remaining $45 million. That $45 million, once it is lent to borrowers, becomes an addition to the money supply in the banking system as described above. If the Fed wants to contract or tighten the money supply, it can raise the reserve requirement ratio from 10 percent, to say 15 percent. At 15 percent, then $7.5 million must be held on reserve and only $42.5 million can be poured into a pool of loanable funds. To expand the money supply, the Fed can lower the reserve requirement ratio. The Fed rarely changes the reserve requirement ratio by any substantial degree, for if it were to do so it could lead to significant uncertainty, and uncertainty in banking can quickly lead to instability.

On any given day, if a bank finds that it is falling short of its reserve requirement it can take emergency measures by borrowing the excess reserves of other banks held on account with the Fed, or face a penalty. Falling outside the reserve requirement and paying penalties as such is so rare as to be nonexistent. This rarity is due in part to the fact that banks can borrow to shore up their cash reserves. Member banks can either borrow directly from the Federal Reserve through the "discount window" at low rates, or they can borrow reserves from other banks on an overnight, emergency basis.

The interest rate the Fed charges member banks when they borrow from the Fed's discount window is the discount rate, and adjusting the discount rate is another lever of Fed monetary policy. By adjusting the discount rate, the Fed can manipulate the amount of cash banks borrow from the Fed for subsequent re-lending. For example, if a bank borrows from the Fed at a 3 percent discount rate, and then lends those same funds to its own borrowers at 5 percent, it profits from the 2 percent difference. If the Fed raises the discount rate, the profit margin diminishes and banks are less likely to borrow and re-lend. As re-lending is discouraged by a higher discount rate, lending in general can slow down. As lending slows down, the amount of money in the banking system will diminish, making cash relatively more scarce. As cash becomes scarce, interest rates in commercial banks rise and overall lending slows down even further.

The short-term, emergency loans are called "federal funds," and the interest rate charged for these funds is called the "federal funds rate." Unlike the discount rate, the federal funds rate is not directly controlled by Fed policy; rather it is determined by forces of supply and demand of loanable funds in the open market. Because the federal funds market spans the entire banking industry, the federal funds rate is the barometer of loanable funds market activity and credit markets in general. When this rate rises and falls, all other short-term rates follow in lock step. Although the Fed does not control the federal funds rate directly by decree, it can control it indirectly by controlling the supply of reserves in the short-term open market. This process of controlling the supply of reserves in the open market is at the core of Fed monetary policy and is referred to as open market operations—the third and most important lever in Fed monetary policy.

Simply put, open market operations involve the Federal Reserve Bank of New York buying and selling U.S. government bonds in the open market. The transactions take place between what is called the "trading desk" at the New York bank and a select group of some thirty-five to fifty securities dealers in the private sector. These securities dealers, known as "primary dealers" are large Wall Street commercial and investment banks that have sufficient amounts of capital to participate in bond trades with the Fed's trading desk. These bond transactions are carried out as a result of directives set by the most powerful body within the Federal Reserve System—the Federal Open Market Committee (FOMC).

Referring back to Figure 2, the Federal Open Market Committee is comprised of the Board of Governors and five Fed branch bank presidents. At some point, the FOMC will convene, make a policy decision with respect to the federal funds market, and seek to adjust the availability of reserves held by banks. Once the decision for a particular direction is made, it sends a directive to New York's trading desk and open market operations commence.

If the directive is to contract the money supply, the goal to be achieved in open market operations is to reduce the amount of reserves available to banks in the federal funds market. To achieve this, the trading desk will send out a message to the primary dealers that it will be selling government bonds and invite the dealers to make bids on bond purchases. The trading desk stays in continuous contact with the primary dealers who are typically given only about ten to fifteen minutes to respond to the invitation before the trade is closed. As the primary dealers make their bids to buy bonds, the successful bidders pay for the bonds by drawing down their balances—or reserves—at their commercial bank accounts. By drawing down reserves, banks remove money from the federal funds market, scarcity arises, and the federal funds rate starts to rise. Rising rates discourage borrowing in the federal funds market and, in turn, discourage lending in banking in general. As lending is discouraged, the inverted pyramid of money shrinks. If the directive is to expand the money supply, the process is reversed and the Fed buys government bonds, reserves increase in the open market, and the money pyramid enlarges.

These three levers of monetary policy—particularly open market operations—are designed to achieve broader economic goals. If banks are lending too aggressively and the money pyramid is getting too large, this could cause rapid price inflation and potential instability. To combat this, the Fed would pursue "contractionary" monetary policy, which involves tightening the money supply and raising interest rates. On the other hand, if the real economy looks as if it might slow into a recession, the Fed would pursue "expansionary" monetary policy by loosening the money supply and lowering interest rates.

The fact that the Fed has the power to control money and rates for the entire U.S. banking system as it pursues broader economic goals, raises questions as to what specifically the goals are and who benefits from them? Former chairman Alan Greenspan repeatedly asserted that his primary target is to fight inflation, and this anti-inflation legacy of the Fed continues. Why inflation? Of course, no one likes to pay higher prices for things, but the negative effects of inflation for the broad base of the working population can be neutralized with cost of living adjustments in their pay contracts, which are typical. But for banks and any other institution or person who earns income from interest-bearing bonds, loans, mortgages, or any other instrument that pays a fixed annual rate of return, their real income (income after adjusted for inflation) is eaten away by inflation. Inflation eats away at the purchasing power of any investment that pays a fixed rate of return, and so any member of the investor class who owns financial assets paying fixed rates of return is going to fear price inflation.

Say, for example, a bondholder earns 5 percent annual interest on the bond and there is 2 percent inflation, then the real income for the bond holder is 3 percent. If the inflation rate is 6 percent, then the real interest income for the bondholder is -1 percent. The same would be true for a bank or mortgage company charging 5 percent on a loan, or any other financial instrument that is created to yield a rate of return, which is nearly the total sum of Wall Street. And Wall Street is command central of American capitalism. In other words, the Fed's primary constituent and beneficiary of its policies is the wealth-owning class.

To fight inflation the Fed will pursue contractionary monetary policy and raise interest rates. This is tough medicine for the broad base of the population because the real weapon against inflation is not the higher rates themselves, but the higher unemployment rates and subsequent downward pressure on wages and salaries that follow. In other words, to help the investor class get over the pain of price inflation, the Fed sacrifices the incomes and job security of working families. Moreover, on more than one occasion Greenspan has been an outspoken critic of raising the federal minimum wage.

Greenspan sought to encourage the federal government to reduce the amount of money it borrows from the banking system by advocating cuts in the already meager social security benefits paid to the aged and disabled.

CONCLUSION: MONEY AND DEMOCRACY

As the Fed's principal constituents are a wealthy and narrow slice of the American population, it is not pressured to be accountable to a broad base of the population. This is consistent with the history of monetary institutions in the U.S and with capitalism in general. Pursuing narrow goals of war or wealth accumulation for the investor class has seldom worked to benefit a broad base of the population. More often than not, monetary institutions have worked to the detriment of people and communities, and will continue to do so unless they are made democratically accountable.

Although the Fed was created by an act of Congress and is subject to some degree of Congressional oversight, the strand of substantive democracy connecting people and monetary policy is a hair's breadth. Each Federal Reserve Bank is owned by, and has boards selected by, private-sector banks. The people that sit on the boards are not elected by popular vote, as would be the case of other public institutions such as school boards or utilities commissions. This is an odd arrangement considering that the Fed is an important public institution, dealing with an extremely important public good—money—that is supported by public debt. Moreover, monetary policy is directed by a secretive committee that works in nearly complete isolation from any body of democratic government. There is no democratic structure in which people and communities can press their political will to influence Fed policy.

As the U.S. proclaims itself to be the vanguard of democratic movements around the world, it is striking that its two most important economic institutions—the corporation and the Federal Reserve System—are fundamentally non-democratic.

To create a more democratically accountable system of money in the U.S., people will be required to do the hard work of building their own, localized financial institutions that are directly accountable to the people and communities they serve. This is, in fact, what people have done throughout the tortured history of American money when they created credit unions and locally based savings banks. The most prevalent depository institution in terms of numbers is the credit union, numbering over ten thousand in operation today. Credit unions were established to give people direct and substantive democratic control over money and banking in their communities. Creating democratic monetary systems does not have to mean reinventing the wheel. In cities scattered across the country, people are building their own locally based monetary systems including local currencies.

In a mindful economy, we value the needs of people and their communities as a top priority. A mindful monetary system is an integral part of a mindful economy that does not serve the purposes of war, corporate profits, or the aggrandizement of a small investor class. Rather it is guided by different, non-capitalist principles, and is rooted in the original purpose of money as a medium of exchange between people and businesses that are working to build just and sustainable communities. This and other mindful alternatives will be explored in detail in later chapters.

6

THE U.S. FINANCIAL SYSTEM PART II
Wall Street, Stocks, and Bonds

In the previous chapter, we asserted that money is a vitally important institution for capitalist systems. Its importance derives from the fact that capitalist systems are centered on market exchanges and money is the medium of these exchanges. As capitalism has come to be the dominant system within the U.S. economy, its key monetary and financial institutions have also evolved and developed to serve the needs of profit-making and capital accumulation. Part of this evolution includes the development of the Federal Reserve System and the U.S. banking industry. Also, out of this evolution emerged a structure of powerful and wealthy financial institutions collectively referred to as "Wall Street."

Along with cities like London and Tokyo, New York City is revered as one of the premier financial centers of the world. Wall Street is an actual street located at the center of New York's financial district. Historically, the street was the epicenter of financial activity as it headquartered all the major U.S. financial institutions such as commercial banks, investment banks, stock exchanges, and brokerage houses. These institutions created the "securities" industry. Securities are the stocks, bonds, and other financial instruments that are created and traded by these institutions. The term "Wall Street" is now used mainly as a metaphor for this securities industry since much of the buying and selling is electronically dispersed around the globe and no longer physically takes place in New York.

The officially stated purpose of Wall Street institutions is to assemble and concentrate large amounts of money from widely dispersed *sources* and redirect them toward various *uses*. More specifically, the ultimate purpose of Wall Street is, and always has been, to serve the profit-making interests of a relatively small class of investors. To this end, Wall Street has functioned spectacularly well.

Wall Street offers state-of-the-art technology, a highly skilled labor force, and sophisticated institutions to advance the never-ending agenda of profit-making and accumulation. With this as its mandate, Wall Street assists in the capitalization (initial financing) of corporations, the merging and expanding of existing corporations, as well as speculative buying and selling of securities. Wall Street is also perhaps the most dynamic component of the U.S. economy, as it is continually inventing and reinventing new types of securities for speculation.

It is beyond the scope of this book to explore all these securities in detail. We will, however, explore Wall Street as a key part of the U.S. economy and our focus will be on the basic and most prevalent securities—stocks and bonds—and on the institutions that create and trade them.

CORPORATE CAPITALIZATION AND INVESTMENT BANKS

An important function of the U.S. financial system is to pull together funds to be used in capitalizing corporations. Capitalization is the process of raising the money—finance capital—corporations need to start or expand their businesses. It was to this end that the securities industry was originally created. In the process of developing and marketing stocks and bonds, Wall Street institutions assist corporations in concentrating large amounts of money from scores of investors in order to finance large-scale enterprises.

When a corporation capitalizes for the first time it will typically require the services of an investment bank. Investment banks are finance companies that "underwrite" newly issued stocks or bonds which involves creating the securities and brokering them to investors. Unlike the commercial banks and depository institutions we explored in the last chapter, investment banks are not in the business of taking deposits and making loans. Their principal activity is to assist in raising finance capital by providing consulting and brokerage services to corporations that seek to issue stocks or bonds in order to raise capital. Unlike depository institutions whose earnings come from interest on loans, investment banks' earnings come from fees they charge for these services, and from capital gains made from brokering stocks and bonds.

Investment banks begin the underwriting process for corporations by advising corporate managers on how to present their financial statements to potential investors. The goal is to make the stocks as attractive to investors as possible. Investment bankers advise the corporations on strategies for resolving labor disputes or other possible legal problems that could jeopardize the salability of the shares. In other words, an investment bank helps a corporation dress up its securities for public sale.

The details of the underwriting process are filed with the Securities

Exchange Commission (SEC), a federal government agency that monitors Wall Street activity. Once the SEC gives its approval, a prospectus (an official report that outlines the profile of the business) is drafted and presented to potential investors. Investors, in turn, inform the bank whether or not they would be interested in buying shares. With this feedback from potential investors, the investment bank then suggests a price for the stock to be offered at the initial public offering (IPO). Investment bankers seek to attain prices for their clients that are high enough that the corporation can realize its capitalization requirements, but low enough to attract prospective buyers. Typically, the prices are set such that the IPO investors will realize a quick increase in the stock price when the stocks are publicly traded. Once the bank and the corporation agree on a stock price, the stock is open for sale; at this point, the investment bank will buy the shares and market them to investors in primary markets.

A primary market is one in which newly issued financial stocks or bonds are first sold to investors. Once these sales are made, the stocks and bonds can be subsequently bought and sold repeatedly in secondary markets. Most of what we hear about in the financial press about stock market activity is secondary market activity. Trades take place in huge dollar amounts as investors and brokers buy and sell existing shares. This activity, however, has little or nothing to do with capitalization as the trades are carried out for speculative purposes.

In addition to capitalizing newly created companies, investment banks also assist in the expansion of existing corporations. By underwriting additional shares of stocks or new bonds to be sold in markets, an investment bank helps businesses expand. Investment banks also assist in taking a formerly privately held corporation "public." Taking a corporation public extends stock ownership from a small, self-defined group of individuals to a much larger group—the general public. By doing so, a corporation can gain access to a much broader field of money sources.

So far, we have described the more traditional function of investment banks. In the last few decades, however, investment banks focus on the more lucrative business of underwriting large corporate mergers and managing investment portfolios for other businesses. Prior to the 1980s, investment banks had a relatively low profile in Wall Street compared to the large commercial banks and the stock exchanges. But all that changed with the onset of multi-billion-dollar corporate mergers that began with the buyout and acquisition mania of the 1980s and huge merger deals such as in the case of

Nabisco's merger with tobacco giant R.J. Reynolds. Behind the scenes of each high-profile merger have been investment banks facilitating a process in which one large corporation executes a leveraged buyout, hostile takeover, or straight merger with another. Often such merger deals are too large to be underwritten by one investment bank and are handled by a group or a "syndicate" of banks. Investment banks also advise and assist their corporate clients in managing portfolios. A portfolio is simply the collection of stocks and other securities owned by an investor. A corporation's portfolio that is managed by an investment bank is financed by corporate profits that are subsequently invested in other businesses.

Whether it is for an initial capitalization of a corporation, or a merger of existing corporations, or investing in a portfolio of stocks, the principal security investment banks underwrite to carry out these transactions is the corporate stock.

STOCKS

When someone invests in a corporate stock, that person is buying a security that certifies ownership of a share of the corporation and a right to a proportional share of the earnings of that business. A stock also certifies a percentage ownership of the company. For example, if a corporation has ten thousand shares "outstanding" (which means they have been purchased by an investor and can be traded in secondary markets), and if an investor buys one share, then the stock would certify that the person owns $1/10,000^{th}$, or .01 percent, of the business. If the person bought 5,000 shares the stocks would certify that the person owns 50 percent of the business.

Such proportionality of ownership is an important aspect of owning stocks. If one owns 50 percent of a company that is valued at $1 million, then that person's investment, or equity, represents $500,000. If the company grows over time and increases in value to $5 million, then the equity increases to $2.5 million even though the investor's percentage share of ownership did not increase. Such growth in investor equity is the single, most important force of a corporate enterprise. It is the principal reason why investors make such investments and is the reason why corporations drive to maximize profits.

Aside from equity growth, owners of stocks can also benefit by receiving dividend payments that are a kind of shareholder cash income. Each year the executive management and directors of a corporation must make decisions about what is to be done with the earnings of the corporation. Their two main choices are either to retain cash to be used for growth and expansion or pay out a portion of the earnings to shareholders as dividends. Such dividend payments are distributed to investors on a per-share basis. If a company decides to pay out a dividend, it will pay an equal amount per each outstanding share—say $.05 or $.07 on each share. The greater the number of shares one owns, the greater the amount of the dividend income one will receive. A payment of $.05 per share paid to an owner of 1 million shares would amount to $50,000 in dividend income.

Whether or not a company will pay a dividend depends on the management style of the business. Software giant Microsoft Corporation had a tradition for the first twenty years of its operations to retain its cash earnings, and was reluctant to pay dividends. After accumulating about $60 billion cash, Microsoft finally decided it was time to share this money with its shareholders. In the summer of 2004, Microsoft announced its intention to pay a massive $32 billion one-time dividend payout—the largest such payout in corporate history.[65]

The type of stocks an investor owns, common or preferred, can also determine whether or not they will receive a dividend. The vast majority of stocks issued and traded on Wall Street are common stocks. As specified in Chapter Two, common stocks have no priority status for receiving dividends. Common shareholders may or may not receive dividend payments depending on the decision of management and directors. Preferred stocks typically have a fixed dividend payment, which means that the corporation is contractually bound to pay preferred stockholders a share of the profits. Since most corporations would opt to avoid this obligation, common stocks are more prevalent.

As common and preferred stocks are traded in markets, their prices will fluctuate with changing market conditions. Stock prices are the most closely watched financial market indicators as they signify Wall Street trading activity and symbolize the financial standing of corporations in general. Stock prices are also watched as measurements of how well, or how poorly, the overall economy is functioning. If corporations are profitable and they plow back their earnings into real investment and grow, then stock prices will rise and shareholder equity increases. If they decide to pay dividends instead, the income makes the stocks attractive to investors; again, stock prices will rise and shareholders gain. Either way, shareholders benefit from profitable businesses, and gains for private business owners is the central purpose.

Stock prices tend to be volatile with short-term trading activity as investors react to an endless number of variables ranging from corporate profits to weather conditions. But the long-term rate of return (growth in value) to investors is relatively stable and constant. Stock returns tend to be significantly higher than other financial instruments or securities as shown in Table 1 below. Measured by growth in real stock values (adjusted for price inflation), the last two hundred years of capitalism has generated a consistent long-term growth rate of close to 7 percent.

Though stock prices are stable over the long run, short-run instabilities can be severe and lead to recessions, depressions, and economic ruin. Part of stock price volatility stems from the fact that they are liquid financial assets; that is, they are relatively easily converted into cash. Liquidity also means that a speculator can sell off, or liquidate, holdings of stocks at the slightest provocation. This can push stock prices through dramatic up and down swings. The damage that this volatility can do to the rest of the economy will be explored in more detail in Chapter 11.

Closely related to stock volatility is risk. A characteristic feature of stock markets and of Wall Street markets in general is the inverse relationship between potential returns and the potential risk. As a general rule the greater the potential for gain, the greater the risk of total loss. Stocks that have greater-than-average potential for gains tend to be more volatile and have a greater-than-average risk factor, and less risky stocks offer less volatility and generally less growth in value for investors. For example, stocks issued by the large and very well known corporations like those represented in the Dow Jones Industrial Average index tend to be less volatile and less risky, but offer relatively low rates of returns to investors. On the other hand, stocks issued by smaller, riskier businesses like the so-called "dot.com" start-up companies in the later 1990s, offer very high rates of return, but with much risk. Financial experts typically recommend that investors maintain a diverse "portfolio" containing riskier stocks with growth potential balanced with more stable investments yielding lower returns.

TABLE 1
Inflation-Adjusted Percentage Rates of Return

	1802-1871	1871-1925	1926-1996	1802-1996
Stocks	7.0%	6.6%	6.9%	6.9%
Bonds	4.8%	3.7%	1.9%	3.4%
Gold	0.2%	-0.8%	0.6%	0.6%

Source: *The Complete Finance Companion: Mastering Finance,* London: Pitman Publishing, 1998, p. 7.

STOCK CLASSIFICATIONS AND INDEXES

The financial press typically groups stocks according to different classes based on the type of industry, the size of the corporations, or other shared characteristics. Stock price indexes are used to measure general stock price movements within those classes. The idea behind classification and indexing is that if there are certain market conditions that could affect the price of one stock, these conditions could also affect other stocks in the same class. By classifying and indexing, analysts develop a basis for analyzing broader stock market trends.

STOCK CLASSIFICATIONS

One example of a popular classification of stocks is the "blue chip" category. This is a class of stocks issued by large, prestigious corporations that are firmly established in an industry and often enjoy a dominant share of their industry's market. As these companies are so firmly established, they are considered to be the least risky and their stock prices experience very little volatility. Low volatility means there are not significant price fluctuations, and as prices tend not to change much there is little to be gained or lost in speculative trades of blue chip stocks.

Another classification of stocks is the "utilities" category. This is a grouping of the stocks of corporations that are involved in providing electricity, water, sewage, and other services that are most often regulated by local government agencies. Like blue chips, utilities are usually well established, have low risk and offer low return for speculators. Both blue chips and utilities generally pay dividends as they generate cash earnings, but are seldom in a rapid growth mode. Other stocks can be classified as "growth stocks," however, and they typically pay little or no dividends. Instead of paying out cash income to shareholders, their earnings are used to finance real investment, inventory, product development, and other forces leading to the companies' growth. These tend to be smaller companies that offer investors the potential for higher rates of growth and returns, but with more risk of loss.

The financial press also classifies stocks according to size measured by their capitalization—the market value of all outstanding shares. Capitalization is measured by the total number of shares multiplied by the market price. For example, if a firm's stock is priced at $25 per share and has 1 million outstanding shares, its capitalization is $25 million. If the share price falls to $20 per share, then capitalization falls to $20 million. As a general guideline, stocks grouped as micro cap, small cap, mid cap, and large cap use approximately the following values:

TABLE 2

Category	Market Capitalization
Micro Cap	0–$300 million
Small Cap	$300 millio–$1 billion
Mid Cap	$1 billion–$5 billion
Large Cap	$5 billion and over

The purpose of such categorization is to allow observers to identify trends that may affect a group of companies that are of a particular size. As stock classifications are not necessarily mutually exclusive, companies listed as large caps—capitalized at $5 billion and over—can also be blue chip companies, such as General Motors or Exxon/Mobil, as they are not only large but firmly established in their industries. Collectively, large caps dominate the stock market industry and account for over half of the total market capitalization of all American corporations. Mid caps are stocks—capitalized between $1 and $5 billion—that have growth potential, typically pay more dividends than small caps, and are less likely to experience extreme volatility. Micro and small caps—between 0 and $300 million and $300 million and $1 billion, respectively—tend to be relatively young businesses, are riskier and volatile, pay little or no dividends, but possibly offer much growth and high returns. Most initial public offerings made by investment banks tend to be small caps.

Small cap IPOs are often called "pops" because the stock prices can soar within minutes after being put on the market. Small cap pops received much media attention during the bubbly years of the late 1990s as investment banks offered special deals to their preferred clients—large volume dealers who were allowed to buy large amounts of stocks at below-market value at the time of the IPO. These investors could turn around at the end of the same day and sell their stocks at 50 percent to 70 percent over their purchase price. These pops came at the expense of small investors who typically buy later and at much higher prices, and at the expense of the companies that received financing at levels below their true market value.

STOCK MARKET INDEXES

Investors and speculators are as likely to follow trends affecting an entire class of stocks as they are to follow the stock prices of a particular company. To serve this end, stock market indexes were created. A stock market index serves as a kind of price barometer. It is typically a benchmark number or average of the combined market prices for a specified number of stocks representing a particular class, or of stocks traded in particular markets or exchanges.

Some indexes are based on the size of the firm measured in terms of annual revenues. For example, the Fortune 500 index is a stock market index comprised of *Fortune* magazine's list of the five hundred largest U.S. based corporations ranked by annual revenues. Other indexes are based on the size of the market capitalization of the stocks. The popular S&P 500 (Standard and Poors) is an index of a broad selection of large cap stocks and the Russell 2000 is an index that tracks small caps. The S&P 100 is an index of one hundred blue chip stocks and the S&P 400 Midcap Index, obviously, tracks midcap stocks. The Wilshire 5,000 is a very broad index that tracks the stocks of about seven thousand U.S. companies, stretching across all classifications. Some indexes represent the stocks that are listed on specific exchanges. The NYSE Composite is a broad index of about two thousand common stocks listed in the New York Stock Exchange and the AMEX Composite, similarly, is an index of over five hundred American Stock Exchange listings.

Some indexes are narrowly limited to particular industries. The Dow Jones Transportation Index (Dow Transport) is an index that tracks a narrow group of twenty of the largest airlines, railroads, and trucking companies that dominate the transportations industry. The Dow Jones Utilities Index (Dow Utilities) tracks fifteen utilities companies located throughout the United States. The Philadelphia Semiconductor is an index created by the Philadelphia stock exchange in 1993 that tracks seventeen U.S. semiconductor corporations that dominate that industry.

Another popular index is the NASDAQ Composite Index, or simply NASDAQ (see below). NASDAQ is a relatively new index that is a broad composite of stocks of small cap firms, young high-tech companies, and depository institutions listed in a specific electronic, over-the-counter exchange system. From its inception in the early 1970s, NASDAQ was a relatively obscure index and drew little attention from the financial press. With the onset of the Internet and the raging dot.com stock market of 1990s, NASDAQ burst through its obscurity to become one of the most closely watched indexes in the securities industry.

The world's most popular index, as well as one of the narrowest, is the Dow Jones Industrial Average (DJIA). Founded in 1896, the Dow Jones Industrial Average is the oldest stock price index that continues to be used and tracks the stocks of the top thirty most dominant blue chip corporations in major industries. The specific companies listed in the DJIA can change from time to time, but is always limited to thirty stocks that are widely held by both individuals and institutions. As of this writing, the DJIA includes the following companies:

> Alcoa Inc., American Intl Group Inc., American Express Company, Boeing Co., Citigroup, Inc., Caterpillar Inc., E.I. du Pont de Nemours and Company, Walt Disney Company, General Electric Company, General Motors Corporation, The Home Depot, Inc., Honeywell Intl Inc., Hewlett Packard Co., IBM, Intel Corporation, Johnson & Johnson, J.P. Morgan & Co. Incorporated, The Coca-Cola Company, McDonald's Corporation, 3M Corporation, Altria Group inc., Merck & Co., Inc., Microsoft Corporation, Pfizer Inc., The Procter & Gamble Company, SBC Communications Inc., United Technologies Corporation, Verizon Communications, Wal-Mart Stores, Inc., and Exxon Mobil Corp.

The *Wall Street Journal* and other publications report daily information about the performance of the stocks as they are represented in these indexes. For many observers, the stock market information contained in these daily reports is a distillation of information about the economy overall. That is, if the DJIA stock index is up, this could be interpreted as a signal that the real economy of production and distribution is prospering, and if the index is down it could signal that the real economy is doing poorly. As stock indexes are the barometers of economic performance, economic performance itself is thus seen in financial terms—meaning how well the economy creates equity growth for investors. Stock indexes are therefore closely watched and are reported daily as a principal measure of how well the economy is generating money wealth for the investor class.

STOCK VALUATION

The daily movements of a stock market index represent price changes of an entire class of stocks that can be caused by an infinite number of variables. Deriving the value and price of an individual stock, however, is a different matter. An individual company's stock price can rise or fall as investors and stock market analysts make their decisions about the value of the stock. One approach to determining the value of a stock is by analyzing the company's fundamentals.

The fundamentals approach assesses the basic financial standing of the company. Using this approach, analysts assess the value of the company's assets, its sales and earnings (net profits) generated from those assets, the amount of debt owed to creditors, and so forth. By closely tracking the fundamentals of a company over time, analysts can develop a sense of its trend toward more or less earnings in the future, and this could be a decisive factor in whether or not to buy or sell a stock. If analysts develop a reasonably good understanding of the company's potential earnings from examining costs and revenues, the next step would be to project a flow of future earnings per share, and compare it to the current market price of the stock. High projected earnings could suggest that the stock might rise in price and thus offer an investor a profitable return. Predictions of future stock prices are, of course, a key aspect of stock market trading activity and speculation.

One possible fundamentals strategy for predicting the future value of a stock price is to use a price/earnings ratio (P/E ratio). The P/E ratio is the market price of a stock divided by the company's earnings per share. Say, for example, a stock is selling at $20 per share and the company is generating a net income of $2 per share; the P/E ratio would be 10. This means that investors are paying a price that is 10 times the earnings per share. Depending on the class of stock—large cap, utility, blue chip, etc.—investors will identify a P/E ratio that is typical for that class. Say the typical P/E ratio is expected to be about 15 for a particular category of stocks, and if a stock in that category is reported to have a P/E ratio of 10, this could signify that the stock is underpriced and investors could expect the stock price to rise. Based on this expectation, investors would probably buy the stock and, by doing so, would drive the stock price upward until it meets the benchmark P/E ratio. There is a tendency for stocks to gravitate toward their expected P/E ratio. Also, if investors expect the stock's P/E ratio hold fast at 15 and they also expect earnings to rise, they can reasonably expect that the stock price will rise in the future.

Perhaps a more direct method of determining the market value of a stock based on the fundamentals approach is to use the company's "book value." The book value is simply the net worth of the corporation or shareholder equity. Book value is calculated by subtracting the outstanding liabilities or debt of the company from the value of its assets. A company that takes on much debt will lose net worth or shareholder equity and the book value of the stock could start to decline. Long-term debt can also affect future net profits as corporations have to make their debt service payments.

In sum, the healthier the fundamentals, the higher the value investors will place on the stock, and the stock price—other factors unchanging—will rise.

In addition to the fundamentals approach, individual stock prices can also be valued using the "technical" approach. The technical approach to stock pricing focuses on patterns of stock prices and trade volume changes over time. Rather than focusing on the earnings, assets, and debts of a company, stock market analysts look at past patterns to identify a range with upper and lower limits within which a particular stock's price will fluctuate. Analysts watch for short-term movements of prices as they fluctuate around a long term trend or average (see Figure 1). If a stock price approaches or exceeds the upper limit, it can be expected to fall back toward the long-term trend. Investors will be inclined to sell. On the other hand, if a stock falls to, or below, the lower limit, the stock price can be expected to rise and investors will be inclined to buy.

Stock market analysts, investors, and fund managers typically use some combination of both fundamental analysis derived from financial reports and technical analysis derived from broader market trend data. Regardless of the information about fundamentals contained in the corporations' annual reports or long-term trend lines, stock prices also can significantly increase or decrease by sheer momentum and volume of daily trading activity in the markets driven by the mass psychology of investors. Speculative buying and selling for short-term gain can move the prices of stocks across a spectrum of categories either upward or downward at any moment, on any day, or over a trend that can last months or even years, and these movements have little or nothing to do with fundamental or technical valuation. The list of forces that can cause speculative momentum in stock trades is innumerable: politics, clear weather, rainy weather, the day of the week, the month, bond prices, commodity prices, labor market reports, interest rates, demographics, international financial market turbulence, and thousands of other factors. This is, of course, what makes speculation in the stock market unpredictable. Playing the stock market is risky business in which great fortunes can be made or lost, sometimes in an instant.

STOCK MARKETS AND STOCK TRADES

As was emphasized in Chapter Two, the history of capitalism is indistinguishable from the history of the corporation. Naturally, this history will also contain the history of stock markets. As the capitalist system evolves, so do the financial institutions that facilitate the capitalization of private enterprise and draw together sources and uses of funds. As part of this evolution, organized stock exchanges and over-the-counter (OTC) stock markets were developed. Stock exchanges and markets have made it easier for buyers and sellers to come together and carry out stock trades in an orderly and predictable manner. These institutions have also created an organized system for establishing and quoting stock prices. By making stocks available for purchase to a wide range of potential investors, stock markets gave corporations a wide reservoir of cash from which to draw for capitalization and this proved to be a tremendous boost for capitalist growth. Although the effort to capitalize business enterprises was the original and immediate purpose of creating stock markets, we will see that there is also a much deeper purpose—the ultimate purpose of any financial institution within a capitalist system is the concentration and accumulation of wealth for the investor class.

Stock exchanges are private, for-profit businesses. They are in the business of providing an organized marketplace in which stock trades are carried out. Like dating services that bring together potential mates, organized exchanges bring together potential buyers and sellers of securities. Their revenues come from subscription fees paid by corporations that want to have their stocks listed on the exchange and thus made available for purchase to the investor public.

The earliest stock exchanges sprang up in Europe in the seventeenth and eighteenth centuries where capitalism and the modern corporation first took root. As we saw in Chapter Two, the first major corporations, or joint stock companies, were large-scale seagoing enterprises that required substantial capitalization. The capitalization requirements necessary to finance companies like the British East India Company and the Dutch East India Company required access to organized markets to make their stocks as accessible to as broad of an investor population as possible. The stock exchanges in Amsterdam and London successfully drew together investors and companies for a common cause of profit-making. These exchanges became the models for a new phase of business finance, and as capitalism and the corporation developed, stock market exchanges sprouted and grew.

Most of the well-known exchanges in the United States and Britain are more than two hundred years old: the Philadelphia Stock Exchange was established in 1790, the London Stock Exchange opened its doors in England in 1802, and the New York Stock Exchange (NYSE) emerged in 1782 when a group of brokers interested in establishing an organized investment community gathered under a tree located somewhere on Wall Street. Today, the New York Stock Exchange remains the premier stock exchange in which the stocks of America's flagship corporations are traded.

In exchanges like the NYSE, stock trades are carried out by brokers who are employees of brokerage firms. The firms pay fees to become members of the exchanges and to be the facilitators of the trades on which they earn commissions. The bulk of trades that take place in organized exchanges are large in scale. When an investor makes a decision to buy or sell a sizeable amount of a particular stock, he or she contacts a brokerage firm that is a member of the exchange. After the investor submits the order, it is immediately transmitted to the firm's broker on the floor of the exchange—the "floor trader"—who then proceeds to the appropriate trading post to complete the trade in batches with other individuals' orders. Trading posts are the specific locations on the trading floor of the exchanges at which the stocks of specific companies listed on the exchange are traded. Actively traded stocks typically have several floor traders swarming around a particular post, seeking to buy or sell shares with each other.

Part of the institutional purpose of an organized exchange is to maintain an orderly market. That is, to provide assurance, or at least as much assurance as can be made, that for every buyer there will be a seller. If a trader shows up at the trading post to buy a significant number of shares in a particular stock and there are no other brokers seeking to sell, then the transaction is turned over to a specialist working at the trading post whose job is to step in as buyer or seller to facilitate uninterrupted trading. If, for example, the order is to buy more shares than the specialist has available to sell, the specialist will begin raising the bidding price to attract sellers and will continue, like an auctioneer, to raise prices until enough sellers have come forward to supply the buyers with enough shares to complete the transaction. If a seller approaches the post and does not find other brokers interested in buying, then the specialist can either buy the stock directly or bid the stock price downward until enough buyers are attracted to cover the transaction. In this way, the buying and selling activities of floor traders and specialists at these trading posts determine the prices of stocks.

This large order process involves a fair amount of human effort on the trading floor and has the most significant impact on stock prices in general. For smaller orders, typically 1,000 shares or less, stock trades are carried out in a more direct manner that bypasses the floor traders and goes directly to the specialist via an electronic system known as SuperDot—Designated

Order Turnaround System. In this way, the investor's broker will send a buy or sell order directly to the specialist who quotes the market price at that moment given the floor trading activity. If there is little or no trading volume for a particular stock, then the market price quoted to brokers through Super-Dot remains unchanged. As with any market, if there are heavy sell commands this will drive down the stock price, and lower prices will be quoted in SuperDot, and heavy buy commands will drive prices higher.

Aside from organized exchanges, buyers and sellers can trade stocks in Over-The-Counter (OTC) markets. OTC markets largely execute trades of stocks of small cap firms, young high-tech companies and the stocks of depository institutions. OTC trades take place exclusively within telecommunications infrastructure—on the phone, over the Internet, or through some other electronic medium. Although there is no centralized physical location for trading as with the NYSE, OTC markets have centralized electronic bulletins in which stock prices, buy and sell commands, and the names and phone numbers of brokers seeking to execute specific stock trades are listed. The two most well known bulletins are the National Quotation Bureau (NQB) for small caps, and the National Association of Securities Dealers Automated Quotation System (NASDAQ).

The NQB maintains daily "pink sheets" on which about eleven thousand OTC stocks and trade orders are listed. The sheets are posted daily as general guidelines for trades in particular stocks, but specific bids and prices are established directly between buyers and sellers. The development of high-powered desktop computers and Internet technology has dramatically transformed OTC trades by increasing speed, accessibility, scope, scale, and efficiency, and some observers are calling into question whether organized exchanges with their labor-intensive floor trading will become obsolete in the not-so-distant future.

The National Association of Securities Dealers (NASD) is a Washington DC-based private business that establishes and enforces rules for OTC stock trades. NASD has over five thousand brokerage firms on its registry, and each has a vested interest in seeing that the OTC markets are orderly. Stock markets are particularly subject to wild instabilities, mischief, and unfair trading practices. NASD was created to establish and enforce rules in order to create fairness and stability. Its role in creating order in OTC markets has been substantial enough that Federal law requires that all U.S. brokerage firms operating in U.S. markets must be NASD members, and this membership contractually binds the brokerage firms to abide by the rules or pay heavy fines.

NASD also owns the National Association of Securities Dealers Automated Quotation System (NASDAQ). Founded in 1971, NASDAQ has become the most important OTC market institution. Like the NQB, NASDAQ is a computerized trading system used specifically for NASD brokerage firms that trade OTC stocks. In the 1980s and 1990s, many smaller start-up companies that could not afford the high fees to be listed in the more prestigious organized exchanges turned to NASDAQ for capitalization. A frenzied market boom ramped up in the late 1990s and, with the development of desktop computing and Internet technologies, NASDAQ rose to become enormously popular in the media.

NASD also maintains several indexes as barometers of general share price movements of stocks in particular industries including telecommunications, manufacturing, computer banking, and biotechnology. The most popularly referenced NASD index is the NASDAQ Composite Index (simply referred to as "The NASDAQ"), which is a broad index of all stocks traded on the NASDAQ system. Once an obscure sideline in the securities markets, the NASDAQ composite index is now quoted with the same regularity and significance as the DJIA.

INSTITUTIONAL INVESTORS

Much of the stock and bond market trading activity on Wall Street is driven by the concentrated financial power of "institutional investors." Institutional investors are either for-profit or nonprofit organizations that make investments in securities on behalf of a group of individual investors. Institutional investors pool together savings from a large group of individuals and use those savings for specific investments. The most common institutional investors are mutual funds, pension and retirement funds, commercial and investment banks, hedge funds, insurance companies, and private endowments.

Mutual funds are either privately or publicly held corporations. Mutual funds sell shares to investors and the money received from the sales is pooled with others and subsequently used to make large-scale investments in stocks and other securities. Each share in a mutual fund represents an equal share of the ownership of all the mutual fund investments, and the gains from the fund investments are divided equally per share. Since the investors in a mutual fund are also its shareholders, the fund's primary responsibility is to maintain holdings of investments that will maximize returns and shareholders' equity.

From the perspective of an investor, one advantage of mutual funds is that they can be highly diversified. Diversification is typically advisable because it spreads out or dilutes risk and makes for a more stable investment portfolio. This means that the money raised by the fund can be invested in a wide range of stocks of different industries, mortgages, commodities like gold or oil, and bonds. Without a mutual fund, individuals interested in making diversified investments in gold, oil futures, various stocks, and other securities would have to have a very large amount of money in order to make investments in all these markets. Going through a mutual fund, however, a relatively small investment say as little as $1,000, can be highly diversified. Not all mutual funds are so diversified, however. Some choose to invest in specialized stocks in which mutual fund managers have expertise such as a fund that exclusively trades shares in small cap stocks, stocks in a particular industry, large cap stocks, or only in stocks that pay dividends, and so on.

Hedge funds are a special kind of privately held mutual fund reserved exclusively for the wealthiest individual or institutional investors. Typically, hedge funds are small in terms of the number of people who are investors, but they control disproportionately large amounts of investment funds. A hedge fund of one hundred investors can have as much as $100 billion of capital aggregated into a single fund. There is little regulatory oversight of hedge funds because the assumption is that they are capitalized by wealthy investors who are expected to know the risks they take with their fortunes. Hedge funds often borrow heavily to invest in the stock market and often borrow as much as twenty times their cash investment. This means that a single fund of one hundred individuals making a total of $100 billion in paid-in cash investments can leverage as much as $2 trillion in investments with borrowed money.

Other institutional investors include retirement funds, insurance companies, and the trust department of commercial banks. Like mutual funds and hedge funds, these institutional investors pool together funds from working people, insurance premiums, and depositors. Retirement funds constitute a significant amount of institutional investment capital and come from both public sector and private sector plans. The most common private-sector retirement funds are 401(k) plans. A 401(k) retirement fund is a retirement savings account established by businesses as a benefit for their employees and is managed by financial investment companies. The name "401(k)" comes from a section of the Internal Revenue Code that created them in 1978 as tax-sheltered plans. Employees are allowed to contribute a certain amount of their pre-tax income, along with a matching amount by their employers, into an account that is subsequently invested in a diversified portfolio of stocks and other instruments. Often the same investment companies that manage mutual funds also manage 401(k) accounts.

Insurance companies invest premiums paid by policyholders into securities. Although some life insurance policies share gains and risks with policyholders these investments are made primarily for their own accounts. Commercial banks can also act as institutional investors. Although they have traditionally been prohibited from taking depositors' money and investing in stocks, they do hold vast amounts of interest-bearing bonds. Most state governments manage large public employee retirement funds. These are nonprofit, professionally managed funds that control trillions of dollars worth of financial assets.

Institutional investors wield much power in the market. They are estimated to account for as much as 70 percent of all securities trading activity in the U.S. Acting on behalf of millions of individuals and controlling trillions of dollars of invested money, institutional investors are major players in financial market activity, and make decisions that can cause significant momentum in market activity. Often referred to as professional sponsorship, institutional investors have built a profession around buying and selling stocks, research and data analysis, and maximizing returns for themselves as well as for their clients.

All institutional investments, including mutual funds, are managed by professional money managers for fees. Theoretically, the gains from having expert money managers make investments on behalf of individual investors should outweigh the costs of paying management fees. In most cases, this is probably true. But the individual investor is also vulnerable because he or she is at the mercy of fund managers, and has to trust that the managers are going to make sound investments. Following the long list of fraud-induced corporate scandals and bankruptcies in the years 2001 and 2002, the SEC and NASD discovered widespread mischief among fund managers. Manager deception and fraud eventually led to the destruction of retirement nest eggs for millions of working people who had placed their trust in institutional investors.

A popular misconception about institutional investors is that by pooling money from a relatively wide cross section of the population, capitalist ownership is also extended to this population as well. It is true that millions more Americans are now invested in stocks and bonds than ever before and much of that is due to access made through institutional investors. But those same millions are not capitalists as their income is primarily derived from working, not owning. They may realize some returns on their investments, but this is not their primary source of income. The vast majority of people who are vested in mutual or retirement funds depends on wages and salaries for their livelihoods, not returns on their investments. Moreover, as we will see in a later chapter, ownership in stocks and bonds is distributed highly unevenly, and is concentrated in the hands of a small but very affluent investor class. Such top-heavy imbalance of ownership is one of the hallmark characteristics of capitalism.

BONDS

In essence, a bond is a certificate that promises to pay a certain sum of money at some time in the future, and to pay a fixed rate of interest at regular intervals. The amount of the sum to be paid in the future is referred to in the financial press as the "face value" or "par value" of the bond, and the future date at which the sum is to be paid is the "maturation date." Bonds can be either registered bonds which have the owner's name printed on the bond certificate and interest payments can only be paid to that person, or they can be bearer bonds for which interest payments are made on the presumption that whoever possesses the bond is the owner.

Like stocks, bonds are an important part of the financial system that links sources and uses of funds. As individual or institutional investors buy bonds as financial investments, they are the sources of funds. Any government agency or corporation that issues bonds for sale as a means to raise money is the user of funds. Measured in the dollar value of trade volume, the bond market activity is several times larger than stock markets. Bonds are considered more conservative investments because they generally have a fixed rate of return which makes them less volatile than stocks. This dependability and protection from losses is primarily what attracts investors to bonds.

Like stocks, bonds are also an important means of capitalizing a corporation. When a corporation issues a bond, it is essentially borrowing money by issuing a kind of certified IOU to bondholders with a promise to pay the credited amount plus interest. When an investor buys a corporate stock, the investor becomes part owner of a corporation, and when an investor buys a corporate bond the investor becomes a creditor or lender to that corporation. Stockholders can share in the growth and rising profitability of a corporation that can theoretically rise without limits, but bondholders generally get a fixed rate of return. An advantage to bondholders as creditors is that they are first in line to get paid in the event of a liquidation of a corporation or in bank-ruptcy proceedings. Stockholders, particularly common stockholders, are the last in line and are the most likely to lose their entire investment.

When a bond is first issued in primary markets, the process is underwrit-ten in a manner similar to that of a new stock. The bond issue is handled by an investment bank and is brokered mainly to banks and other institutional investors. Once issued in primary markets, bonds can be subsequently bought and sold in secondary markets like any other Wall Street security.

The two most important features of bonds as they are traded in second-ary markets are their prices and their percentage yields. Prices for bonds are quoted in "points" where each point is equal to $10 and is broken down to increments of 1/32 fractions. For example, a particular bond price could be quoted at 100 25/32 points which means its market value is 100 25/32 x 10 = $1,007.81. If that same bond increased in price to, say 106 11/32 points, its market value would be 106 11/32 x 10 = $1,063.43.

Bond yields are the returns to the investors in bonds expressed as a per-centage of the rate of return. Yields differ from interest rates in the sense that interest rates are the percentage interest paid on the principal of the bond, but yields are calculated by dividing the interest paid on the bond by the bond's market price as it is set in secondary markets. Interest rates on bonds are fixed at what is called the "coupon rate" but yields are continuously changing with changing bond prices.

Bond prices and percentage yields are mathematically locked together in an inverse relationship. As bond prices rise, the percentage yield will fall; and as bond prices fall, percentage yields will rise. Percentage bond yields and interest rates are also closely linked. Both are percentage rates paid to credi-tors, and both are inversely related to bond prices.

Although not as volatile as the stock market, bond prices rise and fall as speculators in bond markets respond to information on Fed policy, price inflation, or economic and political news. As we saw in the previous chapter, Federal Reserve monetary policy has an immediate and deliberate impact on short-term bond prices and interest rates. But bond prices can also rise or fall as bond market speculators respond to information about price inflation. Price inflation—a sustained increase in the general price level—not only causes goods and services to be more expensive, it also erodes the real value of bond investments with fixed interest rates. When price inflation occurs, the real interest rate (interest rate minus inflation) will decline, and the purchas-ing power of bonds as a financial asset will also decline. For this reason, bond speculators have an allergy to price inflation, and often respond to news of possible inflation by starting bond market sell-offs, driving down bond prices in the process. As bond prices are driven down, rates will rise. This is why bond markets are sensitive to any news reports suggesting that the economy is headed toward an inflationary trend.

Bond prices will also rise and fall in response to "good news" or "bad news" in the real economy. Bonds are considered to be more stable financial investments than stocks. If the news is good news, such as an indication that the economy is growing or becoming more stable, investors tend to be emboldened and will try riskier investments. Many will sell their bonds and buy stock causing a rally (increase in prices) in the stock market but pushing down bond prices. If the news is bad, such as a recession or instability, investors flock to bonds as a safe haven for their investments. Bond prices will then rally.

Although bonds are less volatile than stocks, they are not risk-free investments. Bondholders, like banks, must also consider the risk of the bonds they purchase from issuers. This is so important, in fact, that private credit rating companies (sometimes referred to as bond rating agencies) assess the creditworthiness of bond issuers, and publish their assessments as formal bond ratings. Perhaps the most well-known bond rating agencies are Moody's and Standard and Poors. A typical bond rating chart is summarized in the table below. Bonds that are rated BBB (Standard and Poors) and above are "investment grade," which means that they have relatively low risk of default and would be considered by banks as a relatively secure investment of their depositors' money. "Speculative grade" bonds, also known as "junk bonds" tend to be much riskier investments because of a much higher chance of default; the riskier the investment, the higher the rate of return to compensate investors for taking on extra risk.

Another aspect of bond market analysis is the yield curve. Yield curves are the difference in percentage yields between short-term and long-term bonds, and are seen as possible indicators of future economic activity. Generally speaking, the short-term bonds such as one-, three-, or six-month bonds have lower yields than long-term bonds such as ten-, twenty-, or thirty-year bonds. Under normal circumstances, the difference between short and long-term bond yields is about 3 percent. The reason for the difference stems from the risk that investors must expose themselves to when investing in bonds. The longer the term to maturity, the greater the chance something could happen to cause the issuer to default on bonds and thus raising the risk exposure for the investors. To compensate investors for long-term exposure to this risk, a 3-percent "risk premium" is added. If the difference rises above 3 percent, the yield curve is said to be "steep," showing a wider than normal gap between short-term and long-term bond yields. If it narrows below 3 percent, the yield curve is "flat" and long and short-term yields come closer together.

TABLE 3
Standard & Poors Long-Term Debt and Moody's Ratings Equivalents

	MOODY'S	STANDARD & POORS
Investment Grade:		
Exceptional	Aaa, Aaa1, Aaa2, Aaa3	AAA, AAA-, AA+
Excellent	Aa, Aa1, Aa2, Aa3	AA, AA-, A+
Good	A, A1, A2, A3	A, A-, BBB+
Adequate	Baa, Baa1, Baa2, Baa3	BBB, BBB-, BB+
Speculative Grade:		
Questionable	Ba, Ba1, Ba2, Ba3	BB, BB-, B+
Poor	B, B1, B2, B3	B, B-, CCC+
Very Poor	Caa, Caa1, Caa2, Caa3	CCC, CCC-, CC+
Extremely Poor	Ca, Ca1, Ca2, Ca3	CC, CC-, C+
Lowest	C	C

A steep yield curve suggests that investors in long-term bonds anticipate growth and inflation in the future and will bid long-term yields upward. When yield curves are very steep it is most likely to be an indication of an acute fear of inflation in long-term bond markets, and buyers are demanding higher yields as a hedge against inflation. A flat curve indicates that investors are anticipating an economic slowdown and little inflation, lessening the pressure to bid long-term yields upward. An inverted curve happens when yields on short-term bonds exceed long-term bonds and this suggests that they antici-pate a major slowdown—recession or depression.

GOVERNMENT AND CORPORATE BONDS

The market for U.S. Treasury Department securities is the largest bond mar-ket in the world. Currently the United States federal government carries over $6 trillion in national debt that is financed primarily by selling Treasury Department bonds. On any given day, about $5 billion worth of bonds are bought and sold. The most common types of Treasury bonds are Treasury

Bills (T-bills), Treasury Notes, Treasury Bonds, and Treasury Inflation Protected Securities (TIPS). These are all considered very high investment-grade bonds with virtually no risk of default.

T-bills are short term bonds issued by the U.S. Treasury Department maturing in thirteen, twenty-six, or fifty-two weeks; Treasury Notes are longer term U.S. government bonds that mature in two, three, five, or ten years; and Treasury Bonds are thirty-year bonds, although the Treasury Department no longer issues thirty-year bonds. Treasury Inflation Protected Securities (TIPS) are relatively new securities that were introduced in the late 1990s. TIPS are bonds that provide a fixed interest rate, but the rate has a built-in hedge against inflation that automatically adjusts the interest rate to keep up with the general inflation rate.

While U.S. Treasury securities are federal government bonds, municipal bonds are those issued by states, counties, cities, public utilities, school districts, and other local government agencies. These are mainly of interest to local investors. The most significant difference between municipal bonds and other bonds is that the interest payments are exempt from federal income taxes. Another unique feature of municipals is that they are subject to serial maturity, which means that the bond matures in incremental stages over the life of the bond, rather than all at once like most other bonds. Municipals are underwritten by investment banks and sold to investors—mainly banks and other institutional investors—and the revenues used to make the interest and principal payments come from state and local tax levies. In general, state agencies rely on state sales and income taxes to pay off their bond debt, and local agencies rely on property taxes and local business taxes. Often the decision as to whether or not to levy such a tax comes from voters who decide on fundraising measures for their schools, libraries, and other local services and infrastructure.

Another important but smaller segment of the U.S. bond market is the market for corporate bonds. Selling bonds to investors is part of how corporations are capitalized. The buyers of corporate bonds are creditors like banks and often are banks. And like bank loans, corporate bonds can be secured with collateral to minimize investors' risk. The fact that corporate bonds may be secured with collateral gives their owners first claim on the assets of the company such as the inventory, equipment, building, land, liquid assets, accounts receivable, or anything else of value owned by the business in case of bankruptcy proceedings.

Not all corporate bonds are secured. Many corporate bonds are "debentures" or unsecured corporate bonds. Faith in these bonds is established not with the value of the businesses real assets, but by the creditworthiness of the corporation. This is a centrally important criterion for investors as they attempt to manage their risk exposure. This risk exposure is the main reason why bond market investors rely on information provided by formal bond rating agencies. Moreover, not all corporate bonds pay a fixed rate of return. Some bonds known as "income bonds" pay a return only if the corporation makes a net profit. These are only desirable to investors if the potential rate of return is significantly high enough to offset the possibility of no return at all.

Bonds, like any other financial instrument, are traded in securities markets. Although some corporate bonds are traded on organized exchanges like the NYSE, most are bought and sold in OTC markets alongside stocks. One way of viewing securities markets is to separate them into two broad categories: long-term capital markets and short-term money markets. Long-term capital markets are markets for stocks and long-term bonds, and short-term money markets—or simply "money markets"—are markets for short-term bonds (maturation terms of one year or less). Short-term bond markets are referred to as "money markets" because the instruments are designed to raise money quickly on a short-term basis, are liquid, and easily converted to cash money.

The most common money market bonds are the U.S. Treasury bills (T-bills) mentioned above, as well as short-term certificates of deposit (CDs), and short-term debentures known as "commercial paper" issued by commercial banks. A CD is a security that certifies that an investor holds a certain sum of money on deposit in a commercial bank account for a specified duration, and will earn a specified interest rate on that account. In a sense, a CD is like a short-term loan to a bank from investors but is sustained over a certain period of time. Commercial paper is an unsecured corporate bond issued typically by large corporations that want to raise cash on a short-term basis, usually maturing in thirty to ninety days. Because of the somewhat higher risk, commercial paper typically pays a higher rate of interest than T-Bills. They are used by large corporations to augment or stabilize their cash flow as it fluctuates from month to month.

CONCLUSION: WALL STREET AND CAPITALISM

Wall Street has always been an important part of the U.S. capitalist system. By creating stocks and bonds and by creating the markets that trade them, Wall Street institutions have succeeded in carrying out the financial system's original purposes—bringing together sources and uses of funds, and making money for large-scale capital investments.

The universe of financial instruments and institutions created by Wall Street also allows investors to own a vast array of business assets. Without Wall Street, it would be much more difficult for the investor class to become the owners of the bulk of income-earning assets, and to accumulate increasingly large amounts of financial wealth. Wall Street also made it much easier for business to buy the stocks of other businesses and to become the large corporate giants that dominate the economy. In its service to capitalism, Wall Street has facilitated the concentration of enormous wealth in the hands of a small investor class.

Capitalism in America is in a mature state of development, and aggregating cash for real investment and growth has become a small and peripheral function of Wall Street institutions. With the exception of smaller start-up companies, businesses seldom issue stocks or sell bonds in order to raise capital for growth or expansion. Economic growth is largely internally financed with corporate earnings or "plowed back" profits. Writer and critic Doug Henwood makes this point in his thoroughgoing study of Wall Street:

> Over the long haul, almost all corporate capital expenditures are internally financed, through profits and depreciation allowances . . . Between 1981 and early 1996, U.S. nonfinancial corporations retired over $700 billion more in stock than they issued . . . In other words, even the new-issues market has a lot more to do with the arrangement and rearrangement of ownership patterns than it does with raising fresh capital . . .[66]

A more important function of Wall Street today is financial market speculation. Like gamblers playing the roulette wheel at a casino, individual and institutional investors place bets on stocks or other instruments with the expectation that they will increase in value in the future. More than anything else, the U.S. financial system has become a mechanism through which speculators attempt to enrich themselves through buying and selling stocks and bonds. Wall Street nourishes the buy-low-sell-high-get-rich fascination inherent in a capitalist system.

One of the myths of American capitalism is that if Wall Street assets are rising in value, the benefits will accrue to everyone. The reality is that most Wall Street assets are owned by a very small percentage of the population;

overall ownership of the majority of Wall Street assets is skewed toward the top wealthiest 10 percent.[67] As we have emphasized earlier, most Americans are not capitalists, and do not have the luxury of deriving their income exclusively by buying, owning, and selling stocks. The income people use to pay their bills and make mortgage payments is earned by working for a wage or salary, not from owning stocks. But more importantly, the interests of working people and the interests of Wall Street investors are in conflict. Higher pay and better working conditions for working people take a bite out of corporate profits. Lower profits will reduce dividends paid to shareholders or equity growth, and this will push down stock prices.

Not only do gains from speculation largely benefit the wealthy, but Wall Street also serves to redistribute wealth toward the affluent. In the typical boom and bust pattern of financial market speculation, a boom often comes when a larger than normal percentage of the population puts money into speculative investments. The booms represented by soaring stock or bond prices turn into "bubbles" as more money gets pumped into the markets from a broad base of the population. Such bubbles inevitably pop and prices fall or "crash." In each boom-and-bust cycle, there are winners and losers. Most of the losers are the minor investors who lost their savings and were exhorted by financial experts and political leaders into keeping their money in a market that was doomed to crash.

In the years and months leading up to the stock market crash of October 1929, people across the country were convinced to invest their savings in stocks. Irving Fisher, a leading economist at the time, wrote in the *New York Times* on September 5th that, "There may be a recession in stock prices, but not anything in the nature of a crash." And on October 17, 1929, less than two weeks before the great crash, Fisher wrote "Stock prices have reached what looks like a permanently high plateau." Acting on this information, people flocked to the stock market to place what money they had in the stock market. Billions flowed from all across America and concentrated in financial centers, particularly Wall Street. The stock market ballooned into a gigantic bubble that would most assuredly pop. When the crash finally came, the winners were the wealthy Wall Street insiders who were manipulating the markets through organized pools and could force prices up or down with sheer market power. The winners became wealthier and the losers were virtually everyone else who was caught flat-footed.

From 1929 to 1932, about $74 billion of paper wealth was obliterated by the stock market crash. This figure, however, is eclipsed by the crash that occurred between 2000 and 2002 when over ninety million people lost $7 trillion in stock wealth. The pattern of stock market activity over the last decade has demonstrated a classic boom and bust pattern that has been almost identical to that which occurred in the 1920s and 1930s. From January of 1997 to January of 2000 the Dow Jones Industrial Average (DJIA) stock market index rocketed up from 6448 to 11,723. The NASDAQ had gone from 1,291 in January, 1997 to a peak of 5,048 in March, 2000. By October of 2002, the DJIA had fallen to 7286 and the NASDAQ collapsed all the way down to 1,114. Former Goldman Sachs investment banker Nomi Prins observed that contained within this spectacular crash was an obliteration of $295 billion, the result of pump-and-dump fraud committed by corporate executives in just four companies: Enron, World Com, Global Crossing, and Adelphia.[68]

Senior executive personnel at Enron pocketed over $1 billion in wealth as it used fraudulent financial statements to pump up share prices before they dumped Enron stock and defrauded California ratepayers of over $45 billion in hyper-inflated electricity prices. Senior executives at Global Crossing pocketed $5.2 billion and its chairman walked away with nearly $1 billion as they sold their stocks immediately before wiping out $47 billion in investor wealth that resulted from accounting fraud and bankruptcy. World Com's executives cashed out a more modest $1.5 billion before orchestrating the largest bankruptcy in U.S. history. The founders of Adelphia, attempted to extract over $1 billion in company assets before being charged with financial fraud that ultimately cost an estimated $60 billion in shareholder wealth.

The story does not end with these four companies. *Fortune* magazine reported that executives from hundreds of corporations cashed $66 billion of wealth out of their companies, of which $23 billion went to insiders at some of the two dozen biggest firms in the country. According to Prins:

> Qwest led the Top 25 club with $2.3 billion transferred from the pensions of its workers to the pockets of its leaders. . . . When the senior circles cashed out at the peak just before the crash, they reduced the value of the shares and thus the value of the workers' pensions. The faster the chief executive officers (CEOs) cashed out, the faster pensions fell in value.[69]

These bankruptcies of the early 2000s, resulting from insider sell-offs created the largest volume of bankruptcy loss in U.S. history. During this historical event, corporate executives sailed away with over $3.3 billion as they drove their companies into the ground leaving a wake of financial ruin behind.[70] Most of those who are responsible for these financial disasters ascended to become enormously wealthy. Such accumulation of financial wealth is, of course, the ultimate purpose of capitalism.

The U.S. financial system has served to redistribute wealth to the rich in another way—it pushes debt. Government bonds and consumer debt ultimately pull debt service payments from a broad sector of the population to a small percentage of wealthy bondholders. Doug Henwood explains this process:

> Government debt, for example, can be thought of as a means for upward redistribution of income, from ordinary taxpayers to rich bond-holders. Instead of taxing rich people, governments borrow from them, and pay them interest for the privilege. Consumer credit also enriches the rich; people suffering stagnant wages who use the VISA card to make ends meet only fatten the wallets of their creditors with each monthly payment. . . . the richest ½ percent of the U.S. population claims a larger share of national wealth than the bottom 90 percent, and the richest 10 percent account for over three quarters of the total.[71]

Far removed from the stated purpose of merging sources and uses of funds for real investment, the financial system facilitates the most predatory aspects of the capitalist economy. Wall Street has become a casino in which high-stakes games are played, and the winners in these games walk away with tremendous fortunes simply by having access to privileged information and by acting on this information to strategically buy and sell securities. The winners are generally major speculators and corporate insiders who thrive on instability, as they would not be able to make their tremendous capital gains without dramatic booms and busts of securities prices—often taking profits in both directions. These profits, however, are not earned by making a productive contribution to the real economic output of goods and services, yet the people who make them gain the purchasing power to buy those real goods. As such, Wall Street functions not to create wealth, but to extract it and redistribute it—mostly to enrich the already wealthy. We will return to the topic of financial market instability in Chapter 11.

We do see a place for finance in a mindful economy. In our view, a mindful financial system is one that is governed in sound principles about how money is raised, and for what purposes it is to be used. These principles are rooted in the needs of people and communities, and not in the predatory or speculative greed that today guides much of Wall Street activity. To create a mindful financial system would entail building new institutions that operate according to a new and different set of rules. We will turn our attention to these alternatives in detail in Part Three.

It is never certain what exactly will happen on Wall Street at any given time. One thing that does appear certain, however, is that the current, gigantic levels of government debt and debt-financed trade deficits are not sustainable. The reconciliation of this sustainable debt must come sooner or later, and when it does it most likely will come, once again at the cost of much instability and potential ruin for a broad base of the population. It could be that this is the reason for the highly unusual inverted yield curves mentioned above. To more fully understand the problem of financing ever-larger amounts of national and international debt we will next briefly explore U.S trade and its financial connection to the rest of the world.

7
AMERICA'S UMBILICAL CORD
The International Economy

America does not exist in isolation. Our understanding of the U.S. economy would not be complete without information about its economic connections to the rest of the world. Virtually every country on the planet is connected in some way to every other country through global network of imports, exports, cash flows, and investments. This global system of interconnectedness is, in part, a natural historical development. As populations grew over time, the scope of economic activity expanded into wider geographical territory. Growth in international trade among expanding populations followed as cultures came into contact with one another and realized that there is much to be gained from trade. It is natural to expect that as economies expand, so should international trade and investment.

Since the mid-twentieth century, however, the rate of growth in international trade exceeded world economic growth. This suggests that economies around the world are becoming more integrated and interdependent despite growth. Economic activity is becoming increasingly internationalized. In a significant way, this economic internationalization has been fostered by the creation of institutions such as the international gold standard in the nineteenth century, and the International Monetary Fund and the World Trade Organization in the twentieth century. These institutions were primarily designed to expand the capitalist system globally—giving businesses an ever-widening market in which to sell and profit and giving investors an ever-growing field in which to buy and sell securities. The country that is most responsible for leading the global expansion of capitalism in the twentieth century, particularly after World War II, is the United States. Yet, like a child in its mother's womb, the U.S. has become utterly dependent on the surrounding global economy for markets, resources, and also for borrowed funds.

THE INTERNATIONALIZATION OF ECONOMIC ACTIVITY

Throughout much of the nineteenth and early twentieth centuries, the inter-

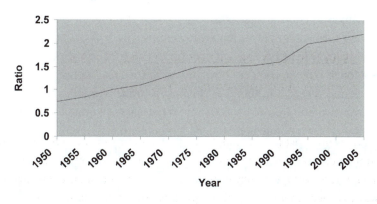

World Trade/Output Growth, 1950 - 2005

Figure 1

Source: Terborgh, *WTO International Trade Stats.*, 2005

national gold standard was the primary institution within which international trade was carried out. Originally created by the Bank of England, the gold standard became an international structure in which national currencies were pegged at a fixed ratio to an ounce of gold. The gold standard stabilized exchange rates of currencies among nations and facilitated the development of a multilateral system of trade and investments. After the financial collapse of 1929 and the onset of the Great Depression, the gold standard began to disintegrate. With the decline of trade that followed, many countries around the world adopted isolationist policies and embraced political nationalism— one of the key factors that led to World War II.

For a few years immediately following World War II, international trade remained a relatively small part of the global economy as many countries were preoccupied with rebuilding their war-torn domestic economies, and the world was in the early stages of rebuilding international financial institutions. Beginning in the late 1940s, a phenomenal surge in the rate of growth in international trade occurred, and between 1948 and 1960 world trade more than doubled.[72]

From around 1950 onward, world trade began to grow at a rate that exceeded growth of world output. Figure 1 above shows a steady rise in the ratio of the rate of growth in world trade to the rate of growth of world output. One reason for this growth in trade was technological. Communication and transportation technology advanced to narrow the distances between countries, and decreased freight and transaction costs made it easier and less costly for countries to import and export. As trade was made less costly, more and more nations were able to realize the potential mutual benefits derived from exchanges of goods across borders.

Technology aside, mutual exchange in voluntary trade is the primary reason nations engage in importing and exporting. The last fifty years of growth in international trade, in part, has been driven by the fact that people around the globe found that it is in their best interest to trade with other countries. For well over two hundred years, economists have asserted that by engaging in international trade, populations can enjoy a higher material standard of living than if they tried to produce all that they consume in their own economies. One of the first economists of note to make this argument was Adam Smith, author of the famed classic, *An Inquiry into the Nature and Causes of the Wealth of Nations* (1776), or more commonly known simply as *The Wealth of Nations*.

Smith's book was primarily an attack on mercantilist ideology that was popular among European monarchs from the sixteenth through the eighteenth centuries. The paramount goal of mercantilism was for a particular nation to maximize the inflow of gold and silver coins or bullion. To achieve this, each nation would seek to maximize exports, receive gold and silver as payment for those exports, and at the same time, minimize imports to stanch gold and silver outflows. By maximizing exports and minimizing imports, a country was believed to experience a systematic increase in gold and silver reserves. More gold and silver reserves translated directly into political power as monarchs could use those reserves to finance shipbuilding and arms buildups, and to bankroll professional armies.

Mercantilism was not a sustainable system, however, as it was built on an unavoidable contradiction. If all countries attempted to minimize imports, there would be no country to which one could export. Without importers, exporters would have no buyers. Mercantilism also led to the European conquests and colonization of parts of Asia, Africa, and the Americas. Europe's most powerful nations needed to find importers. Britain, France, and others forced the people they colonized to become involuntary importers of the goods and services produced in the factories of industrial capitalism. The military expense of keeping people in a state of involuntary colonial servitude, however, amounted to a drain on these kingdoms' reserves.

Based on these contradictions, Adam Smith challenged the efficacy of mercantilism. He also contended that specialization based on a free system of international division of labor would allow trading partners to focus the use of their resources on the production of goods in which each is most capable and efficient. By doing so, each nation would achieve high levels of productivity. Each can then trade with others that are also specializing in what they do best. A multilateral system based on the international division of labor and specialization allows each nation to benefit from the efficiencies of every other nation, and by doing so, all will be able to import certain goods that cost less than what it would cost to produce domestically. The result is that after specialization and trade, each nation ends up with quantities of goods that exceed their domestic capacity to produce. The quantity of goods available for consumption was, for Adam Smith, the true measure of the wealth of nations, not gold and silver bullion.

The gains to be made from trade based on specialization remains as the foundation for the current global trading system. Today Americans import certain goods or services from other countries either because they cannot produce them domestically or because they can be produced more cheaply or efficiently in other countries. People in other countries find it advantageous to buy goods made in the United States for the same reasons. The expectation for all trading partners is that there is some level of mutual gain from international trade, and this remains the primary reason virtually every economy on the planet has an international sector.

Another reason for the rise in international trade since World War II has been due to the internationalization of economic institutions, or, what many have called "economic globalization."

GLOBAL ECONOMIC INSTITUTIONS

Corporations are not only the dominant economic institutions in the U.S., but many have expanded beyond their national boundaries to become transnational enterprises. As capitalist enterprises, they are always accountable primarily to their investors and must continuously seek profit-maximization opportunities wherever they can be found. By expanding business operations beyond their nation's borders, corporations can gain access to a much larger marketplace in which to sell their goods. They also gain access to resource and labor markets where costs are substantially lower. An expanding global economy also provides businesses with opportunities for investments that potentially yield higher rates of return for investors. With the allure of high returns, a wide access to markets, and cheap labor, corporate enterprises are compelled to take on a global profile, transcending the interests of people and communities in their national economies and answerable only to a global investor class.

As early as 1967, George Ball, then working in the U.S. State Department, spoke on behalf of transnational corporations, "[T]he political boundaries of nation-state are too narrow and constricted to define the scope and activities of modern business."[73] More recently, executives have clearly stated their transnational ambition, for example Charles Exley of National Cash Register boasted that, "National Cash Register is not a U.S. corporation. It is a world corporation that happens to be headquartered in the United States."[74] And C. Michael Armstrong, a high-ranking executive at IBM asserted that, "IBM, to some degree, has successfully lost its American identity."[75] As these businesses expand and adopt a global identity, they have also pushed for the creation of new global economic institutions that provide a worldwide structure within which they can seek to achieve their profit-making goals.

In observance of the profit-imperative of the capitalist system, governments and large corporations have been working together to build a global economic system that functions independently of the governments or cultures in which their trading activities and investments take place. The capitalist dream of a global system, free from what George Ball lamented as the constricting boundaries of countries, has become closer to a reality with the creation of global institutions such as the International Monetary Fund (IMF), The International Bank for Reconstruction and Development (more popularly known as "The World Bank"), and later the World Trade Organization (WTO). Although each has its own specific objectives, they all share the same ultimate goal of providing access to markets and opportunities for investments for capitalist businesses.

THE INTERNATIONAL MONETARY FUND AND THE WORLD BANK

As World War II was coming to an end, it became clear to most capitalist countries that it was necessary to build a global institution designed to provide a stable international system of finance and currency exchange. As we saw in Chapter Five, the collapse of the international gold standard during the 1930s created global financial instability, and eventually widespread economic instability. This was an important precondition for war. It became clear to business and government leaders that a global system of stable exchange rates was not only necessary for the continuation of profit accumulation, but also for political stability. To this end, several hundred officials from forty-four nations convened at a conference in Bretton Woods, New Hampshire in the summer of 1944. At the Bretton Woods meetings, a resolution was passed to create the

International Monetary Fund (IMF) and the International Bank for Reconstruction and Development, also known as the World Bank.

Originally, the official function of the IMF was to create an international system within which the participating countries could maintain stable currency exchange rates with each other. Capitalized with contributions made by the treasuries of participating countries, the fund was designed to be a lender of last resort for countries that experience collapsing currency values. For example, if a country's currency, say the British pound, is falling relative to the U.S. dollar, the central bank of Britain can borrow dollars from the IMF and use them to buy their domestic currency. By doing so, they could shore up the value of the pound and prevent it from falling further.

Creators of the IMF also attempted to achieve currency stability by creating a gold exchange standard. The gold exchange standard was a system that pegged the currency of each participating country to the U.S. dollar, which, in turn, was pegged to an ounce of gold. The dollar was convertible at a rate of $35 to one ounce of gold, and other currencies were fixed to the U.S. dollar but with some limited flexibility. By creating such a system, international trade could commence without concerns of the dramatic swings of currency exchange rates that destabilized trade in the 1920s and 30s. The IMF created a kind of global financial pasture into which transnational corporations could expand and graze—fattening the returns for investors.

The World Bank was initially created to provide loans to countries that were rebuilding from the wreckage of World War II. Unlike the IMF, the World Bank is not capitalized by government funds, but with the funds of an international consortium of commercial banks. Post-war reconstruction commenced at amazing speed and much of it was financed by an infusion of funds through the famous Marshall Plan,[76] however, so the Bank provided very little resources for reconstructing war-torn Europe. Losing its sense of purpose, the Bank had to refocus its lending practices or dissolve. In the 1950s and 1960s, the Bank took on a much broader global purpose of providing and orchestrating loans for developing countries, or so-called Third World countries, as they attempted to build infrastructure and industrialize. Such development projects remain largely the World Bank's purpose today.

Whether through the IMF or the World Bank, funding and stability was provided on a global scale that allowed for countries around the world to participate in the global marketplace like never before. During the Cold War, the U.S and other capitalist countries used the Bretton Woods institutions as a financial Great Wall, keeping the Soviet socialist influence on the outside and capitalist expansion on the inside. The U.S. had the most to gain from Bretton Woods because it was the only major economic power that emerged from World War II relatively undamaged, and its mighty corporations were poised to take over markets around the world. The Bretton Woods institutions provided the money countries around the world needed to buy U.S. exports and to make profits for American companies. The IMF and World Bank came less to resemble international institutions and more as extensions of U.S. economic power.

By the 1980s, Germany, Japan, and other countries became established contenders in world markets and the U.S. found that its position of economic supremacy was being challenged. Seeking markets wherever they could be found, American companies pressured the IMF and World Bank to become more aggressive in imposing the will of corporate interests on developing countries around the world. Both Bretton Woods institutions began imposing restrictions on the recipients of their financial services in the developing countries of Asia, Africa, and Latin America. Imposed mainly by the IMF, these restrictions came to be known as *structural adjustments*. Structural adjustments, among other things, imposed policy restrictions on borrowing countries and forced them to privatize government-owned enterprises, open their countries to foreign investments, and remove barriers to imports and exports—particularly exports from the U.S. If borrowing countries refused to comply, the IMF could cut off access to badly needed loans.

Structural adjustments paved the way for transnational corporations to move in and set up business operations, dominate markets, buy property, and make capital investments throughout the developing world. The profits from these activities were not kept in the developing countries where they could be used for subsequent development, but rather profits were expropriated as returns to investors in the U.S. and other countries. Such expropriation led to an increasingly polarized pattern of wealth and income distribution between the world's wealthy and poor populations. The IMF and World Bank in effect became agents for the corporate colonization of the developing world just as the British East India Company did centuries ago.

THE GENERAL AGREEMENT ON TARIFFS AND TRADE (GATT) AND THE WORLD TRADE ORGANIZATION (WTO)

Another global institution that allowed for the global expansion of capitalist profit making was the General Agreement on Tariffs and Trade (GATT), drafted in 1947. The purpose of GATT was to provide an international forum within which countries could pursue bilateral and multilateral trade agreements, and for setting uniform rules to be followed in these agreements. The official philosophy underlying the formation of GATT was to create an international system of trade, and the resulting prosperity would bring nations closer together. By reducing trade barriers such as bans, tariffs and quotas on imports, the mutual gains from trade, it was believed, would create such widespread prosperity that it would lessen the likelihood of conflict or even warfare among nations.

From the time of its inception, GATT succeeded in signing on over 130 nations. Those who signed the agreement were typically government officials acting on behalf of business interests in each country that sought to join a much larger international capitalist community. In 1995, GATT was replaced by its successor, the World Trade Organization (WTO)—a much larger and more comprehensive international economic institution.

The WTO was designed to go further than any other institution in allowing businesses to pursue their goals without interference of the government or cultures of specific countries. Like GATT, the WTO retains its role of setting trade rules designed to expand trade globally as much as possible. The rules revolve around a few core principles: (1) each participating country must open its market to the businesses of other countries; (2) the businesses of other countries must be treated in a nondiscriminatory manner—they must be given the same "most favored" treatment, and be allowed to bid on contracts, sell in markets, and promote their products on the same footing as domestic businesses; and (3) exports should not be unfairly pushed onto other markets with government subsidies. By establishing such trade rules, the WTO has become a quasi-governing institution with legislative power. And unlike any other international economic institution, the WTO was granted judicial powers as well. Trade disputes between countries are settled though a kind of tribunal within the WTO known as the "Dispute Settlement Body." These governmental powers of the WTO are not democratically sanctioned, and have done more than any other international institution to realize George Ball's vision of transcending the restrictions of national governments in favor of the globalization of private enterprise.

The development of these global institutions allowed businesses unchallenged access to labor, resources, markets, and investment opportunities. Such a system provides an open field for corporations to move goods, investment, and technology to wherever the rate of return proves highest, without being hindered by local or national interests. The global system provides an apparatus for surveillance over individual countries' policies regarding trade and investment, provides legislative powers to set rules that transcend these policies, and grants judicial powers to enforce the interest of capitalism over virtually all else.

Yet in a very significant way, the global multilateral system has backfired against the U.S economy. Since the mid-1970s, the U.S. companies have been steadily losing market share, as their global competitors have been able to combine state-of-the-art technology with a low-wage workforce. Moreover, as U.S. businesses shed their national identity, they have moved their production operations offshore to become exporters to U.S. markets alongside foreign competitors. The result has been steadily rising trade deficits that are larger than any country has experienced in world history. Along with these deficits come mounting debt and an increasing dependency on foreign creditors. These global institutions were once created as a means by which U.S. companies could conquer markets around the world. Now they serve as a kind of financial umbilical cord to feed the debt-ridden American economy.

AMERICAN TRADE DEFICITS AND DEBT

Although the argument that there are mutual gains from voluntary trade is based on sound reasoning, it does not tell a complete story. In their arguments for free and open international trade, Smith and the many others who followed him failed to add that although there can be mutual gains, there is no guarantee that those gains will be distributed equally or fairly among trading partners. In most cases, certain countries take the majority of the benefits, while others gain very little in return. Many of the developing countries are connected to the international economy, but remain mired in poverty. At the same time, the businesses from North America and Western Europe that engage these countries in trade have extracted enormous fortunes through buying cheap and selling high in premier markets around the world. Transnational corporations pursue their profit maximization goals by setting up production in places where people are poor and receive low wages, or where they can extract resources at low prices. The low wages and prices serve to keep the poor in a perpetual state of poverty. The products are then sold in high-priced markets at huge mark-ups, creating tremendous profits. This opportunity for making such profits, of course, is the primary force behind the capitalist-driven system of international trade.

Of the high-priced markets in which exporters make their big profits, the

U.S. is by far the largest and most lucrative. Businesses around the world see the U.S. as the most sought-after final destination for their export goods, including American companies that have chosen to move their production operations offshore and export back to U.S. markets. For decades, the U.S. has distinguished itself as the leading importer of everything from fruits, vegetables, clothing, cars, computer chips, to millions of barrels of oil. Yet, as an exporter, the U.S. has found it difficult to compete or to gain access to markets in other countries. The result is increasingly wide disparity between imports and exports—trade deficits.

The volume of imports, exports, and capital flow that link the U.S. to the global economy is summarized in the "Balance of Payments" maintained by the U.S. Commerce Department, and is shown in Table 1. The Commerce

TABLE 1
Balance of Payments of the United States (2006, millions)

Current Account

Exports of Goods	1,023,536	
Imports of Goods	1,861,380	
Balance of Goods	-837,844	
Exports of services	422,594	
Imports of services	342,845	
Balance on Services	79,749	
Net Income Receipts and Transfers	-52,596	
Balance on the Current Account		**-811,051**

Capital Account

Flows of U.S. Assets Abroad	-1,055,176	
Flows of Foreign Assets Into U.S.	1,859,597	
Statistical Discrepancy	-6,630	
Balance on the Capital Account		**811,051**

Source: U. Bureau of Economic Analysis, "U.S. International Transactions,
Third Quarter 2007," Douglas Weinberg

Department's Bureau of Economic Analysis maintains two categories for tracking the economic connections the U.S. economy has with the rest of the world: the current account and the capital account. The current account summarizes the flows of money representing imports, exports, income, and other transfers of dollars as they move across the nation's boundaries. Exports of goods and services bring money into the U.S. economy and are shown in the Balance of Payments as positive numbers. Imports send money out of the economy and are shown as negative numbers. In 2006, the U.S. imported about $758 billion in goods and services more than it exported. Income receipts flow into the U.S. when American residents are receiving wages, salaries, or some other form of income from a source outside the country, and if an American business is paying an income to someone abroad, then income is flowing out of the country. Unilateral transfers are amounts of money flowing in and out of the U.S. economy in the form of private donations, grants, or residents sending money to individuals such as relatives in other countries. Taken together, the net income and transfers amounted to an outflow of about $53 billion. The Balance on the Current Account sums together deficits in goods and services and the outflow of income and transfers. The final total is a staggering Current Account deficit of $811 billion.

Such current account deficits have been the rule, and not the exception, for the U.S. economy for the last thirty years. Figure 2 shows that the U.S. has had negative current account balances every year since 1975. In addition, with

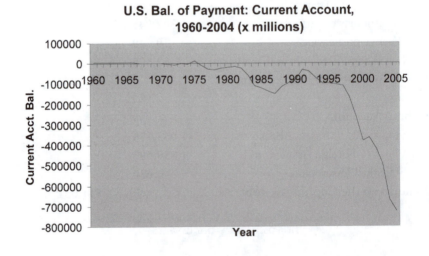

Figure 2

Source: U.S. Census Bureau, Foreign Trade Division

the exception of a few years in the early 1980s, and once in 1995, the trade deficit figure has been getting progressively larger. The most dramatic change in the current account has occurred in the ten years after the ratification of the North American Free Trade Agreement and the creation of the World Trade Organization. Trade deficits have plunged to depths never before seen in history. In 2004, the deficit of $618 billion and in 2006 soared to $811 billion—a number eight times larger than it was in 1995 when the WTO was created, and over two hundred times larger than it was in 1960.

In a manner similar to a household that spends more than it earns, trade deficits must be financed with debt. The U.S. has essentially two choices when it incurs trade deficits: it can pay the deficit amount by depleting its foreign exchange reserves held by the central bank, the Federal Reserve System, or borrow from abroad. To deplete the foreign exchange reserves would signal a financial crisis in the same way a household would go broke by depleting its savings. The other option would be to debt-finance the deficit by selling government bonds. This is the preferred option, although it can hold a financial crisis at a distance; it has long-term cumulative effects. Each year the U.S. experiences trade deficits, it goes deeper into debt, and it becomes more financially dependent on foreign countries.

The borrowed funds are shown in the Balance of Payments in the Capital Account. Referring back to Table 1, the Capital Account measures all of the money used to buy financial assets abroad (Flows of U.S. Assets Abroad) as a negative number because it is flowing out of the country, and all the money flowing into the U.S. that used to buy American financial assets (Flows of Foreign Assets into U.S.) as a positive number. If the investment inflow does offset the investment outflow by an amount sufficient to cover the trade deficit, then the U.S. will begin depleting its foreign exchange reserves. To prevent this, and a possible crisis, the U.S. must sell government bonds to foreign banks in order to make up the difference. This amount should be equal to the Balance on the Capital Account, but these transactions are based on estimates, not an exact science, and so the Commerce Department makes a "Statistical Discrepancy" adjustment to bring the current account and capital account into balance.

In short, if the current account shows a deficit of $811 billion, the capital account must offset this by selling $811 worth of debt to the rest of the world. This means that the U.S. goes deeper into debt relative to the rest of the world with each annual trade deficit. This is debt that the U.S. must sell to its trading partners in ever-larger amounts. The principal way the U.S. sells its debt to buyers around the world is to sell government bonds and other interest-earning assets—particularly business assets. This is being partially offset by the progressively weakening dollar relative to other currencies. This makes U.S. exports cheaper in global markets, but the downside is more expensive imports and price inflation.

In one sector after another, foreign investors are taking majority ownership of what were American industries. The following is a partial list showing the percentage of basic U.S. industries that is now owned by foreign companies:[77]

- Sound recording industries – 97%
- Commodity contracts dealing and brokerage – 79%
- Motion picture and sound recording industries – 75%
- Metal ore mining – 65%
- Motion picture and video industries – 64%
- Wineries and distilleries – 64%
- Database, directory, and other publishers – 63%
- Book publishers – 63%
- Cement, concrete, lime, and gypsum product – 62%
- Engine, turbine, and power transmission equipment – 57%
- Rubber product – 53%
- Nonmetallic mineral product manufacturing – 53%
- Plastics and rubber products manufacturing – 52%
- Plastics product – 51%
- Other insurance-related activities – 51%
- Boiler, tank, and shipping container – 50%
- Glass and glass product – 48%
- Coal mining – 48%
- Sugar and confectionery product – 48%
- Nonmetallic mineral mining and quarrying – 47%
- Advertising and related services – 41%
- Pharmaceutical and medicine – 40%
- Clay, refractory, and other nonmetallic mineral products – 40%
- Securities brokerage – 38%
- Other general purpose machinery – 37%
- Audio/video equipment mfg and reproducing magnetic and optical media – 36%
- Support activities for mining – 36%
- Chemical manufacturing – 30%
- Industrial machinery – 30%

Whether it is borrowing or selling off more of its assets to foreign investors, a return must be paid and these returns show up as income outflows on the current account. Current account outflows cause deeper deficits and an even deeper downward spiral, triggering another round of borrowing and sell-offs. Just as with an individual who finances a lifestyle with ever-larger amounts of credit card debt, eventually a time of financial reckoning will come. When this happens, sacrifices will have to be made. If history is a guide, the sacrifices will be made by a broad base of the population in the form of soaring interest rates, heavy debt service payments, high price inflation, and possibly higher taxes or cuts in government services as our nation's government is also buried deep in debt.

Currently, the U.S. is borrowing so heavily from abroad that many foreign banks are signaling that they no longer want to continue financing the U.S. as their bond portfolios are excessively weighted with U.S. Treasury Department bonds. This dependence on the foreign inflow of finance capital also makes the U.S. more dependent on the policies of foreign governments. A recent article in the *Financial Times* reported that, "China indicated on Thursday it could begin to diversify its rapidly growing foreign exchange reserves away from the U.S. dollar and government bonds—a potential shift with significant implications for global financial and commodity markets."[78] China is the United States' leading trading partner, and with which the U.S. mounted a $232 billion-dollar deficit in 2006. The implications of China's policy shift away from U.S. assets could be profound, for the money inflow from China is being used to widen the pool of loanable funds that is, in turn, used to finance government deficits and hundreds of billions of dollars in household debt.

CONCLUSION

Since World War II, the U.S. was the leading proponent of the expansion of a global, capitalist trading network. The aim, as always, was to expand capitalism into new markets, and extract a steady flow of profits. But in an ironic turn of events, this process has reversed as the global system now sees the U.S. as the place to extract profits.

Being the largest consumer of imported goods from around the world, the U.S. is the world's premier market, and resides at the very center of a global capitalist system that is becoming increasingly integrated. Like an infant in its mother's womb, the U.S. is surrounded by, and dependent on, the rest of the world—the umbilical cord that connects the U.S. to the world is debt. And like the relationship between an unborn child and its mother, it cannot go on forever. To assume that the U.S. can sustain its current high levels of consumption is a dangerous folly. At some time in the future, America has to curb its deficits and debt, and when that happens, the global capitalist economy will be facing perhaps the greatest crisis in memory.

The net debt the U.S. has with the rest of the world stands between $2 and $3 trillion and is rising. This means that the United States owes the rest of the world trillions more than the total sum the rest of the world owes the United States. Yet it is hard to convince Americans at the moment that there is anything wrong with these debt levels. This has to do with the uniquely privileged nature of American debt. Even though the U.S. has a huge net debtor position in the world, there is still a net inflow of interest payments coming into the U.S. financial system. This means that the amount of interest flowing into the U.S. is greater than the amount of interest flowing out. Such a situation is only possible because the interest the U.S. pays on its debt is a much lower rate of interest than the returns it gets on the financing it extends to the rest of the world. Much of the foreign-owned U.S. debt is in low-interest government bonds while much of the U.S.-owned investments abroad are riskier and pay higher rates of returns.

Although this situation is, for now, advantageous, it is risky and unsustainable. High risk, high yield investment positions tend to break down eventually and rates of return tend to equalize over time. When this has happened in the past, such as the collapse of the Mexican bond market and peso crisis in the mid-1990s, the IMF and U.S. Treasury Department were on standby with reserves to bail out investors and stem a broader financial and economic crisis. This was only possible because the amount of money involved was relatively small. There is no lender of last resort on the planet, or even a consortium of investors, that has the resources to come to the rescue in a $3 trillion financial crisis. Financially, the U.S. has created a structure that almost guarantees that there will be significant instabilities in the future. Even the IMF is now issuing warnings that "global current account imbalances are likely to remain at elevated levels for longer than would otherwise have been the case, heightening the risk of a sudden disorderly adjustment."[79] The IMF report was focused primarily on the U.S. sustaining ever higher deficits as a result of high oil prices. IMF director, Rodrigo Rato warned that even though the U.S. shows good economic performance in 2006 it, ". . . rests on a shaky foundation because of large and continuing global imbalances." We will turn once again to these problems in later chapters.

8

THE U.S. CAPITALIST MACHINE

There is a long-established practice in the field of economics of referring to an economy as a machine. Many economists see economic systems as analogous to vast, continuously running contraptions like motor vehicles, aircraft, or locomotives. Fascinated with this idea, economist and famous prognosticator, Irving Fisher, while a doctoral candidate at Yale University in the early 1890s, constructed various machines as models of the U.S. economy. Fisher attempted to use these machines fixed with hydraulic pumps, valves, levers, and gears to demonstrate a theory about how prices are determined in the free-market system. The machine remains a standard paradigm for illustrating economic theory, and economic jargon is infused with mechanistic metaphors. Federal Reserve policy is often referred to in economic reports as "pushing and pulling monetary policy levers." If the economy is growing rapidly, it is often said that the economic "engine is overheating," or, if the economy begins a gradual slowdown, it is often referred to as a "soft-landing," like an aircraft gently landing at an airstrip rather than "crashing." John M. Keynes popularized the machine metaphor by referring to an economy as something like a steam locomotive, the "drive wheel" of which was capital investment.

The economy-as-machine metaphor was used by Fisher and other economists to illustrate a *laissez faire* idea of self-regulating markets—a kind of market automation. In the same way that people are fascinated with how machines can perform work automatically without much more human effort than pushing a button or pulling a lever, mainstream economists describe the capitalist market system as something that can run automatically without intervention except for a little fine-tuning by skilled technicians. The skilled technicians, of course, are the economists themselves. Economists act as the advisors to government and central bank authorities who stipulate precision adjustments in tax or banking policies in order to gain optimal performance out of an otherwise highly automated free-market machine.

As we have shown in previous chapters, however, the market system is far from automated and self-regulating. Markets are more likely to be controlled deliberately by businesses, labor unions, or government institutions. Yet this economy-as-machine metaphor can still be useful to highlight certain characteristics of a capitalist system. The metaphor works, but not as a self-regulating automaton, rather as a system. Like a machine, a capitalist economy is an assemblage of integrated components, and it can accelerate, decelerate, malfunction, and break down. Like a machine, it uses energy and resources to keep itself going. Like a machine, the capitalist system doggedly pursues a narrowly defined purpose of profit-making and wealth accumulation. Like a machine, the system is not endowed with an innate ability to morally reflect on the consequences of this purpose. Any constraints on the machine stemming from moral, ethical, or environmental considerations not related to capitalist profit-making must be imposed by outside forces and are not engendered from within.

KEY ECONOMIC INDICATORS

Keeping with this machine metaphor, imagine a console of gauges or dials like those found on the dashboard of a car or the cockpit of an aircraft. These gauges are used to monitor the performance of the machine such as speed, oil pressure or engine temperature. For the economic machine, the console of gauges would consist of those that track the movements of key variables such as stock market indexes, gross domestic product, the consumer price index, the national unemployment rate, and other indicators of economic performance.

The most frequently referenced economic indicators are the stock market indexes such as the Dow Jones Industrial Average and NASDAQ discussed in Chapter Six. Measured by these indexes, the up and down movements of stock prices are reported throughout every working day. Stock Market indexes can give an indication of whether or not the economic machine is achieving its ultimate purpose of generating profits and returns for investors. Investor returns, however, largely hinge on corporate profits generated by the production, sale, and distribution of goods and services. A more thoroughgoing indicator of the performance of the capitalist machine would be the one that tracks the overall volume of goods and services that the economy churns out into the marketplace—gross domestic product.

GROSS DOMESTIC PRODUCT

Gross domestic product (GDP) is a measurement of the dollar value of all finished goods and services produced and distributed in the economy. The GDP of the United States is calculated on an annualized basis by the U.S. Department of Commerce and, as of this writing, is approximately $11.6 trillion.[80] This figure indicates that over the last year the U.S. generated $11.6 trillion worth of finished goods and services.

To arrive at the GDP figure, the Commerce Department's Bureau of Economic Analysis (BEA) compiles data from a variety of sources on production, income, prices, and spending. The BEA keeps track of these figures in National Income and Product Accounts (NIPAs) and makes quarterly estimates on overall production and income in the U.S. economy. These estimates are revised as new data is collected and analyzed, then quarterly GDP statements are published monthly in the *Survey of Current Business*. Every July, the BEA revises its estimates for the previous three years and after the final revisions, the GDP statistics are fixed as historical records.

The BEA uses total spending in the U.S. economy as its primary measurement of overall production and income. This is based on the idea that there are two sides to every transaction in which a finished product is bought and sold. On one side of the transaction, money is spent by a consumer and on the other side a dollar value of output is sold by the producer. As the producer sells the product at its market value, he or she is also receiving income. By measuring spending in this way, economists are also measuring output and income. That is, spending, output, and income are three dimensions of the same thing.

In its quarterly statements, the BEA presents GDP in the form of "outlays" arranged into four broad categories: Consumer Spending, Investment Spending, Government Spending, and Net Export Spending—the balance between exports and imports. Table 1 shows 2007 GDP data as it broken down into these categories.

TABLE 1

Real Gross Domestic Product, 2007 (2000 Dollars)	x billions	Percentage of Total
Real GDP, Total	$11,660	100 %
Consumer Spending	$8,301	71 %
Investment Spending	$1,859	16 %
Government Spending	$2,034	17 %
Net Export Spending	($534)	-4 %

Every month the BEA also estimates the annualized growth rate of gross domestic product. The long-run growth rate of gross domestic product hovers at about 3 percent annually, which has come to be the benchmark growth rate. Growth rates that are less than this benchmark are held as "anemic" and rates in excess are referred to as "hot" or "rapid." Yet a targeted 3 percent growth rate of material output is also an exponential growth rate, meaning that every year the additional output to the economy must be 3 percent larger than it was the year before. Mathematically, an economy that continuously grows at this rate will double in size every twenty-four years. So with a 3 percent growth rate, by 2030 the U.S. capitalist machine will be running at a rate of $22 trillion dollars worth of goods and services annually. The implications of this are profound and will be explored in more detail in the next chapter.

Whether the number is $11 trillion or $22 trillion, gross domestic product is calculated in dollar values. One technical problem with this calculation is that money measurements are always subject to price inflation. Inflation distorts GDP as a measurement of the actual physical production of goods and services. To remove this distortion, the BEA deflates GDP by "chaining" prices to a base year, or by calculating GDP using constant dollars. The inflation-adjusted figure is called "real GDP." Note that in Table 1, the 2007 real GDP is expressed in 2000 dollars. This means that the real GDP for 2007 measures the goods and services produced in 2007, but sets the prices of those goods and services at 2000 levels. By doing so, all the price inflation that occurred by 2000 and 2007 is eliminated or deflated.

PRICE INFLATION AND THE CONSUMER PRICE INDEX

Like aging, price inflation seems to be a constant fact of life. Most people always pay more for things now than they did the previous year. By definition, price inflation is a sustained increase in the general price level of a broad spectrum of goods and services that occurs over a stretch of time. Inflation rates are calculated based on averages, so a 2 percent rate of inflation means that although some prices are rising faster than others, prices in general are increasing by an average of 2 percent. Also, since inflation is generalized over an array of goods and services it cannot be pinned to a single cause. However, we can be certain that price inflation is the result of a dynamic process in which one round of inflation can bring about economic conditions that will result in another round of inflation later on, and this leads to yet more inflation, and so on.

For example, consider population growth. A growing population will create "demand-pull" inflation as more and more people demand goods made from limited resources. More human consumption will place a greater strain on resources, say oil or natural gas, and the costs of these resources will rise. Rising energy costs can lead to higher manufacturing costs and subsequently create "cost-push" inflation driving up prices of finished products. Higher prices of finished products, in turn, will put upward pressure on wages and salaries in labor markets as employees demand pay raises to keep up with a higher cost of living. Wage and salary increases create even more cost-push inflation, and will push up prices of finished goods even higher, triggering another round of general price increases and so on in an upward inflationary spiral.

An inflationary spiral can also be caused by central bank monetary policy. If monetary authorities produce a disproportionately large increase in the money supply, they will cause prices to jump as more money circulates around a limited amount of goods and services. Once again, labor and other resource costs will subsequently rise and general price inflation will be underway.

Price inflation is not always considered as a bad thing and it does not affect everyone in the same way. People who are trying to get by on low, fixed incomes experience a deterioration of their standard of living as the purchasing power of their incomes erode with higher prices. For people who are paying long-term mortgages and at the same time have incomes that are subject to annual cost of living adjustments (COLAS), modest price inflation can be a good thing. With an upward wage and price spiral, a fixed monthly mortgage or interest payment becomes a proportionately smaller debt burden over time. For lenders receiving fixed interest income, price inflation diminishes the value of their income-earning assets. Accordingly, inflation is worrisome to those in commercial banking and the multi-trillion-dollar bond industry. The Federal Reserve System, particularly under the leadership of Alan Greenspan and his successor Benjamin Bernanke, has therefore made fighting inflation its primary monetary policy goal.

Since the banking and bond industries share a central position in the U.S. economy, inflation rates are closely watched by the Fed and carefully measured by the U.S. government. The U.S. Bureau of Labor Statistics' (BLS) consumer price index (CPI) is the most commonly referenced measure of price inflation. The CPI was originally created as an index of the costs of a "basket" or selection of consumer goods and services purchased by typical households. The selection consists of various categories of goods including food, clothing, energy, transportation, healthcare, housing, and other categories of goods on which a typical household spends its income. The CPI-U is a more specific index that measures prices paid by urban populations. The

CPI is anchored to a base period, currently the years between 1982-1984, for which the base index is set at 100. So, for example, if the CPI in 2004 is 190, this means that a basket of consumer goods costing $100 in the 1982-1984 base period cost $190 in 2004. This is interpreted to mean that consumer prices were 90 percent higher in 2004 than they were in 1982-1984.

The main difficulties faced by the BLS in maintaining an accurate measure of inflation are defining what categories of items should be contained in the basket, and the relative importance of each category. As the economy and technology change over time, the basket will inevitably change its contents and certain categories will begin to weigh more heavily than others. Food and energy costs carried more weight in the price index in 1984 than in 2004, and in 2004 healthcare costs weighed more heavily than ever before.

Given these difficulties, Congress appointed a commission to track these changes and report their impact on CPI statistics. The commission, known as "The Boskin Commission," found that consumer spending habits were continuously changing as people substituted one good for another as price inflation occurred unevenly across a spectrum of consumer goods. The commission reported that the CPI was overstating the cost of living as consumers would substitute less expensive goods when prices of comparable goods would rise. For example, if the price of apples increased and oranges did not, and if consumers then switched to oranges, according to the commission, the cost of fruit would not rise in the basket. The commission's recommendation, therefore, was to build these substitution factors into the CPI-U calculations. Many have questioned the validity of this recommendation, for substitutions of less expensive goods would more likely signify a deterioration of living standards rather than lower price inflation. The commission's motives were questioned as well, as the federal government has a financial interest in understating price inflation. Social security beneficiaries are subject to annual cost of living adjustments and these adjustment are fixed to the CPI-U, so to understate inflation could save the government billions in benefits. Lower benefits, of course, mean lower living standards for retirees and the disabled.

Such a policy recommendation is consistent with an economic system where the highest goal is to maximize wealth accumulation for investors and where care for the elderly and disabled is of secondary importance.

UNEMPLOYMENT AND THE UNEMPLOYMENT RATE

Another key measurement of the performance of the economic machine is the level of employment. High levels of employment, or low levels of unemployment, are generally viewed as positive indicators of economic health. However, as with inflation, the burden of unemployment means different things to different people. For most working families, chronic unemployment is the most severe of all potential economic hardships. Long-term unemployment contributes to a host of personal and social maladies ranging from depression and domestic violence to community breakdown and social unrest. And for millions of low-income Americans the only alternative to joblessness is employment in dead-end jobs where the pay is so low that they are almost certain to remain poor.

For banks, bondholders, and businesses, however, rising unemployment can be an encouraging sign. This fact has guided many Fed monetary policy decisions, for as unemployment falls below a certain level, banks get nervous about inflationary pressure and the Fed will thus be inclined to raise interest rates in an attempt to slow down the economic machine. This will push unemployment back up and slow down an upward wage/price spiral. High unemployment alleviates bankers' concern about rising labor costs as increasing joblessness can function as a direct assault against cost driven inflation. With many unemployed workers, businesses can hire from a more competitive labor market and will not be compelled to offer higher wages or salaries, which will widen their profit margins.

Like the CPI, the official unemployment rate is also maintained by the Bureau of Labor Statistics. During the week of the twelfth day of each month, the U.S. Census Bureau, acting on behalf of the BLS, conducts a Current Population Survey (CPS) of sixty thousand households that is held to be a representative sample of the overall U.S. population. The surveys include questions regarding the number of people old enough to be employed legally, how many are currently employed or looking for employment, how many hours were worked in the last week, and other employment-related questions. The BLS also conducts monthly surveys of business and government payroll information such as employee earnings, hours worked by employees and pay periods. The purpose of all these surveys is to gather information about the size of the labor force, the number of jobs created and to calculate the unemployment rate. The data from the surveys is collected, and summarized by the BLS in a monthly report titled, "The Employment Situation," in which the official employment rate is reported along with other labor market data.

The national unemployment rate is calculated by dividing the number of unemployed members of the labor force by the total labor force. To be considered as a member of the labor force, a person must be at least sixteen years old and either working full- or part-time, or has been actively looking for work in the last four weeks. If someone is of employable age but has not been looking for work, he or she is no longer considered part of the labor force. Once people are dropped from the labor force, they become labor market non-entities. The official unemployment rate therefore is the percentage of people in the labor force who are not employed, even at part-time jobs, and who are actively looking for jobs. As of this writing, the national unemployment rate is currently averaging around 5 percent.

The unemployment rate is a closely watched indicator of economic performance, but it masks many of the hardships associated with joblessness. Many who have been facing hopeless employment prospects become discouraged and stop looking. Though still jobless, if they stop looking they disappear from the official labor force and no longer register in unemployment statistics. Also, the unemployment rate does not make a distinction for those who are involuntarily working part-time (underemployed). A person who works as little as one hour per week is considered by the BLS to be employed as someone who is working forty hours, or someone who is working several low-pay jobs to make ends meet. Every job is treated the same as every other job. Also, the unemployment rate is not spread uniformly among geographic areas or demographic groups. Some towns or communities have unemployment rates as high as they were during the Great Depression, and the unemployment rate for black and latino Americans is consistently higher than it is for whites.

These and other economic indicators can measure how well the U.S. economy is performing as a capitalist system. However, they do not necessarily measure the well-being of people. The Dow Jones Industrial Average and NASDAQ are closely watched and daily reported economic indicators, even though stock values only have daily significance for a very small and wealthy sector of the population. Of much greater concern to the vast majority of Americans are things like job security, healthcare benefits, and the wages and salaries they depend on for their livelihoods. Although millions of working people have retirement funds invested in stocks, it is far less important to them than the daily concern of being able to buy food and make mortgage payments. Yet these concerns are not emphasized in the business press except when they influence the values of financial investments. This emphasis on financial market activity exemplifies the reality that the U.S. economy is, first and foremost, a system in which the interests of investors are of a top priority. By daily reporting on Wall Street activity, the business press is doing precisely what it should be doing in a capitalist system—reporting on those indicators that signify how well the economic system is performing its primary function.

The unemployment rate, job creation, and CPI statistics reported monthly by the BLS contain important information, but they are used primarily by banks, bond dealers, and the Fed as a way of watching for signs of inflationary pressure building in the system. GDP stands above the other indicators because it, more than any other, signifies the rate with which the capitalist machine is producing ever larger amounts of goods and services for sale and profit. That is, GDP is continuously watched for signs of growth.

Growth in output is a centrally important and necessary feature of capitalism. But growth rates are seldom steady and are not always positive. The capitalist machine can accelerate into a red-hot growth phase, or enter a phase in which it slows to a crawl or even recedes. These undulations in growth rates in GDP are known as business cycles.

BUSINESS CYCLES

One of the main arguments presented in this book is that the U.S. economy is a system. This means that to understand economics, the economy has to be seen as a network of integrated components and also that problems or consequences are systemic. One such systemic problem is a pattern of recurrent cycles of economic instability. Moreover, to understand business cycles it is necessary to see also that the U.S. economy is a *dynamic* system. As mentioned in our discussion of price inflation, dynamic systems are subject to continuous flux and change, and part of what causes these changes are feedback mechanisms. Feedback mechanisms are inherent in all dynamic systems and generally follow a circuitous or non-linear pattern: A leads to B, B leads to C, and C causes a change in A, which again leads to a further change in B, and so forth (See Figure 1).

If we take a long view of the U.S. economy, we can see this kind of dynamic pattern and built-in feedback mechanisms. For example, if the economy is growing—measured by growth rates in GDP—businesses are producing more output of goods and services and generating more income (See Figure 2). With more income flowing to households, people will spend more on goods and services, and as people spend more on goods and services, busi-

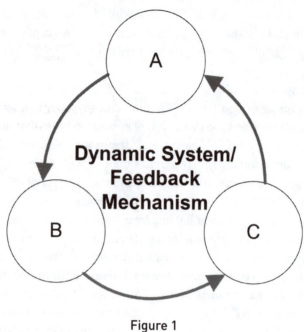

Figure 1

nesses will see their inventories being depleted and will develop a more positive outlook for future sales. With a more positive outlook, and as they replace depleted inventories, businesses will increase output of goods and services and GDP rises. More GDP means more income and more spending and so on in a "virtuous circle of expansion"—economic growth is a supreme "virtue" in a capitalist system.

The economic system can also reverse this course. If the economy is shrinking, businesses are producing less output of goods and services and generating less income. With less income flowing to households, people will spend less on goods and services and as people spend less on goods and services, businesses will see an accumulation of unsold inventories, and they will develop a negative outlook for future sales. With a negative outlook and inventories piling up, businesses will decrease output of goods and services and GDP falls. With less GDP, there is less income and less spending and so on in a "vicious circle of contraction."

Business cycles, therefore, are the processes through which the economy alternates between the virtuous circle of expansion and the vicious circle of contraction. The business cycle is the prime mover of all of the elements of

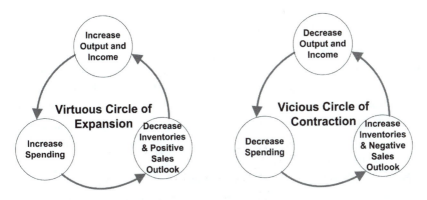

Figure 2

the economic machine that we have been describing in the preceding chapters of this book. With every fluctuation in a business cycle, changes will occur in virtually every aspect of the economy. As the economy enters a growth phase, jobs are created in labor markets and the unemployment rates will fall. Falling unemployment puts upward pressure on wages and salaries, and this could trigger a price inflation, which also could trigger changes in bond prices and interest rates. Expansion of output and income will also affect government tax revenues and expand the budgets for state and federal government institutions. Governments receiving more tax revenue will have more resources to spend on public services and this invariably involves spending on goods and services produced by businesses.

Expansion of production also means higher corporate profits and rising stock prices. With more corporate profits and a more positive sales outlook, businesses will also expand investments in new capital. And, as share prices rise, people experience what economists call the "wealth effect" in which many people feel wealthier and consequently spend more of their money. Individuals see their retirement funds grow proportionally to rising stock prices and as they feel less inclined to save for retirement, they spend more of their incomes. Therefore, with rising government spending stimulated by additional revenues, rising consumer spending stimulated by rising incomes and the wealth effect, and rising business investments stimulated by a more favorable economic climate, all of these spending increases combine to increase overall spending on goods and services in the economy. The economy charges forward into the virtuous circle of growth and expansion, and all the key indicators—rising stock market indexes, rising GDP, job growth, as well as price inflation—point to a booming economy. Such an economic boom can last for several years, but eventually the process will slow down and for a time reverse direction. This reversal can occur for many reasons, one being Fed policy directed at slowing down the boom in order to fight inflation. By reversing the direction and sustaining a slow down, the economy can spiral into the vicious circle of recession. Government and Fed policies will be used at this point to fight rising unemployment. These alternating patterns of boom and bust phases in business cycles constitute a familiar pattern in U.S. economic history.

As we emphasized in Chapter Four, government has always been a major player in the U.S. economy. As we examine the years following World War II in the next section, we can see that government and Fed policy-making can have a significant effect on the direction of the U.S. economy. If the U.S. economy is a capitalist machine, government policy-makers and Fed authorities play a key role by putting their foot on, or taking it off, the machine's accelerator.

POST–WORLD WAR II BUSINESS CYCLES

For most of the decades between the Civil War and World War II, the U.S. economy experienced severe business cycle instability. Contractions were harsh and debilitating, and expansions were associated with rapid price inflation along with wild financial market instability. After the Great Depression and the horrors of World War II were finally brought to an end, the U.S. economy gained unprecedented strength in growth and development. Nonetheless, it experienced several major recessions between 1945 and 2001.

Throughout World War II, the U.S. economic machine steadily accelerated. This acceleration reached a peak in February 1945 just as the war was coming to a close and the machine slowed into a mild contraction that lasted for about eight months. During this recession, GDP decreased from about $212 billion to $208 billion. Prior to the recession the unemployment rate was about 1.2 percent but after the economy slid into the vicious circle of contraction, unemployment had jumped to nearly 4 percent.[81]

Beginning in October 1945 the machine began to accelerate again and the economy embarked on a three-year period of an uninterrupted virtuous circle of expansion and growth. Economic output measured by real GDP increased from $208 billion in the recessionary trough of 1945 to a peak of about $258 billion in 1948. Job growth continued but was not rapid enough to keep up with the increase in the civilian labor force; the unemployment rate remained at nearly 4 percent even though the economy was growing. Price inflation often accompanies economic growth and during this three-year expansion prices, measured by the consumer price index, increased by about 32 percent.[82] This inflation was due in part to shortages of commodities that were still lingering from the war years. Demand-driven inflation occurred as economic growth gave households more income to spend, and as the pent-up demand for consumer goods that was created during the war was being satisfied as consumers bought automobiles, household appliances, and many bought new homes using the newly created "GI Bill of Rights"[83] that gave war veterans access to home mortgage credit. Facing pressure from banks, President Harry Truman ordered a special convening of Congressional leaders to implement wage and price controls to combat inflation. The Republican Congress was reluctant to grant such powers as they were seeking to scale back government intervention in the economy, not to increase it. Yet rapid price inflation was alarming and Congress eventually moved to restrict consumer credit and debt-driven spending. The move to restrict credit was deliberately targeting consumer spending and demand-driven inflation. This was certain to trigger a vicious circle of contraction, and a recession began in autumn of 1948.

The first post–World War II recession lasted from November 1948 to October 1949. During this recession industrial production dropped by 10 percent and real GDP fell by 4 percent. The demand-driven buying spree that occurred in the years immediately after the war abated during this recession. Unplanned inventories began to accumulate and businesses responded by slowing production. As the machine slowed, less labor was needed and workers were laid off. The unemployment rate jumped to nearly 6 percent in 1949 and remained well above 5 percent for several months. As the vicious circle of contraction continued, working people were put out of their jobs and households lost their buying power. With less household consumption, production slowed even further resulting in downward pressure on prices. The anti-inflation strategy was successful as price inflation slowed to a crawl between 1949 and 1950. A new precedent was established in which throwing people out of work came to be seen as the most effective weapon against price inflation that is so feared by the banking community.

The recession eventually ended and the next growth phase began in October 1949. From 1949 to 1953, the U.S. economy experienced four years of a virtuous circle of expansion. Gross Domestic Product increased from a low of $257 billion in 1949 to $285 billion in 1950, soared to $328 billion in 1951, and then peaked at $365 billion in 1953.[84] The driving force behind this growth phase was not consumer spending, however, but rather government spending as the U.S. began its preparations and build-up for another war. This growth phase precisely coincided with the years of the Korean War. The war began when North Korean forces crossed the border into South Korea in June 1950, and it ended when an armistice was signed in July 1953. Government spending on defense increased from $13 billion in 1949, to its peak of $49 billion in 1953— an increase of 270 percent.[85] Government spending increased significantly and, at the same time, household spending increased as people anticipated wartime shortages and rushed out to stock up on basic commodities and consumer durables. This surge in household and government spending triggered a surge in output growth as businesses scrambled to replace declining inventories.

During the growth years between 1949 and 1953, the unemployment rate dropped to less than 3 percent. Wages and salaries started to rise, and the CPI increased by about 13 percent.[86] The rate of inflation was not as rapid as it otherwise might have been due to tight Federal Reserve policy. The tradition of the Fed was to increase the money supply given the Treasury Department's need to spend for war efforts. By 1951, however, the Fed was resisting out of fear of repeating the rapid price inflation that occurred in the late 1940s. The result was economic growth, and price inflation that otherwise would have skyrocketed was tempered by high interest rates.

Defense spending by the U.S. government slowed at the end of the Korean War and this brought about an economic slowdown beginning in May 1954. Defense outlays decreased from $49 billion in 1953, to $41 billion in 1954, and to $39 billion in 1955.[87] Industrial output, driven by fewer defense contracts, slowed by about 10 percent over a nine-month period and overall national output fell by about 4 percent. The unemployment rate rose from 2.9 percent in 1953 to 5.5 percent in 1954. Price inflation remained in check for four years and then began a slight but steady rise in 1955. The inventory increases that were caused by slower spending gradually disappeared and businesses began stepping up production, although at a slower rate than what was seen in previous periods of expansion. The rate of growth slowed to a crawl and eventually fell into another recession by the summer of 1957. The recession of 1957 lasted for only nine months but was deep. Unemployment jumped to 4.3 percent, climbed to 6.8 percent, and peaked at 7.5 percent in 1958.[88] Viewed from the perspective of how labor markets were affected, this was the worst since the Depression years of the 1930s.

The machine once again rebounded by April 1958, but the recovery was slow. National output increased by a little over 1.3 percent and unemployment remained above 5 percent. Although businesses were decreasing their investments in physical capital, the virtuous circle of expansion was perpetuated by a steady rise in consumer spending. Toward the end of the Eisenhower administration in 1961, the U.S. government moved toward a fiscal policy of a balanced budget. This meant that the government would restrain spending to keep within the bounds of available tax revenues. Government spending declined and along with it came another recession that lasted from April of 1960 to February of 1961. That was also the year that John F. Kennedy defeated Eisenhower's Vice President, Richard Nixon, in the election for president on a promise to bring the economy out of the recession.

From the end of the recession of 1961, the U.S. capitalist machine accelerated once again and embarked on a growth phase that lasted until December of 1969. The growth was the result of a combination of fiscal policies that included tax cuts, transfer payments and an increase in government defense spending as the U.S. entered into another war in Asia—the Vietnam War.

Under the guidance of his council of economic advisers, President John F. Kennedy began the first of a series of tax cuts that came to be known as the "supply-side" approach to economic policy. The centerpiece of the supply-side approach to economics is a tax-cut policy particularly aimed at the upper-income sector of the population. Tax cuts for the wealthy, it was presumed, would release funds that could be used for new investments and growth. President Kennedy was assassinated in 1963, but his tax cut policies were continued by his successor, Lyndon B. Johnson. Johnson pushed the tax cut agenda further by lowering tax rates for a broader base of the income-earning population. The idea behind Johnson's extension of tax cuts was that they would lead to more disposable income for households, more consumer spending, more sales and profits for businesses, and eventually more growth. The policy was heralded as a success as the unemployment rate fell to below 4 percent by 1966. National output was $591 billion in 1963, and climbed to over $750 billion by 1966.

The Kennedy and Johnson administrations also significantly increased government defense spending while cutting taxes. With the onset of the U.S. involvement in the Vietnam War, defense expenditures increased from $50 billion in 1965 to $78 billion in 1969, an increase of 56 percent. The Johnson Administration also expanded government spending on transfer payment programs by increasing social security payments, and by creating public assistance programs such as Medicare, Medicaid, food stamps, and government subsidies to farmers and small businesses. The programs put more purchasing power in the hands of low-income households who spent nearly all of it on goods and services. Business sales increased which further augmented growth in the economy as it ascended into the virtuous circle of expansion.[89]

These tax cuts coupled with increases in defense spending led the U.S. government into budget deficits. The supply-side belief that tax cuts could engender enough growth such that tax revenue would actually increase did not materialize, and government deficits continued to rise throughout the late 1960s. Deficit-driven government spending and rising consumer spending caused the economy to continue to grow nonetheless. With these high levels of spending, demand-pull inflation was inevitable. The CPI showed annual price increases from 1.5 percent in 1965 to a 6.2 percent increase in 1969.

Price inflation caused interest rates to rise as commercial banks attempted to recover the loss of real interest income. The prime interest rate increased from a little over 4.5 percent in 1965 to almost 8 percent in 1969. This constituted nearly a 77 percent increase in the cost of borrowing. As we have seen from earlier experiences, rising interest rates push down spending causing the capitalist machine to decelerate. The fifth post-war recession came in December 1969 and continued until November 1970 and the U.S. economy began to spiral downward into a vicious circle of rising unemployment, falling consumer spending and overall decline in economic activity.

To combat this downward spiral, the Federal Reserve System expanded the money supply, which effectively lowered interest rates and the machine began to accelerate once again. Given the historic instability of the monetary system of the United States, economic growth that is built on a foundation of an expanding money supply is likely to lead to rapid price inflation and financial market instability.

Price inflation soared in the early 1970s as money expanded. The value of the U.S. dollar weakened and this led to significant increases in global oil and food prices. In 1971, President Richard Nixon ended the gold-exchange standard (See Chapter Five), the value of the dollar fell more rapidly and prices started to soar. To make inflationary matters worse, in 1973 an international oil embargo caused oil prices to increase fourfold, and worldwide shortages of meat and other food products sent prices of basic consumer goods skyrocketing. The CPI increased by 8.7 percent in 1973 and by 12.3 percent in 1974. Spikes in the prime interest rate followed these spikes in prices. The prime rate rose from below 5 percent to over 8 percent in 1973 and then to almost

11 percent in 1974. As before, high interest rates slammed the brakes on the economic machine. A deep recession was under way and the unemployment rate shot up to 8.5 percent by 1975.

Throughout the mid-to-late 1970s, unemployment remained high and the real wage (wages adjusted for inflation) remained unchanged. Another oil shock hit in the late 1970s and prices once again soared by 9 percent in 1978, 13.3 percent in 1979 and by 12.5 percent in 1980. The Federal Reserve responded with equal severity and dramatically decreased the money supply; prime interest rates soared to 13 percent in 1979, 15 percent in 1980 and to a staggering 19 percent by 1981. Such historic high rates of interest, of course, drove down borrowing, spending, and investments, and by 1982, the U.S. economy plunged into the worst recession since the Depression of the 1930s. National output contracted sharply and the unemployment rate peaked at over 10 percent. Inflation was eventually brought under control at the cost of heavy casualties in the labor markets. Oil prices began to decline and the consumer price index slowed its growth rate to between 3 percent and 4 percent throughout the 1980s.

From the deepest point of the recession of 1982, the U.S. capitalist machine embarked on the longest phase of peacetime expansion in American history. But much of the energy behind the growth that occurred during the 1980s stemmed from borrowed money. Federal government deficits and debt plunged to its deepest levels in history as President Ronald Reagan pursued a much more aggressive implementation of supply-side policies involving massive tax cuts for upper income households and businesses. Consumer debt also reached an all-time high during this period. In a matter of a few years in the 1980s, the United States transformed itself from the world's largest creditor nation to the world's largest debtor nation and debt of every kind continued to rise. High levels of debt also kept interest rates relatively high by historic standards, as the prime interest rate remained around 9 and 10 percent. Sustained high rates brought about another relatively short recession that occurred in between July 1990 and March 1991. But the machine accelerated into a red-hot growth period in the 1990s, and then slowed down again from March to November 2001.

The Fed responded to this recession much more actively and lowered interest rates to the lowest levels in forty years. Low rates may have prevented a deeper or longer recession and the economy is currently growing. Much of this growth is being fed by a combination of massive federal government and consumer debt. In the current period, massive trade and budget deficits and debt continue to break historic records. As we mentioned at the end of the previous chapter, continuously increasing debt cannot be sustained forever and the bill collector will eventually arrive. At that point the debt will either have to be paid or face the possibility of a widespread financial collapse. Yet debt repayment will pose a drain on the economy and result in a downturn. With every layer of accumulated debt, the likelihood of a severe downturn becomes increasingly more likely. Fed authorities are becoming concerned about this potential problem and have starting raising interest rates in order to slow down borrowing and debt accumulation.

CONCLUSION: THE CAPITALIST MACHINE AND THE WELL-BEING OF THE POPULATION

GDP is the premier measure of the economic machine's performance and growth of GDP is heralded as a supreme virtue. It is rare to find an economist who would question this virtue of economic growth as a positive contribution to human well-being. Yet, GDP growth masks other indicators that would suggest that its ongoing growth is not necessarily good for human well-being.

GDP is the dollar value of all finished goods and services produced in an economy in a year's time. As a single number, roughly $11.6 trillion, it is a numerical measurement expressed as an undifferentiated mass of products and services. GDP does not take into account under what conditions the products and services are produced, whether they actually improve people's lives, the damage done to people and our environment resulting from growth, or how the output is distributed among the population. In other words, when we attempt to reduce something as complex as a measurement of well-being of an entire population to a single number, much important information falls through the cracks.

One problem is that GDP is calculated in a way that is heavily biased toward capitalist production. Although GDP imputes some value that is created in the public sector, it primarily measures the dollar value of transactions that only occur in the marketplace. The capitalist machine will appear to be slowing down when people prepare their own meals, clean their own homes, or do their own yard maintenance rather than pay businesses in the private sector to perform the same work. If people grow food in their own vegetable gardens, there is no change in GDP, but if they buy those same vegetables in a grocery store, GDP rises. If people do their own do-it-yourself repairs on their homes, GDP does not change, but if they hire a contractor to do the work, GDP rises. Whether people do the work themselves or pay businesses to do it, the net amount of work does not change but the way the U.S. economy is measured, the machine will only accelerate when people pay businesses and will decelerate when people work for themselves. In fact, the more self-sufficient households become then the lower the GDP becomes which by this measure constitutes economic failure. British writer and critic, Richard Douthwaite, illuminates this seeming contradiction:

> British visitors to rural Ireland are often amazed at how well-off the locals seem in spite of lower wages, higher taxes and higher prices in the shops. The mystery is explained by the fact that many of the sparkling new bungalows have been built on family land by the owners and their friends: only the materials and specialist jobs cost money. Many of these people cut their own fuel and grow their own vegetables too, but the value of these and of the house construction is left off their income tax returns.[90]

As the capitalist machine accelerates, it does damage to people and the environment. These negative side effects of growth are not accounted for in GDP statistics. Moreover, the work people have to do to heal or protect themselves from the damage done by growth shows as an increase in GDP. For example, the more people do keyboard or assembly work that causes hand and wrist strain, the more people will seek out treatment for carpal tunnel syndrome, and GDP rises. If people work longer and longer hours, GDP rises, and if they opt for more leisure time, or for time to volunteer in their communities, the capitalist machine slows down. As more and more people commute to and from their jobs, more traffic accidents will occur. Traffic accidents lead to auto repair and medical bills, parts replacements, and insurance and legal fees—the capitalist machine speeds up. As people pollute rivers, damage forests and wetlands, deplete resources such as fresh water, topsoil, and fuel, GDP increases; but these will assure a decrease in the quality of life on earth. In addition, qualitative dimensions to our lives such as having clean surroundings, natural beauty, a sense of personal dignity and community connection, show no contribution to GDP, as they are not part of the capitalist cash nexus, and thus are ignored as measures of human well-being. If people were to cut down all the redwood trees that exist in the state of California, turn them into boards and paper to be sold for profit, take the profits to Las Vegas and gamble them away, the nation's GDP would rise and people would be seen as better off.

GDP calculations do not take into account how the goods and services are distributed. If GDP growth is supposed to be beneficial to society, then it must follow that those benefits of growth must be widely distributed among members of society. The data presented in Chapter Ten shows that the opposite is occurring in the U.S. economy. The U.S. has one of the most unequal income distribution patterns in the world. As national output and income increases, the wealthier classes are typically the primary beneficiaries of this growth. On the surface, it would seem to make little sense to cheer economic growth as a barometer of people's well-being when most of the benefits of growth get passed on to a relatively small and well-off percentage of the population. It makes perfect sense, however, if we understand that making wealthy investors even wealthier is the ultimate goal of capitalism.

Although GDP growth is touted as the quantitative measure of well-being, it does not resonate with a broad base of the population. Polls consistently show that when people are asked what contributes most to their happiness, material gain invariably takes a backseat to qualitative factors such as a stable home life, community ties, good health, and a general sense of peace and contentment. In addition, these values are becoming increasingly incompatible with the imperatives of capitalist growth. For example, longer hours performed on the job can lead to more income and growth, but puts an increasing strain on home life, pulls people away from their communities, and imperils people's health and our sense of contentment. None of which, of course, can be measured accurately in dollar terms.

There is no accurate way to assign a quality-of-life measure to national output because to do so would be attempting to quantify something that is inherently non-quantifiable. Beyond some level of a universally recognized level of poverty, there is no clear correlation between national output and the well-being of the population. What is clear, however, is that in the process of producing more and more goods and services, the strains placed on the planet's carrying capacity intensifies, as does noise, water and air pollution, and resource depletion. Over time this damage will bring down the well-being of everyone; wealthy and poor alike.

The need for economic growth is intrinsic to the capitalist system. The key problem is that the capitalist machine cannot continue to accelerate forever. At some point in time, the growth imperative of the capitalist system will force people to confront its consequences: resource depletion and environmental ruination, as well as the moral and health implications of this have up to now been swept under the rug by standard economics. Without growth, the machine will slow down and people's livelihoods will be jeopardized. Thus, people face a conundrum: Either remain trapped under the top-down growth imperative that is foisted on them by a mindless capitalist machine that has no regard for how people and communities are affected by this growth, or see their livelihoods ruined. In our view, the only way out of this conundrum, is to confront the capitalist system itself. That is, a mindful economy is one that is free from the growth imperative. We envision healthy people, vibrant communities and a clean and healthy natural environment as the top goals of economic activity, not growth for the sake of profits. To create a mindful economy and to free people from the dictates of the machine, would involve creating a non-capitalist, democratic economy. The growth imperative is ultimately derived from the needs and logic of capitalism and is not a democratic imperative originating from the needs of communities. It is to this growth imperative and its consequences as an inherent feature of capitalism that we now turn.

9

THE GROWTH IMPERATIVE
Prosperity or Poverty

Generating a measurable rate of return for investors is the core element of any capitalist economy. Investors derive their income from percentage returns on stocks, bonds, or other business investments. If investors do not get these expected returns, they will sell their investments and seek returns elsewhere. By disinvesting, or cashing out, investors can drive down the book value of a company, which can ultimately cause the business to fail. To prevent this outcome, the prime directive of a capitalist business is to sustain robust returns and growth of financial wealth for their investors. This is the paramount goal of capitalist enterprise.

To provide these returns for their investors, businesses essentially have three choices. One would be to pay investors with money held in their business bank accounts. This choice, however, would amount to self-impoverishment, as businesses would make themselves poorer by drawing down their bank account balances just as a person would become poorer by trying to live on a savings account. Another choice would be to generate profits from sales growth gained by taking market share away from competitors. Although the threat of losing market share in a competitive marketplace can force an individual business to be innovative and create new cost-saving technology, one business's gain is another business's loss in a zero-sum strategy. This would ultimately be self-destructive to the interest of the capitalist class as a whole. The third and only viable, long-term choice would be for each business to generate its returns by producing and selling more goods and services for profit.

In other words, driven by the financial necessity of providing investors with a robust rate of return, capitalist businesses must also sustain a robust rate of growth in the production and sale of goods and services. Financial growth is the taskmaster that drives growth in real production.

To sustain ongoing growth in production and sales, businesses must use a portion of their profits for reinvestment in capital stock (plant, equipment, inventory, etc.). With more capital stock, businesses can increase their production capacity to meet the demands of new growth in output and sales. As the funds for making these capital investments are mostly derived from profits on sales, sales growth and investment are locked into a dynamic relationship: profits from current sales provide financing for new investments, these new investments drive future production and future sales, and future sales and profits will finance yet more investments, and so on. Looking at the system in its entirety, keeping the engine of the economic machine running requires a steady flow in real investments that are derived from a steady rise in production and sales. In other words, the economy has to keep growing.

This growth imperative is systemic and extends beyond merely generating returns for investors. Not only are individual businesses driven to grow, but also the entire capitalist system depends on it. If the dynamic relationship between investment and growth were to break down, the economic system would break down as well. For example, if sales growth were to slow down, the source of funds for capital investment would begin to evaporate and new investments in capital stock would begin to fall. Falling investments would lead to an overall slowdown in production and sales. With falling sales, incomes would fall and a downward vicious circle of contraction would follow. Contraction or recession, if sustained over time can turn into a depression, and depression signifies systemic failure of the capitalist system.

As the capitalist machine speeds up or slows down, the changes are felt in every corner of the economy. Every institution within the U.S. economy is connected to every other institution as parts in the machine, and all have evolved to be dependent on the growth imperative. Therefore, if the economy grows, there is a chorus of cheers. Consumers look to growth because it means more goods and services available in markets; workers see growing job opportunities and rising incomes; public agencies receive more money from increased sales and income tax revenue to pay for police, schools, and roads; nonprofits receive more donations and grants from rising incomes; bank loans are repaid; and, most importantly, investors' profits are realized.

When growth turns to contraction (recession), however, trepidation is felt by all. Workers experience layoffs and default on their bank loans; falling profits and share prices in the stock markets deplete the value of pension funds; bankruptcies soar along with government budget deficits and budget cuts. Growth is so centrally important that it has shaped the development of America's most powerful institutions. Without steady growth, the economic system will proceed to wither away like a plant deprived of water and sunlight. For this reason, most observers are very hesitant to question this growth imperative of capitalism.

The acceptance of the growth imperative has become deeply infused in American culture and thought. Most Americans would rather ignore the inevitable environmental damage that ongoing growth causes than question it. As long as people are feeling benefits of growth, and that those benefits outweigh the damage it causes, people are likely to accept the idea that ongoing economic growth is benign. If this changes, however, and if it becomes clear that the damage outweighs the benefits, then a crisis in the perception of growth will emerge. This shift in perception is bound to occur at some point because of the scientific fact that *ongoing growth is not possible.* This is perhaps the single most deleterious consequence of the capitalist system. The system is based on a fundamental contradiction that, on the one hand, it must continue to grow, but on the other hand, it cannot. Many people seem to be more willing to accept even illusions of growth rather than directly face and reconcile this contradiction.

One such illusion of growth is a financial market "bubble." Market bubbles occur when speculators inflate prices far above what would be considered reasonable. A steady rise in stock values or housing prices can make those who own these financial assets feel wealthier. If growth in the value of financial assets is not supported by growth in the real economy of goods and services, then it is growth on paper only and the feeling of greater wealth is merely an illusion. Such illusions can suddenly transform into a harsh reality when the bubbles inevitably burst, prices fall, and the paper wealth collapses. For the few who sell prior to the collapse—as top Enron executives did moments before the company famously plunged into bankruptcy—the growth in wealth is real, as they can take their profits and buy real goods or property. But for the majority who lose, their losses are also real as their life savings evaporate. With winners and losers offsetting each other, bubbles in stocks, bonds, gold, or real estate are typically zero-sum situations that do not represent real growth in wealth, but rather an upward redistribution of existing wealth. Some real growth can hitch a ride on bubbles such as a booming housing construction industry that rides along with a bubble in the housing market, but these industries also suffer tremendously when the market bubbles burst.

Bubbles aside, capitalism is a money-based system. Growth is tracked and measured in monetary or financial terms such as the dollar-value of GDP or securities. For economic growth to be real and not an illusion, increases in these monetary measurements must be anchored to real growth in production. If not, then there will be a fundamental disconnect between the financial and the real, and this disconnect will become a source of instability. In other words, if the stock market shows a steady increase in values of say 7 percent per year but real production of goods and services grows by only 3 percent, then the money wealth represented in stock prices begins to pull away from what one can buy with that money. Money begins to lose its real purchasing power and, as we saw in Chapter Five, a sustained decline in the value of money eventually leads to economic collapse. A key factor in maintaining economic stability is to maintain a stable proportion between monetary growth and growth in the goods that you can buy with that money.

The paramount purpose of capitalism is to provide steady returns to investors. These returns are measured by growth in the value of the financial instruments the investors own, and for this growth to be real and stable, it must be supported by real growth in the production and sales of goods and services in the economy overall. A common misconception about the growth imperative is that it is driven by American consumers who are driven by a deeper impulse to buy and have more things. The cultural phenomenon of consumerism does not push the capitalist economy to grow, but rather is a byproduct of the capitalist system's growth imperative. Consumers do not push into the malls to buy things as much as they are pulled into the malls by the producers' desperate need to sell more and more.

CONSUMERISM: NURTURE NOT NATURE

The term consumerism is used to describe a cultural norm that equates personal well-being with purchasing more and better material possessions. If this were a natural human impulse, then economic growth would naturally follow human nature. At some primal level, we can see that economic growth is in fact necessary for our survival and success as species. Economist Thorstein Veblen asserted that a deeply rooted tendency of human beings is to see that our offspring have a fair chance at a good life. Veblen referred to this tendency as a "parental instinct." Driven by this instinct, Veblen argues, each generation seeks to make their material standard of living better than the last, causing the economy to grow to higher and higher levels of production. If what Veblen tells us is true, then at some level we are by our nature driven to achieve economic growth. This primal instinct, however, has very little to do with the systemic imperative to grow into what is now an already massive $11 trillion-dollar economy. In fact, the parental instinct to assure a good life for our offspring and ongoing growth are actually *contradictory* goals as endless growth promises to deplete available resources and undermine the welfare of future generations.

Ongoing growth entails using more and more inputs or resources. As these resources are depleted, the productive capacity of future generations is compromised, as will be their chance at a decent livelihood. Moreover, the things people really want for their children—good schools, clean and functional neighborhoods, healthy and vibrant natural environment, economic stability and security—are those that are least likely to be offered in the growth-driven capitalist system.

Veblen identified that alongside the parental instinct is a "predatory instinct," which is also a deeply rooted human tendency toward certain behavior. Predatory behavior is not concerned with caring for future generations as much as with conquests and self-aggrandizement. Coining terms such as "pecuniary emulation" and "conspicuous consumption," Veblen was one of the first economists to identify the predatory impulse to achieve social status through owning and consuming more and more goods. In Veblen's view, bigger and better and more goods are consumerist trophies celebrating the prowess and skill of the predator like the taxidermy heads of animals displayed on the hunter's game room walls. For Veblen, the simultaneous existence of these instincts—the parental instinct to care for our young and the predatory instincts of ostentatious consumption and competitive acquisition—stand in an antagonistic relationship and are emblematic of modern life.

Whether their primary impulse stems from a parental or a predatory instinct, the generally accepted view in American culture is that consumers are sovereign in the marketplace. Most proponents as well as critics of capitalism hold the belief that consumer demand is the prime mover in the basic economic processes. That is, consumers will express their demands in the markets and businesses dutifully follow. Proponents argue that growth serves to satisfy the demands of people, and critics argue that people are selfishly, or perhaps unwittingly, creating their own destruction with excessive demands. In either view, the line of causality begins with consumption and consumption drives production.

We challenge this viewpoint and argue that consumerism is a cultural phenomenon that was created as part of a broader systemic need of the capitalist economy to grow. Profits from sales are the source of returns to capitalist investors, and these returns cannot be sustained if people do not sustain high levels of consumption. The relentless drive for profits created the consumer culture that fuels the economic machine.

If consumerism did in fact stem from a natural instinct of the human species, it was not evident among most Americans in the nineteenth century. One of the problems facing capitalism throughout the nineteenth century was chronic overproduction. Businesses were producing goods for the market, but people tended to be frugal, self-sufficient, and were reluctant to spend their earnings on more and more consumer goods. More often than not, people tended to follow the ethic expressed in Christian Proverbs, "He that tilleth his land shall have plenty of bread: but he that followeth after vain persons shall have poverty enough . . . Remove far from me vanity and lies: give me neither poverty nor riches; feed me with food convenient for me."[91] For many Americans at that time, conspicuous consumption—overtly consuming and buying to display social status—was unseemly.

By the turn of the twentieth century, businesses began searching for new ways to get people to spend more of their earnings on consumer goods. In order to sell goods in volume, businesses began deploying revolutionary methods designed to entice people into consumer indulgences that were previously considered frivolous or unnecessary. In his description of America in the early twentieth century as "The Dawn of a Commercial Empire,"[92] cultural historian and author, William Leach writes:

> After 1880, American commercial capitalism, in the interest of marketing goods and making money, started down the road of creating . . . a set of symbols, signs and enticements . . . From the 1880s onward, a commercial aesthetic of desire and longing took shape to meet the needs of business. And since that need was constantly growing and seeking expression in wider and wider markets, the aesthetic of longing and desire was everywhere and took many forms . . . this aesthetic appeared in shop windows, electrical signs, fashion shows, advertisements, and billboards.[93]

To satisfy the growth imperative of capitalism, the marketing and advertising industry was born. By the "roaring 1920s," consumerism, molded by the nascent advertising industry, was in full swing and established itself not as a fad, but as a permanent and central feature of American culture. Today, advertising is a several hundred-billion-dollar industry, which is about ten times the entire GDP of the U.S. economy at the turn of the twentieth century when the industry began.

Capitalism has a systemic need to sell things. If people show no inclination to buy these things, then the capitalist machine will break down. To survive, capitalism must find ways—manipulation and seduction if necessary—to get people to buy more and more things that potentially have little or no relevance to their physical or spiritual well-being, or to that of their offspring. Consumerism is a product of modern marketing techniques that stimulate deep psychological impulses to consume, not because it makes them better off, as consumption may or may not make them better off, but because the growth imperative of the capitalist machine requires it.

Ongoing growth in production and consumption is not just some haphazard thing that people do by chance, it occurs deliberately in response to the capitalist system's requirement to produce and sell ever-larger amounts of goods and services. The roots of this requirement run very deep and it is a requirement that has exceeded the planet's ability to sustain it.

THROUGHPUT AND LIMITS

Recall from Chapter One that the production process draws from available resource inputs to produce final goods, or outputs. It is logical to assume that continuous growth on the output side of the production process must necessarily draw more resources from the input side. This process is limited by the availability of resources of our planet. It is for this limitation, more than any other reason, that ongoing capitalist growth is not sustainable.

Parallel to this input/output production process shown in Figure 1 is the process of *throughput*. Throughput is a one-directional process in which usable resources and energy are converted into unusable waste. For example, a wooden match is a usable resource and when it burns, it eventually is converted into ash, which is waste and is no longer usable. The immutable laws of matter and energy govern throughput and all other physical and economic phenomena. In a sense, matter is the substance of physical reality and energy determines how that substance will act. Without energy, matter would be lifeless, motionless, and inert; and without matter, energy is like a ghost with no medium through which it can become manifest.

Any serious consideration of matter and energy should include the laws of thermodynamics. The first law of thermodynamics informs us that the quantity of all available energy is constant, and the second law states that this energy is continuously transforming from a usable state to a non-usable state. The rate of throughput and the rate with which this one-directional transformation takes place will vary with various rates of economic production. The

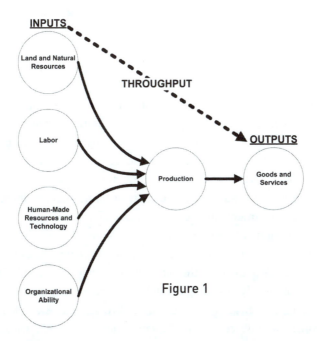

Figure 1

faster the economic machine turns resources into products, the faster people turn usable resources into unusable waste.

The capitalist growth imperative is not the only force behind throughput. Population pressures obviously play a role, and ongoing growth is evident in non-capitalist systems as well. But these other factors do not take away from the fact that capitalism is driven by a growth imperative, and this growth imperative is a major force behind throughput.

Biologist Mary E. Clark describes the process of hastening throughput as analogous to running up a balance on a credit card that will have to be paid in the future:

> We have been—and are—living on a one-time 'bank account' of fossil energy and mineral deposits both formed over eons of geologic time. To have become as dependent on them as we now are is singularly imprudent. Not only are we using up these one-time resources at a galloping rate; we are also living far beyond our day-to-day income of potentially renewable resources—of soil, of water, and of other living species. Instead of husbanding them so they will last forever, we exploit them. We are borrowing from the future.

We are not paying our way at all. We are living off past and future natural capital that we have suddenly learned to exploit. Like irresponsible credit card users, we live high today by borrowing from tomorrow.[94]

Not only are we borrowing from tomorrow, we are doing so at faster and faster rates. Clark's analogy is perhaps more literal than she thought as the need to use up resources stems from the underlying need to sustain returns to financial investors. As we argued above, steady growth in the value of financial assets drives growth in real production. Mathematically, if investors expect to receive a relatively constant rate of return on their investments, the value of the investment must grow *exponentially*. No matter how small, any fixed rate of return must grow at an exponential rate. A 2 or 3 percent growth rate means that every year the value of the investment must be 2 or 3 percent greater than it was the year before. Using the "72 rule," we can calculate approximately how long it will take for something to double in size by dividing the number 72 by the percentage growth rate. An $11 trillion economy growing at 3 percent annually would double to a $22 trillion economy in approximately twenty-four years (72/3 = 24). That is, in twenty-four years, the U.S. economic machine will be cranking out $22 trillion worth of goods and services. If the growth rate continues at 3 percent for an additional twenty-four years, national output will climb to $44 trillion. Driven by this internal mathematical logic of exponential returns, capitalist production is being pushed beyond the carrying capacity of our planet, or, in the language of thermodynamics, pushed toward "heat death," the ultimate state in which all useable energy is turned to waste.

Physicist and mathematician, Albert Bartlett, refers to those who believe in the possibility of perpetual growth as members of a "New Flat Earth Society." Bartlett argues that a belief in the ability to grow into perpetuity is logically consistent with believing that the earth is flat. If the earth is flat, then mathematically it exists as a plane in two-dimensional space and is therefore boundless. Only something that has no bounds as such can grow to infinity. If one were to envision the earth as a sphere, however, then it is contained in three-dimensional space and is finite. Bartlett's conclusion is:

If the "we can grow forever" people are right, then they will expect us, as scientists, to modify our science in ways that will permit perpetual growth. We will be called on to abandon the "spherical earth" concept and figure out the science of the flat earth. We can see some of the problems we will have to solve. We will be called on to explain the balance of forces that make it possible for astronauts to circle endlessly in orbit above a flat earth, and to explain why astronauts appear to be weightless. We will have to figure out why we have time zones; where do the sun, moon and stars go when they set in the west of an infinite flat earth, and during the night, how do they get back to their starting point in the east. We will have to figure out the nature of the gravitational lensing that makes an infinite flat earth appear from space to be a small circular flat disk. These and a host of other problems will face us as the "infinite earth" people gain more and more acceptance, power and authority. We need to identify these people as members of "The New Flat Earth Society" because a flat earth is the only earth that has the potential to allow the human population to grow forever.[95]

Bartlett touches on a point that is important for the discipline of economics. When presented with the factual and indisputable mathematics of limits to growth, as well as resource depletion and ecological ruin caused by endless growth, most economists slip into vague and cliché references to scientific or technological fixes. For over two hundred years, the discipline of mainstream economics has been tailored to fit the logic of capitalism and is not equipped to deal with a world without perpetual growth. Scarcity and economic growth are fundamental tenets in virtually every mainstream economic textbook. Yet in these same textbooks, the contradiction between these two tenets is universally ignored. Mainstream economists, it would seem, are full-fledged members of "The New Flat Earth Society."

THE GROWTH IMPERATIVE AND THE DEPLETION OF NON-RENEWABLE RESOURCES

Non-renewable fossil fuels such as oil, coal, and natural gas are the most widely used energy resources in the world. Fossil fuel use has become deeply integrated into virtually every aspect of economic production and distribution. Fossil fuels constitute the lifeblood of industrialization and are the main reason that economies have been able to grow and expand exponentially for the last two centuries. The commercial use of these fuels is central to the capitalist commodity-producing machine as 80 percent of the energy used in the processes of production and distribution of goods and services comes from oil, natural gas, and coal.[96] Natural gas and coal are widely used to power turbines in electricity-generating plants. Petroleum is a primary raw ingredient for the production of an entire generation of plastics, cosmetics, fertilizers, pesticides, herbicides, and paving, and roofing materials, as well as fuel for heating, electricity generation, and transportation.

There is a finite quantity of fossil fuels contained in the earth's crust, yet the growth imperative requires that consumption of these fuels must continuously increase as if the supplies were limitless. Resource exploration technology has proven effective in discovering pockets of oil and gas that were previously considered nonexistent. This technology has served so well that all significant oil and gas fields that exist on the planet have now been discovered. Every possible place on the planet that can be explored has been explored and tested. All the bigger fields have been discovered and are currently drilled, or soon will be drilled, and what remains are smaller fields with minimal potential to change the world's resource supply. With finite fuel resources and exponential growth in consumption of these fuels, the logical conclusion is clear: depletion.

Here "depletion" means reaching a threshold where it is no longer feasible to extract fuel resources. It will be impossible for us to deplete all non-renewable fossil fuels in an absolute sense. Quantities of oil and natural gas exist throughout the planet, but much of it is dispersed in such a way that it would take more energy to extract or pump it to the surface than what would be gained. The central question regarding the availability of these resources is not whether or not they will be depleted, or even when the depletion will occur. Depletion is inevitable. A more important question is, "How do we best prepare ourselves and our future generations for this inevitability?" And perhaps an even more pressing question is, "How do we prepare ourselves for the inevitable depletion of *oil*?"

OIL

Oil, or petroleum, is a liquid substance containing high concentrations of energy from the sun that was long ago absorbed by oceanic plants and animals. Theoretically, oil is a renewable resource, as it is continually being produced by nature. But the biological processes and geological conditions necessary to produce oil are so extremely slow and unique that, in a practical sense, oil is a non-renewable and finite resource.

Ocean-dwelling organisms absorb solar energy while they are living. When they die, their remains sink to the ocean floor and small amounts of solar energy contained in the organic matter become trapped in layers of sediment. For millions of years bits of solar energy were trapped and compressed in this way, but only a tiny fraction of this energy ends up as usable oil. Energy contained in organic matter must be contained in sediment at depths of between 1,500 and 7,500 feet below sea level where the pressure and temperature are just right to "cook" or process the trapped energy into liquid oil. Most of this liquid will remain locked in sediment unless it can escape through porous rock and collect in pools or concentrate in sand.

Since industrial capitalism came into full force over two hundred years ago, about one-half of all oil reserves that took millions of years to generate have been depleted. Throughout most of that history, the rate with which new oil reserves were discovered and the technology used to find and extract oil has allowed the supply to stay ahead of demand. As of this writing, however, that situation has now reversed and for the first time in the history of industrialization, the demand for oil is greater than its supply. The demand for oil continues to soar with population and growth and as more and more of the world's populations are brought into the capitalist system. At the same time, oil production is peaking. Every oil-producing country in the world has either reached its peak production capacity, or will peak during the next decade, and an irreversible decline will begin thereafter. Though it took two hundred years to deplete the first half of oil reserves, at the current rate of consumption growth, it will take only a few decades to deplete the other half.

Geologists forecast that by 2040 U.S. oil production will fall by 90 percent from its production peak, which occurred in the early 1970s.[97] Geologists have also reported that Mexico's oil production peaked in 2001, and will drop by 92 percent by 2040; Venezuela's oil production is peaking now and is projected to decline by 46 percent by 2040; and Colombia will peak in 2009 and will fall by 62 percent. In the great oil-rich region of the Middle East, Iran's oil production peaked in 1974, and is projected to decline by 62 percent by 2040; Iraq will peak in 2010 and will fall by 45 percent; and Saudi Arabia will peak in 2011 and will fall by 48 percent; and so on. The conclusion is that world oil production is peaking in 2006, and the total amount of oil production will decline by at least 63 percent by 2040. Yet, along with exponential economic growth, consumption grows exponentially thereby hastening the rate of depletion.

There is some disagreement among geologists about the projections of oil production and the rate of decline, but there is no disagreement on this fact: legitimate geological research concludes that oil production will peak within our lifetimes and oil reserves will be seriously depleted within the lifetimes of our children and grandchildren. It is impossible to say with certainty when the world will deplete its oil reserves, or precisely how much will be around by the mid–twenty-first century, but we can say with certainty that it will become increasingly scarce and increasingly expensive. This is trouble for the capitalist machine that has been fueled by cheap oil for over a century. It is also trouble for those without the money to pay for it.

As global oil production passes through peak production, each new barrel of oil will cost more to extract than the last. As the availability of oil becomes scarcer, additional extraction will come from fields that contain lower concentrations, which means that the amount of energy expended to recover oil in these fields will continue to rise, as will the costs. So with receding oil production, economies will move closer to a threshold in which oil production will become so inefficient that it will cost more to extract a barrel of oil than what a barrel of oil is worth. This threshold is expected to be reached sometime in the next fifty to eighty years.[98] Once that threshold is reached, petroleum will no more be a viable source of energy than whale oil—a major fuel in the nineteenth century.

As oil becomes scarcer and sold at higher prices, it will become more profitable to extract it from concentrations in tar sands and shale. Unlike crude oil which can be relatively easily pumped out of the ground, extracting oil from tar sands requires strip mining mass quantities of tar sand deposits for small amounts of bitumen—a kind of tar that is "cooked" to produce crude oil. Processing bitumen into crude uses about three times the amount of water than conventional pumping methods. Moreover, the water must be heated with natural gas. Strip mining tar sands and processing them into crude oil requires that the land literally be turned inside out, as tons of sand is flushed out with warm water. Once the oil has been extracted, massive quantities of sand and shale tailings or remnants will be left behind as ruins. To restore these mined areas to grassland or forest land would drive the costs far above cost-effectiveness for commercial use. Thus, the only economical way to produce oil from tar sands and shale would be to leave behind large-scale environmental destruction. Processing tar sands is an expensive and highly destructive process, but it will become more profitable as oil prices soar. This also means that if our economy stays on its current course, tar sand processing will grow proportionally to declining oil supplies in general.

The oil shortages that occurred in the 1970s raised concerns about the future availability of oil, and people began asking questions about how long cheap oil will last. Since that time, however, instead of developing viable alternative systems of production, transportation, or moving toward conservation, the U.S. economy shifted oil guzzling into high gear.

Americans consume about 25 percent of the world's oil but constitute about 5 percent of the world's population.[99] After a very brief effort at oil conservation in the 1970s, consumption surged to higher levels each year as Americans heated larger and larger homes and drove larger and larger vehicles, particularly SUVs. The popular gas-guzzling sports utility vehicles proved to be too profitable for the auto industry to resist. Part of their profitability stems from the fact that they are bigger and more valuable, and more value accounts for more capitalist profit. Throughout the decades since the early 1980s, the profitable SUVs and minivans were heavily marketed to the American consumer.

Not only are people driving larger vehicles they are also traveling greater distances. The amount of miles Americans are traveling in their cars and trucks is growing faster than the rate of population growth. Oil prices fell significantly in the mid-1980s and U.S. oil consumption increased by 25 percent, of which about 54 percent was imported oil. At the same time, domestic oil production has continued to decline since the early 1970s. Since 1988, Americans have burned over nine trillion barrels of oil, and consumption is expected to continue to climb over the next twenty years.[100]

As the problem of oil scarcity has now raised its profile with high oil and gas prices, many politicians and critics are looking for a culprit. Some are pointing their fingers at misguided government oil policies. Others blame actions taken by the auto industry for forcing people out of efficient public transportation systems and into cars, subsidizing freeway construction, and sidestepping fuel efficiency standards set by government legislation. It needs to be clarified, however, that the actions taken by the auto industry have always followed the same guiding principle of profit maximization as any other capitalist enterprise. When General Motors and a group of tire manufacturers bought out the streetcar companies in California in the 1930s in order to force people into cars, they were doing what their shareholders expected—maximizing profits. So was Ford when it designed and manufactured the Ford Explorer—the most profitable motor vehicle in auto industry history. For decades, Ford and GM created new industries, jobs, and wealth for the middle class, and throughout most of those years, no fingers of blame were pointed. Nor were people blaming the auto industry as it made it possible for people to move to the suburbs away from polluted cities to enjoy a more comfortable lifestyle, or when the profits of these companies allowed their stock prices to soar and thereby fattened the portfolios of retirement and mutual funds.

The problems of oil scarcity and over-consumption do not have a single culprit—they are systemic. The capitalist machine needs to grow, and it found a vehicle for this growth, as it were, in the auto industry. It makes no more sense to blame the auto industry or the oil companies for excessive oil consumption in the U.S. than it would to blame the factory workers who built the cars and trucks, or the construction workers who built the freeways, highways, and bridges throughout the country. Every sector of the economy has played a role: consumers who bought SUVs and minivans, workers in the multitude of industries related to car and truck manufacturing, union representatives, government officials, business managers, and Wall Street investors. Americans will be unable to find a true, viable solution to the problem of oil depletion until they recognize the fact that the problem is systemic—the problem is rooted in the growth imperative of the economic system itself.

NATURAL GAS AND COAL

As oil reserves are depleted, the economy will turn to other fuel sources to power growth. Natural gas and coal are the most likely sources as they are still relatively abundant and inexpensive. According to geological estimates, at the current rate of consumption the life expectancy of natural gas is somewhere between 160 and 310 years.[101] However, if natural gas were put in place of oil to keep the economic machines running, then the rate of growth of fuel consumption would have to stay consistent at the current rate, which is about 3.5 percent per year. If a 3.5 percent annual increase in natural gas consumption is sustained, the amount consumed will double every twenty years and the lifespan would be cut to about sixty years.

Natural gas, or methane, is a less-than-perfect substitute for oil because in its natural state it is a vapor not a liquid. Vapors are more difficult to store and transport because they have to be liquefied and transported in pressurized tanks, which is a much more expensive process compared to storing and transporting oil. Power plants and distribution infrastructure would have to be moved closer to natural gas source sites, which would also create added expense and logistical barriers. At best, energy analysts such as Paul Roberts, author of *The End of Oil: A Perilous World*, see natural gas as a temporary "bridge" energy resource as the U.S. transitions away from a fossil fuel-based economy.[102]

Coal is the most abundant of all fossil fuels and its effluents are also the most toxic. At the current rate of consumption, coal supplies could last for several hundred years.[103] However, as oil and natural gas supplies are depleted and if the growth imperative remains, then the lifespan of coal will be truncated. A more immediate concern with heightened coal consumption is pollution. Coal-burning plants are used extensively in the U.S. and around the world for generating electricity. Each plant spews effluents of smoke soot, organic compounds, carbon dioxide, and sulfur and nitrogen oxides. Sulfur and nitrogen oxides are extremely hazardous air pollutants that, when combined with atmospheric oxygen and water vapor, transform into highly toxic acid rain. When acid rain falls to the earth it collects in lakes and ponds, killing fish, plants, and other forms of life. "Scrubbing" technology has been developed to reduce emissions of acid rain from coal plants, but these gases cannot be eliminated completely. If coal use increases as a replacement fuel for oil, then inevitably so will acid rain. A long-term concern with coal burning is the emission of carbon dioxide, the principal "greenhouse" gas that scientists have concluded to be a principal cause of global warming.

THE GROWTH IMPERATIVE AND GLOBAL WARMING

One of the most important features of the earth's atmosphere is that it is kept warmer than it would otherwise be allowed given its distance from the sun. As heat radiated from the sun enters the earth's atmosphere, some of it is absorbed by the planet and some of it is reflected back into the atmosphere in the form of infrared radiation. As carbon dioxide and other greenhouse gasses accumulate in the atmosphere, heat energy that would otherwise radiate back out into space is trapped and the ambient temperature of the planet rises—global warming. The Intergovernmental Panel on Climate Change (IPCC)—a body of hundreds of scientists brought together by the United Nations, as well as the World Meteorological Association and the National Academy of Sciences—has concluded from their analysis of data on carbon dioxide emissions and the historic temperature changes that the earth's temperature is warming, and the primary cause is the accumulation of atmospheric carbon dioxide and other greenhouse gases.

As shown in Figure 2, carbon dioxide emissions have been growing exponentially for the last two hundred years. This last two hundred years also precisely coincides with the exponential growth in real U. S. Gross Domestic Product based on industrialization and the extensive use of fossil fuels. Throughout most of the period between 1800 and 2000, there has been a

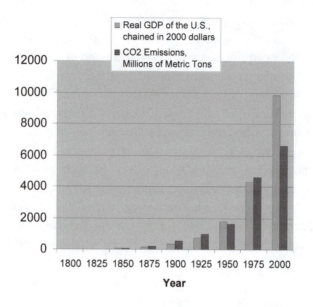

Figure 2

Source: U.S. Bureau of Economic Analysis, www.bea.gov/bea/dn/gdllev.xls;
Economic History Services, Goddard Institute for Space Studies

slow but steady climb in global temperatures. As shown in Figure 3, the largest increase occurs in the last fifty years during which both national output and carbon dioxide emissions have recorded gigantic increases.

In their most recent report titled, "Climate Change 2007: The Physical Science Basis," IPCC scientists conclude that the planet is getting warmer and the cause is very likely to be an increased amount of greenhouse gasses emitted by human activity. The report specifies that the planet will get progressively warmer by 3.2 to 7.1 degrees Fahrenheit over the next hundred years. Although the evidence of global warming and its causes are conclusive, it is still uncertain what exactly the consequences of global warming will be, the severity of those consequences, or when they will occur.

The IPCC report outlines a possible sequence of events such as rising seawater levels by anywhere between 7 and 23 inches and flooding of coastal regions including many highly populated urban areas, changing weather patterns, warmer ocean temperatures, arctic conditions developing in some temperate climates, drying trends, falling crop yields, and drought. The report

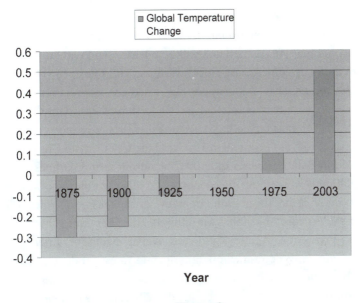

Figure 3

Source: Oak Ridge National Laboratory, NASA Goddard Institute for Space Studies

added that human-made emissions of greenhouse gases is already identified as the cause of intense heat waves, hurricanes, and tropical storms.[104]

Melting of polar ice caps is at the center of the global warming problem. As the ice continues to melt, several inches of additional fresh water will continue flooding into, and disrupting, the Gulf Stream which carries warm air northward from the tropics. The result will most certainly be a sharp cooling trend in Western Europe and Eastern North America causing those temperate climates to change into arctic climates similar to present-day Alaska or Siberia. Changing climate conditions could also create deserts within the interiors of large landmasses. The Pentagon has raised concerns that these changes, combined with depleting fuel sources, will result in food shortages and food shortages could easily develop into national security problems. Melting ice caps will also raise sea levels, which threaten to submerge coastal urban areas causing immeasurable property damage and displacing hundreds of millions of people.

Warming seawater and melting frozen tundra, or permafrost, will release methane that has been trapped in ice for thousands of years. Methane is also a major contributor to global warming. Methane release acts as a kind of global warming supercharger because it does not come from burning fossil fuels; it is simply released into the atmosphere as the planet gets warmer. This sets in place an unstoppable vicious circle—as the planet gets warmer, more permafrost will melt, more methane will be released, and with an increased amount of methane comes more global warming, and so on.

Although the Defense Department has raised concerns based on IPCC reports, the U.S. Government, under the leadership of President George W. Bush, chose not to participate in international efforts to reduce greenhouse gases such as the Kyoto Protocol in 1997 and the UN Climate Change Conference held in Bali, Indonesia in 2007. The administration argues instead, "[that] such steps will cripple the economy." In other words, the official government position is that the growth imperative of capitalism overrides serious natural disasters caused by global warming. Political appointees at the Environmental Protection Agency and the Departments of Interior and Agriculture are tied to powerful oil, mining, and forest products industries, and have been methodically removing information or concerns about global warming from their reports.[105] Moreover, as political favors to their corporate supporters, these agencies are overturning regulations and relaxing enforcement actions directed at reducing air pollution. Yet, as callous as this may seem, government officials and industry leaders are doing precisely what they ought to do in a capitalist system: ensuring a steady flow of returns to investors.

Efforts are being made to reform the capitalist system to bring about reductions in greenhouse gas emissions. The most commonly suggested proposal from both business leaders and environmental groups is to enact mandatory reductions in carbon emissions using a combination of taxes, markets, and investment incentives. In these proposals, the core institutions of capitalism should remain intact, but should be modified to make the system more environmentally friendly. One suggestion is to levy a tax on fossil fuel consumption and use the revenue generated from the tax to subsidize investments in alternative energy research and development. Such a policy promises to achieve two goals: a forced reduction in burning fossil fuels by making it more expensive and simultaneously developing more energy-efficient alternatives.

The logic of these proposals is sound and undoubtedly would achieve some level of success, yet the root problem of the growth imperative remains unchanged. Up to now, energy-efficient technology has not curbed growth in energy consumption. Motor vehicles, for example, have been made more fuel-efficient, but fuel consumption has increased as growth in the auto industry has resulted in more cars, larger vehicles such as SUVs and minivans, and people are driving more miles than ever before. Oil production and distribution technology has become more efficient as well, and the result has been growth in output, decreasing production costs, and growth in consumption. As long as capitalism remains as the dominant system, it will continue to find ways to grow and growth will inevitably give rise to more greenhouse gas emissions.

Another problem lies with the regressive nature of the fossil fuel tax. Any consumption tax is regressive, which means that it will put a disproportionately heavier burden on low-income households, individuals, or societies than on the wealthy. The result would be a situation in which those at the bottom of the income scale will be fleeced in order to deal with environmental problems caused by a capitalist system that primarily benefits those at the top. Globally a tax on fuel consumption will pose a greater hardship not only on poorer individuals, but also on entire societies that are strapped for cash. This will exacerbate a growing gap between the wealthy and poor—another innate feature of capitalism.

One variation on this proposal is to make the fossil tax "revenue neutral." This would entail a more complex tax levy/tax credit structure such that there is no net increase in the tax burden by extending tax credits by the same amount as the levy to those who reduce their consumption. Those who reduce their fuel consumption or convert to renewable energy sources would benefit from the credit and those who continue to burn fossil fuels would pay more, and there would be no net increase in tax revenues to the government.

The fossil tax/credit proposals have serious shortcomings. They are based on the assumption that consumers choose to burn fuels in certain quantities rather than by necessity. It is true that people choose to buy vehicles and homes of a certain size, and by making it more expensive to buy and operate larger vehicles and heat larger homes, people will have an incentive to downshift to smaller, more fuel-efficient sizes. But fuel consumption faces an inelasticity problem. In other words, people are not very flexible in their consumption of gasoline and other fossil fuels, particularly with transportation, as the infrastructure is built in a way that offers very few alternatives. What is more likely is that people will simply be stuck paying higher prices, and although they may cut back their consumption, the actual reduction would not be statistically significant enough to overcome problems of global warming which would require far more dramatic changes in energy consumption habits. Also, the proposals make no provisions about what people would do with the tax credits once they receive them. In the U.S., chances are people or businesses will spend the money, which means more consumption, more production, and more burning of fossil fuels.

Another proposed strategy to reduce greenhouse gases is a carbon trading system. This is a system designed to use a global marketplace to cut carbon emissions by a specified amount. Under the carbon trading system, each business or government is given a certain allowable, but reduced, quantity of carbon emissions. Those who voluntarily adopt better methods and technology, and thereby fall below the allowable amount of emissions can sell their carbon surplus on the open market as an emission credit. The buyers of these credits would be businesses or governments that find it too costly to reach their mandated targets and have to pay for their excess pollution. The results are predicted to financially reward the carbon good-doers at the expense of the carbon bad-doers. The good-doers can further invest and gain more tradable credits and become stronger competitors. The bad-doers will find that their higher costs will make it increasingly difficult to compete in the marketplace, and if they have to continue to pay for their carbon emissions, they will eventually be forced to either clean up their plants or cease operations. Using the familiar Darwinistic logic of free markets, it is believed that the bad-doers will eventually be weeded out of the global economy. After years of attempts at using this program to make businesses greener, the results are, according to industry insiders, dubious.[106]

The carbon trading system has been implemented at local levels and up to now has failed to reduce overall carbon emissions. The main problem with this system is that most of the major polluting industries do not operate in competitive market environments and are not facing such pressures to survive. Moreover, most of these industries are also very profitable and the businesses have deep pockets from which to pay for a seemingly endless quantity of carbon credits. There has been no indication that businesses will voluntarily reduce carbon emissions as long as it is more profitable for them to buy the credits and continue polluting.

The most obvious problem with these tax/credit/market proposals is that they do not address the core problem of the growth imperative of capitalism. According to *Business Week*, the use of energy credits is mere "window dressing" to make companies look greener and therefore improve their standing with the public.[107] Any policy that does not specifically address this root problem is doomed to fail to achieve its goals in the long run. It takes a long stretch of imagination to envision that capitalist institutions of for-profit enterprises and markets, which have been a major driving force behind the problem of excess fossil fuel consumption in the first place, will suddenly be a central part of the solution. Using capitalist institutions to solve problems created by capitalist institutions is proving to be as futile as training a lion to become a vegetarian—they are simply not programmed to work that way.

Tax/credit/market reform proposals at best will result in small and temporary reductions in carbon emissions and lack resonance as lasting earth-friendly solutions. Such a system is as dubious as trying to make slavery more human-friendly by taxing slave owners who mistreat their slaves and giving credits to those who do not. By their very institutional natures, the growth imperative of capitalist economies prevents them from being earth-friendly just as the fundamental violation of human rights inherent in slavery prevents slave systems from being humanitarian.

It is a scientific reality that the supplies of oil and natural gas are being depleted. It is also a scientific reality that the planet is warming and climates are changing. Yet the growth imperative of capitalism continues unabated and largely unquestioned, and the hungry eyes of growth are turning once again to nuclear energy as an alternative to fossil fuels.

THE GROWTH IMPERATIVE AND A PLUTONIUM ECONOMY

Perhaps equally as daunting as global warming is the prospect of powering the capitalist machine with nuclear energy. The process of converting nuclear energy into a productive resource entails processing uranium fuel rods in fission reactions that result in radioactive waste as a by-product. One such waste is plutonium, the most deadly and toxic substance currently in existence, and once it is released it will remain deadly for at least half a million years. Plutonium is so lethal that in one estimate a pound, if distributed equally, could cause cancer in every person on the planet.[108] Every kilowatt of electricity generated in a nuclear power plant produces some measure of radioactive waste that will have to be safely isolated from its environment into perpetuity. If not safely stored, the result will be catastrophic environmental and public health disasters. Given the complex safety measures required to operate a nuclear reactor and to store radioactive waste safely for all time, nuclear power plants are enormously expensive to build and maintain. Originally sold to the public as safe and inexpensive, nuclear energy technology is neither.

In order to truly estimate the cost of producing electricity with nuclear power, economists would have to calculate the present value of the costs of storing every ounce of radioactive waste for the next 500,000 years. The present value of these future costs would be staggering. Even an extraordinarily small number of, say, $.03 each day to store one kilogram of radioactive waste which would produce about 50,000 kwh of electricity, stretched over a half million years would total over $5 million dollars per kilogram. This would amount to about $100/kwh in storage costs alone, which compared to $.05 to $.10/kwh for conventional and renewable energy technology, makes nuclear energy extremely expensive. The pressure to cut costs would be enormous and if safety measures are compromised, the result would likely be horrific cost to life and property. Moreover, the risks of nuclear accidents such as that which occurred at Chernobyl, Ukraine would increase proportionally with any increase in the use of nuclear power.

In April 1986, the nuclear power plant located in Chernobyl, Ukraine exploded after an accidental meltdown and burned uncontrollably for ten days.[109] The Chernobyl plant provided only about 3 percent of all the electricity for Ukraine, yet the accident contaminated an area of 100,000 square miles with highly toxic radioactive fallout. At least thirty people at the plant site were killed instantly, and several thousand people subsequently died due to exposure to the radioactive fallout from the explosion. After the explosion, the Chernobyl region experienced a sudden increase in thyroid cancer and other illnesses among children who lived in the affected areas. Millions of people were displaced and as they were forced to relocate with no employment prospects waiting for them at their new locations, they quickly fell into poverty.

Chernobyl was the worst on record thus far, but was not the only such accident. A leakage of radioactive waste occurred in 1979 at the Three-Mile Island nuclear plant near Harrisburg, Pennsylvania. Due to industry coverup, the amount of radioactive waste released into the atmosphere remains unknown.[110] Fires broke out at a nuclear plant in Tokai, Japan in 1997 and plutonium remnants from the fires released into the atmosphere were detected as far as twenty-three miles from the site.[111] A nuclear power plant in Argentina that had been plagued with safety problems since the 1980s leaked radioactive waste into the local water supply of an area spanning eighty square miles. Similar problems have affected nuclear plants in Spain, France, Canada, and nearly every country that uses nuclear power. The central problem with nuclear power is that no truly safe method for the permanent storage and isolation of radioactive waste has been found, and as the amount of waste accumulates, the dangers to human and other life will accumulate proportionally. According to physicist Fritjof Capra:

Nuclear power also creates other problems and hazards. They include the unsolved problem of disassembling, or "decommissioning" nuclear reactors at the end of their useful lives; the development of "fast breeder reactors," which use plutonium as a fuel and are far more dangerous than ordinary commercial reactors; the threat of nuclear terrorism and the ensuing loss of basic civil liberties in a totalitarian "plutonium economy"; and the disastrous economic consequences of the use of nuclear power as a capital-and-technology intensive, highly centralized source of energy. The total impact of the unprecedented threats of nuclear technology should make it abundantly clear to anyone that it is unsafe, uneconomical, irresponsible, and immoral . . .[112]

Growth in economic production is inseparable from the throughput process of converting resources into waste. If nuclear power were to be harnessed as the principal energy source for the capitalist growth machine, the waste would be the most toxic substance in the planet. The toxicity of plutonium does not die with the organisms it kills. Seepage of radioactive waste into groundwater or into the food chain could circulate for hundreds of millennia, repeatedly causing cancer and other diseases in humans and virtually all living organisms.

THE GROWTH IMPERATIVE AND THE OVERUSE OF RENEWABLE RESOURCES

To the extent that oxygen, trees, plants, fish, and topsoil are continually reproduced in nature they are considered "renewable." Though they are considered renewable, they are not without limits. The limit on renewable resources is time. These resources can only be considered renewable if they are used at a rate such that they can be naturally replenished and sustained. However, with endless economic growth, the pace of renewal is slow compared to the rate with which they are being used or destroyed. In every category, renewable resources are being exploited to extinction. Here we will explore the impact growth is having on just a few of the more critical resources—topsoil, water, and forest vegetation.

TOPSOIL

Topsoil is a renewable resource in the sense that it has the capacity to regenerate itself. Like oil and other resources, however, it is being used up and destroyed at a rate faster than it can be restored. As capitalism demands more growth, this growth is fed by the throughput process of transforming usable land into unusable waste. Continuous and accelerated economic production involves destructive agricultural practices—overgrazing, land and water pollution, deforestation, and strip mining—all of which accelerate topsoil ruination.

According to one estimate, over the last millennium humans have transformed about 10 billion acres of productive farmland into unproductive wasteland and about 11 percent of the planet's topsoil surface has suffered from moderate to extreme soil degradation in the last fifty years.[113] Since the end of World War II, about 3 billion acres (1.2 billion hectares) of usable land has either been significantly degraded or destroyed.[114] The rate of topsoil ruination has accelerated from 25 million tons per year in the eighteenth century, to 300 million tons in the nineteenth and twentieth centuries, and to 760 million tons in the past fifty years.[115] In other words, two hundred years of exponential economic growth has come at the cost of two hundred years of exponential and irreversible increases in wasteland.

The economic imperatives to grow, sustain higher profits, and expand market share have also driven farmers into agricultural practices that are not sustainable. The necessity to grow overrides attempts to conserve the integrity or fertility of soil and capitalist agriculture strives to use whatever combination of land, water, and chemicals required to yield maximum output on a short-term basis.

Farmers generally do not have much control over the prices of the crops they produce for the market. Prices are set in global commodities markets and seem to be chronically low. Farmers must therefore get the maximum yield from their land during the growing seasons in order to maximize revenues and profits. Each season farmers face increasing pressure to borrow funds in order to purchase the latest version of patented seeds, chemicals, fuel, and water to avoid losing their places in the market. To pay back their loans and make their interest payments, they must get the highest yield possible on a short-run basis. Yet the following season, the soil worsens requiring more water and chemicals and so on in a downward spiral of topsoil degradation. Many farmers have not survived this process financially, resulting in steadily rising bankruptcies, particularly among the smaller family farms. Compared to large corporate farms, small farms must pay higher interest rates on their credit and have the least purchasing power to pay for increasingly expensive chemicals and seeds. To increase their profitability, farmers are allowing for shorter and shorter fallow periods in which land is allowed to rest and regenerate from cultivation.

Historically, agricultural technology has succeeded in multiplying the output per acre. Since the beginning of the application of the internal combustion motor to agriculture and the use of tractors, combines, and other heavy machinery, agricultural output and productivity have increased dramatically. The extensive use of petrochemical fertilizers and pesticides began in agriculture about fifty years ago and was heralded as a "green revolution" as it contributed to significant increases in productivity and output. Yet the destruction caused by this technology remains largely hidden. Topsoil is being hardened from the compaction caused by the heavy machinery. Hardening decreases the rate of water absorption and causes problems of water runoff and inadequate drainage and increases the occurrence of erosion. In Nebraska, for example, wind erosion removes about 186 tons of soil per acre every year, a rate far above natural rates of soil erosion.[116] As we shall see in the next section, fresh water is another resource that is being depleted. As the water tables fall, and as farmers use petroleum-based chemical pesticides and herbicides, the soil is becoming dryer and more susceptible to wind erosion.

FRESH WATER

Fresh water is considered renewable as it is continuously restored by the natural hydrologic cycle of evaporation, condensation, and precipitation—all of which are driven by energy from the sun. If fresh water is used at a rate equal to the rate it is restored by the hydrologic cycle, water supplies could be sustainable into perpetuity. Unfortunately, this is far from the case as fresh water is being consumed or polluted much more quickly than it can be restored. Water is the most basic and necessary resource for sustaining life on the planet, but is being used up as if its supplies were limitless, and like topsoil fresh water is used as a sink into which wastes are dumped.

Approximately 70 percent of the planet's fresh water supply, or "wet gold," is used in agriculture for irrigation of crops.[117] The rate of water consumption is not equally distributed around the planet. The fastest rates of consumption are in predominantly growth-oriented capitalist economies in Western Europe, North America, and Japan where per capita water consumption ranges between 80 and 150 gallons per day. In most of the rest of the world, people consume about 2 to 5 gallons per day.[118]

Throughout most of human history, water was directed from rivers, stored in small dams, and channeled into farmland by canals. This changed after the development of industrial capitalism and water stored naturally underground began to be pumped to the surface. By sinking wells deep into the ground, high quality fresh water that seeped underground into porous soil and sand and collected in pools, is raised above ground with diesel or electric pumps and used for human consumption. At upper levels, ground water has higher saturation rates and millions of shallow wells sunk throughout the world have tapped into virtually all available supplies. As the demand has increased, and with the development of pumping and drilling technology, deeper wells were sunk providing access to larger underground reservoirs or aquifers that have formed naturally in much deeper geological basins known as aquifers. Like oil drilling and extraction, groundwater stored in aquifers is being pumped out at a rate faster than it can be replenished.

The United States is fortunate compared to many places in the world as it is blessed with much rainfall. About 25 percent of the water used in the United States comes from groundwater pumping—about 28 trillion gallons a year—and the rest comes from surface water from precipitation.[119] Nonetheless, all of the major aquifers in the United States are being depleted. In the arid southwestern states, the groundwater levels, water tables, have dropped as much as 110 feet in ten years.[120] As water tables drop, previously productive wells go dry and farmers must either dig deeper wells and draw down water tables even further or drill new wells where the process of depletion starts anew. In Arizona's Santa Cruz basin water tables are being depleted by a half million acre-feet (an acre-foot equals about 326,000 gallons) every year. California's San Joaquin Valley, a rich agricultural region, depletes its groundwater supplies by 1.5 million acre-feet annually.[121] Also, falling water tables cause spring-fed rivers, lakes, and wetlands on the surface to dry up. This, in turn, causes ground surfaces to sink, creating lifeless sand boxes.

The most dramatic instance of groundwater depletion is the Ogallala aquifer which spans several states from west of the Mississippi River to the Rocky Mountains, and from South Dakota to Texas. This huge 225,000 square mile aquifer was created millions of years ago. Snow run-off from the Rocky Mountains has not fed into the Ogallala in over one thousand years, and since then the aquifer has been largely cut off from any significant replenishing source. Most of the water in the Ogallala is considered "fossil water" as it melted ice that dates back to the last ice age. For decades, over 170,000 wells scattered throughout the Ogallala region have been pumping out millions of gallons every year. The rate of pumping increased by 300 percent between 1950 and 1980 and this rapid increase is, in part due to the fact that the water is relatively accessible to the surface—about 300 feet on average.[122] From the time that pumping from the Ogallala began in the 1930s to about 1950, the levels drawn out remained fairly constant. Between 1950 and 1985, the Ogallala water table dropped by about 160 feet. Although the rate of depletion has slowed down in recent years, the water table continues to fall. As aquifers like the Ogallala are stocked mainly with fossil water, once they are pumped dry they will become extinct and populations that have depended on them will either have to make due with rain water, suffer health problems, or migrate.

According to a 1997 United Nations report titled, "Comprehensive Assessment of the Freshwater Resources of the World," the following conclusions were drawn:

> About one-third of the world's population lives in countries that are experiencing moderate to high water stress partly resulting from increasing demands from a growing population and human activities. By 2025 as much as 2/3 of the world population would be under stress conditions. Water shortages and pollution are causing widespread public health problems, limiting economic and agricultural development, and harming a wide range of ecosystems. They may put global food supplies in jeopardy and lead to economic stagnation in many areas of the world.[123]

The report stresses that not only is water being used up, it is also being spoiled with contamination, rendering it useless for human consumption. Heavy use of petrochemical pesticides and fertilizers not only kill soil-dwelling insects and microbes and causes sterilization of the soil, it also contaminates groundwater. In the 1980s, concern about groundwater contamination led to a federal government investigation and report titled, "Protecting the Nation's Groundwater from Contamination." This report found that some 245 toxic substances were contaminating groundwater and about a fourth of those came directly from compounds used in herbicides and pesticides.[124] About 13,000 square miles in Mississippi contain a body of dead water in which chemical runoff and soil erosion has killed virtually all aquatic life.[125]

According to UN projections, at current levels of population growth and per capita demand growth, a severe water shortage will occur before the end of the twenty-first century.[126] As that time approaches, water, like oil, will become steadily more scarce and expensive. The economic burden of expensive water will affect poorer countries most severely. Water shortages will reduce food production, causing famine in addition to an increase in diseases associated with contaminated drinking water.

Scarcity of water and other resources is closely linked with the growing inequality of living standards around the world. We will explore this problem in more detail in the next chapter.

FORESTS

Like topsoil and fresh water, forests are renewable resources in the sense that they can self-regenerate through natural processes. Also like topsoil and water, forests are being depleted. The economy's need of profit-making and accumulation causes forestry to be practiced in ways that are highly destructive and unsustainable. The most profitable way to harvest lumber and wood fiber is to extract it in a manner similar to strip mining—clear-cutting—in which huge swaths of forest land are razed to the ground. Clear-cut logging permanently drives forests to extinction by destroying the fragile and complex ecological systems on which forests depend for their existence. Forests that remain in their original pristine state, untouched by logging, are known as "old growth" forests, and only a very small percentage of them have survived.

Some of the world's most magnificent old growth forests are located in the Pacific Northwest. The earliest records of logging in the United States' Pacific Northwest forest date back to around 1875 in what is now the Willamette National Forest. Since that time about 90 percent of the old growth forests in the region has been logged; only a very small fraction remain in preserves and parks.[127] These old growth forests are not merely stands of trees but rather are complex systems composed of living trees and plants, fungi, bacteria, decomposing matter and detritus, animals, and a delicate balance of shade and sunlight. If any one of these elements is significantly disrupted, the forests are irreversibly transformed. Physicist Vandana Shiva explains a similar complex relationship in the food chain,

> It is precisely because these essential links in the food chain have been ignored and destroyed by 'developed and 'scientific' agriculture that the croplands of the world are rapidly being destroyed. . . . The little earthworm working invisibly in the soil is actually the tractor and fertilizer factory and dam combined.[128]

Most old growth forests have been logged, transformed into tree farms, and managed by the profit-driven wood products industry. Tree farms are not forests as they are planted crops to be harvested like fields of corn or wheat. Modern agriculture creates huge land areas planted with a single species of crop, or monocultures, that requires high doses of chemical fertilizers and pesticides. Chemicals are used to generate high yields and fight against locusts and other biological imbalances associated with monocultures. The same is true of modern forestry. Clear-cut logging results in loss of soil fertility and erosion, and in response the forest products industry turns to chemicals to boost yields and industry profits.

The destruction caused by clear-cut deforestation extends far beyond damage to the land. Biological diversity and natural biological processes that have sustained forests for thousands of years are also being permanently destroyed. Erosion associated with logging causes excessive siltation of streams and riverbeds in which fish attempt to fertilize and hatch their eggs. The fish population thus declines in areas affected by clear-cuts. Moreover, clear-cuts cause floods and drought as rainwater is no longer absorbed and controlled by tree roots. Destruction of forests means the destruction of the habitats for over half the species of plants and animals that live on the planet.[129]

Forests absorb carbon dioxide from the atmosphere which, as we have seen, is one of the primary causes of global warming. Deforestation destroys the planet's natural ability to moderate climate, and rather than absorbing carbon dioxide it releases more into the atmosphere. Deforestation also depletes soil nitrogen, an essential element for all forms of plant life.

To replace the lost nitrogen foresters began using expensive nitrogen fertilizers. Most nitrogen fertilizers are chemicals derived from oil. Once the practice of chemical nitrogen fertilization has been adopted, the natural process of nitrogen-fixing in plants is suppressed. Forest management will be forever dependent on chemicals made from increasingly scarce and expensive petroleum. The only alternative to this permanent chemical dependency would be to abandon the logged areas as wasteland that will take generations to bring back to life.[130] According to forest ecologist Elliot Norse:

> Even this cursory nitrogen budget suggests that intensive timber management is not renewable resource management, the stated aim of most kinds of commercial forestry. It is not even farming. It is mining.[131]

Although mining forests for wood fiber is not sustainable, it is very profitable. Capitalism does not reward prudent, forward thinking regarding resource conservation. Its goal is profit-maximization, and clear-cut logging is the most direct way to achieve this goal. A single high-quality, old growth conifer in the Pacific Northwest contains as much as $10,000 worth of wood fiber. A small stand of one hundred such trees can be worth about $1 million requiring little by way of harvesting costs if it is clear-cut. Given its profitability, it would be virtually impossible to convince any profit-maximizing enterprise that long-term sustainability is a better use of forest resources. This is particularly true of large, publicly traded corporations that have shareholders who never see, or know, or even care about the long-term, irreversible damage the company they own is doing.

The long-standing practice of depleting vital resources such as fossil fuels, topsoil, water, and forests for profit will necessarily come to an end. Either by conscious and mindful changes in our economic institutions, or by calamity, a change in our practices is inevitable. Of course, waiting for calamities to arrive before making meaningful changes will be too late.

It is uncertain how much longer the U.S. capitalist machine can remain on this path before experiencing dire environmental consequences. In his latest work, *Collapse: How Societies Choose to Fail or Succeed*, evolutionary psychologist Jared Diamond predicts that we will continue to mindlessly misuse our resources to a point where the foundation of our collective existence inevitably disintegrates. Society, according to Diamond, will undergo some form of cataclysmic event such as violent political upheaval, warfare or some other form of self-destruction. Diamond asserts that it seems easier for people to indulge in collective denial about such outcomes than face them.

As most of us go about our daily lives, we tend not to think of such extreme events as predicted by Diamond. When confronted with warnings, most are inclined to dismiss them as paranoia or pointless ruminations on distant future possibilities, or if taken at all seriously, most are likely to seek comfort in a technological solution.

THE FALLACY OF THE TECHNOLOGICAL FIX

The belief in technology pervades economic thought. It is seen as the ultimate solution to virtually every economic problem ranging from poverty to growth limits. This is true of most economists whether they are proponents of capitalism or critics. In 1848, Karl Marx and Frederick Engels wrote glowingly of the technological wonders associated with capitalism:

[The capitalist class] has created more massive and more colossal productive forces than have all preceding generations together. Subjection of nature's forces to man, machinery, application of chemistry to industry and agriculture, steam navigation, railways, electric telegraphs, clearing whole continents for cultivation . . . what earlier century had even a presentiment that such productive forces slumbered in the lap of social labor.[132]

In the twenty-first century, David Korten, author of *When Corporations Rule the World,* echoes a similar sense of technological awe and wonder:

A mere fifty years ago . . . many of the things we take for granted today as essential to a good and prosperous life were unavailable, nonexistent, or even unimagined. These include the jet airplane . . . computers, microwave ovens, electric typewriters, photocopying machines, television, clothes dryers, air conditioning, freeways . . . chemical pesticides—to name only a few.[133]

Korten is correct, as were Marx and Engels a century and a half before him, to point out the many positive aspects of technology. Technology provides hope. Not many people would advocate that we should allow our productive technology to regress back to pre-modern standards. Yet, without a critical perspective, belief in technology becomes an irrational faith that every problem we face will always have a technological fix. Like a secular religion, blind faith in technology provides comfort and reassurance that perpetual growth is possible.

Like a religion, belief in technology provides comfort to people. It allows people to believe that they can continue doing things in the same way, will never have to change their behavior, beliefs, or their institutions. Technology allows people to have confidence that the growth imperative of capitalist economies can continue uninterrupted by resource limitations. By analogy, the irrational belief in technology instills a sense of confidence in perpetual growth in a way similar to a heavy smoker who is reassured by a doctor that he can continue smoking as medical science will always provide a technological solution to any health problem. Like heavy smoking, perpetual growth has consequences, and those consequences become more severe over time. Technology can provide short-term remedies, but long-term solutions require behavioral and institutional change. Perhaps most importantly, it requires an end to the belief that perpetual growth is possible.

Perpetual growth under capitalism is inseparable from the technology that allows growth to continue. Technological development is not random, and is always fostered within a specific environment. There is very little by way of technological development that is insulated from the demands of our economy or political environment. The cotton gin, steam powered locomotives, petrochemicals, the guillotine, and nuclear warheads are all instances of technology that did not develop in a vacuum. These technological developments came about as ways to solve immediate economic and political problems. One of the biggest problems capitalism is facing is the simultaneous need for ongoing growth and the limitation of available resources to power that growth. To solve this problem, the capitalist system turns to technological fixes. Yet just as much as a technological "fix" remedies an immediate problem of scarcity, it can give rise to new and perhaps deeper problems.

For example, as mentioned above, the problem of agricultural productivity was confronted with the application of chemical technology. Yet this technological fix gave rise to a host of other and deeper problems such as environmental damage and the dependency on increasingly scarce and expensive oil. And the proposal to fix the problem of energy shortages with nuclear technology will set a framework for the most dangerous and toxic input to growth the world has ever encountered.

CONCLUSION: PROSPERITY OR POVERTY OF GROWTH

One of the greatest ironies of capitalism is that perpetual growth is heralded as the ultimate solution to the problem of poverty, yet its future is bleak with poverty caused by resource depletion and environmental destruction. Economic growth as a solution to poverty has always been popular among the affluent as it suggests that the problem can be solved by expanding wealth, not redistributing existing wealth from the rich to the poor. John F. Kennedy popularized this sentiment in his political adage "a rising tide that lifts all boats." Kennedy's message was misleading, however, for anyone who has visited the ocean knows that tides ebb and flow, and that a rising tide will eventually give way to a receding tide. When this happens, the receding water will not lift boats, but will ground them. Just as there is no such thing as a perpetually rising tide, there cannot be a perpetually growing economy.

Any serious reflection on the capitalist growth imperative will lead to the conclusion that available resources will be exploited to the point of exhaustion, and thus growth cannot be sustained. As resources are exhausted, people's ability to produce goods and services will be undermined, and prosperity will eventually turn to poverty. A mindless belief in technology as a panacea for chronic resource shortages will only hasten this inevitability.

Technology cannot change the immutable laws of nature and physics any more than it can bring a dead person back to life. Scarcity of resources that are used to sustain growth is an immutable scientific reality—as real as the fact that our planet is not flat, but rather is three-dimensional and finite. Oil and natural gas are resources that have definite limits, and once they are depleted, they will never be brought to life again. As coal, fresh water, topsoil, and other finite resources disappear or become filled with waste, they become increasingly scarce and more expensive, and the cost of finding new usable replacements will also rise. Rising scarcity and costs of resources are tightening its grip on the throat of capitalist growth and—technology notwithstanding—will eventually bring centuries of exponential growth to an end. And then where do people go? Do we wait for the calamitous scenarios of poverty as envisioned by Jared Diamond, or do we become proactive and work for institutional change while there is still time?

Technology can and does lead to good solutions, and this should not be ignored, but technology is always fostered within a specific institutional context and this should not be ignored either. If our institutions are warlike, then we will develop weapons technology. If they are oriented toward growth for growth's sake, then we will develop growth-oriented technology. But if they are oriented toward survival and sustainability, then we will develop survival and sustainability-oriented technology. Mindful institutional change, away from the capitalist growth imperative, will allow for a rising tide of new and appropriate technological developments.

10

SWEET DELIGHT AND ENDLESS NIGHT
Polarization in America

The economic boom of the 1980s and 1990s were much touted in the business press as economic "good times." Real Gross Domestic Product increased from roughly $5 trillion in 1980 to about $7 trillion in 1990, and then to over $10 trillion by 2000. The red-hot growth of the decade of the 1990s—publicized in the press as the "New Economy"—added $3 trillion dollars worth of new wealth to the U.S. economy. Yet rarely did the press report how this growth in national income was distributed among the population. Aggregate statistics like the rising stock market prices and rising GDP suggested much newly added prosperity, but masked the burdens and struggles experienced by working families, many of whom were working two jobs to pay their bills.

The boom years of the last twenty-five years lavished tremendous wealth on the upper classes, and incomes for the wealthy soared to unprecedented levels. During the same period, however, the middle class experienced little or no real (inflation-adjusted) income growth, and poverty spread like an epidemic among the poor. GDP growth has shown the greatest boom in prosperity in memory, yet income distribution has become the most polarized since the Great Depression of the 1930s, and continues its march toward more extreme levels. Once again, Kennedy's adage of the rising tide that lifts all boats proves to be misleading—the rising tide of economic growth primarily lifted the expensive yachts and luxury cruise ships for the affluent.

Yachts by themselves do not create a problem of inequality. It is when they stand aside poverty that the problem becomes manifest. Virtually every society accepts a certain amount of inequality as a fair and necessary reality. But when the gap between the rich and poor widens beyond the point of tolerance, and wealth, income, and power become extremely polarized, this tears at the social fabric. Extreme polarization causes social and political instability and becomes incompatible with widely held notions of justice and democracy. During the last two decades of so-called "prosperity," American capitalism has already crossed this point of intolerability and the implications for its democracy are profound.

Income inequality polarizes through the familiar dynamics of virtuous and vicious circles.[134] Rising levels of wealth and income for the upper-income families provides them with access to a structure of opportunity for further gain that is inaccessible to middle and low-income classes. Wealthier families have the resources to send their children to prestigious schools and universities, assuring access to the highest-paying jobs and income security. The affluent typically use their top-tier incomes to gain even more wealth as they buy income-earning property and make financial investments. The income derived from these assets can be used to acquire more assets, and so on. Wealth begets wealth in the virtuous ascent to prosperity.

Low-income families, on the other hand, are largely shut out of the structure of opportunity, and the vast majority experience little upward class mobility. Most tend to borrow and rent, and thus are paying the rent and interest income that flows to the wealthier property owners. Low-income families find it more difficult to accumulate wealth in the form of income-earning assets as ownership remains and accumulates in the hands of the wealthiest segment of American society. Low-income families stand as the most likely to be drained of resources as they spend all their income mainly to pay their bills, have higher debt burdens, and thus are far more likely to descend into a vicious circle of poverty.

Inequality is not only measured in terms of family income and wealth. It can also be seen in terms of disproportionately large concentrations of industry and market control by large corporations. Gigantic Fortune 500 corporations wield enormous power over input and output markets and smaller family-owned businesses are rapidly being squeezed out of the marketplace. Concentrations of power over industries also directly translate into concentrated political power, and moneyed interests dominate government institutions at every level. In other words, affluence not only begets more affluence and privilege, it also begets market power and political influence. Taken to its logical conclusion, rising income and wealth inequality promise to undermine the very existence of democracy.

Such income and wealth polarization is not evidence of a flaw or malfunction of American capitalism, but rather is an innate and purposeful feature of it. One of the core defining features of capitalism is the separation of ownership and work. Without this separation, capitalism could not exist as an economic system. This separation is also what inevitably leads to disproportionate concentrations of asset ownership. Another central defining feature is the market system. As we have seen in previous chapters, the market system is rarely a free and openly competitive environment, but rather is the field within which large businesses are free to seize control and monopolize entire industries.

Capitalism can provide jobs and incomes for working people and foster the development of a prosperous middle class, including small business owners. Such developments, however, are incidental and are not what the system is designed to accomplish. Capitalism has always worked to serve the economic interests of a small and wealthy investor class. As the wealthy become wealthier, this is a sign of the success of capitalism not its failure. To the extent that working people have sought to gain a larger share of the wealth, they had to do so by directly confronting the considerable power of the capitalist upper classes. After a century of such confrontation, a relatively prosperous middle class emerged with the help of union representation, government policies designed to regulate corporate power, and progressive tax/transfer redistribution policies—all of which were fought against by the wealthy members of the capitalist class.

Over the recent decades of booming growth, however, labor unions and government institutions have been under attack by businesses and are weakening. Accordingly, the historical trend that gave rise to a middle class and a more equitable pattern of income and wealth distribution is reversing. The U.S. is returning to a more pure system of capitalism redolent of the nineteenth century, and to extreme polarization.

It should be emphasized here that extreme inequality did not originate with capitalism. From the beginning of human civilization, there have always been class distinctions and conflict between the wealthy and the poor: between slave owners and slaves, landowners and peasants, and between factory owners and workers. Capitalism is simply the modern variation of this same historical theme. Since the Industrial Revolution in eighteenth-century England, capitalism has consistently worked to create splendid affluence for the upper classes who own property and grinding poverty for those who work for the owners. Poet and critic William Blake observed this in this stanza from his poem "Auguries of Innocence":

> The Harlots cry from Street to Street
> Shall weave Old Englands winding Sheet
> The Winners Shout the Losers Curse
> Dance before dead Englands Hearse
> Every Night & every Morn

Some to misery are Born
Every Morn & every Night
Some are Born to Sweet Delight
Some are Born to Sweet Delight
Some are Born to Endless Night[135]

By definition capital is property. Capitalism is an economic system that revolves around an exclusive right to property ownership, and to the profits derived from that ownership. Capitalism did not create inequality, but as long as it remains the dominant economic system, it will assure that the separation of ownership and work will continue. Along with that separation, the long-standing legacy of polarization will also continue and the gap between the wealthy and the poor will grow wider.

MEASURING ECONOMIC INEQUALITY

The most common way to measure economic inequality is to measure patterns of income distribution among classes or social groups. Income distribution analysis is typically based on segmenting the income-earning population into quintiles: the bottom (poorest) 20 percent, second 20 percent, middle 20 percent, fourth 20 percent, and typically the top quintile is divided into subgroups such as the top 10 percent, 5 percent or 1 percent of wealthiest households. This analysis clearly indicates a trend of increasing inequality in the U.S. For example, as mentioned above the real national income for the entire economy doubled from about $5 trillion to over $10 trillion between 1980 and 2004. During that twenty-four-year period the bottom 20 percent received a total of about a 9 percent increase in real income, which amounts to less than one half of 1 percent annually. The top 5 percent, however, received a 46.3 percent increase in income during that same period.[136] In addition, throughout most of that twenty-four-year period, people working for hourly wages experienced an actual decline in real income as their wage growth did not keep up with inflation.

The most commonly used measurement for income distribution patterns is the Gini Index. Sometimes referred to as the Gini Coefficient or Gini Ratio, the Gini Index is named after economist Corrado Gini who invented and published the formula in 1912. The Gini Index is a numerical index scaled between 0 and 1 where an index of 0 would signify an extreme case of "perfect equality" of income distribution and 1 is the opposite extreme of "perfect inequality." With an index of 0, or perfect equality, the incomes received by all households in the United States are exactly equal. This could only be achieved by completely leveling all household incomes regardless of skill levels, occupation, or location. Such a situation, of course, would be impossible and would likely be viewed by virtually everyone as both undesirable and unfair. With a Gini Index of 1, or perfect inequality, one household receives 100 percent of all income earned in the economy and all other households receive absolutely nothing. For obvious reasons this also would be neither possible nor desirable. The Gini Index therefore stands somewhere between 0 and 1.

The Gini Index for the U.S. has typically ranged somewhere between .40 and .50. Figure 1 shows the Gini data for the U.S. between 1913 and a forecast to 2013 based on current trends.[137] Income distribution was most polarized during the Great Depression—a period of high concentrations of wealth and widespread poverty and unemployment. The Gini Index rose slightly above .50 during the Depression's darkest years when farmers were driven into bankruptcy, unemployment plagued 25 percent of the labor force, the poor had no access to social security, unemployment compensation or other social safety nets, and unions had yet to claim the legal right to collectively bargain with their employers. High inequality meant splendid affluence for a small sector of the population as well as mass destitution, cholera,

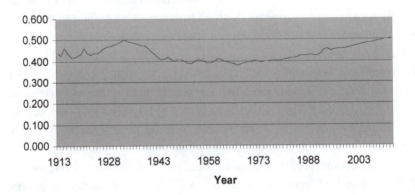

Gini Index, U.S., 1913-2013

Figure 1

Source: U.S. Census Data

typhus, child labor, and labor unrest. In other words, the U.S. economy at that time more resembled what are referred to today as "Third World" countries, decades before the term was invented.

The Gini Index fell dramatically during the immediate post-World War II years, remained stable and relatively low at about .40, but has been on a steady climb since the early 1980s. Currently the Gini Index for the U.S. is about .47 and, given the current trend, it is on track to reach the .50 mark in the next several years. At that point, the U.S. economy will more resemble a system in which one household receives all the national income than a more equitable distribution pattern.

When compared to other countries in North America, Western Europe, and Japan, the U.S. is second only to Mexico in terms of having the highest Gini Index. Table 1 shows Gini Indexes for nations that are members of the Organization for Economic Co-operation and Development (OECD), a group of about thirty countries that are often referred to as "developed" or "industrialized democracies." The U.S. Gini Index stands nearly 50 percent higher than the average for this group of OECD countries.[138]

Table 2 shows countries that all have Gini ratios over .45. Most of the countries listed here are developing countries, and though it is difficult to make comparisons with a country like the United States, what characterizes virtually every country on the list is the absence of democratic institutions. Although the United States is one of the wealthiest countries on the planet, it has an income distribution pattern that resembles those countries plagued with widespread poverty and lacking basic democratic rights for their people. Upon examination of the causes of income disparity, this fact becomes less surprising.

It is widely believed that America is the "land of opportunity," and that for those who work hard, the U.S. economy promises a place among the opulent class. Rags-to-riches stories about social mobility and opportunity in America are celebrated in the media with great fanfare. Most of these stories are fictional, however, and nonfiction versions tell a different story. According to the Luxembourg Income Study, among the members of the OECD countries, the U.S. has among the largest percentage of poor families, has the smallest percentage of middle-income families, and has the largest percentage of the wealthy.[139] The U.S. also has the distinction of having the largest percentage of low-wage workers as a percentage of overall employment. According to a report in the *Economist*, the United States also has the highest child poverty rate of twenty similar industrialized economies.[140] Moreover, of all the OECD countries, the U.S. has the lowest percentage of upward mobility for low-wage workers. In other words, the U.S. is more class-divided than every industrialized nation except Russia and Mexico and these class divisions tend to be permanent and are growing wider apart.

CAUSES OF INCOME INEQUALITY

The causes of income inequality are complex and in many ways are unique to each country. Yet virtually all countries share the political difficulty of confronting distribution problems. The task of addressing uneven patterns of income and wealth distribution is invariably fraught with political controversy and is an enormously difficult challenge.

Among mainstream economists, the root causes of income inequality in the United States remain largely unexamined or dismissed with trite contentions of laziness, poor individual choices, or a lack of industriousness. Instead of confronting the problem of inequality directly, economists tend to explain the problem away by asserting that more jobs and opportunities for earning better incomes will flow naturally from greater capitalist development, freer markets, and lower taxes. Although some economists give attention to race and gender issues, most economists view income as something that is earned from hard work and good choices. Disparity among rich and poor is therefore seen simply as a fact that some people work harder than others, or have made better choices in the process of selecting education and training goals.

The standard approach used by economists is to draw a connection between income levels and productivity. That is, some people earn more than others do because they make a greater contribution to output. In this view, the more skilled and therefore the more productive one becomes, the greater contribution one makes and therefore the more income one earns. Although there is an element of truth to this viewpoint, it fails to explain much about what causes inequality. The reality is that millions of people in the U.S., and billions of people worldwide, will spend their entire lives working tirelessly and contributing massive amounts to productivity and output, yet will never rise to join the ranks of the opulent classes. According to *Business Week*, CEOs in the U.S. manufacturing sector earned on average about 531 times the earnings of their employees on the factory floor.[141] It is hardly plausible to argue that the top corporate executives are 531 times more hard-working and industrious, or 531 times more skilled than their employees. The standard argument also fails

TABLE 1
Gini Index for Thirty OECD Member Countries

COUNTRY	GINI	COUNTRY	GINI
Australia	0.35	Luxembourg	0.31
Austria	0.31	Mexico	0.52
Belgium	0.25	Netherlands	0.33
Canada	0.32	New Zealand	0.36
Czech Republic	0.25	Norway	0.26
Denmark	0.25	Poland	0.32
Finland	0.26	Portugal	0.39
France	0.33	Slovak Republic	0.26
Germany	0.38	Spain	0.33
Greece	0.35	Sweden	0.25
Hungary	0.24	Switzerland	0.33
Ireland	0.36	Turkey	0.40
Italy	0.36	United Kingdom	0.36
Japan	0.25	**United States**	**0.47**
Korea	0.32	**Average**	**0.31**

Source: UN Human Development Report, *World Bank Development Indicators, 2003*; and U.S. Census Data

TABLE 2
Gini Index for Countries Over .45

COUNTRY	GINI	COUNTRY	GINI
Uruguay	0.45	El Salvador	0.51
Costa Rica	0.46	South Africa	0.59
Malaysia	0.49	Bolivia	0.45
Panama	0.49	Honduras	0.59
Russian Federation	0.46	Mexico	0.52
Colombia	0.57	Nicaragua	0.56
Brazil	0.61	Botswana	0.63
Venezuela	0.49	Mali	0.51
Peru	0.46	Burkina Faso	0.48
Paraguay	0.58	Niger	0.51
Philippines	0.46	Sierra Leone	0.63
Guyana	0.45	Central African Republic	0.61
Dominican Republic	0.47	Ethiopia	0.49
Namibia	0.71	Zambia	0.53
Papua New Guinea	0.51	**United States**	**0.47**
Swaziland	0.61	**Average**	**0.53**

Source: UN Human Development Report, *World Bank Development Indicators, 2003*; and U.S. Census Data

to explain why the real incomes for most middle and low-income workers declined throughout most of the decades in the 1980s and 1990s, while labor productivity levels steadily increased throughout that same period.

Another way to avoid addressing the problem of inequality directly is to argue that more educational opportunities will lead to more equality. This argument is popular argument among the more liberal economists. Indeed, there is a significant correlation between people's level of education and their income levels, but this remains only a partial explanation of inequality. During the post-World War II years when income was more evenly distributed, middle-income jobs were being created for people with only the most basic education levels, and advanced education was accessible primarily by the wealthy and privileged. Moreover, education attainment levels have increased and access to advanced education has become less unequal during the same period that income disparities once again became more polarized.[142]

A more plausible and thorough explanation of the problem of inequality is one that confronts it directly as a systemic problem. That is, the growing income disparity originates in the institutional structure of the U.S. economic system. Rising inequality is a direct consequence of an economic system that is drifting back toward a purer form of capitalism.

Equality in the post-war period did not come about as a result of free-market capitalism, but from institutional forces that ran counter to the capitalist system, particularly labor unionization and government tax-and-transfer programs. Over the last twenty to thirty years, that trend reversed course and the U.S., more so than most other economies of the world, has since been drifting toward a more pure form of capitalism. With industry deregulation, busting labor unions, and dismantling government programs and other non-capitalist institutions, the U.S. has demonstrated a heavier reliance on the capitalist institutions of private property, the market system, and the relentless drive for profits.

Transnational corporations, in their pursuit of profits, have been moving middle-income jobs offshore where labor costs are much lower. This has been particularly true of the manufacturing sector that has traditionally been a source of middle-income, unionized jobs. These developments have become more pronounced as the economy changes its structure to favor owners of capital over working people, and polarization in income inevitably follows.

As the U.S. economy changes over time, so does the pattern of income distribution. These changes in income patterns set in motion the circular and cumulative causality of polarization: the virtuous circles in which more wealth begets more wealth, and the vicious circles in which more poverty begets more poverty—and as the rich get richer, capitalism shines triumphantly.

UNEQUAL OWNERSHIP

The private ownership of business capital is the cornerstone institution of capitalism. If ownership of capital were equally distributed among the population, it would follow that the profits and other forms of income generated from the business assets would also be equally distributed.

Some of the most income-polarized countries in the world are in Central and South America where there is high concentration of ownership of farmland and other assets owned by the wealthy. Many Central and South American landowners tend to be members of a small but extremely wealthy class. With their wealth gained from agriculture, landowners expanded their economic interests, acquired industrial monopolies, and formed cartels. As was the case in the U.S. economy during the nineteenth century, monopoly businesses can forcibly keep wages low by limiting workers to a few or no alternatives for employment. Working people are generally given a basic choice: a bare subsistence wage or abject poverty. A highly unequal pattern of land and capital ownership is a salient characteristic of developing countries, as well as an unequal pattern of income distribution and the existence of non-democratic institutions. As the U.S. reverts to the nineteenth century system of monopoly capitalism and the deterioration of its democratic institutions, it is coming to more resemble the so-called Third World countries in Central and South America than the industrial democracies of the OECD. This fact is reflected in the data in Table 2.

According to recent data, the wealthiest 10 percent of the American population owned 95.8 percent of bonds, 88 percent of stocks,[143] 85 percent of nonresidential real estate, and 78.6 percent of the shares in mutual funds.[145] Virtually all of those listed in the "Forbes 400" wealthiest people in America derive their primary income from the ownership of capital and other forms of income-earning property, not from wages and salaries. Given the logic of the growth imperative of capitalism, this also means that the value of their enormous wealth holdings must continue to grow exponentially. In a capitalist system, the wealth of the rich is necessarily anchored to a growth rate or rate of return, but for people working for wages and salaries this is not the case. Most working people—the other 90 percent—do not have the luxury of putting substantial amounts of money away into capital investments as they need nearly every dollar they earn to sustain themselves and their families.

During the boom period of the last two decades, the share of total income going to owners of capital and property increased substantially and the share going to wages and salaries has decreased. In addition, during the same two decades, the percentages of the overall population of these two groups—the owning classes and the working classes—have not significantly changed. This indicates that the rising tide of an economic boom is lifting only a small percentage of the population into prosperity. The rich get richer and at ever-faster rates—a clear indication that capitalism is succeeding splendidly.

DECLINING UNION MEMBERSHIP AND NON-CAPITALIST INSTITUTIONS

Countries that traditionally have strong democratic institutions also tend to have well-established non-capitalist institutions. These institutions play a significant role in achieving a relatively equitable pattern of income distribution that is more consistent with the spirit of a democratic society. For example, Sweden, Norway, and Denmark have government institutions that pursue a highly progressive tax structure. Taxing the incomes of upper income groups, and using the revenues to fund social programs such as universal healthcare and publicly subsidized college education and maternity leave equalizes living standards. These programs historically came about as a result of legitimate substantive and procedural democracy. Obviously, these programs are not favored by wealthier families who would prefer a more capitalist-leaning and less democratic system like the U.S., but the programs are favored by low-income families who benefit the most from these programs. As shown in Table 1, these countries have the lowest Gini Indexes and the greatest income distribution equality. By contrast, the U.S. has been reversing this trend over the last few decades and has changed its tax policies in ways that overwhelmingly favor wealthy families, and is reducing public support for social programs. The result is more polarization and one of the highest Gini Indexes.

The same countries that have low Gini Indexes also have among the world's highest levels of union membership as a percentage of the overall workforce. In Figure 2 below, data from twenty OECD countries show that those with low union membership tend to cluster around high Gini Indexes and those with higher membership cluster around low Gini Indexes. In other words, there is a statistically significant relationship between union membership among the ranks of the working population and equality of income distribution. When we compare Figure 1 with Figure 3 below, we can see that the sustained decline in union membership in the U.S. that began in the early

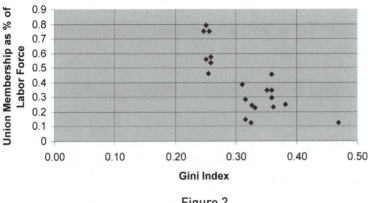

Figure 2

1970s precisely coincides with the sustained rise in the Gini Index that also began in the early 1970s.[145]

The drive for capitalist profits is also driving traditional middle-class manufacturing jobs offshore. As manufacturing jobs are exported, so are union-scale incomes that have historically been the bulk of America's middle class. These jobs are being replaced by a large low-wage sector as typified by aggressively anti-union companies like Wal-Mart. Wal-Mart employment has increased dramatically since 1980 to become the largest private-sector employer in the United States—an employer that has demonstrated its preference to shut down stores rather than allow it to become unionized.

DARWINISM IN THE WINNER-TAKE-ALL MARKET SYSTEM

Another cornerstone institution of capitalism is the market system. Even the most devout believer in a *laissez faire* market system will admit that such a system was never directed toward creating equality. Without government or union institutions forcing the capitalist economy in the direction of more income equality, the market system will naturally lead to ever-widening income disparities. In the competitive struggle for survival in the marketplace, the fittest takes all and leaves little behind for the rest.

Recall that the market system is a network that links product, or output, markets with labor and resource, or input, markets. A grim feature of a competitive market system is that it locks people and businesses on both the output and input sides into a Darwinistic struggle to survive, or a struggle to

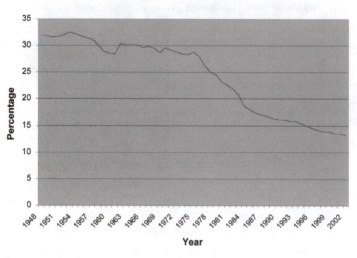

Figure 3

avoid being selected for extinction. In their drive to make ever-increasing profits, businesses struggle with one another for a larger share of revenues in product markets. Out of this struggle, some businesses ascend the virtuous circle as winners, and others fall down the vicious circle of impoverishment and ultimately fail. The winners are those who typically have low production costs and therefore have a competitive advantage. The winners remain in the market, exploit their advantages, and become more powerful. The losers are those with high costs, are less able to compete, and are eventually driven out of the market and into extinction.

The logical conclusion of this process is that only one dominant firm, or a select few, will remain to take the majority of the share of product markets. Product markets eventually become dominated by corporate monopolies (one dominant firm) or oligopolies (a few dominant firms). These are the corporate giants that drive small businesses from the market, destroy middle-income jobs and replace them with substandard or minimum wage jobs, and then splendidly compensate their managers and corporate executives for their skill in executing competitive ruthlessness. A small number of corporate winners take all and leave the rest to a large number of losers who must scramble with one another for the remains. The final result is a widening of the income gap between the wealthy winners and the poor losers.

In the capitalist market system, winners and losers in product markets also determine winners and losers in labor markets. What distinguishes the winners from the losers in labor markets has little to do with skill levels or hard work, and more to do with the outcome of the winner-take-all process of output markets. Those who happen to be in a field that is not valued by the corporate powerhouses in product markets will be in low demand and will be poorly compensated. Those who are lucky enough to be in demand by big corporations will be the winners and will be tremendously compensated. In other words, there is a direct relationship between the winners that take all, or monopolies, in product markets and the winners who take all in labor markets.

For example, highly talented engineers, scientists, or technicians will only succeed if their particular skills are in high market demand relative to the supply. The demand for these skills is determined by the hiring practices of the firms that employ these workers to produce for product markets. If the workers make a contribution to the profitability of the firm, then they have a chance to ride the wave of affluence, that is, if there are not too many people with the same skills competing for the jobs. But if they cannot make the firm more profitable, then no matter how skilled they are or how hard they work, they will not be rewarded. The same would be true of skilled or semi-skilled factory or production workers. If they are in high demand relative to supply, then it will be easier for them to carve out decent middle-class incomes for themselves. If not, then their work is seen by businesses as less valuable, they are rejected by employers, and can quickly fall into low-income status.

As product markets become increasingly concentrated into monopolies and oligopolies, the high-income winners become fewer and wealthier, and the ranks of low-income workers grow. In a dispersed market with numerous firms, there are plenty of opportunities for talent to be spread around and utilized. Labor markets are still competitive, but a relative abundance of access and available opportunities make it such that individuals can hold out for better working conditions. But when an industry becomes concentrated, control of the entire market falls into the hands of the few firms. In this case, a much smaller group of winners ascends and a much larger and growing group of losers falls in labor markets. In either group, differences in skill levels or effort bear no reflection of the differences in compensation.

Take the highly concentrated media industry as an example. There are many talented and creative actors, musicians, and writers throughout the United States, and most of them are probably working for what would amount to minimum wage or even less. Yet, movie stars, musicians, and best-selling novelists can get paid tens of millions even though many possess only rudimentary skills. The primary reason for this difference is market access. Large corporate media companies have access to multi-billion-dollar markets and can choose film, musical, or literary stars on the basis of "marketability" to a mass audience. Once producers make their selection they will attempt to market their production to a high-revenue, globalized market. The stars, musicians, and writers then have the advantage necessary to command tremendous compensation. Even more talented actors who play for smaller, local audiences bring in far less revenues, and thus many work for starvation wages. The "stars" are presented to the entire world market at the expense of those who are only slightly less or even more talented. A writer of a popular trashy romance novel can name his or her figure if their work is chosen by one of the few large publishing companies that control virtually the entire book publishing market and have access to millions of readers. Yet nearly all the other writers of equal or even greater talent who do not have this access to a huge market will receive practically no compensation for their work.

This type of winner-take-all market system is not limited to media and entertainment. There are also "stars" among large investment banking companies, engineering and law firms, corporate CEOs, and many other professions. The winners in these professions can select their salary figures with little concern about competitive forces.

High salaries for a handful of individuals are a small portion of the operating costs for a giant corporate monopoly. A small business would not have the resources to pay its "stars" millions in annual salaries. For those in the second tier who may be equally talented as the stars, the competition is intense and pay scales drop dramatically. Moreover, the competition for the second tier is increasingly global in scale. According to *Business Week*, global outsourcing is a menace to those who are seeking professional jobs in engineering, financial services, architecture and other traditionally high-paying jobs.[146] The winner-take-all capitalist market system has effectively shed its union constraints and created an intensely competitive global labor market that pushes down labor costs and pushes up profits. At the same time, the system has created a substantially less competitive global product market that also allows for higher profits. If we follow the winner-take-all process in a market system to its logical conclusion, the result would be a market system characterized by a Gini Index of 1 where one producer takes all—100 percent of all income earned in the economy—and all others receive nothing.

The winner-take-all society is an extension of capitalism's natural tendency toward industry concentration. The Darwinistic struggle for market share eventually leads to only a handful of winners, or perhaps just one. Without counterveiling institutions to prevent winners from achieving monopoly power, they will take all. When this happens, polarization becomes more severe. The same winners who achieve monopoly power in product markets also wield buying power in labor and input markets; that is, they achieve monopsony power as well.

MONOPSONY CAPITALISM

Corporate giants in the U.S. economy have enormous economic and political power. They have the ability not only to dominate product markets and squeeze out competitors, but also can sidestep antitrust laws and other government regulations, bankroll political campaigns, mold public opinion through the media, and perform a host of other things necessary for maximizing profits. They also have sufficient power to dominate the buying side of their businesses. By dominating markets on the output side of the market system, businesses also become the major buyers of resources and major employers. In other words, the power to dominate on the output side of the market system leads to power to dominate the input side as well. This kind of input-side power is called *monopsony* power.

Monopsony power allows businesses to use bullying tactics when negotiating resource prices or labor contracts. As corporate giants gain monopoly control of output markets, they also become the biggest buyers of resources, raw materials, or goods sold in wholesale markets. If suppliers choose not to sell on the terms dictated by the monopsony, their market share will collapse. The corporate giant then reaps enormous profits, pays its executives with world record-breaking compensation packages, and pushes down incomes for its suppliers and employees. Monopsonies are therefore a key force in widening income disparities.

The leader of monopsony capitalism in the U.S. is the corporate retail giant, Wal-Mart. Wal-Mart, with sales revenues over $250 billion, is perhaps the best example of a highly successful capitalist enterprise in existence today. Part of Wal-Mart's success is derived from competitive pricing and rapid growth in retail markets. It has also been able to aggressively cut costs with automated inventory control systems and with offshore sourcing of wholesale suppliers and manufacturers. Wal-Mart waged war on costs and won. By doing so, it gained a cost advantage over its competitors. During late 1980s and throughout the decade of the 1990s, Wal-Mart went from being a regional player in the "big box" consumer retail market, to become the world's largest corporation and therefore could assert its dominance over nearly the entire consumer goods retail industry.

Part of Wal-Mart's cost-cutting success was the development of a new kind of business model. Known as the "pull" model, large retailers that have a high profile in product markets gain the power to decide what products to sell to consumers, and at what price. Once the decision is made at the retail end, the retailer then commands suppliers to either comply or lose their contracts. With Wal-Mart's huge dominance of the retail product markets, suppliers could not afford to lose Wal-Mart's business as it would cause their share of the wholesale market to collapse and they would be forced out of business. This model contrasts with the more traditional "push" model in which manufacturers produce something and then push retailers to sell or market the products to consumers at the manufacturer's suggested retail prices. With the ascent of companies like Wal-Mart, and the shift toward industry concentration throughout the U.S. economy, the push model is fading and the pull model is winning out. Given that the pull model is rooted in cost-cutting strategies, it is taking its toll on the incomes of workers and businesses in the supply chain.

The pull model is also leading to more inequality. In its ascent to dominance, Wal-Mart deliberately targeted small, independent retailers primarily located in rural areas. These small businesses did not have cost advantages that allowed them to compete with Wal-Mart, and as they were driven to extinction, so were the middle-class incomes earned by the small business owners. Wherever Wal-Mart has a presence in the market, middle-class incomes of small-scale entrepreneurs are replaced by the bottom-tier incomes of Wal-Mart employees, and middle-income manufacturing jobs are eliminated through outsourcing to low-wage markets offshore. This process is now known as the familiar "Wal-Mart Effect," and the upshot of this effect is income polarization. Regional managers who work for Wal-Mart are paid six-figure incomes while the retail workers are paid less than $9 per hour on average. The principal shareholders are still the family members of Wal-Mart founder Sam Walton, and the Walton family is the wealthiest in the world.

Following Wal-Mart's lead, industries across the spectrum are becoming concentrated and dominated by monopoly/monopsony corporate giants. Manufacturers and suppliers are finding that there are fewer buyers, even though the markets are growing in sales volume. Monopsony buyers use their market power, and their power is derived from the fact that they buy in significantly larger quantities than any other buyer. Large monopsonies can force sellers to accept the "take it or leave it" terms dictated by monopsony buyers not market forces.

Other corporate giants are following Wal-Mat's lead. Ruppert Murdoch's media empire, NewsCorp had already controlled much of the content of cable programs such as FoxNews, FX, Fox Sports, and National Geographic, but after NewsCorp acquired satellite distribution network DirecTV in December 2003, its reach extended beyond its traditional domain of cable to take a dominant position in the telecommunications industry. Like Wal-Mart, Newscorp has captured such a large share of the outlet market for programs that it is able to squeeze companies that produce media programs. According to *Business Week*, "No longer beholden to other distributors, industry insiders predict, [Murdoch] will drive down the prices of others' entertainment and sports programming. With so many viewers hooked up to DirecTV, the argument goes, no programmer will dare risk getting kicked off his system, so they'll bend."[147] NewsCorp wins and becomes more affluent, the programming companies lose out, experience falling incomes, and income inequality intensifies.

Consider another example of monopsony power—InterActiveCorp. InterActiveCorp, under the rule of CEO Barry Diller, positioned itself through acquisitions of companies like Expedia, Hotels.com, and Ticketmaster to control the retail markets for Internet services. As an e-commerce intermediary, Diller's InterActiveCorp brokers services for airline, hotel, and concert establishments, among many others. By becoming a dominant player in this service sector, InterActiveCorp can squeeze its client companies on their prices. Like Wal-Mart and NewsCorp, the suppliers of travel and local entertainment services cannot risk being dropped from InterActiveCorp's services for fear of a substantial drop in their share of the market. By aggressively hammering suppliers down on prices, passing a portion of the savings on to the customers and pocketing the rest, InterActiveCorp has become exceptionally profitable. Expedia alone has a staggering 18 million customers.[148] With control of such a substantial share of the market, hotels cannot afford not to do business with Expedia. According to another *Business Week* report:

Expedia . . . demands a wholesale rate of about $151 and then charges the customer $189. The customer saves $30, while Expedia pockets a 24 percent markup, far more than the 10 percent travel-agency commission that was standard before the arrival of the Net. Why do hotels play ball? 'Expedia has 18 million unique users a month—that's humongous,' says Kurien Jacob, distribution director at the Radisson Lexington, which fills about 100 rooms a day with Expedia customers. What happens if a hotel balks at heavy discounts? It may just find itself at the bottom of Expedia's list of hotels.[149]

InterActiveCorp's monopsony power gives them "... the ability to punish," according to Jim Young, senior vice-president at InterContinental Hotels Group.[150]

The polarization process associated with monopsony capitalism is now systemic. Monopsony aggression is setting off a kind of downward-spiraling chain reaction within supply networks throughout the U.S. economy. Consider this example. Wal-Mart is the world's largest retailer of chicken and beef products. The world's largest supplier of beef and poultry is Tyson Foods. Wal-Mart uses its monopsony power to pressure Tyson to lower its prices and forces it to find its own cost-cutting strategies. Tyson Foods, in turn, is aggressively buying out competitors and has gained monopsony power of its own. Using its power, it can squeeze the prices and incomes received by its suppliers such as cattle ranchers and poultry farmers, as well as placing intense cost-cutting pressures on its own workers. According to *Business Week*:

> ... marketing agreements with ranchers that cover 50 percent or more of its cattle supplies give it increasing control over that end of the business. The bottom line, some contend, is a strategy that squeezes workers on one side and farmers on the other ...[151]

The downward spiral does not end there. Tyson is also a major buyer of cardboard boxes and other packaging materials. The largest packaging materials company, Weyerhaeuser Corporation—a $20 billion per year company—itself is a firm that is gaining monopsony power, as it has bought out most of its major competitors. As Weyerhaeuser is pressured by Tyson to slash prices, it takes additional cost-cutting measures by blocking other buyers from the market and pressures local saw mills in the states of Washington and Oregon to sell logs at below market prices. According to the local press:

> As big box retailers expand market share though discount pricing, they are pushing down consumer prices and applying more pressure

to suppliers to find their own efficiencies. Weyerhaeuser, for instance, competes to provide thousands of cardboard boxes to Tyson Foods, the world's largest seller of beef and chicken, for distribution through Tyson's biggest customer, Wal-Mart, the world's largest retailer.[152]

At the bottom of the food chain, then, are the cattle ranchers, poultry farmers, independent saw mills, hotels, and of course their employees. In the case of the media, at the bottom are the studios, production companies, and their employees. And the hotels, restaurants, airlines, and concert halls are being bled of their profitability by the Internet monopsonies. In this high-pressure cost-cutting environment, the large and powerful are able to gain on the disadvantages of the small. Bankruptcies abound among farmers, small manufacturers, and airlines that are being pushed below their shutdown points.

To avoid being forced to shut down by corporate monopsonies, many firms are looking overseas to find cheaper labor and resources. Ironically, as a result of the capitalist drive to accumulate ever greater amounts of financial wealth, businesses are turning to perhaps the most totalitarian state socialist country in the world—the People's Republic of China. Oded Shenkar, author of *The Chinese Century*, warns of the difficulties of trying to compete with China, "If you still make anything labor intensive, get out now rather than bleed to death. Shaving 5 percent here and there won't work. You need an entirely new business model to compete."[153]

Such monopoly/monopsony power, and the imbalance and inequalities it creates, is not a quirk or an aberration of the capitalist system, it is its supreme triumph. Capitalism is and always has been designed to generate profits for a small class of investors. This means that businesses must try to squeeze as much revenue from sales in product markets as possible, and at the same time squeeze down the wages and incomes of workers and others in the chain of supply as much as possible. These are simply the rules of the capitalist economy and companies like Wal-Mart have excelled in playing by these rules. The profits of monopoly/monopsony corporations are soaring, shareholders are cheering, and at the same time the disproportionately top-heavy pattern of income in the U.S. is intensifying and the Gini Index marches higher. Such imbalance in wealth and income distribution also engenders imbalance in political power.

POLITICAL INEQUALITY

The concentration of wealth and income is an integral feature of a capitalist system, and this translates directly into concentration of political power. The wealthy investor class is naturally inclined to use its economic power to sustain and augment its position of advantage. Wealthy individuals and corporations tap into their mighty treasure chests to sway election outcomes, influence legislation through campaign contributions, fund political action committees, and pay for expensive media advertising and political messaging, as well as outright bribery.

Less than one tenth of one percent of the American population has the willingness or financial ability to donate more than $1,000 to political candidates.[154] Yet this minute fraction of the population composed mainly of wealthy individuals and powerful corporations dominates U.S. political institutions. Although large labor unions and other so-called "special interests" spend significant amounts of money in the political arena, businesses spend far more. According to one observer, "The 82 largest American corporations contributed $33,045,832 to political action committees in the year-2000 election cycle, outspending labor unions by 15 to 1."[155] Their ability to dominate stems not only from the fact that they have money to spend, but also because political candidates are becoming more dependent on their contributions as the costs of running political campaigns soars.

Because of the high costs of campaigning, being a senator or member of Congress has nearly become a full-time fundraising job. It is estimated that senators representing some of the larger states must raise about $34,000 per week for every week they are in office in order to keep themselves in the Senate.[156] In the 2000 election, no challengers who spent less than $850,000 in their campaign won a seat in the House of Representatives.[157] When political candidates or parties depend on wealthy individuals and corporations to finance their campaigns, they become less independently-minded and become more beholden to those with money to spend. Moreover, a candidate who does not take money has virtually no chance at success. The intense need to raise money in order to wage an effective campaign naturally rewards those with more corruptible instincts and who are more likely to grant favors to wealthy campaign donors.

The U.S. Supreme Court also protects wealthy donors from charges of corruption. In the landmark Supreme Court case *Buckley v. Valeo (1976)*, the Supreme Court struck down election spending ceilings contained in a 1974 amendment to the Federal Election Campaign Act.[158] The Court ruled that government restrictions of campaign contributions was a violation of the First Amendment to the U.S. Constitution that protects the freedom of political expression. When the First Amendment to the constitution was ratified in 1791, it is unlikely that it was intended to benefit large corporations. Yet from 1976 forward, electoral politics became a fundraising and spending free-for-all, and corporate money became a central feature of electoral politics. With the Buckley ruling, the scales of power tilted heavily in the direction of individuals and businesses with money whose takeover of the electoral and legislative processes was all but preordained. With the donation of campaign money ruled by the Supreme Court as a protected form of political expression, multi-billion-dollar corporations can easily ascend to positions of unprecedented political power. Considering that companies like Wal-Mart, whose annual revenues—over $250 billion—exceed the Gross State Product of thirty-seven American states, the political influence a single company has at its disposal is profound.

The corruptive influence of money in American politics is therefore not a deviation from, but a logical extension of the capitalist profit motive. Businesses are generally reluctant to spend money unless the expenditures improve their bottom-line profits. Buying favorable electoral and legislative outcomes that will help improve their profitability is merely a rational course of action in doing business. That is, they use money as leverage to put government into the service of their goal of profit maximization. Consider this evidence:

• The oil and energy corporations contributed heavily to the Republican Party and its candidates in the 2000 election. Later, the same corporations were granted access to the Vice President's task force on the national energy policy that relaxed regulations on energy development permits. These government favors thus made the corporations more profitable.[159]

• The Airline Passenger Fairness Act was a piece of bipartisan legislation that was introduced in the Senate in 1999 to make the airline industry more accountable for its poor service and treatment of passengers. The airline industry donated over $400,000 in contributions during the first weeks following the introduction of the legislation, and shortly thereafter, all of the substantive provisions in the bill were removed.[160]

• A bill was introduced by Senator Richard Bryan in 1990 to propose that mandatory fuel mileage, known as CAFE (Corporate Average Fuel Economy) standards, for automobiles including SUVs be raised by 40 percent by

2001. The proposed legislation was an attempt to reduce U.S. dependency on foreign oil. A senator representing the auto industry's home state of Michigan led a filibuster to kill the legislation. Auto industry campaign contributions influenced the vote for the filibuster; with the exception of Senator John McCain who co-sponsored the bill and two Oregon Senators, all of those who were among the top recipients of auto industry money voted for the filibuster.[161]

• In 1999, in a private communication with the CEO of pharmaceutical giant Bristol-Myers Squibb, then chair of the Republican Party requested $250,000 in donations to "keep the lines of communication open . . . to keep passing legislation that will benefit your industry."[162] The drug companies spent about $262 million in lobbying, political messaging, and campaign contributions leading up to the 2000 election. The legislative boon that followed was stunning. Pharmaceutical companies were granted unprecedented extensions on their monopoly patents for a wide range of drugs. Patent extensions of course, allow companies to maintain high prices and pull in high profits.[163]

As checks are written for political influence and access, the payback to corporations has been substantial. This is particularly true when large corporations form coalitions to combine their resources and target specific legislation. In 1997, a group of America's most powerful companies formed an alliance to rewrite the Alternative Minimum Tax (AMT) laws that were instituted a decade earlier. AMT laws were designed to prevent corporations from having excessive tax write-offs and loopholes such that their tax liability would fall to zero. After changing the AMT laws, corporations were able to erase roughly $26 billion in taxes in just two years in the late 1990s.[164] According to IRS records, corporations' AMT tax payments fell by 60 percent after the laws were changed, and less than one half of one percent of all the corporations that filed tax returns made AMT payments.[165]

The list of connections between industry lobbyists and political payback is a long one. Businesses see their contributions as nothing more than a cost of doing business that will help assure a favorable political climate and future profitability. In other words, they are doing exactly what their shareholders expect of them. Joel Bakan, law professor and author of *The Corporation*, writes:

> Lacking the legal license to spend shareholders' money without a reasonable prospect of return, corporations spend money on politics for

the same reason they make other investments: to advance their own and their owners' financial self-interest.[166]

In other words, the corrupting and non-democratic influence of big business money in politics is merely a logical part of the day-to-day operations of capitalism.

INFORMATION INEQUALITY IN COMMERCIAL MEDIA

In the section on monopsony capitalism, we discussed the economic power of the large commercial media corporations. The commercial media industry is one of the most concentrated industries on the planet, and its might extends beyond its economic and political power, which is enormous. The commercial media industry also has another source of power—it controls people's access to information.

Less than a dozen very large corporations control the majority of television broadcasts, cable networks, book publishers, music labels, film studios, magazines, and major newspapers around the world. These companies are the gatekeepers of nearly all information and cultural production outside the Internet. Commercial media companies control people's access to information as well as the information content itself. And as a matter of rational business policy, these companies use this power to serve the interests of their investors. As a result, much of what is produced as news, information or culture is highly imbalanced and skewed toward generating corporate profits. Any other purposes, including having a functioning democracy, are of less importance.

A unique advantage for a highly concentrated commercial media industry is that it can make profits while simultaneously molding public opinion and viewpoints to further its profit-making interests. A media system that is corporate-owned and sells advertising to other corporations is naturally going to be suspicious of viewpoints that are critical of capitalist business. The tendency of corporate media is, therefore, to emphasize information that serves business interests and de-emphasize that which does not. This is not to say that such opposing viewpoints are completely suppressed or will never exist in a capitalist society, but rather they are pushed to the margins and generally treated as "controversial" or "offensive." Scholar and media critic Robert McChesney specifies the core problem with capitalist media:

To the extent that the contemporary media system answers to investors first and foremost, it may become a weaker democratic force. Commercial media also may be useful to capitalism in generating a political culture that is more enthusiastic about capitalism and suspicious of capitalism's critics.[167]

For most Americans, centralized control of information and censorship are associated with the governments of totalitarian regimes and not with the United States. It would not come as a surprise to an American to discover that in the former Soviet Union viewpoints that were critical of state socialism were censored from media and controlled by the Communist Party. The Soviet's ability to control information stemmed from its undemocratic command structure. Yet the concentrated corporate media in the U.S. is a similarly undemocratic command structure.

Most Americans have been raised to equate capitalism with democracy, and therefore it seems natural that criticisms of capitalism rarely, if ever, appear in the corporate-owned media. Criticisms of capitalism exist in the U.S., but only on the margins just as dissenting viewpoints existed only in underground media in the Soviet Union. The implications are profound considering that the U.S. traditionally sees itself as the vanguard of democracy for the world.

This highlights another unique characteristic of the media industry. On the one hand, it is considered as the "Fourth Estate" in political governance and is a centrally important component of political democracy. On the other, it is largely controlled by non-democratic corporations. The power of the media was clearly recognized by the framers of the U.S. Constitution who wrote the First Amendment in the Bill of Rights to guarantee freedom of speech and the press. The simultaneous existence of the democratic principle of free speech and corporate controlled media presents a profound contradiction: commercial media is comprised of a handful of gigantic corporations that have a fiduciary responsibility to maximize returns to their shareholders represented by a proportionally small investor class, yet democracy can only be served by a media that serves the interests of a broad base of the population.

Open access to media for all citizens has always been seen as an important and necessary aspect of democracy. Yet commercial media profitability is the guiding principle, not openness. A core feature of capitalism is that only that which can generate profits for investors will be produced. Serious political discourse and critical viewpoints that are essential to democracy tend not to be profitable commodities, and thus are pushed out of view of mainstream audiences. Democratic will, however, resides in the mainstream, not in the fringe. Under capitalism, it is profitability that determines what will or will not be produced, not the democratic needs of a polity.

Thomas Jefferson addressed this contradiction between business interests and democracy. Jefferson was outspoken about the need to have freedom of the press as a necessary condition for democracy, yet also well-known for his distrust of corporate monopolies. Jefferson writes:

> Our liberty depends on the freedom of the press, and that cannot be limited without being lost . . . I hope we shall . . . crush in its birth the aristocracy of our moneyed corporations, which dare already to challenge our government to a trial of strength and bid defiance to the laws of our country.[168]

This contradiction between concern over the corporate usurpation of the electoral process and the need for free access to information is now confirmed in America's current political and economic environment. As it now stands, the majority of Americans still get the bulk of their political information from television. Accordingly, cable and network television producers have all but completely purged serious political discourse from their programs. The result has been a depoliticization of American minds. People are becoming less and less informed by corporate news programs, and serious journalism is replaced by gossip, bland coverage, and noisy diatribes by pundits. Jefferson concluded that, "If once [the people] become inattentive to the public affairs . . . you and I, and Congress and Assemblies, Judges and Governors, shall all become wolves."[169]

Nonetheless, the commercial media industry relies on its First Amendment rights to produce whatever generates the most in profits. For the media corporations, what maximizes profits is advertising revenue and advertisers attempt to penetrate whatever is most scintillating to the public: gossip, sports events, sex, violence, celebrity trials, and virtually nothing by way of serious information. What is held to be in demand is that which has mass appeal and marketability. Mass marketability tends to be that which appeals to the lowest common denominator, media companies therefore cannot raise the standard of their programs to educate and inform the public about complex and serious issues.

There has always been a commercial dimension to the media business. In the past, however, journalistic standards were balanced with the need to satisfy marketing strategies of advertisers. In other words, the media as an institution had to some extent defied the demands of the capitalist system. By the 1980s, this antagonistic relationship began to change, and media became wholly devoured by a wave of corporate giants. The media merger wave that began in the 1980s generated a mountain of debt that had to be paid back, and so the pressure to maximize revenues was heightened dramatically. Media programs, like never before, became commodities for mass consumption and the democratic need for free political expression dissolved into the packaging and repackaging of formulaic cop and lawyer shows, wrestling, ranting pundits, and, of course, an endless stream of commercials. The industry has reduced the First Amendment need for political expression to ashes.

Mass marketing leads to mass advertising revenues and mass corporate profits. This is, however, only part of the story of commercial media. The profit motive not only selects what is, or is not, to be produced, it also relentlessly seeks to cut costs, and this bottom-line orientation has taken its toll on news programs. Corporate media mergers and the cost-cutting imperatives that followed forced a model of news programming employing fewer reporters, and pursuing very little by way of investigative journalism. Serious political and investigative journalism is expensive, and television and radio stations are pressured to cut the budgets of news divisions. Such low-budget approaches to news programming resulted in gossipy stories that require little or no research, and programs that host what Robert McChesney refers to as "celebrity pontificators."[170] Serious facts and information fade into oblivion as the corporate media serves up cheap "infotainment" for mass consumption. The need for profit maximization thus prevails over the needs of information for a functioning democratic society.

Without investigative journalism, most political coverage takes the form of press releases in which reporters do microphone interviews and regurgitate official government statements. Gaining and maintaining access to government officials' press releases keeps reporters disciplined. Those who show up asking serious or tough questions of government officials or candidates from major parties are bumped out and other well-heeled reporters take their place. Television, cable, and radio news reports become the media instruments through which established structures of power mold public opinion in ways that serve their narrow political or business interests, but not the interest of democracy. News programs resemble low-budget stenographers, repeating word-for-word-he-said-she-said daily scandal and chatter. Investigation, fact finding, turning hard ground, or penetrating the resistance from those in power have all but disappeared from the media system dominated by gigantic corporations. In its place are programs that will, no matter how idiotic they may seem, turn a fast buck. According to McChesney, new trivia programs will ". . . give the appearance of controversy and conflict but rarely have anything to do with significant issues. Study after study reveals a general decline in the amount of hard news relative to fluff."[171]

According to a Pew Research Center survey of about three hundred journalists, close to half of them admitted that they tailor their reports to the needs of the profit needs of their corporate employers.[172] Media increasingly bends their news reports to serve the commercial interests of their revenue sources—advertisers. It appears that no major corporation is going to advertise with, and thereby financially support, a media outlet that makes a regular practice of taking a critical view of the same major corporations. The logic of capitalism is clear and direct, and although on occasion exceptions arise, there is no reason to assume that capitalist institutions would knowingly pursue a line of business that would undermine their financial interests. This economic reality was expressed explicitly by a major newspaper executive:

> The press does not depend on government officials . . . for its standing or its resources. But it has a much more intricate relationship with big business. Today's news media are themselves frequently a part of large, often global corporations dependent on advertising revenue that increasingly comes from other large corporations. As public companies themselves, the news media are under the same kind of pressure to create "shareholder value," by reducing costs and increasing earnings, as are other public companies. And they face numerous conflicts of interest as they grow larger and more diversified.[173]

One major source of independent information is the Internet. But this is changing as the Internet is being absorbed into the media oligopoly in the U.S. and Internet neutrality is under attack. Only a handful companies have the infrastructure to provide high-speed Internet access to people's homes and are using this as leverage to charge fees for users to access specific sites or for sites to be posted. Once these companies acquire this power, they will be able to use a fee system to control what sites are accessible by Internet users in the same way that cable and broadcast networks control what programs get in the wires or on the airwaves. Just as the airwaves were once open and non-proprietary, and eventually came under complete control of corporate giants, the domain of the Internet is soon to meet with the same fate. When Internet Service Providers control site access, the open door to independent media sources will be closed for good. Internet neutrality, the last bastion of free access to information, will eventually go the way of network television.

CONCLUSION

Inequality in America is the most sharply polarized it has ever been since the Depression of the 1930s. Class distinctions are becoming more rigid, and social mobility for those at the bottom is becoming increasingly difficult, if not impossible. Income disparities are rapidly getting wider as the more innovative sectors in the U.S. economy such as the high-tech and manufacturing sectors—traditionally reliable sources for middle-income jobs—are moving offshore. Disparities of wealth and income combined with concentrated industrial and political power, and control over media by a few mega-corporations, seriously call into question whether democracy can survive in America.

Any critical assessment of this situation must also include a critical assessment of capitalism. It is true that there are many other causes of inequality in America and elsewhere other than the institutions of capitalism. Nonetheless these characteristic features of capitalism—the separation of ownership and work, the winner-take-all market system, the relentless drive for profits, and the systematic breakdown of non-capitalist institutions—have unquestionably contributed to heightened inequality. But with the media access controlled by giant, for-profit businesses, critical assessments of capitalism continue to be marginalized.

The majority of Americans are taught to accept capitalism as a natural, normative part of life, and to view other systems with suspicion. This makes the molding of public opinion by corporate media a relatively uncomplicated task. By merely broadcasting and printing conventional pieties that are designed to fortify the existing institutions, they call into question any competing or alternative system. This makes critical viewpoints all the more difficult to bring out into the open.

Once the economic processes of production and distribution are no longer possessed by the wealthy investor class who control it for their self-enrichment, they can be redirected toward serving the needs of the people. The institutions that control production and distribution can be re-created in a way that they will become intrinsically democratic. An economic system that is intrinsically democratic will not produce stark inequality because it does not need to drive the livelihoods of working families into a downward vicious spiral so as to keep the wealthy investor class in its virtuous upward spiral of prosperity.

A mindful economy has intrinsic democracy as one of its primary tenets. But to create a democratic economy people must rebuild our economic institutions from the ground up, and for these institutions to be truly democratic they must be non-capitalist. Perhaps even more daunting is the notion that the problem of stark inequalities in America is systemic and therefore a lasting solution to this problem must be systemic change. That is, as people set out to build new economic institutions, these institutions must also cohere into a system and that system must be grounded in a new set of principles. Such rebuilding will be explored in later chapters.

11

FINANCIAL MARKET INSTABILITY

The U.S. stock market crash in 2000 and 2001 was among the most severe financial market crises in the history of capitalism. Shortly before the crash, billionaire financier George Soros warned of the dangers of a global movement toward a more pure, *laissez faire* capitalist market system (see Chapter Four). The movement was spearheaded by U.S. government officials and corporate executives who boasted that capitalism has emerged triumphantly from the Cold War to become the dominant economic system for the global economy. America's leaders began pushing an unregulated, free-market system on the rest of the world. Soros and others saw that this development came at a high cost—the cost was a loss of stability, particularly in financial markets.

Financial market instability and capitalism share a common legacy. The institutional structure of capitalism is based on buying and selling in markets and taking profits. If these markets are left uncontrolled or unregulated, they tend to undulate though boom and bust patterns of instability. Prices can move up or down as market conditions change—sometimes overnight and sometimes by the minute. These up and down patterns can sometimes swing wildly just as would a vehicle that has no driver at the wheel. Financial markets—markets for stocks, bonds, commodities, currencies, and other securities—are particularly vulnerable to such instability as they are designed to be liquid or easily converted to cash, and are subject to constantly changing conditions and uncertainty.

Over time, financial markets have evolved as key elements in the institutional fabric of the U.S. economy. As we saw from Chapter Six, however, these market institutions have drifted far from their original purpose of financing economic development. Most of what takes place in financial markets has little or nothing to do with raising capital for real investments, and has almost everything to do with speculative buying and selling. That is, people and institutions buy and sell stocks, bonds, and other instruments purely on the speculation that money can be made by buying and selling. In this way, the financial system of the United States has come to resemble a nexus of gambling casinos rather than a system designed to foster genuine economic progress.

Financial markets allow for an almost seamless conversion of assets in the form of stocks into cash, from cash back to stocks again or into bonds, and so on. Financial market activity is largely a rapid succession of conversion of cash to a security, back to cash, back to a security, in a flurry of speculative buying and selling. This succession is referred to in the financial press as "trading activity." As we will see, this rapid trading activity is what causes financial markets to be exceptionally unstable. Yet this instability is precisely the environment in which speculators either thrive, or are ruined.

Speculative buying and selling is not aberrant behavior in capitalism. It is a generally accepted practice in a system where the practice of "buying low, selling high" constitutes its primary occupation. Throughout the several-hundred year history of capitalism, buying, selling, and taking profits has become an accepted path toward wealth accumulation—a path that is completely removed from productive work.

As capitalism ascended to become the world's dominant economic system, speculation and the profit motive moved from the margins of pre-capitalist society to occupy a central place. As new institutions quickly developed to accommodate speculative trading, boom and bust instability followed accordingly. Volatility moved from relatively minor, localized events to major national and international financial crises. Virtually every large-scale financial market crisis occurred where capitalist institutions predominate. Moreover, throughout the history of capitalism, these crises have followed a consistent and familiar pattern. Each took place in the same core institutions and each was driven by the same motivation—greed. In other words, with the development of capitalism, speculative greed became an institutionalized, systemic problem.

SPECULATION AND THE PATTERN OF INSTABILITY

Whether the instrument is a stock, bond, piece of land, or even a tulip bulb, the pattern of instability caused by speculation is usually the same. The pattern begins with an instrument—a security or commodity—which is relatively liquid and somehow captures the interest of speculators who begin to buy. This speculative interest can become contagious and draw more speculators who will also buy, and by doing so, the market price of the instrument will rise. Higher prices fuel even more speculative buying which drives prices higher yet, and soon a boom is underway. A speculative boom will cause prices to soar to a level that is far above any reasonable value of an instrument. Eventually, the process reverses and what was once speculative interest

that drove prices up turns to fear, and this is typically followed by panic selling that drive prices back down again. Prices fall to some rock-bottom level
and the boom-and-bust pattern will start over again as a new instrument captures the interest of speculators.

From the tulip mania of the seventeenth century, the bond mania of the
eighteenth century, the great stock market crash of 1929, and to the current
housing market crisis, the boom and bust pattern of instability has been nearly
identical in each instance. This pattern is outlined as follows: (1) New opportunities for speculation or "displacement," (2) speculation amplified by credit,
(3) a positive, self-reinforcing feedback loop, (4) overtrading or speculative
"bubbles," (5) mania and collective euphoria, (6) price reversal (7) a negative, self-reinforcing feedback loop or "panic" and (8) the boom-and-bust
cycle ends.

NEW OPPORTUNITIES FOR SPECULATION

Perhaps the best model for analyzing the patterns in financial market instability was developed by economist and monetary theorist, Hyman Minski.[174]
Minski saw that financial market booms usually begin with new opportunities or "displacements." A displacement is an event that sparks interest in a
particular financial instrument or a category of instruments. It could be the
creation of a new product or an important technological innovation or discovery. It could also be the result of an institutional change such as the
creation of a new market exchange, the development of new forms of money,
the creation of new government systems of finance or of restructuring government debt. Displacement could also occur as a result of major political
events such as the outbreak of war, or perhaps the end of a war. In other
words, displacement is any significant occurrence that attracts speculators to
a particular instrument. Once an instrument attracts speculators in sufficient
numbers, it draws money to itself like a magnet, or *displaces* money from other
sectors of the economy. When this happens, the familiar pattern of instability
generally follows. The examples below—tulip bulbs, new schemes for restructuring government debt, the development of transportation technology,
discoveries of gold, new eras of industrial development, globalization, and the
Internet—are all forms of displacement that drew speculative interest and set
in motion the familiar boom-and-bust pattern of instability.

SPECULATION AMPLIFIED BY CREDIT

Once the displacement occurs and new opportunities for speculation open up, it is not unusual for speculators to leverage their purchases of financial instruments with borrowed money. If speculators want to borrow money to invest in stocks, for example, it is relatively easy for banks (assuming they are not under strict regulatory controls) to produce the money needed. Recall from Chapter Five that when banks make loans they actually create money virtually out of thin air. So by making loans to speculators for financial investments, banks create new cash that is pumped into financial markets and, like air being pumped into a balloon, inflate the prices of the financial instruments.

Typically, the loans commercial banks make to speculators are "call loans" which are loans that allow speculators to buy stocks in the stock market using a fixed loan-to-investment value ratio. This ratio is also called "margin." For example, say a bank lends a speculator $10,000 on a 50 percent loan-to-value ratio or margin. This means that the bank will allow the outstanding balance of a loan to be a maximum of 50 percent of the market value of the financial investment at any given time. In this case, it would be a $10,000 loan to a $20,000 investment value. The danger of using call loans for speculation, however, is that if the value of the investment falls, the loan-to-value ratio will rise above what is allowed by the banks and they "call" their loans back. That is, the bank will demand that at least a portion of the loan be repaid. In this example, if the value of the speculator's investment fell from $20,000 to $15,000, then the loan-to-value ratio would rise to about 67 percent ($10,000/$15,000) which is significantly above the 50 percent maximum and the lender will call the loan to be repaid. Frequently with margin calls, banks require that the investment automatically be cashed out to repay the loan. Speculators are forced to sell their stocks, which then drive stock prices down even further.

The result is that bank credit tends to amplify financial market price volatility. By making loans, banks pump cash into the markets and prices will balloon upward, and by calling loans back, banks draw money back out causing prices to deflate. In either instance, the boom or bust will be made more severe with borrowed money.

A POSITIVE, SELF-REINFORCING FEEDBACK LOOP

Within all dynamic systems that experience exponential growth patterns, there is an underlying self-reinforcing feedback loop. Such a feedback loop is the engine that drives prices upward—sometimes to astronomical levels. Part of the feedback loop occurs as a kind of self-fulfilling prophecy in which expectations of higher prices will cause speculators to act in a way that will actually bring about the expected higher prices. As speculators discover a new investment opportunity, they begin to buy on the hope, or speculation, that the prices will rise. When they buy, they increase the market demand for the instrument, and when market demand increases, the prices naturally begin to rise. When prices rise, speculators' expectations are confirmed. This confirmation generates more interest and more speculators are attracted to the market driving up prices further and triggering a positive feedback loop: rising prices confirm higher profits, higher profits attract more buyers who drive up prices further, confirming more profits again, and so on.

OVERTRADING OR SPECULATIVE "BUBBLES"

As prices soar they get pushed to a level that is far above any fundamental value of the instrument. In the stock market, for example, the fundamental value of a stock is anchored to the assets and claims on future earnings of the business. An overtraded stock is one in which the stock price rises significantly above a value measured by assets or earnings (see Chapter Six on stock valuation). Overtraded markets are referred to as "bubbles" because the prices are highly inflated and at some point they become unstable and will suddenly burst. When bubbles burst, rapid price deflation or a "crash" inevitably follows. It is sometimes difficult to determine if an instrument is overtraded or if it has experienced a significant increase in fundamental value. However, in all of major financial market crashes, the warning signs of overtrading were abundantly clear but speculators, blinded by greed, chose not to pay attention.

MANIA AND COLLECTIVE EUPHORIA

As speculative bubbles expand and speculators see huge paper fortunes grow before their eyes, a kind of greed-inspired mania or collective euphoria sets in among speculators. Economist and financial historian Charles Kindleberger describes this process:

> In my talks about financial crisis over the last decade, I have polished one line that always gets a nervous laugh: 'There is nothing so disturbing to one's well-being and judgment as to see a friend get rich.' When the number of firms and households indulging in these practices grows large, bringing in segments of the population that are normally aloof from such ventures, speculation for profit leads away from normal, rational behavior to what has been described as manias . . .[175]

Psychologists refer to this kind of denial and the frame of mind of people drawn into speculative manias as "cognitive dissonance." Speculators have a powerful incentive to believe in a fantasy that stock prices will only continue to rise. That is, they will believe in a fiction that everyone can become a millionaire, and have an incentive to disregard information to the contrary no matter how truthful it may be. Compelled by fantasies of riches, people will continue to believe that there will always be a "greater fool" than themselves— someone who will enter the market to buy at foolishly high prices. History has proven repeatedly that bubble markets *always* burst, and when they do, prices will fall. At some point along the way, speculators begin to see this reality and their speculative greed-based fantasies are quickly transformed into a reality-based fear.

PRICE REVERSAL

Once an instrument has expanded into a speculative bubble, it is inevitable that the price will have to come back down again. There is no such thing as an elevator that only goes in the upward direction. Despite economists and business leaders promising "permanent plateaus of prosperity" and other forms of hype surrounding stock or real estate markets, if these investments experience a bubble, the prices *will* fall. It is nearly impossible to predict exactly when or why the prices will begin to decline. The only certainty is that the decline will happen, and usually the fall in prices is caused by a significant sell-off. Rarely is there a single event that triggers a sell off, as it is usually a combination of events. Sometimes a sell off is cut short and speculators start buying again when the prices have fallen to some lower level, and this can cause another surge in prices. Eventually, however, a turning point will occur when a critical mass of speculators simultaneously decides that it is time to get out of the market. In order to sell, however, there must be buyers, and if there are not enough buyers or "greater fools," who want to purchase the instruments or securities during a sell-off, then the prices can go into a free fall. This will trigger a panic.

A NEGATIVE, SELF-REINFORCING FEEDBACK LOOP OR "PANIC"

A panic occurs when the price of the security begins to fall rapidly and speculators begin to fear that if they do not sell immediately, they will lose everything. Here another dynamic process with self-reinforcing feedbacks occurs. Falling prices indicate to speculators that there is no longer money to be made by holding on to the financial instrument. Not only do the owners of the instrument want to sell, but falling prices will fail to attract buyers. Sellers must bid the prices down further in hopes of attracting buyers, but this causes speculators to be more discouraged and more cautious about buying an instrument that will continue to fall in price. As prices fall, more sellers want to get out and drive down prices further, lower prices will cause another rush of speculators to sell which drives down prices even further, and the panic will quickly become widespread. This is sometimes referred to as a "shut door panic" during which a stampede of sellers are all trying to get out at once, but at the same time creating conditions such that there are no longer any buyers and prices go into a free fall. The end result is a crash.

THE BOOM/BUST CYCLE ENDS

In major crashes, billions and even trillions of dollars worth of financial value are wiped out. For those who got in and out of the markets in a timely manner— usually the wealthier insiders who are the leading movers of market dynamics—fortunes can be made. Those who bought at relatively high prices on the assumption that prices would continue to rise further and then were forced to sell at lower prices, or just held on, they would experience losses and these losses are often tremendous. Depending on the magnitude of the crisis and the amount of wealth that is obliterated, such a financial market crash can lead to a broader economic recession or depression. This can have long-term consequences for a broad base of the population who had nothing to do with the financial market instability in the first place. In many cases, during the immediate post-crash period where prices hit rock bottom, some buyers will rush back into the market as "bargain hunters." As bargain hunters scramble to gobble up the remains of the wreckage from the crash, they begin bidding asset prices back up again and if there is a new displacement, the cycle starts anew.

An epidemic of speculative greed that turns to panic is the key problem in financial market instability. It is also a direct, though unintended, consequence of capitalist development. As we emphasized above, greed and speculation are certainly not limited to modern capitalism. However, as capitalism developed and its key market institutions sprouted and flourished, speculation and greed-inspired manias followed like a dark shadow. Capitalism has been built on market institutions that allow speculation to run largely unchecked. Financial markets were originally designed to aggregate money from a widely dispersed pool of investors in order to finance large capitalist business ventures. However, these markets eventually became arenas for speculators to play out get-rich-quick schemes. As a result, the boom/bust crises outlined in this eight-step pattern signify a systemic problem in the capitalist world. Upon close examination of the historical record, we can see that the magnitudes of boom-and-bust financial crises grew in direct proportion with the growth of capitalism itself.

The most important lesson of history is that people can learn from their past mistakes as well as from positive experiences. These lessons are being lost and a deeply ingrained culture of greed and entitlement in capitalist societies continues to block a clear vision of the past. Hoping to restore some clarity, we will journey through a few of the more significant historical instances of speculative manias in financial markets.

EARLY SIGNS IN BIBLICAL TIMES

Throughout human history, there have always been those who speculate on the value of financial instruments with the hopes of buying low and selling high. The New Testament tells a story of how Jesus rode into Jerusalem on a donkey and was dismayed by the rampant speculation and corruption he saw there:

> And Jesus went into the temple of God, and cast out all of them that sold and bought in the temple, and overthrew the tables of the moneychangers, and the seats of them that sold doves, And said unto them, It is written, My house shall be called the house of prayer; but ye have made it a den of thieves.[176]

Petronius Arbiter, the famous satirist and author of *The Satyricon*, observed an epidemic of speculative greed in ancient Rome. Early capitalistic institutions were being created by the Roman state in which shares of business assets were bought and sold in a manner similar to modern stock trades. The shares were more like contracts with the Roman government for public works projects and tax collection, and along with the trading of these shares came speculation and the lure of easy money. Petronius gives his account of the speculative mania infecting those who were involved in the trades:

> . . . caught the common people in a double whirlpool and destroyed them . . . the madness spread through their limbs, and trouble bayed and hounded them down like some disease sown in the dumb flesh.[177]

Buying and selling for profit, as well as charging interest on loans, were considered to be based on fraud and were condemned as sinful practices in pre-capitalist Europe. Throughout the Middle Ages and into the pre-Modern era, speculative buying and selling were not part of the economic mainstream, and occurred only on the margins of Latin Christendom. This changed as capitalism emerged as the dominant force in Western Civilization.

When capitalism first began to cohere into a system in seventeenth-century Europe, a fascination with easy money took hold in the minds of those aspiring to become members of the affluent classes. Their aspirations were based on a relatively simple concept. A speculator could take some amount of money, buy a financial instrument, watch the value of that instrument grow, and then sell it for a handsome profit without having to exert any labor or actually create something of value. With the expanded wealth, the speculator could perform the same transaction again and again. By so doing, one could amass a fortune and, with the right luck, perhaps do so over a very short period of time. It should also be noted that whenever these speculative booms attracted money from a broad base of the population—an achievement made possible by modern financial institutions—they always left behind a wide patch of financial ruin.

The first major, widespread speculative mania occurred, not coincidentally, where the earliest capitalist institutions became an integral part of economic life. The mania, however, was not for stocks or real estate, it was for tulips.

TULIP MANIA OF SEVENTEENTH-CENTURY HOLLAND

Among the first nations to develop a modern capitalist economy was Holland in the early seventeenth century. The Dutch were among the very first to bring together commercial banking and monetary institutions, privately owned joint-stock companies, open market exchanges and other institutions that combined to create a modern capitalist system. Within this system, the nascent entrepreneurial class could rise to prominence and unleash its voracious pursuit of financial wealth.

As capitalism developed in Holland, so did financial market activity and speculation. The Amsterdam Exchange was established in 1610 where stocks, bonds, and contracts to deliver commodities of all kinds were bought and sold. The exchange was described by one observer as ". . . a madhouse full of strange superstitions, peculiar practices and compulsive attractions."[178] Perhaps the most peculiar of these compulsive attractions was for tulip bulbs.

Tulips were first seen as exotic, brightly colored flowers brought to Western Europe from Turkey in the sixteenth century. Tulip bulbs quickly became collectors' items among Holland's growing affluent middle class, and as their prices started to rise, they became commodities for speculation in the Amsterdam Exchange. Tulip bulbs lured speculators with modest sums of money as they were reasonably affordable compared to the prices investors had to pay for shares in joint-stock companies. Tulips were easily cultivated, but there was a mysterious uncertainty about them. One never knew for certain if the flower would be ordinary red or yellow, or would bloom with an explosion of various colors caused by chance from a particular viral infection. Such beautiful freak tulips could be sold to wealthy collectors for an amount greater than the life savings of most Hollanders. Thus, with the temptation of this mysterious flower, an opportunity for investment and speculation was created. The tulip bulb mystique constituted a displacement that triggered a boom-and-bust mania.

Buyers entered the market with the belief that one or more of the tulips could turn out to be a magnificent freak and a valuable asset that could be sold for an enormous profit. This belief alone did not create a mania, however, as a general rise in tulip prices was turning a quick profit for speculators and these rising prices attracted much attention. The rising prices attracted enough attention that those eager to give it a speculative try were bidding up the prices for bulbs, thus creating a self-fulfilling prophecy. Even without the jackpot of the colorful freak blossoms, it was discovered at the Amsterdam Exchange that modest profits could be made as the market gained momentum and prices climbed steadily upward.

Prices in the tulip bulb market began to soar in the characteristic positive, self-reinforcing upward spiral. Rising prices allowed for the quick turn of a profit, the profits attracted more speculators who entered the market to buy, which drove up prices and confirmed their expectations. This confirmation would attract even more buyers, push prices up further and stimulate even more interest, and so on. What was at first an amusing outpost for collectors eventually became a widespread mania as people were borrowing large sums of money, often mortgaging their homes or land, to buy more bulbs on the hope that they would continue to rise in price.

The Amsterdam Exchange was originally established to be a magnet that draws money from a widely dispersed group of investors and concentrates the money for economic development. This original intention was to finance large-scale real investments, but rather than using the money for the intended purpose, the Exchange was fueling an epidemic of greed.

Prices of tulip bulbs became overtraded and soared far above any reasonable value for the commodity. In a manner of only a few weeks, the price of a pound of yellow bulbs increased by nearly 6,000 percent and continued to soar. At one point, a single tulip bulb could be sold for a price equal to the price of a house in Amsterdam. Yet, irrationality and cognitive dissonance, familiar characteristics of a speculative mania, had a grip on the imaginations of speculators who continued to buy.

In 1637, the tulip market met its inevitable fate and crashed. A few perceptive investors who saw the coming price reversal and subsequent crash were among the first to sell all of their tulip holdings. They made tremendous fortunes. Most of those lower on the socioeconomic order, however, who had mortgaged their property, sold their livestock and put up their life savings were ruined. Tulip prices never again experienced such a speculative boom.

THE MISSISSIPPI AND SOUTH SEA BUBBLES

In their attempt to rise to absolute power, monarchs of Europe had to rely on the credit extended by bankers and merchants who were active in creating new capitalist institutions. Merchant and investment banks were inventing new financial instruments such as joint-stock certificates, paper currencies, and bonds. The institutions that traded these instruments were also cropping up in Holland, Britain, France, and elsewhere. By the seventeenth century, the "commercial revolution" was unfolding and modern capitalism was coming into full development. The new capitalist system and its institutions fostered tremendous real economic growth and expansion as well as new speculative manias. Just as tulips attracted speculators in Holland, new paper currencies and government bonds in Britain and France became the new displacements that attracted speculators.

THE MISSISSIPPI BUBBLE

The Mississippi Bubble began as a scheme for privatizing the national debt of France. An Englishman, John Law, who was also a notorious gambler and murderer, conceived the scheme. Law had arrived in France to escape prosecution for murder in Britain and had convinced the French government to privatize its national debt by paying off loans and bonds with a newly printed paper currency. It was generally necessary to back a paper currency with something of value in order to sustain people's faith and get them to accept it—usually gold. The problem was there was not enough gold in France to back the currency. Given the gold shortage, Law's plan was to persuade the creditors to buy shares in his start-up venture known as the Mississippi Company. Rather than gold, shares of this company were used to back the currency that was then used to pay off the government debt. France's creditors were drawn into Law's scheme with promises of great returns on these shares from overseas trade. With this new scheme and the Mississippi stock created by Law, a new displacement and opportunity for speculative investment was created.

Like other "crown monopolies," the King of France granted Law's Mississippi Company the exclusive right to control trade in the Louisiana Territory, which constituted nearly half of the United States in the early eighteenth century. The government's creditors swapped their holdings of French government debt—loans and bonds—for newly printed paper currency, and then used the currency to buy shares in the Mississippi Company. The company was able to promise high returns as they had monopoly trading rights in what was expected to be a lucrative area. These promises of high returns attracted other investors and Mississippi stock prices began to rise.

In the familiar self-reinforcing pattern, the increased stock prices created widening interest and a buying spree gained momentum. The momentum drove up share prices that further reinforced speculative interest, this led to more buying and higher prices. Before long, nearly everyone who had anything of value was scrambling to sell their valuables and property for paper currency so they could buy shares in Mississippi and get rich quick. It did not take long for the stock to become overtraded and overpriced.

A bubble was thus created, and the prices of shares in Mississippi rose to over forty times their original value. The fundamental value of the company would be the value of its assets and the earnings from those assets, and a stock that is not overtraded should be proportional to these fundamentals. The company, however, did not have fundamental value because it was not generating earnings. The great profits that were promised to investors did not materialize.

Seeing that Mississippi was not generating much in revenues and that its stock was overtraded, the more perceptive investors, including the original creditors to the French government, began selling their shares for enormous profits. These investors began a sell off that caused the stock price to decline quickly which triggered alarm among other, less well-informed investors. A downward, self-reinforcing feedback loop ensued. Share prices continued to fall causing speculators to fear that prices would plunge further. People began selling, and by selling, they caused the prices to fall, creating more fear, more selling, etc. A wild panic unfolded. Just as those who bought tulip bulbs by mortgaging their property, the majority of those caught up in the Mississippi scheme were financially ruined. The Mississippi Bubble amounted to a tremendous victory for the wealthy, however, as massive amounts of wealth was transferred to them from a larger group of less wealthy investors who were drawn into the speculative frenzy.

The crisis was as much attributable to the systemic nature of speculative manias as it was to individual folly. New instruments were created, and new institutions were developed to sell these instruments to as wide a segment of the population as possible. Riches were promised to a mass of unsuspecting speculators and the scheme was sanctioned by no less than the King of France.

SOUTH SEA BUBBLE

In 1710, three years after England and Scotland united to form Great Britain, the South Sea Company was chartered. Like the French Mississippi Company, South Sea was a privately owned joint-stock company that was granted an exclusive charter by the British monarch to engage in trade, particularly the slave trade, with the Spanish colonies in South America. South Sea was also an investment company created to underwrite several million British pounds of government debt.

As with the Mississippi scheme, paper money was being issued in Britain and the currency was backed with shares in companies like South Sea. However, the money was created for purchasing the very same shares that were backing the currency. This resulted in a circular and highly unstable scheme: South Sea shares were purchased with money that was backed by South Sea shares. This circular scheme triggered a self-reinforcing feedback loop. Investors were drawn to South Sea because they saw an opportunity to buy low, sell high, and make easy profits. As interested investors demanded more shares, prices would naturally rise. Rising prices would yet attract more investors and so on, inflating a speculative bubble. Share prices soared to many times greater than their original value and quickly became overtraded.

Like the Mississippi Company, there was little or no fundamental value in South Sea. The company was not making the fortunes in the slave trade as was promised for its investors and the shares were therefore highly over-traded. In 1720, British Parliamentarian Archibald Hutcheson warned that investors were suffering from delusion to think that inflated share prices were anything but overpriced, and that they were doomed to fall. Cognitive disso-nance prevailed, however, and Hutcheson's common sense was ignored by a mass of speculators caught up in their own greed. At the peak of its bubble, South Sea share prices increased to over £1,000 per share, nearly ten times its original value.

The South Sea bubble spread to the shares of other joint-stock companies that were also traded in London's financial markets. In London, a general stock market boom was underway inflating utilities, insurance companies, and other businesses that experienced a steep rise in share prices on the coattails of South Sea. A kind of riotous delirium of debauchery took hold and people began crowding the streets in drunken mobs to celebrate their riches in stock market speculation. Public drunkenness and hedonistic feasts sometimes went on for days.

Similar to the Mississippi experience, the most powerful bankers and financial market speculators of London were the first to sell their shares. This privileged group included wealthy financier Thomas Guy who cashed out his South Sea holdings and made a fortune of nearly £200,000.[179] Other nota-bles such as mathematician Isaac Newton—who was also Master of Britain's Royal Mint—cashed out their shares for sizable profits. When the wealthy and powerful exit a market, it generally signals the peak of the bubble market and that the bubble is about to burst.

The inevitable price reversal came. By 1720, London's bacchanalia turned into widespread panic and stock prices in general began to fall including shares in South Sea. South Sea stocks started a gradual decline, then the crash began to accelerate and within four weeks share prices plummeted by over 75 percent. The bubble burst and along with it fell the dreamy fantasies that easy money was at hand and that everyone could easily become as rich as Croesus by play-ing the stock market. Financial ruin was widespread except for those who bailed out early. The result was, once again, a transfer of wealth from a mass of unsus-pecting small-time investors to a slender group of the affluent class.

The South Sea Bubble was the first large-scale stock market crash in the history of modern capitalism. It was also an indication of the possibility of much greater crashes in years to come.

SPECULATION AND INDUSTRIAL CAPITALISM

The memory of the Mississippi and South Sea Bubbles was short-lived. Like a new dawn, industrial development of the nineteenth and twentieth centuries ascended over the horizon, and it came with glowing promises of new opportunities for speculation. A host of new industries and technologies presented themselves to investors and new speculative interest was created.

The industries and technologies in the nineteenth century were created anew, but the boom and bust pattern of stock market instability followed the same pattern as the bubbles of the seventeenth and eighteenth centuries. New gold or silver mines were discovered and this sent mining company stocks skyrocketing as speculators rushed in. A crash in mining stocks followed as speculators eventually panicked and pulled out leaving a trail of financial ruin. The rapid expansion of railway lines fueled investor enthusiasm for railroad stocks and a speculative boom followed there as well. Huge fortunes in railroad stocks were amassed by the privileged few, but hopelessness and ruin fell on many others who were caught in the get-rich-quick euphoria that was followed by the inevitable panic and collapsing prices.

Speculative euphoria reached a new level in the United States. Optimism in financial markets grew during the decades of industrial development following the American Civil War and up to the turn of the twentieth century. Those years were eclipsed, however, by the tremendous expansion that occurred between 1900 and 1929. In the first three decades of the twentieth century, the United States passed Britain as the world's leading manufacturing country and the U.S. dollar became the premier international currency. In the four years between 1925 and 1929, the total number of manufacturing businesses grew from 183,900 to 206,700, the Federal Reserve's index of industrial output rose by 64 percent between 1921 and 1928, and Gross National Product grew by 62 percent between 1914 and 1929.[180]

In the immediate pre-Depression years, unemployment was low and price inflation was practically nonexistent. Between 1899 and 1927, steel output grew by 780 percent as a result of technological advances in metallurgy and steel processing. Cotton textile production stood at 845,000 bales in 1860, and rose to 3,687,000 bales by 1900. Between 1899 and 1927, textiles and related products grew by 449 percent. Other industries also experienced rapid growth during that period as well: chemicals grew by 239 percent, machinery by 562 percent, and transportation by 969 percent.[181] Another spectacular growth phenomenon was the automobile industry.

When Charles Duryea first invented the automobile in 1892, it was certain that the automobile was going to have a dramatic effect on American industrial and cultural development. In the early years, the auto industry was made up of small manufacturers that also produced bicycles and horse-drawn carriages. All of them were in competition with each other to build the best alternative to track-bound trolleys or to animal or steam-powered vehicles. Henry Ford emerged as the winner in the competitive game with elegantly simple vehicles and the technology to mass-produce them inexpensively. In 1896, the Duryea brothers produced and sold thirteen vehicles mainly as novelty toys for the affluent. By 1909, Henry Ford's company was mass-producing the famous Model T and sold over ten thousand cars. By 1913, Ford's output increased to 250,000, which amounted to 50 percent of all automobile production, and by 1929, over 23 million automobiles were produced for American mass consumption.[182]

Another boom industry in the pre-Depression years was electricity and electrical appliances. By the 1920s, technology developed such that electricity could be distributed inexpensively to most urban households. In 1907, only 8 percent of households had access to electricity, but by 1929, the figure had risen to 85 percent.[183] With access to electricity, people could equip their homes with washing machines, toasters, refrigerators, and radios. Westinghouse introduced the first radio to the consumer goods market in 1920. Other companies quickly entered the market and the industry eventually came to be dominated by Radio Corporation of America (RCA). Radio sales skyrocketed from $60 million in 1922 to $843 million in 1928—an increase of 1,305 percent.[184] In 1887, there were 170,000 subscribers to telephone services and by 1917 the number rose to over 12 million—an increase of nearly 7,000 percent.[185]

Rapid growth and development became the norm in one industry after another during the roaring 1920s. Although there was still much poverty and labor strife, there was an emerging optimistic sentiment among the population who celebrated the new wealth created by industrial and technological progress. The period was dubbed "The New Era" as people began to believe that a new time had come that promised to wipe out poverty and economic uncertainty. The incomes of working people increased along with those of the middle class, although many remained in poverty and much of the rise in income flowed to the already affluent. The number of millionaires in the U.S. increased from about four thousand in 1914, to nearly twelve thousand by 1926.[186] The exuberance of the roaring twenties was expressed in the stock market and share prices soared. During these times of prosperity, it was inconceivable to most people that the worst collapse in the history of capitalism was only a few years away. Yet that is precisely what came to pass.

THE CRASH OF 1929

The general mood of optimism in the "New Era" of the 1920s seemed immutable. The newly created Federal Reserve System promised to bring stability to banking and to instill faith in the integrity of the dollar among the people and businesses. Speculators began to develop a false sense of security as they started to believe that the Fed could use its powers of monetary policy to maintain stability, and that there was no longer reason to be wary of financial market bubbles or crashes. Bankers also developed an irrational belief in the Fed as "the banker's bank," and were lending huge sums for margin trading. Widespread confidence, whether well grounded or delusional, caused stock prices across a wide spectrum of industries to rise.

In the same pattern as before, stock prices began an exponential rise into a bubble. The self-reinforcing feedback mechanism began as rapid industrial development generated new interest in stocks and a surge in demand pushed prices upward. Rising prices attracted more speculators, many of whom were armed with borrowed money, and stock prices were bid even higher. The higher stock prices confirmed speculators' expectations and this confirmation attracted more buyers, which generated a new round of rising share prices, and so on.

At the same time, speculators were emboldened by optimistic speeches from business and political leaders and by optimism in the financial press. Yale economist Irving Fisher famously announced on October 17, 1929—one week before the biggest stock market crash in history—that, "stock prices have reached a permanently high plateau and will rise a good deal higher within a few months." Newly elected president, Herbert Hoover, expressed jubilant optimism over the benefits of capitalism in a speech given at Stanford University in 1928,

> We in America today are nearer to the final triumph over poverty than ever before in the history of any land. The poorhouse is vanishing among us. . . . Given a chance to go forward with the policies of the last eight years, we shall soon with the help of God be in sight of the day when poverty will be banished from this nation.[187]

While leaders were using compelling rhetoric to fan the flames of a gigantic speculative mania in the stock market, creditors were lending huge sums to be gambled in speculation. Businesses were also feverishly printing new stock certificates for sale in the markets as a way of meeting the demand as Americans across the country were encouraged to play the stock market. And as with every other speculative boom, when masses of individuals are drawn into the mania, a bubble follows.

Evidence of a bubble was clear. The number of shares listed on the New York Stock Exchange increased from 443 million to over 1 billion between 1925 and 1929. An index of stock prices maintained by the *New York Times* stood at 110 in 1924 and had climbed to 338 by early 1929, and by September, right before the crash, it had reached 452—a fourfold increase in four years. Another measurement showed that the dollar value of all the shares listed on the New York Stock Exchange stood at $4 billion in 1923 and rose to $67 billion at the beginning of 1929. The market boom of the 1920s was one of the largest expansions of paper wealth in the history of the world.

Part of what caused this expansion of paper wealth was the extension of credit to speculators. A common banking practice at the time was to extend credit on the basis of a 90 percent loan-to-value margin. For example, someone who wanted to buy say $1,000 worth of stocks would only need to come up with 10 percent ($100) cash and the other 90 percent ($900) would take the form of a loan. This leverage made it easier for middle and even low-income people to get in the game of speculation. Just before the crash of 1929, the total amount of loans extended by brokers and banks totaled $16 billion, which was about 18 percent of the total market value of all stocks.[188]

Non-financial corporations were also acting as creditors fueling the bubble in stocks throughout the 1920s. Large and profitable companies like Standard Oil were redirecting their profits as loans to speculators to buy stocks, and thus further driving up their share prices. As these companies were not banks, they stood outside the control of Federal Reserve System and were completely unregulated. By 1929, approximately 50 percent of the credit used for stock market speculation came from non-financial corporate loans.[189] Without this infusion of credit into the stock market, the boom of the 1920s and the crash that followed could never have happened—at least not to such a magnitude. Not only were people cajoled to play the market, banks and non-financial companies were aggressively lending them the money to do it.

On the up side, credit supercharged the rise in stock prices by pumping dollars into the market at a rate much faster than the growth rate of real earnings and the value of assets. On the down side, call loans amplified falling prices as banks and brokers would call back loans and trigger more sell-offs of stocks. Speculators who might not have otherwise tried to sell their stocks were forced to when they received their margin calls.

Another factor that served to inflate the bubble was the price-fixing schemes of investment pools. Investment pools were typically formed by groups of wealthy bankers and industrialists who would collaboratively pick a stock, and then pool their money together to buy it. By acting in collusion, they were able to place enough concentrated demand for the stock that they could force the stock price to rise. Seeing the stock price rise, others would be drawn to the stock and the price would begin to soar by its own momentum. The pool operators would eventually sell their shares and make significant profits.

The most infamous investment pool was that which formed to target RCA stocks. In a relatively short period of time RCA stock prices rose from about $20 per share to about $400—an increase of 1900 percent. At that point, the pool operators quietly began selling their stocks and walked away with $100 million in profit in one week.[190]

Forming investment pools often involved bribing financial press reporters of the *New York Times* and the *Wall Street Journal*. The journalists would take payments from the pool operators to hype a particular stock that operators were manipulating to boost the price. When the stock prices inevitably increased, journalists began to develop a kind of false credibility. Though many readers knew that the reporters were being paid, they did not seem to care as long as they could go along for the ride. As in every get-rich-quick scheme, both the deceiver and deceived were playing a part in the deception.

Not only were journalists on the payroll of investment pools to write glowing reports of specific stocks, but also bankers and others were hard-selling stocks to anyone who could scrape together a few dollars. Stock salesmen were peddling get-rich-quick schemes to gullible amateurs in bars and railway stations and John J. Raskob, a member of the board of directors of General Motors, published a famous article in the *Ladies Home Journal* titled, "Everybody Ought to Be Rich." Raskob pitched a scheme in which a combination of cash and call loans could turn a modest sum of $15 a month into a fortune (at that time) of $80,000 within twenty years. And for those who did not want to wait twenty years for their fortunes, he pitched a more aggressive plan involving investment pools.[191] Convinced that they were going to get rich on easy money, amateur speculators from all over were pulling what savings they had from their bank accounts and borrowing on margin to place their bets in the stock market. For a time the schemes were working as promised and people were seeing tremendous increases in financial wealth. As speculators' expectations were confirmed, more money poured into the markets.

There were critics in the late 1920s who were voicing their concerns about the potential instability of the stock market, but they were largely dismissed as curmudgeons. It was difficult for them to make a case when so many speculators were seeing their investments grow many times over their original value. Cognitive dissonance had once again set into the minds of the crowds in Wall Street. Mob psychology and infectious greed served to drown out the voices of those who warned of a coming crash, and their irrationality was encouraged by Wall Street economists and bankers.

Historically significant events like the stock market crash of 1929 are rarely traceable to a single cause. These events come about as a result of a confluence of a multitude of forces that, perhaps largely by chance, meet at a historically unique moment in time. Aside from purely irrational optimism, there were other indicators that suggested that the bubble in the stock market was going to burst. Economic bad news was mounting. There was a money shortage as banks were nearly lent dry with much of their loanable funds absorbed in stock market speculation, and the Federal Reserve's ability to expand credit was severely constrained by a limited amount of bond holdings at the New York Reserve Bank. Interest rates began to rise and this had a dampening effect on consumer and investment spending in the real economy. Real downturns began to show up in every major industry such as steel, construction, and auto manufacturing. Poverty rates were also on the rise. It seemed that the spectacular industrial boom of the 1920s was over and people began to lose their optimism.

As the fog of speculative euphoria was beginning to clear and economic trouble began to come into focus, some decided it was time to get out of the stock market. In the spring of 1929, a steep downturn in stock prices triggered a flurry of margin calls in which banks began calling in their loans. Like so many panics before, the inevitable price reversal finally came and it triggered a massive sell-off. The sell-off was followed by a negative, self-reinforcing pattern of falling prices, more "sell" orders, more falling prices and, eventually, a panic.

A critical mass of speculators simultaneously decided that stocks were overpriced and decided to sell. On Thursday, October 24, 1929, stocks went into a precipitous decline when sellers discovered "air pockets," a situation in which there were no buyers. Stock prices went into a free fall that was temporarily stemmed the following day by National City Bank and J.P. Morgan Co. who sent representatives to the floor of the New York Stock Exchange shouting "buy" orders. Their attempt to end the panic seemed to work for the day and stock prices rose slightly. Over the following weekend, President Herbert Hoover attempted to allay speculators' fears by announcing that the economic conditions were sound and prosperous. Many brokerage firms were exhorting investors to pick up bargains with sales pitches such as, "We believe that the investor who purchases securities at this time . . . may do so with utmost confidence."[192] Their attempts to recreate a mood of optimism were not sufficient to reverse the heavy downward pressure placed by millions that wanted out. Stocks went, once again, into a freefall, and on Tuesday, October 29, the stock market made history as the *New York Times* reported:

> Stock prices virtually collapsed yesterday, swept downward with gigantic losses in the most disastrous trading day in the stock market's history. Billions of dollars in open market values were wiped out as prices crumbled under the pressure of liquidation of securities which had to be sold at any price . . . From every point of view, in the extent of losses sustained, in total turnover, in the number of speculators wiped out, the day was the most disastrous in Wall Street's history. Hysteria swept the country and stocks went overboard for just what they would bring at forced sale.
>
> Efforts to estimate yesterday's market losses in dollars are futile because of the vast number of securities quoted over the counter and on out-of-town exchanges on which no calculations are possible. However, it was estimated that 880 issues, on the New York Stock Exchange, lost between $8,000,000,000 and $9,000,000,000 yesterday.[193]

Measured caution turned to fear, and fear turned to widespread panic. In a single day of trading, the stocks of companies that were once the darlings of speculators collapsed. For example, RCA shares fell from a one-time high of $110 to $26, AT&T share prices dropped by 50 percent and Blue Ridge shares plummeted from $100 to $3.[194] As the panic unfolded, it was clear that the bubble-inflated stocks were finally experiencing a complete deflation.

Stocks continued to fall for nearly three years. From its peak of about 206 in September 1929, the Index of New York Stock Prices (benchmarked in 1926 at 100) plummeted to about 34 in June 1932.[195] Measured in dollar terms, about $74 billion in stockholder wealth was obliterated. As typically is the case, the small investors were hit the hardest. The magic spell of the New Era optimism was broken as the crash left a long and wide trail of financial ruin and bank failures. The crash signified the end not only of the New Era, but also of *laissez faire* ideology and the belief in free-market capitalism. The crash brought the capitalist market system to its knees and opened the way for the Great Depression of the 1930s—the worst crisis of capitalism in history.

BOOMS AND BUSTS AT THE TURN OF THE THIRD MILLENNIUM

The predictable pattern of financial market instability continued for decades. Each boom and bust cycle, however, was of a smaller magnitude compared to the crash of 1929. Speculators once again became optimistic and developed an irrational belief that large-scale financial market crises could not happen again. All that changed with the onset of the East Asian Crisis in the late 1990s and the Great Stock Market Crash of 2000.

Both crises were instances of financial market instabilities that could be traced to two significant developments in the 1990s: the development of computer technology and the Internet, and the post-Cold War hyperbole of the "New World Economic Order." These developments, moreover, were not mutually exclusive. The so-called "emerging markets"—countries whose economies appeared to be on the cusp of developing opportunities for investment, particularly in East Asia—were seen as opportunities for capital investments. Capitalism was largely seen as the winner of the Cold War, and investment opportunities around the world were no longer constrained by the encumbrances of Cold War politics. At the same time, tremendous increases in computing power and Internet technology brought the world of finance much closer together and dramatically facilitated the movement of finance capital around the world. The combination of the post-Cold War promises of prosperity in "emerging markets" and advances in computer technology of the 1990s served as displacements that set in motion a speculative boom and bust unlike any since the New Era of the 1920s.

The similarities between the 1920s and 1990s are profound. The mood of euphoric optimism of the 1920s was given the dramatic name of "The New Era," and the euphoria of the 1990s was similarly dubbed, "The New Economy." Both eras were at the end of global conflict as The New Era came at the end of World War I in 1918, and The New Economy emerged after the end of the Cold War in 1989. Both were boom periods characterized by get-rich-quick schemes, flurries of technological innovation and growth industries, media hype, and a general feeling of capitalist triumph.

The New Economy of the 1990s promised miracles. Behind these often exaggerated promises were America's corporations and their political adjuncts in Washington D.C. Millionaires and billionaires were being made seemingly overnight in the meteoric rise of the dot.com sector. New Internet companies were sprouting every day, and producing everything from electronic greeting cards to online grocery shopping services. American workers were expected to move out of traditional manufacturing and retail jobs to the cutting edge of a high-tech, high-income workforce. According to Robert Reich, Secretary of Labor in the Clinton Administration, American workers were to become better-paid, highly skilled "information" workers and manipulators of symbols (words, computer codes, and numbers) rather than assembly line workers in factories. Millionaires and well-paid information workers alike were all promised to be on the path to riches on America's Information Superhighway.

The Berlin Wall tumbled on November 9, 1989, symbolically ending the Cold War. And with the end of the Cold War, new global divisions of labor were promised. While Americans were promised to become the more affluent information workers, the labor force in the emerging markets of Asia and elsewhere would become the world's premier steel, textile, and consumer goods producers—all of which were fading from the U.S. manufacturing sector.

Also at the end of the Cold War, the American business/political community began celebrating the notion that American capitalism had emerged triumphantly in the world as the premier economic system. The opportunity to direct countries into a global system (New World Order), from which U.S. corporations could profit proved irresistible. With a certain swagger, American foreign policy leaders traveled the globe pressuring countries in Eastern Europe, East Asia, and elsewhere to begin restructuring their economies along guidelines that conformed to *laissez faire* capitalist ideology: cutting government spending on social programs, lowering taxes, reducing government regulations on business activity, privatizing publicly-owned businesses, and most importantly, opening up their economies to trade and financial investments. These policy prescriptions came through the traditional Washington D.C.-based institutions such as the International Monetary Fund, the World Bank, and the U.S. Treasury Department, and subsequently came to be known as the "Washington Consensus."

The Washington Consensus evangelized to the world a vision of a global system of capitalism in which financial investments could travel seamlessly from one country to another. It was important, therefore, for countries to open up, or liberalize, their financial markets so that they could be part of the new system. The principal argument behind policies for capital market liberalization was that finance capital could be allocated around the world most efficiently by following free-market principles. Finance capital is scarce in many parts of the world including, the argument goes, in the emerging markets in Eastern Europe and Asia. Scarcity means higher prices, and for finance capital, that means higher rates of returns. In a global free-market environment, capital will automatically flow around the world to wherever it is needed the most, that is, where it is scarcest and where it pays higher returns.

Large Wall Street investment companies were pushing this vision. Wall Street became a kind of surrogate foreign policy institution. Investment firms pressured governments to pass laws that would deregulate their financial markets so as to make it easier for these companies to move their money in and out of these countries. According to the Washington Consensus, everyone regardless of where he or she was located, could become a stakeholder and could share in the benefits of economic growth stimulated by capital investments. All people of the world would have the opportunity to become rich capitalists. But to do so, they had to play by the rules established by the Washington Consensus. In effect, countries were being told that they had to allow Wall Street firms to move their capital in or out on their own terms if they wanted to gain membership into the global capitalist club.

Nonetheless, the countries' experiences were quite different from that promised by the Washington Consensus, particularly countries in East Asia. Those that followed the recommendations put forth by the Washington Consensus endured some of the worst financial market instabilities in their histories. In the late 1990s, financial market instabilities spread from one Asian country to another like an epidemic—it came to be known as the "Asian Flu." Those that resisted the Washington Consensus remained largely immune and relatively stable.

THE "ASIAN FLU"

Throughout the 1990s, investors poured over $1 trillion of capital into the financial systems of Thailand, Malaysia, Singapore, Hong Kong, South Korea, and others. Much of these capital flows were in the form of bank loans and purchases of stocks and bonds in the local financial markets that paid high rates of return compared to returns on investments in U.S. markets.

Before such investments could be made, however, the regulations on flows of foreign investments imposed by these countries' governments had to be dismantled. The result was that as these countries followed the recommendations of the Washington Consensus, they also became bound to American investment companies.

Part of this binding entailed fixing currencies to the U.S. dollar. Starting as early as the 1980s, Thailand, Indonesia, and other countries began committed to a fixed exchange rate with the dollar so as to maintain stability in international trade and investments. However, by fixing their currencies to the dollar, these countries lost much of their control over the value of their currencies and their economies. In effect, the Asian economies came under the control of policies set in Washington—policies that were designed primarily to benefit American banks and Wall Street firms, not Asia.

In April of 1995, the U.S. began negotiating a process whereby the dollar would rise in value against the Japanese yen in order to assist Japan out of its recession. By weakening the yen relative to the dollar, Japanese exports would become more competitive in U.S. markets. With a boost in its export sector, it was believed that Japan would pull out of its recession. As the U.S. dollar became stronger relative to the yen, other currencies, including the Thai baht (THB), also strengthened as they were fixed to the dollar. Just as weakening the yen boosted Japan's ability to export to foreign markets, strengthening the baht compromised Thailand's ability to export. This was a significant problem for a country like Thailand, whose economic growth was almost entirely driven by its export sector. In their earlier years of development, Thailand and other Asian countries patterned their export-led growth after the Japanese model which was based on a pluralist system of careful government planning and management and private enterprise—a model which is antithetical to America's push for a global system of pure capitalism.

After adopting a more free-market approach, and after tying its currency to the dollar, Thailand's export sales plummeted and trade deficits began to soar. To make matters worse, China burst into the world trading system as the premier producer of low-cost exports and Thailand lost much of its share of the world export market.

Losing its export earnings, Thailand began borrowing large sums of money by selling bonds to Wall Street banks and investment firms at relatively high interest rates. With the borrowed money, Thai banks, in turn, made loans to local businesses for economic development projects (a policy that was also recommended by the Washington Consensus) including commercial real estate development in hotels and resorts to augment tourism, and in export-oriented manufacturing infrastructure. Much of this development was directed toward restoring Thailand's earnings of foreign currency needed to pay their high-interest debt obligations to Wall Street.

As Thailand agreed to follow open-market policies set by the Washington Consensus, its financial sector became vulnerable to instabilities that come with currency speculation. As with the Dutch tulip bulbs centuries before, the Thai baht became an object of speculator interest and was quickly destabilized. Speculators observed Thailand's mounting deficit and debt problems and began to place bets that Thailand would not be able to sustain its fixed exchange rate with the dollar. But the speculators were not anticipating that the baht would rise in value, rather that it would fall. In other words, they were "short-selling" Thailand's currency, and they were doing so in huge volume.

The process of short-selling the Thai currency goes something as follows. Thailand had for some time been maintaining a fixed exchange rate of about 25 THB to the dollar. Speculators who believed that the currency would fall in value began borrowing baht and then used the baht to buy dollars. They would then wait for the currency to devalue, buy the baht at a cheaper price, pay back the loan and walk away with a profit. Say for example, a speculator borrows 25 million bahts and with that money immediately buys $1 million U.S. dollars at the $1 = 25 THB exchange rate. The speculator sits on the million dollars and waits for the baht to devalue, to say $1 = 30 THB. At that point, the speculator can buy the 25 million baht it needs to pay back the loan, and at a $1 = 30 THB, the speculator only needs about $833,000 to buy the 25 million baht and pocket the remaining $167,000.

Like other forms of speculation, short-selling has a way of becoming a self-fulfilling prophecy. Large hedge funds and other U.S. investors were positioning to short-sell the Thai baht. By doing so, they were siphoning dollars out of Thailand's banks. As more speculators decided to short-sell, more were demanding U.S. dollars and therefore placed more stress on Thailand's reserve of foreign currency. Eventually Thailand ran out of dollars. Those who were not short-selling began a panicked sell-off of the baht, and the currency went into a free fall. In a vain attempt to stabilize its currency at its agreed fixed rate, Thailand's government borrowed huge amounts of dollars in order to buy enough baht to raise its value. But those dollars immediately fled back out of its banks as speculators sold off their holdings of baht. The self-fulfilling prophecy for the speculators was realized, and Thailand's currency collapsed. Within a matter of months, Thailand's currency lost half of its value, and at its lowest point it was trading at 56 THB to the dollar.

As the currency collapsed, the panic spread to other sectors of Thailand's financial markets. U.S. banks and investment firms that purchased Thai stocks and bonds stood to lose as these securities, priced in baht, collapsed in value along with the currency. The collapsing currency dragged the stock and bond markets down with it. Free and open markets in Thailand came to mean that Wall Street firms were free to openly move their money into Thailand's markets for speculation, and were free to openly pull it back out, *en masse*, leaving a tsunami of financial wreckage behind. In a wave of panic selling, these Wall Street firms sold out their holdings of Thai securities, which contributed heavily to the destabilization of Thailand's stock and bond markets. In 1997, Thailand's stock market dropped by a staggering 75 percent.[196]

Observing what was happening in Thailand, speculators became skittish in other markets and the speculative panic began to spread to other countries, specifically among those that followed the Washington Consensus's prescription of liberalized capital markets. In October 1997, Hong Kong's Hang Seng stock market index showed a fall of 23 percent and its central bank had spent over $1 billion in U.S. dollars—an amount equal to about half of Hong Kong's broadest measure of its money supply—to prevent a collapse in its currency. Interest rates spun wildly out of control and at one point had risen overnight to as high as 500 percent. In Malaysia, the national currency, the ringgit, also collapsed, the stock market crashed and the country plunged into a deep recession that was felt in every sector of the economy. Malaysia's real gross domestic product declined by 6.2 percent in one year.[197] In Indonesia, the experience was similar: collapsing currency, crashing stock markets, followed by a deep recession.

Accompanying Indonesia's currency crash was skyrocketing price inflation. Steep increases in food prices precipitated riots and political instability. For the countries involved, the end result was among the worst economic downturns in their histories. Joseph Stiglitz, at that time a World Bank economist, describes the aftermath of the crisis:

> As the crisis progressed, unemployment soared, GDP plummeted, banks closed. The unemployment was up fourfold in Korea, threefold in Thailand, tenfold in Indonesia. In Indonesia, almost 15 percent of

males working in 1997 had lost their jobs by August 1998, and the economic devastation was even worse in the urban areas of the main island, Java. In South Korea, urban poverty almost tripled, with almost a quarter of the population falling into poverty; in Indonesia, poverty doubled. In some countries, like Thailand, people thrown out of jobs in the cities could return to their rural homes. However, this put increasing pressure on those in the rural sector. In 1998, GDP in Indonesia fell by 13.1 percent, in Korea by 6.7 percent and in Thailand by 10.8 percent. Three years after the crisis, Indonesia's GDP was still 7.5 percent below that before the crisis, Thailand's 2.3 percent lower.[198]

One country after another fell victim to the financial market instability that was created mainly by Wall Street firms and their partners in Washington.

To be fair, Wall Street firms and the Washington Consensus were not solely responsible for these instabilities. As with other significant events in history, there were a multitude of causes. It is, nonetheless, clear from the evidence that if these countries had not followed the U.S. Treasury and IMF policies, the crisis could have been averted. Moreover, the countries that did not play by the rules set by the Washington Consensus and were still part of the global trading system were spared. According to Joseph Stiglitz:

> I believe that the capital account liberalization was *the single most important factor leading to the crisis* . . . [Stiglitz's italics] Indeed, in retrospect, it became clear that the IMF policies not only exacerbated the downturns but were partially responsible for the onset: excessively rapid financial and capital market liberalization was probably the single most important cause of the crisis, though mistaken policies on the part of the countries themselves played a role as well.[199]

In an ironic turn of events, the Asian countries had no choice but to turn to the IMF, one of the institutions partially responsible for the crisis in the first place, for loans to restore financial stability.[200]

The IMF and U.S. Treasury Department, acting on behalf of America's large banks and Wall Street corporations (premier political campaign contributors) urged the East Asian countries to open their markets to speculative investments. Robert Rubin, a former Wall Street investment banker, was Treasury Department Secretary at the time and brought representation of the investor class directly to the White House cabinet. Acting on behalf of the Wall

Street community, Rubin led the charge to crack open the financial markets in East Asia. Large Wall Street investment companies were drawn to the Asian financial markets because of the potential high rates of return offered there. High returns generally mean higher risk as well, but the element of risk was largely nullified as Wall Street corporations knew that the U.S. Treasury was on their side; they also knew that if conditions in the markets went badly the Treasury and the IMF would be there to bail them out—which is exactly what they did. The IMF gave the governments of the East Asian countries $95 billion in loans so that they could pay back their obligations to Wall Street firms.[201]

The naked interest of capitalism and its relentless drive for profits pried open the economies of East Asia. These were economies that previously pursued their own pluralistic model of growth based not on free markets, but on a system of government planning and private business. Subject to the whims of the Wall Street investors, East Asian economies were destabilized and the people of these countries—people who had not borrowed from foreign banks or benefited from the high rates of return of capital investments—are now shackled to the burdens of debt repayments and the painful austerity programs imposed by the IMF as conditions for the loans.

Yet the Asian crisis can be seen not as a failure of capitalism, but its triumph. The investor class enjoyed high rates of returns while they lasted, and enjoyed the welfare of the IMF that stepped up as lender and bill collector on their behalf. The losers in this game were the people who were experiencing improvements in their lives under a pluralistic system, but found themselves thrown back into poverty as the economies tumbled and the IMF imposed its austerity. This process was characterized by the Prime Minister of Malaysia as a new form of capitalist imperialism:

> In the old days you needed to conquer a country with military force, and then you could control that country. Today it's not necessary at all. You can destabilize a country, make it poor, and then make it request help. And for the help that is given [by the IMF], you gain control over the policies of the country, and when you gain control over the policies of a country, effectively you have colonized that country . . . [Capitalist institutions] are not in the business of attending to the social needs of people. They are only thinking about their profit, and if you allow the market to go free, unregulated, then the world will face monopolies of giants who will not care at all about what happens to people . . .[202]

Not long after the Asian crisis, the chickens of financial market instability came back to roost on Wall Street. In March 2000, a major stock market crash in the U.S. began to unfold. From the peak of the stock market boom to the trough of the bust, the crash of 2000–2001, measured in inflation-adjusted dollars, was the worst stock market crash in the history of the world.

AMERICAN FINANCIAL INSTABILITY IN THE NEW MILLENIUM

The United States played hardball with East Asian countries and pulled them into a system of over a trillion dollars of fast-moving "hot money" that proved to be a destabilizing force. The speed at which this money could move around the world was supercharged by the development of computer technology and the Internet. Just like railroads in the nineteenth century and the auto industry in the twentieth century, at the turn of the twenty-first century, computer and Internet technology became an object of speculator interest. As before, this displacement led to much hype, irrationality, and a massive stock market boom and bust.

Information processing and communications were traditionally cumbersome and expensive. By the 1990s, this changed with a flurry of new technologies that dramatically increased computing speed and access to information. Even more dramatic, perhaps, was the impact these technologies had on the economy and on financial markets.

Not only was technology the vehicle that moved capital around the world, but the stocks of technology companies themselves became the objects of financial speculation. The technology industry was both an area of growth and a source of increased productivity rates for other industries and for the economy overall. As hardware and software technology developed and became more affordable, such as with the introduction of the Pentium processor and Microsoft's Windows operating system, businesses and households spent heavily on computers and software throughout the mid-to-late 1990s. Computing power became much more affordable and user friendly. No longer merely a hobby for techies, personal computers became a regular tool for business use and a household appliance. Households began spending huge amounts of their disposable income on newer and faster machines, and on a succession of new versions of software packages. By the mid-1990s, technology was a red-hot growth sector and this found expression in the stock market.

For businesses, investments in computer technology paid off in higher productivity levels. Productivity rates are measured as ratio of output per unit of labor input. Using this measure, productivity rates increased by an average of about 1.8 percent every year during the 1980s. By the 1990s and the takeoff of the computer/Internet boom, productivity levels rose to an annual average of 3.9 percent, and up to 4.7 percent in the early 2000s.[203] Rising productivity levels allowed for significant economic expansion without concerns of price inflation. Technology enthusiasts began making bold claims that digital technology has changed the U.S. economy in such a way that price inflation would never again be an impediment to growth. With little worry about inflation, the Federal Reserve began expanding the availability of credit, lowering interest rates, and this cheap money was eventually channeled into stock market speculation.

With the development of the Internet, entirely new industries were created seemingly overnight. Entrepreneurs came out of every corner of the economy to create an explosion of dot.com service-sector companies. Internet-based companies that sold travel and dating services, pornography, music and books, movie rentals, banking services, and practically every other service that does not require a physical human presence. Most of these companies were not profitable, but their stocks were publicly traded and they skyrocketed with speculation.

Redolent of the "New Era" of the 1920s, the high-tech "New Economy" of the 1990s was ushered in with much fanfare. Inebriated with optimism about a new dawn of capitalist profit-making, speculators began inflating a new and extraordinarily large stock market bubble.

In addition to dot.com and New Economy grandiosity, the stock market bubble was further inflated by widespread accounting fraud and dubious collaboration between investment analysts and investment bankers. Giant corporations such as Enron and WorldCom were fraudulently hiding debts and overstating their profits with the complicity of large accounting firms like Arthur Anderson, thus driving up stock prices even further. Speculators, blinded by the usual cognitive dissonance, seemed not to notice, nor did they seem to want to notice. Just as journalists were on the pool operator payroll in the 1920s, research analysts of investment banking firms were issuing favorable reports on clients' stocks, particularly new issues by corporations for whom their own investment banks were assisting in capitalizing for lucrative fees.

Another factor contributing to the rise of stock prices during the decade of the 1990s was the heightened role played by institutional investors and the so-called "day traders." A demographic wave coincided with the opening of financial markets in Asia and with digital technology. Baby-boomers were entering their prime income-earning years and by the 1990s had collectively amassed a substantial nest egg in retirement funds and mutual funds. More-over, the institutional investors had considerable influence and were pressuring corporate managers to squeeze maximum returns out of their stocks. As they did so, the stock prices rose. With the Internet and the power contained in desktop computing, online amateur speculators, or "day traders," were drawn to the bull market. Just as in the 1920s, just about any-one with a modest amount of money could potentially become obsessed with playing the stock market.

As with every other bubble in financial market history, when masses are caught up in the euphoria of easy money to be made in speculation, trouble inevitably follows. John K. Galbraith observed, "For built into this situation is the eventual and inevitable fall. Built in also is the circumstance that it cannot come gently or gradually. When it comes, it bears the grim face of disaster."[204] The disaster would be felt not by the rich, but by the millions of average Amer-icans who watched the rapid deflation of their 401(k) accounts. The wealthy inside players that spearheaded bullish momentum on the up side got out quickly and triggered a reversal to bearish momentum on the down side.

The Dow Jones Industrial Average was at 2,588 in January 1991. By Jan-uary 2000 it had risen to 11,302, an increase of 337 percent in ten years. The NASDAQ, which is heavily weighted with stocks of businesses in the com-puter and Internet sectors, rose from 414 in January 1991 to a peak of 5,250 in March of 2000—an overall increase of 1,168 percent in the same ten-year period and an average annual increase of 32 percent. Considering that many of the new, high-tech companies listed in the NASDAQ were not earning profits, the NASDAQ stock market boom could not have been on rising fun-damental values; rather it was a speculative bubble. Measured by the DOW and NASDAQ, the 1990s showed the largest stock market increase over a sin-gle decade in the history of capitalism. Like the New Era of the 1920s, the stock market bubble was evidence of massively overtraded stocks, and like the market of the 1920s, the bubble was doomed to burst.

As the likelihood of a crash became more evident, the hype became increasingly shrill. New Economy exaggeration reached its most intense moments with the publications of books such as *DOW 36,000: The New Strategy for Profiting from the Coming Rise in the Stock Market*, by James Glassman and Kevin Hassett. In 1999, Glassman and Hassett asserted that, "The stock market is a money machine. . . . The Dow should rise to 36,000 immediately, but to be realistic, we believe the rise will take some time, perhaps three to five years."[205] Glassman and Hasset were, of course, dead wrong and beginning in 2000, the stock market crashed with a resonance that could be heard around the world.

Depending on when and how one takes the measurement, the total dollar value loss of the 2000-2001 stock market crash was somewhere between $6 and $8 trillion. It stands as the largest crash of all time and overwhelmingly eclipsed the crash of 1929 which, measured in 1992 dollars, obliterated about $676.5 billion. Tech stocks listed in NASDAQ lost 60 percent of their value, other indexes showed a decline in value of around 10 percent to 20 percent, and banks that lent on margin suffered huge losses. As the NASDAQ crash thundered downward, dot.com companies were wiped out. Panic selling ensued throughout the year 2000 and drove the index to as low as 800 in 2002.

The pattern of the crash was not unlike those of previous crashes going back to the Tulip mania four hundred years ago: speculative buying, expansion of credit to be used in speculation, irrational euphoria as the bubble soared, and the notion that no matter how high the price went, there would always be the "greater fool" to buy. Stocks of the 1990s were driven to sky-high levels with the same self-reinforcing feedback mechanism as were stocks of the 1920s. As the ubiquity of greed—always present in a capitalist economy—turned inevitably to an epidemic of panic, stocks were thrown overboard in a self-reinforcing downward spiral of collapsing prices, panic sell-offs. Millions of workers lost their jobs in the aftermath, and as the economy plunged into a recession millions more saw the hemorrhaging of their pension funds and the obliteration of their retirement nest eggs. Those who did not lose all of their investment cash began looking for a new vehicle for investment growth and they found it in real estate.

THE HOUSING MARKET BOOM AND BUST

As long as capitalism is the dominant economic system, the investor class will speculate in financial markets to make money. On this, Doug Henwood writes:

> Capitalism has always been about maximizing profits. Financiers exerted tremendous control over the real economy in the late nineteenth and early twentieth centuries. Financial assets are the ways by which an owning class constitutes itself in a world of large public corporations; this wasn't a revolution in values but an assertion of the

rights of ownership . . . shareholders demanded higher profits, which
they mostly got . . .[206]

Capitalist profits and other sources of surplus cash have created a global
savings glut largely held by a wealthy investor class around the world. The
IMF estimates that this savings glut amounts to about $11 trillion.[207] In the
first decade of the 2000s, the stock market has been tepid and bonds have
been paying very low rates of interest. The investor class has therefore been
trolling about looking for a new object of speculation, or displacement, which
would give them their always-demanded returns. They found their displacement in residential real estate. Once again, the dangerous combination of
amnesia and euphoria had driven the housing market into a sky-high bubble.
As of this writing, the bubble is leaking steadily and for the first time in
decades, a nationwide housing market crisis is unfolding.

The fact that the U.S. housing market has been in the cross hairs for speculative investment is clear. According to a report in *The Economist*, "A study
by the National Association of Realtors (NAR) found that 23 percent of all
American houses bought in 2004 were for investment, not owner-occupation.
Another 13 percent were bought as second homes. Investors are prepared to
buy houses they will rent out at a loss, just because they think prices will keep
rising—the very definition of a financial bubble."[208]

Though most real estate speculators and homeowners did not want to face
it, real estate prices have been in a bubble. Over the forty-five-year period
from 1950 to 1995, housing prices increased approximately at the same rate
as general price inflation, but since the mid-1990s, housing prices started on
a take off in which prices rose over 45 percent above the rate of inflation. The
housing market index maintained by Robert Shiller hovered around its
benchmark of 100 throughout the century between 1890 and 1990.[209] After
the stock market began to crash, the index soared past 150, and by 2006, it
rose above 200. Moreover, the growth in housing prices has pulled far ahead
of the growth in rental rates, which indicates that rising prices are not simply
caused by an excess of demand of people seeking places to live. The ratio of
housing prices to rents is 35 percent above its average level during the period
from 1975 to 2000.[210] Another indication that housing prices are in a bubble
is that they are soaring past people's ability to afford them as dwellings, yet
they continue to climb to record levels.

Between 2004 and 2005, housing prices in the U.S. rose 15 percent.[211]
Such a run up in prices was triggered by a positive feedback dynamic in

which speculators buy property with the intention of owning it for a year and then selling it to make a 15 percent rate of return. Others get into the game, and by doing so, they drive up prices creating the usual self-fulfilling prophecy of speculation. Prices were also soaring as banks were recklessly lending money to borrowers who could not afford to make their mortgage payments, and everyone was counting on the impossibility that home prices will always appreciate. Speculators have been taking out large mortgages, often through interest-only loans, and buying property on the bet that the rate of appreciation will outstretch the finance charges on borrowed funds. In the premier bubble market of California, over 60 percent of all new mortgages taken out in 2004 were interest-only loans—in 2002, the figure was only 8 percent.[212]

At the core of Wall Street's instability today is the housing and subprime mortgage crisis. For well over a decade, residential real estate prices have been driven by the same pathology that drives every financial market bubble—greed. Eager to profit from expanding home sales, large corporate builders have set themselves up in the mortgage lending business. Builders/lenders aggressively pushed variable rate mortgages to boost home sales. The mortgages were used to collateralize bonds that were both underwritten and purchased by large investment and commercial banks. At the same time, the money banks received by selling these mortgage-backed securities assured the cash they needed to make more loans.

As these securities were bought in multi-billion-dollar batches, there is no way to discern which of these loans are subprime and at risk at default and which are not. The current crisis suggests that the percentage is far more significant than anyone could have imagined. In 2008, foreclosures are at a record high, 60 percent above the previous year, affecting mostly low and middle-income familie. For the first time in four decades, the median home prices for the U.S. housing market overall is declining. In some markets, prices are falling at an annual rate of 22 to 24 percent, which means for those who put little or no money down, their home is valued less than their mortgage. In addition, home sales plunged by 13 percent in 2007, which is the biggest decline since 1982 when the economy was in the midst of a deep recession.

What is different about the real estate bubble is that households have used much of the paper value of the real estate boom as equity for further speculation, borrowing, and spending. Soaring household debt spending has been a significant factor in keeping the U.S. economy from spiraling into a deep recession. Home equity debt alone now stands at over $1 trillion and contin-ues to rise.

Research from the Federal Reserve and other sources suggests that the housing market boom has created a staggering $5 trillion on bubble real estate value. Declining real estate prices could also trigger a reversal in debt-driven consumer spending. Individual home equity, which is largely on paper, will disappear and along with its disappearance will be a decline in the home equity loans and the consumer spending that they support. People will be poorer and will cut back their spending and the economy will spiral downward propor-tionally. New housing construction, which stands at approximately 5 percent of the national GDP, is falling into a steep downturn. Along with that downturn will be a slide in all the housing construction-related industries as well. More-over, U.S. banks that have been aggressively making mortgage loans that are saddled with non-performing or subprime loans, and speculators are stuck with loans for overpriced property that they cannot sell. Mortgage defaults are hitting new records. Merrill Lynch Co. lost close to $10 billion in the third quarter of 2007 and wrote down $14.6 billion in assets. This constitutes the worst quarterly loss and asset devaluation in the company's history.

Eventually all eyes will turn to the U.S. Government for bailouts of the mortgage markets as they did with the Savings and Loans debacle of the 1980s, but they will be turning to a government that is itself already buried deep in unsustainable debt. As *Business Week* notes, "There is far too much evidence right now that low rates are encouraging behavior that could cause trouble. Hold on to your hats."[213] These warnings, like so many speculative booms and busts in the past, were largely ignored.

Former Federal Reserve Chairman, Alan Greenspan, who for over a decade de-emphasized the notion that the housing market is in a bubble, finally began issuing warnings. In a statement issued to the House Financial Services Committee, Greenspan warned of the potential disasters of con-sumers and banks getting swept up in the euphoria of a red-hot housing market. Greenspan warned—what would seem to be obvious—that price increases in bubble markets ". . . do not go on forever."[214]

Like every crash there will be winners and losers. Undoubtedly, the losers will be the amateur speculators who crafted plans to make it big in real estate, and the average working families whose economic lives will be turned upside down by what will be one of the worst financial disasters of all time. Accord-ing to *The Economist*, "The worldwide rise in house prices is the biggest bubble in history. Prepare for the economic pain when it pops."[215] The bubble is popping and evidence of economic pain is showing with the collapse of investment bank giant Bear Stearns and massive layoffs at commercial bank giant Citigroup.

CONCLUSION

The notion that someone can get rich merely from owning, buying, and selling is a central feature of a capitalist system. This is not simply a behavioral phenomenon, but is cemented into the institutions upon which the capitalist system is built. As long as this system and its core institutions prevail, there will be financial markets—commodities markets, stock markets, bond markets, real estate markets, and others—that will be subject to speculation. And as long as there is speculation, there will be instability.

It is clear that the current real estate bubble is massive and is beginning to give way to its inevitable downturn. What is not clear is by how much, or how rapidly housing prices will fall. It is nonetheless certain that such a crisis will be felt worldwide. The global real estate bubble is being fed by credit generated by "petrodollars" from oil producers who are selling increasingly expensive oil and recycling those dollars into the U.S. banking system.

High oil prices are feeding the U.S. trade deficit, but because the oil exporters are putting their oil profits into U.S. banks, loanable funds in the U.S. are scarce, keeping interest rates relatively low. Low rates are, of course, part of what is fueling the real estate bubble. In other words, inflating oil prices are indirectly inflating housing prices in a dangerously unsustainable structure. According to an IMF report published in the *Financial Times*, ". . . global current account imbalances are likely to remain at elevated levels for longer than would otherwise have been the case, heightening the risk of sudden disorderly adjustment."[216] The IMF also warned that what seems like current good economic news—higher employment levels and growth—is based on structural instabilities, "Good economic performance rests on a shaky foundation, because of large and continuing global imbalances. If a disorderly adjustment does take place, it will be very costly and disruptive to the world economy."[217] If the four hundred years of capitalism has taught us anything, it is that such adjustments are always disorderly. When we paint ourselves into a corner, the only way out is to make a mess.

It is our contention that we can embark on an alternative path *before* we are completely cornered. This will require hard and thoroughgoing work, and the first step in this work is to begin to redraw the institutional map that defines our economic system. One of the biggest questions that face us when we begin this work is where to start. Should our focus be on changing our own individual behavior, or on a broader movement for systemic change?

Looking at this question from purely an individualistic viewpoint, one could easily draw the conclusion that the results of all the financial market instabilities were appropriate and just. It is easy to argue that each person should individually bear the responsibility for the consequences of his or her actions and choices that he or she makes. People who played the tulip, stock, and real estate markets were not coerced and those who lost everything were, in fact, motivated by a self-destructive impulse—greed.

A systems view, on the other hand, reveals deeper and broader institutional forces at work. The newly created capitalist system in Holland was based on institutions such as the Amsterdam Exchange that not only facilitated but encouraged get-rich-quick and easy money schemes. At every turn, people were encouraged by business leaders, the financial press, political leaders, and even monarchies to get into the game of speculation.

If an individual is encouraged by the powerful and the elite to drink some magic elixir, the chances are good he will take a drink. If the elixir turns out to be poison, it seems unfair to assert that the individual is entirely responsible for his illness. Social and cultural forces direct people's habits and actions as much as they are driven by their personal impulses. Choices are made, but they are made under very specific social contexts. Speculative greed is not only prevalent in capitalist systems, but it has been fostered by capitalist institutions and encouraged with capitalist ideology for four hundred years. It was only with the historic development and consolidation of the institutions of capitalism that the self-interested pursuit of wealth for wealth's sake was transformed from the sin of avarice to a high virtue sanctioned by religious doctrine and by modern liberal philosophy.

The few that score big in financial markets are heralded as wise businessmen and women and those who lose are scorned as victims of their own imprudence, even though all engage in the same speculative actions. What separates the winners from losers could be mere luck or, perhaps more significantly, certain advantages. This history of financial market speculation demonstrates that the gains and losses are not distributed evenly when a broad base of the population is involved. Gains typically accrue to the few key inside players, and losses are suffered by those on the outside who were lured in by promises of easy access to the leisure class of which they have never been members. The process for extracting wealth from a broad base of the population in order to benefit the few has always been a key characteristic of capitalism. The mystique of capitalism is that it triumphs even when it appears to be failing miserably. The process of creating tremendous fortunes and simultaneous widespread ruin is not a flaw, but a direct consequence of the money-based, self-interested system of capitalism.

Collective irrationality and the momentum generated in each speculative market bubble are systemic problems. They are problems that originate in the human vice of greed, as well as in the very logic of the capitalist credo to buy low, sell high, and otherwise let the devil get the hindmost.

12

THE MINDFUL ECONOMY PART I
Redrawing the Institutional Map

In the previous three chapters we explored the problems of a declining resource base and environmental destruction, rising inequality, and financial market instability. To a significant degree, these problems are the destructive consequences of the capitalist system's relentless drive for profits and growth. We saw that environmental degradation and resource depletion are the direct consequences of the growth imperative that is inherent in the capitalist system, and any serious reflection on continuous growth must inevitably lead to the conclusion that it cannot be sustained. We saw that stark inequalities of wealth and income are also inherent features of a capitalist economy, and any serious reflection on principles of social justice, fairness, or democracy must lead to the conclusion that such inequalities are also not sustainable. Finally, we saw that a chief cause of financial market instability is speculative buying and selling, which are inherent features of capitalism, and any serious consideration on how to avoid another financial crisis must lead to the conclusion that this speculation cannot be sustained. That these problems are both systemic and unsustainable indicates that comprehensive change will be inevitable. Given that such change is inevitable, we must consider whether we want to bring about change in a thoughtful and careful way, or have it thrust upon us in the form of a massive crisis. In a mindful economy, we seek to avoid debilitating crises and set out to follow a thoughtful and careful path toward change.

MINDFULNESS AND VALUES-BASED PRINCIPLES

In a literal sense, mindfulness is a state of mind in which people become aware of their thoughts and actions and are fully occupied in the present moment. To be mindful is to be fully engaged in the here and now. It is a state in which our minds are not cluttered with a running mental commentary or chatter about the millions of things that can capture our thoughts. Mindfulness is free from this chatter, and thereby enables us to be openly and directly engaged in the activities before us. Mindfulness is thoughtfulness without superfluous baggage, and thoughts are clear, open, and directly focused on the tasks at hand.

In a mindful economy, we are present in our minds and directly engaged in our daily tasks of producing and distributing. But these tasks are not random, they are filled with purpose and are guided by specific values-based principles that will take us away from destructiveness and toward a healthier, sustainable economy. In a mindful economy, therefore, economic activity is normative.

The first step in building a mindful economy is to establish these normative principles. For our purposes here, we are concerned with shifting our economic institutions away from the injustices of stark inequalities, environmental destruction, and debilitating boom and bust crises. With this as our aim, it follows that the values-based principles of a mindful economy are to be social justice, equity, and democracy; environmental sustainability; and economic stability. With these core principles as our guide, we can set out to reconstruct our economic institutions in ways that are non-exploitative, non-destructive, and stable. In other words, in the same way that capitalism has institutionalized profit-making, greed, and harmful growth, mindful economics seeks to institutionalize human and environmental well-being. We do not see these as means to an end, but as ends themselves. It is our vision that with a mindful economic system based on these principles, humans, the planet, and the creatures we share it with will have a better chance of surviving beyond the twenty-first century.

A MINDFUL ECONOMY IS INTRINSICALLY DEMOCRATIC, EQUITABLE, AND JUST

In a mindful economy, the core institutions that govern, control, and regulate economic activity are themselves intrinsically democratic. Intrinsic democracy means that the democratic will of the people is not externally imposed on institutions, but is inherent in the institutions themselves. This again, is something that is inconsistent with the non-democratic institutions of capitalism.

Many Americans have been raised on the belief that capitalism and democracy are two dimensions of the same political and economic system. American business and political leaders regularly make statements, particularly regarding foreign policy, in which the terms "free-market capitalism" and "democracy" are used interchangeably. It makes for powerful political rhetoric to justify U.S. foreign policy, but these words are not interchangeable, nor are they even compatible. There is no such compatibility between capitalism and democracy and there never has been. In fact, in a fundamental way capitalism and democracy stand in antagonistic opposition.

The spirit of democracy lies in the sovereignty of the population. Yet under capitalism, the majority of the working population provides labor for businesses owned by a small investor class. This investor class is not democratically accountable to the people who work in these businesses or to the communities in which they conduct business, nor do working people have the power to decide how or what is to be produced or for whom. This privileged class structure of ownership is a core institution of capitalism and it would take a tremendous leap of the imagination to make the claim that it is somehow democratic. If ownership and control were more equitably shared by a majority of the population, such a system would fundamentally change its identity and would no longer be capitalist.

The market system is another key non-democratic institution of capitalism. The market is frequently heralded by economists as a democratic institution by emphasizing that people are always "free to choose" in the marketplace. But the freedom to choose or make demands in the marketplace is only available to those with money. Champions of capitalism claim that the market system is a kind of grass-roots populism in which people exercise their will by spending money on what they want in the marketplace. People vote, as they say, with their dollars. This is a fallacious notion of democracy. A market system functions to allocate goods and resources to the highest bidder—to those who have money—and away from those who do not. Such a system overwhelmingly favors the wealthy, and any system that favors a small minority of the wealthy over the majority cannot claim to be democratic, equitable, or grounded in social justice. A market system might be more democratic if the distribution of money to be spent in the marketplace were equally distributed among the population, as is universal suffrage, but there is no mechanism in a capitalist system that would achieve this equality.

Any political or economic system can claim "freedom to choose" as its primary enterprise. Even the most dictatorial, totalitarian societies can make self-admiring claims to freedom. Slave owners have always claimed their right to the freedom to own slaves and the freedom to do with their private property as they choose. Absolute monarchs of Europe also enjoyed the freedom to exercise their arbitrary power over the people in their kingdoms. Such claims to freedom are, of course, meaningless to those who believe in true democracy. Equally meaningless is the claim that the freedom of multibillion-dollar corporations to pursue profits, despite the opposition of people and communities, is democratic freedom. "Freedom to choose" is also a meaningless expression to the hundreds of millions of people around the world who work in sweatshops because they simply have no access to viable alternatives.

As we saw in Chapters Three and Four, people have expressed opposition to capitalist interests by forming labor unions and pushing for legislative reforms in the political arena. Throughout American history, people have been building democratic political systems and institutions to protect themselves from capitalism. People had to fight tough legal and political battles to gain economic concessions from the capitalist investor class—the right to collectively bargain, consumer protection, antitrust laws—and often people lost those battles. Democratic institutions were created despite capitalism, not because of it, and these institutions were rooted in a sense of social justice. To make substantive improvements in their lives, people had to go outside the capitalist system. That is, the democratic institutions were imposed extrinsically on an otherwise non-democratic capitalist system. To envision intrinsic democracy, consider a vision of a society of small proprietors and landowners in which there is no separation of ownership and work, an economy in which people have the full rights to the fruits of their own labor, and one in which people are not subject to the arbitrary power of wealth. This was the vision of John Locke, Thomas Jefferson, and others who laid the ideological foundation for modern democratic republics.

Another significant contributor to the philosophy of social justice was the eighteenth century philosopher, Immanuel Kant. Kant expressed as an unconditional moral law that one should, ". . . act in such a way that you always treat humanity, whether in your own person or in the person of any other, never simply as a means, but at the same time as an end."[218] Kant's message was that the rights and dignity of human beings are necessarily respected regardless of the merit of their actions. People should not have to earn the right to live decently without being exploited, and to live with dignity should be granted unconditionally.

Capitalism is not built on such an unconditional moral framework. Most people are merely the means to an end, which is always profit-making. In a capitalist system, people are laborers to be exploited, and consumers who must be cajoled into spending larger and larger sums of money to generate revenue and profits. In other non-democratic systems, such as totalitarian state socialism, people are also seen as instruments or resources to be used for building state power. Neither system is defensible from a moral stand-point. Both systems are based on exploitation of working people who are systematically deprived of the fruits of their labor, which according to John Locke is a fundamental and natural right:

> [No] one ought to harm another in his life, health, liberty or posses-sions; . . . every man has a "property" in his own "person." This nobody has any right to but himself. The "labour" of his body and the "work" of his hands, we may say are properly his. Whatsoever, that he removes out of the state Nature hath provided and left it in, he hath mixed his labour with it, and joined to it something that is his own, thereby makes it his property.[219]

Locke's political philosophy was perhaps the greatest influence on mod-ern democratic ideology. In short, Locke wrote a moral imperative similar to Kant's in that the labor people perform is their own, the fruits of their labor is also their own, and thus people should not be exploited as a means to an end. Such a moral framework stands in stark contrast to capitalism in which the primary credo is to buy low, sell high, and get rich. As it is applied to pro-duction it means to buy cheap labor and sell the fruits of this labor as dearly as possible for profit. This, in a word, is exploitation.

In a mindful economy, the exploitation of working people is not the way to build a healthy and vibrant community. The well-being and dignity of each individual is a crucial step in building a viable economic community. Fair and equitable value of each individual's contribution, the right to work without harassment or racial or gender discrimination, and the right to a decent liveli-hood are all important to the overall livability of a community.

A significant step toward creating such a livable economic environment is to reintegrate ownership and work. The process of building intrinsically dem-ocratic economic institutions begins at the grass-roots level where control over economic production and distribution is extended in the area in which it mat-ters the most—ownership. Rather than having people slavishly relying on an investor class to provide jobs and livelihoods, people can take direct demo-cratic control of businesses by re-creating institutions that are rooted in the convergence of ownership and work.

A mindful economy extends ownership of businesses to the citizenry, con-sumers, and other members of the community whose lives are affected by activities of those businesses. In this way, the antagonistic relationship between buyers and sellers or workers and employers—always present in a capitalist system—can be mitigated. In the next chapter, we will explore models of business ownership that are currently in existence and have successfully integrated ownership, work, and the surrounding community.

A mindful economy can also become more democratic, equitable, and just by creating a grass-roots-based system of money and banking. As we have argued in previous chapters, the monetary system of the U.S. is not democratically governed. The principal institutions that control the U.S. monetary system—corporate banks and the Federal Reserve System—are not democratic institutions. Money and banking can, however, be made intrinsically democratic if people begin building their own, locally owned and controlled financial institutions. By integrating a localized system of money, credit, and finance that is owned by members of the local community, the system automatically becomes democratically accountable. We will also explore these alternative models of business ownership and finance in detail in the next chapter.

A MINDFUL ECONOMY IS BASED ON RESPECT FOR ALL LIFE AND NATURAL PROCESSES

Respect for all life and natural processes implies that a mindful economy is also ecologically efficient and sustainable. Kant's moral imperative can be extended not only to human beings, but to all fauna and flora in the natural world—as ends in themselves and not as means to our ends. In a capitalist economy, natural plants and wildlife are treated as resources to be exploited for profit. They are valued only insofar as they contribute to the bottom line. Arguments for preserving tropical rainforests are often that such forests are valuable resources if they are kept intact, and that these forests can provide useful medicines and other goods serviceable to humans. Although such arguments may be an expedient way to preserve the forests, they are nonetheless morally problematic. The logic holds that, by implication, the forests' value is measured in terms of how useable they are to human purposes, but if it can be demonstrated that such forests fail to provide sufficient services to humans, their destruction would therefore be justified. In a mindful economy, natural plants and wildlife are seen as things to be valued and preserved in their own right, not only on the merits that they provide something useful to people.

The question that arises at this point is whether a mindful economy must necessarily preclude harvesting natural resources, or raising animals for food.

To respect and preserve natural processes is to respect the balance that nature provides to sustain life. Sustainability does not preclude cutting trees or raising beef cattle or poultry; rather, it places these practices in a broader moral imperative to sustain all life as much as we want to sustain human life.

Nature does create material wealth just as much as human labor. How we use this material wealth and how we treat the habitat must be considered carefully and mindfully. Capitalism (as well as other economic systems) treats nature as both an endless resource pool and as an endless waste dump. This is neither moral nor sustainable. Human existence and the survival of other animal and plant species depend on healthy ecosystems. For ecosystems to remain healthy, they must retain their natural balance and original integrity which took millions of years of evolution to create. Disrespect and exploitation of our natural environment leads to deforestation, topsoil ruination, air and water pollution, species loss, climate change, and a host of other instances of destruction described in Chapter Nine.

Environmental destruction not only violates the moral imperative to respect nature, it also violates the moral imperative to respect humans as future generations' ability to sustain themselves is systematically undermined. This can only be avoided by reducing the size of the ecological footprint humans make on the planet. And to achieve this, people must build economic alternatives to capitalism. The growth imperative of capitalism necessarily enlarges the footprint; that is, it continually widens the wake of destruction it leaves behind.

Just as capitalism makes profit accumulation its guiding principle, a mindful economy openly and directly makes environmentally sustainable practices its guiding principles. Arguably the best criteria for determining sustainable practices are those defined by "Socio-Ecological Principles for a Sustainable Society," and we will examine these principles and other aspects of sustainability in more detail in Chapter Fourteen.

A MINDFUL ECONOMY IS STABLE

Virtually every major financial market boom and bust crisis occurred where capitalist institutions predominated. Over the several-hundred-year history of capitalism, instances of financial market instability have always been rooted in the same core institutions and driven by the same motivation of getting rich from frenzied patterns of buying and selling.

By contrast, a mindful economy carries on a long tradition of locally based systems of economic stability. For at least a century, people have formed financial cooperatives and local community banks to hedge against the wild instabilities created by Wall Street and large community banks. Community-based systems of finance tend to be less oriented toward Wall Street-style gambling and speculation that have led to much instability and ruin.

One of the most damaging aspects of the U.S. capitalist economy is the stress and insecurity bought about by instability. Layoffs and unemployment associated with downturns lead to both sociological and psychological problems. There is clear evidence correlating heightened instances of crime, community and family breakdown, substance abuse, domestic violence, and health problems with economic insecurity. Revenues used to fund vital public services expand and contract with business cycle instability leaving schools and other public services vulnerable. As we have seen, financial market speculation also creates instability and this can affect economic production as well as long-term development. How we can achieve this stability and build it into the institutional fabric of the mindful economy will also be explored in detail in the next chapter.

Guided by these values, people can begin the hard work of restructuring key economic institutions that direct economic activity on to a new course that is both non-destructive and non-capitalist. That is, people can begin the process of working toward systemic change and healthier livelihoods.

Just as the institutions of capitalism have evolved over time to cohere into a complete economic system, the new institutions of a mindful economy must over time evolve and cohere into a new system. In a mindful economy, systemic change will come to pass as a result of a process that will evolve out of, and away from, the current capitalist system, not by overthrowing it as many critics of capitalism have advocated. The first and most important step in this evolutionary process of change is to reinforce the need for us to embrace a holistic or systems view of economies.

Recall that social systems are made up of networks of integrated institutions that work together to serve a broader social purpose. An economic system is an integrated network of economic institutions that direct the processes of production, distribution, and consumption. In the first eight chapters of this book, we described in some detail the principal institutions that make up the U.S. economy: households; corporations; the market system; monetary, labor, and government institutions; and others. These institutions largely revolve around the central drive to accumulate profits, which is unquestionably the top priority of a capitalist system. Once we grasp that a capitalist economy functions as a system, that its destructive consequences are systemic, and that solutions lie in systemic change, then a door opens and the path toward real change reveals itself.

The path toward building real, non-capitalist alternatives will be long and arduous. Taking this path will require both vision and action. As we begin to envision this alternative economic system, we will also begin to envision a system that serves not the narrow interests of a small and affluent investor class, but a system that serves the needs of all members of communities. We also begin to envision a well-coordinated structure of compatible institutions that guide economic activity toward a common set of value-based goals. As we are guided by the core value of ecological sustainability, institutions of a mindful economy must direct economic production and distribution in a way that retains the integrity of our planet, and that uses resources in a non-wasteful manner. As we are guided by the core values of social justice, equity, and democracy, institutions of a mindful economy must be structured to reintegrate ownership and work and eliminate the inherent conflicts of stark class-segregation. And finally, as we are guided by the core value of stability, institutions of a mindful economy must not be subjected to casino-style financial speculation or recurring booms-and-busts business cycles, but rather are stable and firmly rooted in the community.

Bringing this vision to a reality means redrawing the institutional map of the economy. By this we mean actively mapping out a new set of institutions that are fully integrated and cohere systemically. In other words, redrawing the institutional map of the U.S. economy involves envisioning systemic change from *both* the bird's-eye view of the whole system, and the worm's-eye view of the specific institutional parts. Such change will require not only changing how we see our economy, but also fundamentally changing how we go about our daily work of producing, distributing, and consuming goods and services. Bringing this vision to a reality requires a willingness to accept the fact that the U.S. economy of the twenty-second century will be radically different from the one we have now.

Our vision of a mindful economy is not rooted in revolutionary ideology. It is practically inconceivable that a massive $10 trillion economy can be fundamentally altered in a peaceful or meaningful way through a sudden revolutionary catharsis. Bringing our vision of a mindful economy to a reality will also require much hard work and patience. What is more conceivable and practical than cathartic revolution is a process of implementing real economic change in small steps beginning with the development of locally based alternative institutions. Capitalism and all other major economic systems that have existed historically were originally small and localized systems. In a mindful economy, smaller-scale local economic systems are not enclaves of economic utopias or communes, they are merely the starting places from which a broader and more comprehensive system can evolve and grow.

Vision and action in a mindful economy are two-sides of the same coin. Lasting systemic change cannot come about merely by vision, it also requires active work. Such active work cannot be successful, however, unless it is guided by vision. Economic systems cannot change as a result of people merely thinking about them in new ways, economic systems change because people *both* think about them and act in them in new ways.

Healthy change also requires that our vision be clear and our actions direct. As our values are sustainability, equity, and stability, we need to have mental clarity as to how to achieve these goals, and to act directly to bring them about. Building mindful economic institutions in this way will allow people to directly and purposefully organize economic production and distribution to achieve clearly understood goals. With mindful economic institutions, people can control production and distribution in ways that seek to achieve, not profit accumulation, but people's well-being. People can also control production and distribution in ways that are stable, sustainable, rooted in justice and democracy, and in ways that truly serve the needs of people.

Proponents of capitalism might argue that human and environmental well-being can also be accomplished within a capitalist system. Although this may be true in some instances, a careful examination of capitalism's historical record reveals the opposite: horrid working conditions, stark inequality, institutionalized greed, child labor, strife, corruption, and environmental destruction. The ultimate goals in American capitalism are profit maximization and wealth accumulation for investors. Sustainability, stability, and well-being for anyone other than wealthy investors, if they occur at all under capitalism, are of secondary importance. To think that these goals can be accomplished in a capitalist system is delusion, and delusion is the opposite of mindfulness.

American capitalism is, in fact, a system that spawns much delusion. Most people in the U.S. have as their core values a clean environment, job security, good schools for their children, vibrant communities and cultures, healthy food, adequate healthcare, and affordable housing. Yet the path to achieving these goals is indirect, muddled, and often contradictory. Working toward a clean environment in the U.S. is often pursued by providing tax breaks and other financial incentives for growth-oriented, profit-oriented businesses to adopt new, more environmentally friendly practices. These new practices, however, can only be implemented if they do not interfere with profit-making and growth. Yet the drive for profits and growth are responsible for soiling the environment in the first place. It is also often argued that in order to adequately educate children, it is necessary to first cut taxes for the wealthy, sustain high salaries for top corporate executives, and reduce government spending for public services, all in order to stimulate capitalist growth. Then from this capitalist growth, revenue for funding schools will somehow materialize. Rather than directly providing adequate healthcare for people in the U.S., people are instead told to put their money into annuities that will maximize their returns. These annuities function as a way of saving up for the time when they get old and will need that money to pay for unreasonably high costs maintained by the profit-driven healthcare industry. Thus, under capitalism, people are deluded into believing that the only path toward achieving these core values is to stay on a habitual and accelerating treadmill of capitalist growth and profits—a treadmill that actually turns away from these core values.

It remains that a clean environment, education, stable livelihoods, affordable housing, and adequate healthcare are still among the hardest things to achieve in the U.S. economy. It is easier to find unhealthy processed food or junk food than it is to find healthy food. Violent video games are much easier to come by than good educational resources for children, and millions of people are locked out of access to adequate healthcare. Moreover, corporate offshore sourcing destabilizes communities, and with speculation housing is becoming increasingly unaffordable. Yet corporate profits are skyrocketing and this is the ultimate sign of economic success in the U.S. economy. Over time, this systemic delusion causes people to lose sight of what is most important to them. Many Americans hold on to the belief that capitalism is consistent with their personal values even though their personal values remain largely unrealized.

Mindful economics seeks to cut through this delusion. In a mindful economy, people can work according to core values and do so directly and purposefully. In a mindful approach, if we want a clean environment, then we directly build the institutions that will foster this development. If we want good schools, adequate healthcare, and affordable housing, then we build the institutions that foster these developments as well. In a mindful economy, these values are pursued directly and not as a side effect of capitalist profit-making.

INSTITUTIONAL EMBEDDEDNESS

A mindful economy seeks to integrate the values-based principles of justice, sustainability, and stability into the economic system itself. In other words, a mindful economy is an economic system that is *embedded* in a broader culture characterized by these same values and principles.

The concept of institutional embeddedness is a key component of institutional economics, particularly from the contributions by Thorstein Veblen, Allan Gruchy, and economic historian, Karl Polanyi. Polanyi informed us that, contrary to orthodox economic theory, the market system associated with capitalism is not a self-regulating machine. Markets generally do not function in cultural isolation, they are embedded in a broader cultural and social context that sets rules of governance and control in the marketplace. That is, markets are a part of a broader configuration of institutions. Under capitalism, however, the process is reversed. Rather than having markets be a part of human culture, human culture and everything in it becomes a commodity to be bought and sold in the capitalist market system. Polanyi writes:

> To separate labor from other activities of life and to subject it to the laws of the market was to annihilate all organic forms of existence and to replace them by a different type of organization, an atomistic and individualistic one. . . . What we call land is an element of nature inextricably interwoven with man's institutions. To isolate it and form a market out of it was perhaps the weirdest of all undertakings of our ancestors. Traditionally, land and labor are not separated; labor forms part of life, land remains part of nature, life and nature form an articulate whole. Land is thus tied up with the organizations of kinship, neighborhood, craft, and creed—with tribe and temple, village, guild, and church. One Big Market, on the other hand, is an arrangement of economic life which included markets for the factors of production . . . the market economy involves a society the institutions of which are subordinated to the requirements of the market mechanism.[220]

The market system is, of course, where capitalist profits are made. Had Polanyi taken a further step back he might have seen a bigger picture. He might have seen that although culture has come to be defined by the market system, that market system itself is subordinate to the requirements of capitalism.

To redefine life, culture and nature along the lines of the core principles of mindful economy, the relationship between markets and culture must be radically changed. Markets will always be a necessary component to any economic system. But markets are contained or embedded within a broader cultural and social milieu. Our task is to begin the process of redefining this culture within which the markets are embedded. If the culture is dominated by capitalism, then markets will serve the end of profit-making. If, however, the culture is embedded within a system that is founded on justice, stability, and ecological sustainability, then the market system will be subordinate to these ends.

Redrawing the institutional map means redefining all aspects of economic life: the structure of ownership, the relationships between workers and managers, how consumers and producers interact, the nature and function of financial systems and financial instruments, public policy, clear ideas of what "fairness" and "justice" mean, as well as ecology and people's relationships to their natural environment. All of these elements cohere into, and are embedded within, a broader cultural configuration—that will be the mindful economy.

Envisioning economic embeddedness is not to envision something wholly new. As Polanyi argues, economies have historically always been embedded in a broader culture of one sort or another. What we are proposing is for people to question the current culture that economic activity in the United States is embedded within, to reflect on the consequences of this embeddedness, and begin working toward alternatives. We propose both vision and action.

There have been many experiments in the past in which people have tried to build economic alternatives but most have failed. These experiments failed because they were isolated utopias and were not situated within a broader cultural or systemic transformation. That is, the experiments did not take the necessary systems view for determining into what their economic institutions would be embedded. Daunting as this task may seem, there is no reason to think that communities are incapable of mindfully creating alternative cultures within which people live and work. We know this, because the capitalist business community has been creating and recreating our cultures for us for the last two centuries.

In mindful economics, we seek to redraw the institutional map from both a bird's-eye view and a worm's-eye view. Envisioning economic embeddedness requires a bird's-eye view. But this view cannot come into clear focus without actual work. We cannot understand how to change our material surroundings with an intellectual blueprint, we must also act. And through our actions we derive an understanding of how to make the necessary changes.

In our daily struggles to make a living we generate knowledge about our material surroundings. This knowledge eventually congeals into our technology and institutions, and these become a part of our broader cultural fabric. So, as we work, our culture changes and these changes get shared with members of our community, and the culture itself acts as a mediator defining how we interact with nature and with each other. This, in turn, changes the way we work in our daily struggle to produce a living, and thus our economic system evolves.

CONCLUSION

Many have argued that systemic change and redrawing the institutional map of our economy are not necessary. Their contention is that capitalism is not incompatible with the core values of sustainability, justice, and stability. They point to examples of companies that have reformed to specialize in socially and environmentally responsible investments, and to specific consumer choices or political reforms that could have results consistent with the core values of mindful economics. Although there is some truth in these arguments, they fail to address the systemic big picture. At best, such reforms can be seen as remedies of marginal value or half-measures. More importantly, capitalist enterprises are most likely not to pursue these reforms because the profit and growth requirements of capitalism prevent them from doing so.

Companies that sacrifice profits for broader social and environmental goals deviate from the capitalist norm. If they were to become the norm, capitalism as a system would be thrown into a crisis. Profits are not only what drive the capitalist system, they are what keep it alive with a steady infusion of capital investments. Without a steady flow of profits businesses will fail, and if businesses fail, all good social and environmental intentions notwithstanding, the system will fail.

If we do indeed want to survive the twenty-first century, systemic change is necessary. Given that humans show a tremendous resilience and aptitude for survival, systemic change is also inevitable. And if systemic change is inevitable, then the important question is how to bring it about in a way that will assure our survival. It is our hope that the core values and principles of a mindful economy listed above will serve as a starting place in this endeavor.

More specifically, these principles can be built into the legal language of all the key institutions of a mindful economy. Every business, every financial institution, every government agency, and every labor union can be organized along the guidelines set out in these principles. This can be done by incorporating these principles into the bylaws, articles of incorporation, and mission statements of each institution. [We recommend that the reader review the section "II. D. The Corporation" in Chapter Two.] These principles will become the DNA of new institutions, and the new institutions will foster the development of the core values of justice, sustainability, and stability. As these new values are realized, the economy will have experienced systemic change. Just as profit maximization and the growth imperative of capitalism are systemic, the values-based principles of mindful economics will also become systemic.

Redrawing the institutional map requires new ways of *thinking* and new ways of *doing* things. The guiding principles themselves are not sufficient to bring about systemic change; people must actively and purposefully work hard to achieve this change, and perhaps the very first step is to bring the members of local communities together to begin the process of creating new economic institutions that are centered on these core values.

13

THE MINDFUL ECONOMY PART II
Mindful Ownership and Mindful Finance

A common form of capitalist business ownership in America during the nineteenth century was the "company town." These were typically mining or timber communities in which the businesses that owned the mine or mill, also owned the houses and stores in the community. Employees who worked in the mines or the sawmill, also rented their homes from their employers at high rent. Workers were paid a bare subsistence wage in a local currency or "scrip" which was redeemable only in company-owned establishments. Workers did not have the freedom to choose and were forced to use the company scrip to pay for their food at inflated prices in the company stores. The company town was a self-contained and largely self-reliant economic community. In this quasi-feudal arrangement, the company had complete control over the local economy and the source of its control was the fact that it both owned the businesses and controlled the circulation of the town's money. As we reflect on these historical experiences, it would seem clear that whoever has the power of business ownership and control of money circulation, could control the entire economy.

A mindful economy turns this company town model on its head. In the previous chapter, we asserted that the seeds of a mindful economy are planted at the local level. But rather than having a local economy controlled by businesses that exploit the entire community for profits, the economy is owned and controlled democratically by people from the community. People who work and shop in the local businesses also become the owners. In a mindful economy, people not only own and control businesses that produce goods and services for the local economy, they also own the local banks which gives them control over the flow of money as well.

By empowering members of a local community with business ownership and the control of the flow of money, people gain direct democratic control over their economy. Direct ownership and control is intrinsically democratic and also enables a community to focus economic activity according to the values-based core principles of human and environmental well-being, social justice, and stability.

Such a model stands in stark contrast to the currently dominant corporate institutions of the American economy. In the U.S. economy today, ownership and control of production resides with large transnational corporations, and the authorities at the Federal Reserve control money. Transnational corporations are preoccupied with creating a globalized system of production and distribution without regard for the needs and interests of the people where they set up factories or workshops, and are solely answerable to their shareholders. The Fed is owned by, and answerable to, the commercial banking industry. None of these institutions is community-oriented or accountable to the people in the areas where they conduct business, and none is intrinsically democratic.

Currently, most communities in the United States rely on large transnational corporations to make key decisions about where to locate manufacturing facilities and corporate headquarters. These corporations have the capability to create or destroy jobs and livelihoods without democratic accountability. Corporate decisions are not based on what is good for the people in those communities, but on what will bring the most profits to business. They also have the capability to bend the arms of local government officials to get preferential treatment, tax abatements, and subsidies. At the same time, corporations provide no guarantees that they will not be bought out by another company, decide to relocate to another location or move offshore where costs are lower, throwing scores of people in the community out of work. By being controlled by distant corporations, and by the fundamental separation of ownership and work, people have very little control over their economic lives. In a mindful economy that empowers people with ownership and control, people at the local or community level will be the decision-makers, not corporate executives located halfway across the globe. For such a model to work, however, people must both act locally and think systemically.

Although systemic change is a key aspect of mindful economics, it is highly unlikely that the entire American economy is going to change soon. What is conceivable, however, is that new intrinsically democratic systems can take root and grow starting on a small scale at the local level where people have a better chance at gaining the power of ownership and control. Taking root at the local level is the historical rule not the exception. All economies, including American capitalism, originated as small-scale, localized systems. Wal-Mart, the largest corporation in the world, started as a local "five and dime" store in a small town in Arkansas.

FROM GLOBALIZATION TO LOCALIZATION

Though it has captured much media attention recently, economic globalization is not a new phenomenon. International trade and finance date back over a thousand years. Nor can transnational corporations or banks be considered new institutions. Some of the earliest corporations such as the British East India Company, the Dutch East India Company, and the merchant banks of London had vast international profiles. Nor is the capitalist system extending its reach beyond national boundaries a new development. In the mid-nineteenth century, Karl Marx and Frederick Engels wrote this about the international scope of capitalism:

> The need of a constantly expanding market for its products chases the bourgeoisie over the whole surface of the globe. It must nestle everywhere, settle everywhere, establish connections everywhere.
>
> The bourgeoisie has through its exploitation of the world market given a cosmopolitan character to production and consumption in every country. . . . All old-established national industries have been destroyed or are daily being destroyed. They are dislodged by new industries, whose introduction becomes a life and death question for all civilized nations . . . In place of old wants . . . we find new wants, requiring for their satisfaction the products of distant lands and climes. In place of the old local and national seclusion and self-sufficiency, we have intercourse in every direction, universal interdependence of nations. . . . It compels all nations, on pain of extinction, to adopt the bourgeois mode of production . . . In one word, it creates a world after its own image.[221]

Marx and Engels envisioned a globalized capitalist system 150 years before most Americans had ever heard the term "globalization."

Although there is no universally agreed upon definition of economic globalization, there is near universal agreement among observers that globalization entails the creation of economic institutions that span the globe. Economic globalization has drawn much public attention in recent years, particularly after the World Trade Organization was launched in the mid-1990s. The creation of the WTO is arguably the final step in creating a truly globalized capitalist system—a system in which national economies of the world are linked together with a common pledge to further capitalist growth and development.

Among these observers of globalization are both champions and critics. Champions of globalization argue that a worldwide system of trade and investments creates opportunities for prosperity that extend to even the poorest regions on earth—that globalization is a program for economic development. There is some evidence that this is happening in a few places around the world, but there is also evidence that conditions have worsened and become less stable in other places. Criticisms range from the exploitation of sweatshop labor in developing countries, to deforestation, to a loss of corporate accountability, and to a global homogenization of an American brand of consumerism driven by overseas marketing. A consensus is building, however, from across the spectrum of viewpoints that economic institutions which transcend national boundaries are making it increasingly difficult for people to maintain democratic control over their economies.

Global capitalism is constantly changing and moving as corporations seek out new opportunities for investment that will give them the highest returns. Transnational corporations move their financial and real investments from one location to the next, and communities that are economically dependent on these companies find themselves in a constant state of uncertainty and insecurity. This is also not a new phenomenon, and was described by Karl Marx and Frederick Engels as a state in which ". . . all that is solid melts into air."[222] What is new are the speed and size of capital movements that are made possible by new technologies. Entire communities live under a constant threat of losing their economic vitality when a major employer decides to shut down and move operations elsewhere that promises a higher rate of return to investors. Workers are advised to be continuously upgrading their job skills so as to avoid having their livelihoods melt into air along with their employment in the industries that the capitalist system no longer considers profitable enough to keep alive.

Global corporate mobility uproots the livelihoods of people, creates economic insecurity and, because it has no loyalty to specific location, is indifferent to its own destruction of local environments and to people's sense of place. Shortly after the creation of the World Trade Organization in the mid-1990s, offshore production in low-cost countries increased by around 2.5 percent to 3 percent annually. By 2006, the figure had climbed to over 4.5 percent and continues to rise.[223] Corporations must necessarily follow these patterns of behavior because they are institutionally mandated to do so. Profit maximization is written into their bylaws, not community well-being.

The economic localization movement aims to create economic communities that are more self-reliant and less dependent on global corporations. By taking local and democratic control over economic activity, communities make their own decisions and direct activity for their own benefit.

Economic localization does not, however, mean reverting to provincialism or nationalism. Local economies can become more self-reliant yet remain connected to the rest of the surrounding economy and world. Nor does economic localism mean focusing on a narrow segment of the economy, rather the movement is evolving into complete economic systems that are locally-based. The institutions that people create to coordinate local production and distribution cannot exist as islands isolated from one another. They must cohere as compatible elements of a localized system. By implication, therefore, economic localism can be seen as a critical step toward systemic change, and systemic change, as we have asserted, requires both action and vision.

One of the greatest visionaries of self-reliant, localized economic systems is Michael Shuman. In his important book, *Going Local: Creating Self-Reliant Communities in a Global Age*, Shuman imagines a local economy in which local business ownership takes the form of what he calls a "community corporation." Shuman describes successful models of decentralized, community-based corporations in which people have successfully become self-empowered by acquiring ownership and control of the businesses that operate in their communities.

Corporations come in many shapes and sizes. They are malleable institutions and can be made to serve a multitude of purposes, ranging from community development, to public broadcasting, to profit maximization. For Shuman, the process of creating community corporations that serve the needs of local communities is relatively simple: rewriting the charters and bylaws of corporations in such a way that the activities of the business are anchored to the local community, and by requiring that shareholders must also be residents of the local community. In this way, ownership and control, as well as responsibility, will be localized and communities will become more self-reliant and self-accountable.

Shuman also sees community corporations as economic institutions that are embedded in local cultures. Following the tradition established by Karl Polanyi, Shuman sees locally-owned business enterprises as embedded or rooted in a localized community culture. As embedded institutions, locally-owned businesses are more likely to be accountable to the social needs and the cultural characteristics of the community. Shuman argues that the community orientation of local businesses will provide checks and balances on the potentially destructive actions stemming from profit maximization. Thus, for Shuman, capitalism can be preserved, but its consequences can be mitigated as long as it stays embedded in a local community.

It is here that the vision in mindful economics parts with Shuman's vision. Shuman does not address the much deeper systemic consequences (inequality, environmental destruction, and instability) of capitalism. Moreover, he dismisses any such criticism of capitalism by associating the criticism with the failed economic policies of state socialism such as the former Soviet republics. By taking one step further and addressing systemic change rather than mere localized institutional development, Shuman could make a more serious case for lasting and thoroughgoing economic alternatives. By failing to address the systemic problems associated with capitalism, the underlying causes of inequality, environmental destruction, and instability will remain largely intact. Granted, these problems would be easier to manage at a local level, but it takes much faith to assume that these problems will be kept in check by merely embedding them in a local culture.

In fact, most capitalist enterprises throughout history have been locally based and such localism did not act as a deterrent to ruthless exploitation of workers or environmental destruction. Locally owned mines, steel mills, slave plantations, and feudal fiefdoms all share a historical tradition of localism as well as violations of human rights and dignity, and environmental destruction.

In mindful economics, we propose to take Shuman's proposal for building community corporations a step further by defining them specifically in non-capitalist terms in addition to being community-based. Community corporations *can* take a variety of forms. And if the charters and bylaws can be rewritten to make them have a community orientation, they can also be written to be oriented toward equality, environmental sustainability, and stability. We submit that the legal documents of community corporations can be written to assure that the businesses adhere to all the values-based core principles of a mindful economy. Most importantly, corporate charters can be drafted to redefine businesses specifically in non-capitalist categories. This is, in fact, not a new or radical idea as there are tens of thousands of enterprises around the U.S. that operate as non-capitalist businesses.

Before we explore the specifics of non-capitalist community corporations, we would like to add one last thought on economic localization. Any attempt to successfully create an intrinsically democratic and locally based economic system must be located amid an active and participatory citizenry. A key element to the success of a mindful economy are mindful citizens.

In a truly mindful economy, people *must* play an active role in the same way they must play an active role as citizens in a political democracy. In such a system, non-capitalist and intrinsically democratic institutions can be created to reintegrate ownership and work, and to foster sustainability and stability. Citizens can use their constitutionally granted powers of procedural and substantive democracy and see to it that such values become legally written into corporate charters for businesses in their communities. Basic economic institutions can and do work toward eliminating the long-standing antagonisms between owners and workers or buyers and sellers in the cash nexus. And by embedding the businesses into the local community, citizens can achieve more stability and direct community-based democratic control. To achieve this, however, a mindful economy must fully integrate the individual into the broader economic community. By doing so, the individual's role in the economy expands and becomes more complex.

By becoming an integrated member of a mindful economic community, much more responsibility is placed on the individual. This burden is, in part, the price one must pay for democracy. People will become not only employees and consumers, but also owners who must actively participate in the governance of their local economic institutions. That is, in a mindful economy, the role of the individual is to become a "mindful economic citizen." This more complex role of the individual is shown in Figure 1. In most mainstream economic textbooks, the economic role of an individual is

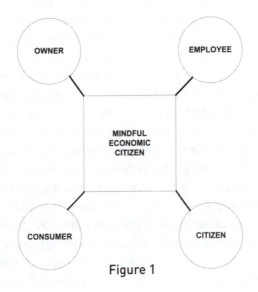

Figure 1

two-dimensional: consumer and producer, with much emphasis placed on the consumer. By contrast, in a mindful economy, the individual's role is four-dimensional by adding the roles of owner and citizen.

Building such a democratic economy requires deep, thoroughgoing institutional change. The most important change is to begin the evolutionary process of replacing capitalist with non-capitalist forms of business ownership.

NON-CAPITALIST COOPERATIVES

Cooperatives (co-ops) are business enterprises that are distinct from traditional capitalist institutions in a number of important ways. The most significant distinction is ownership. Although most co-ops are organized as corporations, they are not owned by absentee investors, but extend ownership and control to *stakeholders* rather than a small group of wealthy investors. For most cooperatives, the stakeholders are people in the community including consumers, employees, and members of the community in general. By becoming members of a cooperative, these people also become the business owners. Co-ops are real-world examples of the democratic union of ownership and community, and their development will be an important step in creating a mindful economy.

Like capitalist enterprises, cooperatives buy and sell in a market system. Unlike capitalist businesses, however, they are not built on the cynical assumption that the antagonisms between worker and owner, or buyer and seller, are natural and unavoidable. Unlike capitalist enterprises whose paramount goal is profit maximization, cooperatives are formed to serve other purposes: to provide basic goods such as food or housing, financial services, education, and other goods and services. Co-ops also differ from capitalist enterprises in that the goods and services are provided openly and directly and not merely as a means to profit-making. In a mindful economy, cooperatives are based on the notion that everyone in the community potentially has a shared interest in the enterprise, and therefore all must play a role in the governance of the business. If serving the needs of people is the goal of a community, then cooperatives can be made as institutions that go to work on that goal directly, not seeking profits with the hope that the goal is accomplished indirectly.

Profit maximization is not the driving force behind cooperatives in a mindful economy as it is in a capitalist economy. This fact often raises questions about how production can take place in the absence of entrepreneurial incentive and the profit motive. The profit motive is obviously important, but it is also overemphasized, particularly in the U.S. Most productive work already takes place in a capitalist system without the profit motive because most of the people who do this work do not work for profits. If we take a careful look at capitalism, very few people can claim a significant share of businesses profits. Most people go to work for a wage or salary because it is a necessary part of life. The notion that work cannot be done unless there is a profit incentive is based on an ideological assumption that initiative and the organization of enterprise could not happen unless an entrepreneur can profit from it. Yet people organize themselves for many reasons outside of profit-making. A church is formed for spiritual and social reasons, government institutions are formed to serve the public, schools are organized to educate children, and so on. None of these institutions have anything to do with entrepreneurs or the profit motive, but are considered by many to be necessary institutions. Similarly, the reason for organizing an economic cooperative is not profit-making, but to provide goods or services for the community as a necessary part of life.

Currently there are about 750–800 million people in the world who are members of cooperatives. In the U.S., there are about 48,000 cooperatives with over 120 million members.[224] Traditionally, cooperatives have been most successful in producing and distributing food and agricultural products, utilities, and financial services. Other fields such as housing, healthcare, education, and a range of other services have also been successfully organized into cooperatives.

Modern cooperatives date back to the populist movements of the mid-nineteenth century and the heyday of monopoly capitalism. Poverty, low wages, low prices for farmers, and dismal working conditions compelled people in communities to pool their resources and form cooperatives as alternative business models. As with organized labor, communities that were organizing cooperatives had discovered that collective action and pooled resources translated into protection against the otherwise grim, Darwinistic struggle for survival in the marketplace.

In the late nineteenth century and early twentieth century in North America, populism was a notable political force. Populism came from various sectors of society, but each was devoted to improving the lives of both urban and rural working-class families. Populist movements were a series of social and political campaigns that were in one way or another directed at challenging the power of giant corporate monopolies that dominated railroad, banking, and manufacturing industries, as well as people's lives.

At that time farmers formed agricultural cooperatives to pool their bargaining power and to gain fair prices for farm products ranging from bushels of grain to eggs to cut flowers. Farmers were at the mercy of large monopoly banks and railroads that showed no inclination to be responsive to the needs of people in rural communities. Also, money circulation and financial services were largely controlled by monopoly banks that were similarly indifferent to the needs of most people. In response, financial cooperatives were formed. Some of these early co-ops were more successful than others, but as alternative institutions they continue to exist. A central challenge for co-ops, however, has always been that they are nonprofit, noncapitalist institutions trying to survive within the dominant framework of a capitalist system.

The most common forms of cooperatives are consumer cooperatives and producer cooperatives. Consumer co-ops are owned by the people who buy the goods and services provided by the co-op, and producer co-ops are owned by people who work for them. There are far more consumer co-ops than producers. This is due to the fact that consumers constitute a wider base within the community and therefore offer more resources for capitalization. Traditionally, most producer cooperatives are owned by cooperative associations in which independent producers—farmers, artisans, or other small-scale trades—form a collective to combine resources and purchasing power in buying raw materials or energy. Producer cooperatives could also be worker cooperatives in which membership and ownership is held by employees of the company, but these are rare in the U.S. economy.

For a mindful economy, the specific type of cooperative that is formed is centrally important. Merely forming a co-op without careful consideration of its purpose, values, and goals stands a poor chance of succeeding. Many cooperatives as they exist today have lost their original populist spirit. The most successful co-ops are chic chain stores that sell expensive sporting goods and health food to wealthy consumers, and pay their employees less than a living wage. These cooperatives sell in lucrative markets, and have become virtually indistinguishable from the dominant capitalist businesses. Many financial cooperatives have also become multi-branch banks that are now almost identical to for-profit commercial banks. Aside from the very small and mainly symbolic benefits for their members, it is hard to see how communities can benefit from these business models in a way that is different from capitalist business. As these co-ops have lost touch with the original populist spirit, their goals are unclear, and they no longer stand as truly viable economic alternatives.

In a mindful economy, the purpose of a cooperative must be clearly stated and defined in its corporate charter. As a true alternative, its most important purpose is to serve the needs of people. A food cooperative that runs its operations as though it were a for-profit money machine and pays its workers far below a living wage is a model for self-interest and not community-interest. Moreover, if self-interest is the guiding principle, then openly capitalist enterprises would be far superior models.

Cooperatives that are not fully integrated into the community can readily pit producers against consumers, or employer against employee, in a manner similar to capitalist enterprises. By paying substandard wages to workers and subsidizing premier discounts and other benefits for consumers, a cooperative can breed antagonism. Cooperatives must still buy and sell in markets and markets are always susceptible to imbalances. An exclusively producer cooperative would create an imbalanced sellers market in which producers maintain ownership, control, and a position of advantage. Exclusively consumer cooperatives also create an imbalanced buyers market that gives consumers control and advantage.

What is important for a mindful economy is that cooperatives have the potential to form genuine community corporations that balance a plurality of interests. Such institutions must integrate all stakeholders and transcend the specific interests of consumers, producers, workers, or employers. A key part of systemic change is the existence of cooperatives that evolve in this more comprehensive way. In our view, a true alternative are *community cooperatives* which balance the interests of all members of the community. A community cooperative allows not just consumers or employees to become members and owners, but also suppliers and any other stakeholder in the community as well. In this way, members of the community also become active participants in the governance of the economic institutions that affect their lives. These institutions fit under the umbrella of Michael Shuman community corporations, yet are more far-reaching as they embody democratic principles.

Balancing a plurality of interests is essential for functional democracy. Creating community cooperatives would be a significant step toward building an alternative economic system that is intrinsically democratic. By pulling together all the stakeholders in a community and empowering them with ownership and control, people take a significant step away from exploitation and toward a system that is founded on a principle of respect for humanity—the principle that people are ends and not means. In a practical sense, such guiding principles must be written into the bylaws and corporate charters. It also would be necessary that the board of directors of community cooperatives be charged with the responsibility of making sure that its business activities follow these guiding principles.

Systemic change toward a mindful economy entails the creation and development of non-capitalist community cooperatives as the paradigm for mindful ownership. These community-owned businesses are specifically created to serve the needs of people in the community and maintain a healthy balance between all stakeholders. These are also corporations that have in their legal documentation the rules and guidelines that anchor the business to core principles of a mindful economy specified in Chapter Twelve. These are also businesses that pursue the core values of human and environmental well-being, economic justice, and stability. Such a system would require a rigorous framework of rules and principles for governance.

PRINCIPLES FOR COOPERATIVE GOVERNANCE

Cooperatives are institutions. Like most institutions, they have mission statements and guiding principles for their governance. Although the mission statements are generally specific to each cooperative, most cooperatives follow the guidelines for governance established by the International Cooperative Association (ICA). The following is a summary of principles that were designed to guide the work of cooperatives and were formed as principles of governance by the ICA in 1966.

VOLUNTARY AND OPEN MEMBERSHIP

As a community-based institution, a cooperative is owned, financed, and operated by people from the community regardless of their race, gender, religion, or political affiliations. Cooperatives also serve the community openly and without discrimination. Membership is not exclusive and does not discriminate as to who can participate and become members/owners/employees. Cooperatives are also voluntary and individuals cannot be forced to become members. What is required of members is that they agree to the guiding principles of the cooperative and understand the values inherent in those principles.

Although membership is to be open and voluntary, some cooperatives can be limited in the number of people they can serve or employ. Ideally, however, for a cooperative to be firmly embedded in the community it must maintain a balance of all stakeholders: workers, consumers, suppliers, and others in the community who contribute to, or are affected by, the functioning and operations of the cooperative.

DEMOCRATIC MEMBER CONTROL

This is perhaps the most significant aspect of cooperatives that make them intrinsically democratic institutions. Extending from the principle of open and voluntary membership, each member has a vote on the policies of the cooperative.

This form of member control contrasts with that of the capitalist corporation that employs a non-democratic electoral process. In a capitalist corporation, each share of common stock is endowed with a vote. Using the one-share-one-vote process, shareholders hold referendums on board of director appointments and other resolutions related to the corporation's business activities. Unlike the electoral process in a true democracy in which each citizen has one vote, voting rights in a capitalist corporation are allocated on the basis of ownership, and favor those who have the most money to buy the most shares. Concentrations of ownership translate directly into an imbalance of governing power.

Even with the one-member-one-vote system of cooperative governance, imbalances can occur. For example, if the consumers are a majority and workers are a minority, then votes can work against workers resulting in unfair working conditions from which consumers reap the benefits. Perhaps also larger cooperatives in the community could be in a position of advantage over smaller cooperatives as they would have more voices in community governance. Specific provisions would have to be made such that the democratic governance of cooperatives would be pluralistic in order to assure that minority rights are protected, and that the basic principles of respect for all humans, fairness, and equity are upheld.

AUTONOMY AND INDEPENDENCE

Keeping with Michael Shuman's arguments for the need of community self-reliance, cooperatives must strive to be autonomous and independent institutions. Independent cooperatives are not dominated by other institutions nor do special interests dominate their boards or decision-making processes. It is impossible, however, to be completely disconnected from other established institutions, including capitalist businesses and government. The process of building self-reliant and locally based systems is long and gradual. During this process cooperatives may need to turn to other institutions for resources or assistance.

Although cooperatives are autonomous they are still community-based businesses and firmly rooted in the local community. Being embedded in a community does not mean losing autonomy, it means that they sustain their localized character, serve the local community, and resist being controlled by other institutions or political pressures. In a mindful economy it is imperative that cooperatives maintain independence from capitalist businesses that are most likely headquartered in another city or country and through their indifference both destabilize and attempt to homogenize all local cultures in which they have business interests.

EDUCATION, TRAINING, AND INFORMATION

A mindful economy that is centered on the cooperative as a key economic institution must have a well-trained and educated membership. To this end, cooperatives must train and educate all members, leaders, and employees. A well-trained membership will help assure that cooperatives will continue to work effectively toward, and educate the general public on, their stated goals. Any democratic institution requires transparency and open access to information. What is of particular importance for a mindful economy is educating young people about the benefits of cooperatives so that these institutions will survive through successive generations and through the long and gradual process of systemic change. Cooperatives also provide community education and other services that are free to members. Members are kept up to date in newsletters and have access to information and membership opportunities by other cooperatives in the community.

MEMBER ECONOMIC PARTICIPATION

In any economic system, there is a fundamental relationship between how a business enterprise is capitalized and how it is governed. Under a capitalist system, owners of capital, no matter how few in number, maintain dictatorial control over their businesses. In cooperatives, that relationship is reversed— capital investment is used to serve the needs of the cooperative and the community it serves. Cooperatives are not-for-profit businesses and so the financial resources contributed by members are not investments that expect or require a return. Surpluses are not paid as returns to investors as would be the case in a capitalist system, but rather are used for cooperative development, savings, or benefits for members. Some cooperatives may choose to pay a small dividend to members as a membership benefit, but such a practice is discouraged and strictly limited; for it is a slippery slope from there to becoming a profit-oriented institution. Also, by limiting returns on capital, outside capitalist investors are discouraged from attempting to take over a cooperative and making it into a money machine for the benefit of investors and not the community. Some give members of consumer cooperatives point-of-sale discounts on purchases or annual patronage refunds. To be fair and equitable structures, however, cooperatives generally keep the member discount at about 2 percent. However the surplus is allocated, it must be done according to the democratically determined approval by its members. This decision-making power stems from the four-dimensional role of the mindful economic citizen, and such participation links the cooperative with its surrounding community.

COOPERATION AMONG COOPERATIVES

Although there is some competition among cooperatives, this should not be a guiding principle for the governance of these businesses. To the extent that competition exists in the current system, it is more often than not destructive: cut-throat pricing, ruthless cost-cutting measures taken out on employees, manipulative advertising, and aggressive attempts to steal market share from each other. By contrast, cooperatives (as their names would suggest) best serve the needs of their members by working together in local, national, or regional associations. By forming associations with other cooperatives, businesses can pool their resources and achieve economies of scale through collective buying in mass quantities, sharing costs of technological and resource development, and collectively bargaining for insurance. Cooperative associations can more effectively manage larger-scale enterprises such as power plants, financial cooperatives, large farms or fertilizer plants, or transportation/distribution infrastructure as a group of enterprises rather than individual ones. Associations can also assist in the development of new cooperatives. The benefits of these economies of scale are to be realized not by investors, but by the members and the communities served by the cooperatives. The process of forming associations and attempts to achieve economies of scale must be tempered by a commitment to autonomy and respect for local culture.

CONCERN FOR COMMUNITY

In a mindful economy, cooperatives are embedded in the local community and have their roots in local values, social justice, and environmental sustainability of the local community. By forming cooperatives, people can take direct control over at least a part of the local economy. With local control, the needs of the community can be met through direct action by cooperatives.

STARTING A COOPERATIVE

Although cooperatives can take on various forms of community ownership, they have proven to be most successful as corporations. The process of starting a cooperative as a corporation is not significantly different from starting any other corporation. The key differences are that they are created not for profit, but for community service, and that the steering committee in charge of the start-up are not capitalist investors, but rather are people interested in serving their community or in systemic change. Starting a cooperative begins with market research of goods or services, and a feasibility study or business plan. This should also include information about how the cooperative will be capitalized and the relative ratios of equity to debt. It should also include information on a projection of the cooperative's ability to repay its creditors. If the project shows promise, the next steps are to arrange for financing for capitalization and to incorporate.

Typically cooperatives are about 20 percent to 30 percent financed by member equity or the contributions by people in the local community who join the co-op. Member equity constitutes base financing, and the balance comes from bank loans, bond issues, grants, and other sources. Potential members who are invited to participate should be stakeholders from the community on an equal opportunity basis without discrimination. All potential members gather at a meeting to vote on whether or not to proceed, and if the vote approves to go forward, the next step is to incorporate.

The process of incorporating starts with legal documentation filed by an attorney with a state government. The attorney drafts the articles of incorporation, which is a legal description of the corporation including the activities to be carried out by the cooperative as well as the designation of the board of directors. Once the articles are approved by the state, it will issue a corporate charter—the permission to be a corporation and an agreement by the cooperative to follow the state corporate guidelines. From that point on, the corporation exists as a distinct legal entity that is contractually obligated to its stakeholders or members of the community. The corporate bylaws—also part of the legal documentation—provide legal and managerial guidelines directing the day-to-day activities along the lines set out by the articles of incorporation and the corporate charter. It is in this process that the cooperative takes on its identity as an economic institution. What is included in the articles, charter, and bylaws is crucial; for it is here that the core principles of a mindful economy, its core values and the principles of governance, are all written into the founding legal documentation of a cooperative. This legally binds the institution to certain values and practices. With this process, the core values of mindful economics become institutionalized. And as an institution, it becomes a key building block of a mindful economy.

Once all the legal documentation is drafted, members vote to approve the articles and bylaws that are subsequently filed with the appropriate agency of the state government. Upon approval by the state, the cooperative can operate as a licensed corporation.

Cooperatives that are established in this way constitute the first step in creating a real, meaningful alternative to capitalism. Starting up cooperatives is a necessary condition for creating an alternative to capitalism, but not a sufficient one. Just as Fortune 500 corporations, government institutions, commercial banks, and the Fed are institutionally tied together to serve profit-making, co-ops must cohere institutionally as well. To be a true alternative to capitalism, production and distribution of food, clothing, transportation, healthcare, education, housing, manufacturing, and financial services must all cohere institutionally. That is, cooperatives must evolve into a *system* of co-ops. The most direct way to achieve this is to align the governance of these institutions with a common set of values-based core principles that become the guidelines for their governance. By piecing together each institution that was individually developed along non-capitalist lines, the system itself eventually evolves into a viable alternative to capitalism. There are other forms of business ownership besides cooperatives that can also cohere into this system such as small businesses and public enterprises.

SMALL BUSINESS AND PUBLIC ENTERPRISE

Individual or family-owned businesses have been an integral part of communities and economies since the beginning of human culture. Contrary to popular misconception, most small-scale bakeries, butchers, building contractors, repair shops, landscape maintenance companies, hair salons, restaurants, and so on, do not fit the definition of capitalist enterprise. Although they are indeed for profit and are privately owned, they miss two key and important features that prevent them from being designated as capitalist. First, small businesses, in the sense we are using the term here, have no separation of ownership and work. Owners spend most of their working lives working at their businesses because if they did not the business could not continue. Secondly, small businesses are not driven by the growth imperative. Small businesses only need to sustain a living for their owners. This sustenance can exist in a steady state and does not have to continuously grow because the businesses are not required to generate exponential returns for outside investors.

To be officially considered a small business by the federal government, businesses must have five hundred employees or less. Many of these firms are large enough that the work performed is done with hired labor and profits are paid to absentee investors, and thus are capitalist enterprises. These companies would not fit the definition of small business in the way we use the term here. Our definition of a small business is specifically a locally based, locally owned business that is operated by an individual, family, or small group of partners who both work and own.

If the scale of operations for a particular enterprise requires capitalization that exceeds what could be raised by a family or small group, then a cooperative or local public enterprise would be more expedient in order to maintain the economic integrity of the local community and to stay embedded in a mindful economy.

Local public enterprises are familiar institutions throughout America's cities and towns. These are public agencies and municipal corporations that provide port facilities, services for maritime transportation, airports for airlines, water and sewage, electricity, infrastructure, schools, and other services for the local community. By definition, they are publicly-owned which means they are owned by the citizens in the community and financed by taxpayers. They are also non-capitalist as they integrate ownership (publicly) and work, and are not driven by the growth imperative.

Sound public-sector management is largely dependent on localized participatory democracy. It is both the civic pride and responsibility of an active local citizenry to keep close watch over their public enterprises and to see how taxpayers' dollars are used to provide public services. Where there is strong local participation in institution-building and oversight, there are efficient and democratically accountable public enterprises. Again, the four-dimensional mindful economic citizen is critically important.

THE MINDFUL ECONOMY AND COMMUNITY-BASED MONEY AND FINANCE

An economic system is a network of economic institutions. The glue that holds these institutions together is money and so a stable monetary system is centrally important. When banks and other financial institutions are stable, the rest of the economy has a better chance at achieving stability. On the other hand, if the financial sector of the economy is unstable, it can send shock waves of instability through the entire economy.

As communities begin to build alternative economic systems, a stable and community-based financial system will be its centerpiece. As mentioned earlier, the company towns of the nineteenth century controlled the local economy because they both owned the businesses and controlled the local circulation of money. Through community corporations, people can gain such control through ownership in cooperatives and by locally and democratically controlling flows of money and access to credit.

A locally controlled financial system would typically be some combination of community-owned financial cooperatives, small community banks, electronic credit systems, localized debit cards, and local currencies. A localized financial system can also restore the financial system to its original purpose of linking sources and uses of funds rather than the current system of speculation, gambling, and all the instability that these vices bring in their train. If people can, through local institutions, control the money that flows through their communities, they can also control where and how that money is saved and spent. And by controlling this, people can directly and purposefully control the lifeblood of their local economies.

A community-based system of money must also be comprised of institutions that are organized according to the values-based core principles. By doing so, the monetary institutions of a mindful economy will be compatible with the other core economic institutions. Such a system would stand in stark contrast to the current national monetary system that is centrally controlled by Wall Street firms and the Federal Reserve System. Whereas the U.S. national system of banking is based on federal government debt and the arbitrary decision-making power of a non-democratically accountable central bank, a community-based system is controlled by people in local communities and is based on local production of goods and services.

Centralized monetary systems work in conjunction with large corporations in such a way that they can bleed local economies of their vitality. Large corporations collect money from local sales and deposit money in a large corporate bank that then whisks the money away to possibly anywhere on the planet. Unless there is a very compelling reason to bring the money back, and there often is not, the money is drained from the community and the local economy loses its vitality. Community-based businesses and community-based money and finance can reverse this process and keep the money circulating, fostering business transactions at the local level.

LOCAL CURRENCIES AND LETS SYSTEMS

Systems of locally based money exist largely as small-scale experiments. Though they are limited in scope, these experiments exist all over the world. Currently they take basically two forms: local paper currencies and computer-based trading credits (LETS).

A local currency is paper money printed and regulated by a local barter community. Local paper currencies are primarily used to facilitate local transactions, and to keep the money circulating locally. As we saw with the history of money in America, the biggest obstacle to establishing a paper currency—or any other monetary system for that matter—is building faith. If people in the local community have faith and see their currency as a viable medium of exchange, then the process of implementing their own paper currency is relatively uncomplicated and legal.

Typically the process of creating a local paper currency begins when members of the local community organize a local nonprofit organization—usually a local financial cooperative—that will issue and control the flow of the local currency. Part of administering a local currency involves recruiting local businesses and individuals to become members and participate in the program. Member businesses are listed in Internet-based barter directories at the cooperative's website so that community members are able to gain access to information regarding what products are available to buy with the local currency and at what prices.

Local currencies can be used as mediums of exchange at local shops, barter clubs, or trade fairs. Community members can use their local currency to buy bread from a local bakery or pay a house painter or dentist for their services. The principal advantage, of course, is that money earned and spent in the local economy stays in there, and it adds to its vibrancy. A disadvantage is that local currency cannot work well as financial instruments to be saved. The main reason for this is that once the money is saved in a bank, it becomes subject to control of the Federal Reserve System and would lose its standing as a local currency. The Federal Reserve System also requires that a local currency not be used to transfer funds from one bank to another. Local currencies are not used to make bank deposits as these deposits, or reserves, are what the Federal Reserve uses for controlling the money supply. If a local currency were used to make deposits, it would be, in effect, posing as U.S. dollars.

In any case, the purpose of a local currency is to circulate and sustain the pulse of local economic activity, not savings as a financial investment. In addition, transactions that involve new production of goods or services are taxable. A dollar-equivalent of the good or service must be calculated and will be taxable according to state and federal tax laws. Moreover, those taxes must be paid in dollars, not in the local currency.

Aside from Fed regulations and tax laws, there are generally no great legal obstacles to establishing and circulating a local currency. The currency cannot be printed in a way that resembles the U.S. dollar, which would suggest an attempt to counterfeit, nor can it be issued in fractional currencies that are valued at less than $1. Also, local institutions are prohibited from minting coins. Some states have banking laws that prohibit local currencies or other instruments from being used as a medium of exchange instead of the U.S. dollar.

The biggest challenge to establishing an alternative currency is not legal but institutional. Establishing a new currency means establishing a new social convention. A newly issued local currency will encounter much reluctance and faith would be difficult to establish.

One strategy would be to forge an agreement that the currency unit will be proportional or "pegged" to the national currency in terms of purchasing power, but not backed by, or exchangeable with, that currency. In other words, the local currency must not be convertible to a national currency within the community. If it is easily converted into dollars, this undermines the purpose of local currencies. The local currency would, at best, become a surrogate of the national currency, like poker chips at a gambling casino, and would lose its meaning as a local currency. Surrogate currencies will always be subordinate to national currencies and therefore will be subordinate to a centralized monetary system. Ultimately, the national currency would become the dominant currency and would drive the local currency out of circulation. This is more often the case than not in most experiments with local currencies.

On the other hand, to peg the currency could be an effective way to establish value. Pegging the currency to some agreed-upon standard establishes and institutionalizes the currency in a way that is familiar to members of the barter community and allows the currency to become an effective medium of exchange. A currency could also be pegged to something else of tangible value such as gold or labor hours.

Perhaps the most successful model of a local paper currency is the Ithaca Hours, started in Ithaca, New York in the early 1990s (see www.ithaca-hours.com). The currency unit's value was established on the basis of an hour of work at what would be considered the local living wage. For example, if the local living wage is determined to be $12/hour, then the paper currency can be denominated as "hours"—one of which enables the bearer to buy the equivalent of goods and services one could by if one worked one hour at $12 per hour. Workers of different skill levels can ask for more if skills are higher and more complex or less if they are lower and simpler. The Ithaca system, though successful, remains as a very small part of the local financial system.

Another locally based monetary system is a computer-based trading credit system. There have been hundreds of experiments with these systems around the world and some have been more successful than others. The first and most successful model is Local Employment and Trading System (LETS), developed in the early 1980s in the Comox Valley located on Vancouver Island, Canada. This prototype became the model for most other experiments around the world.

A LETS system is a nonprofit organization that provides specific electronic "clearinghouse" services for its members. It is a system that is patterned after services that specialize in check-clearing. Standard banking clearinghouse services process check-clearing services for banks in which someone writes a check and sends it to another. In the transaction, the receiver's account is credited or added to a monetary balance and the sender's account is debited or reduced. LETS carries out a similar accounting service by clearing transactions directly through electronic means without paper currency, checks, or commercial banks. In other words, the computerized clearinghouse service itself is a medium of exchange. Members would be merchants, consumers, or anyone who buys and sells and wants to subscribe to the service.

Here is a closer look. LETS directly maintains standard accounting debt-and-credit T-accounts for each member. When a member sells a good or service to another in the directory, a single transaction is recorded with two accounting entries. For example, if person A sells an item to person B for say $100, person A's account is credited by $100 and person B's account is debited by $100. Each member begins with some balance in their account just as one would with a checking account. Say persons A and B begin with $500 in their accounts, then the transaction would be recorded as follows:

Person A				Person B			
	Debit	Credit	Balance		Debit	Credit	Balance
Beg. Bal.			$500	Beg. Bal.			$500
Transaction 1		$100	$600	Transaction 1	$100		$400

The double-entry system always maintains a constant amount of money that will only increase with an increase in membership or an increase in members' contributions to the LETS system.

A central problem in the LETS system is that it is prone to instability. A key problem with any monetary system is determining how much money should be maintained in the system and how to get that money in the system in the first place. LETS systems do not have a regulated money supply and allow unlimited transactions. Without strict controls on the availability of credits in the system people could buy unlimited quantities of goods, running up unlimited balances and—like printing off too much paper currency—the system would very quickly become unstable and potentially collapse.

A more stable system would limit balances held by individuals to credits that are earned through some method that is agreed-upon by members. Credits could be earned, for example, by working a number of hours, selling a product, or by backing the LETS credits with something of tangible value like gold or a national currency. Most LETS systems have failed primarily because they have been unsuccessful in establishing a standard method of controlling such credits and collapsed into instability.

Though a LETS system or a local paper currency can effectively pull people closer together economically through trade fairs and barter directories in which the systems are used, establishing these systems faces tremendous difficultly. At best, a local paper currency should be seen as a limited dimension to a broader, locally controlled monetary system. A much more expedient way to localize money and banks would be to establish financial cooperatives that are created for the sole purpose of serving the local community. These cooperatives could then manage both local currencies and national currencies for the local communities.

COMMUNITY-BASED FINANCIAL COOPERATIVES

Financial cooperatives are similar to other cooperatives in that they are owned by the stakeholders in the community. Traditionally, financial cooperatives have been organized into nonprofit credit unions and savings and loan associations in which the depositors are also the owners (see Chapter Five). Like many consumer cooperatives in the U.S., however, financial cooperatives are losing their original identity and the distinction between them and their capitalist counterparts is being blurred.

Ideally, a mindful system of money and finance would consist of a network of independent, community-based financial cooperatives that are true to their original purpose of economic localization. The mission of these depository institutions would primarily be to keep money and financial services local. As with other cooperatives, this mission can be written into the legal documentation of the institution. As a network or association, financial cooperatives could more effectively achieve local control of money and credit by unifying their banking policies to achieve broader, community-based financial goals.

Community-based financial cooperatives could be created to perform the same function at the local level as the Fed does at the national level. Recall that the primary means by which the Fed controls the money supply is by controlling the amount of reserves from which depository institutions can make loans. That is, the Fed controls the availability of credit. Community-based financial cooperatives could maintain local control by allocating a significant portion of local deposits to be used exclusively for credit and financial services available only to, and spent within, the local community. These provisions can be specified in the charter and bylaws of all community-based depository institutions. As such, they would set rules and guidelines for managing deposits and credit, and make assurances that as the money passes through the bank it is to be used primarily for locally purposes. Ownership of community-based financial cooperatives would be limited to direct stakeholders: depositors, borrowers, employees, other cooperatives, local public agencies, and other members of the local community. Financial services can be directed specifically for local business or household development, and accounts would be set up with the provision that these accounts will be established specifically to cover local transactions.

Another important aspect of local control of money is the "multiplier effect." When locally-earned money is spent, or re-spent, in the local economy it has a multiplicative or amplifying effect. Say $100 was earned in a local economy, but the money was spent outside the local economy in a distant location. In this case, the total spending in the local economy during that week would be $0 as the $100 was spent elsewhere. Development economists refer to this problem as the "leaky bucket" or "capital flight" as it constitutes a drain on the vibrancy of the local economy. If, however, the $100 was spent locally and the person who received the $100 also, in turn, re-spent the $100 on locally produced goods and services, total spending doubles to $200. And if those producers who received the re-spent $100 in the local economy, then spending triples to $300, and so on. With every transaction in which the same bills are exchanged, the local spending and domestic product will increase proportionally and this will enhance the liveliness of the local economy. When it is spent outside the local economy, the local domestic product will decrease proportionally. The more money that is drained, the more depressed the economy becomes, and like a hemorrhaging organism, it will eventually die.

The purpose of a mindful economy is to sustain quality livelihoods for people in the local community. A certain amount of local economic vibrancy is required for this to be accomplished. Centralized corporate capitalism drains money out of local economies and redirects the money in other locations. People become increasingly dependent on these businesses to bring the money back in to prevent financial hemorrhage. By taking local control, money can be used to sustain local activity. The disadvantage of such localism, of course, is that buyers will have fewer options and will probably be forced to pay higher prices than what might be paid if one could buy products made in a more distant location, such as those retailed by big-box stores like Wal-Mart.

Although concern over this disadvantage is valid, it is in many ways moot. People are most likely going to be forced to focus on local economic activity anyway as skyrocketing fuel and energy prices will render long-distance exchanges less economically viable. Also, discount prices of big-box retailers often come as a result of environmental destruction, worker exploitation, or by externalizing costs into another sphere. In these instances, lower prices are not true prices for they create more problems and higher costs elsewhere. To some degree, economic self-sufficiency will be a necessary and inevitable part of life in the future. Our contention is that we should begin now to purposefully and mindfully construct the financial institutions necessary to foster its proper development.

CONCLUSION

Two very significant consequences of the capitalist system are widening inequality and instability. These problems can be mitigated in a direct and purposeful way. Inequality stems largely from the separation of ownership and work that is endemic in capitalism, and is largely caused by dramatic disparities of ownership of income-earning assets. By creating community-based institutions of business ownership organized through cooperatives, local small businesses and public enterprises, ownership, and work are reintegrated. Income-earning assets will be shared democratically among all stakeholders in the community and problems of severe inequality will start to disappear.

The problem of financial instability arises from money being extracted from a broad base to be used for speculative buying and selling of financial instruments. As we have argued in Chapter Eleven, although individuals are partially responsible for this instability, institutions can be modified to reduce speculation. By creating a community-based system of money and finance, Wall Street institutions will become irrelevant. Money will be controlled democratically and locally and, as such, can be used to efficiently bring together sources and uses of funds that serve the needs of people in the local economy. This, not speculation, is the original intent of financial systems.

People have always needed to have a place where they could store their money for safe-keeping. And communities need financing for infrastructure, schools, security in old age, and for building homes. These needs can be satisfied directly if they are made a priority among people in the community through local institutions.

Yet these financial needs, although met to some degree in American society, rank lowest on the list of priorities of U.S. financial institutions. At the top of the list is capitalist wealth accumulation. Capitalism is a system that rewards those who are skilled at buying and selling to make a profit. To this end, the U.S. financial system has become more like a casino for gamblers and speculators who seek to buy low and sell high, and has become less about serving the needs of people. In a mindful economy we reverse this order and seek to rebuild our financial instruments and institutions to make the needs of people the primary goal of the financial system.

There are many more advantages to moving toward a locally based economy as well. Local economic activity is directly accountable. This builds trust and social cohesion rather than what is now a local community's distrust of, and alienation from, the big-box companies and corporate chains. Local economic activity breeds locally based invention, which can strengthen locally based economic activity. Small-scale, decentralized institutions also foster the development of small-scale, community-centered technology. This development will allow for even more self-reliance and self confidence, which, in turn, establishes more faith in the local economy. Pride in local development will instill a greater sense of investment in the local economy and stimulate more locally-based inventions.

Markets that are embedded in the local community are immune from outside speculation, such as in housing and stock markets, which have led to history's worst experiences of economic instability. Localization acts as a hedge against recessions and inflationary booms caused by forces outside local control, and thus is more stable. Stability breeds stability.

When economic activity is centered locally, people gain more local control over business hiring practices and over how businesses interact with the natural environment. Local economic activity is economical in the sense that it saves on transportation, marketing, distribution, warehousing, and preservation costs associated with long-distance distribution. It also saves on the much broader environmental and social costs associated with fossil fuel consumption, including those caused by global warming. By eliminating these costs, local producers can have the flexibility to absorb higher costs by using more environmentally sustainable practices. It is to the issue of sustainability that we now turn our attention.

14

THE MINDFUL ECONOMY PART III
Sustainable Practices

Capitalist economic systems need to grow. Steady returns to investors must be grounded in perpetual economic growth in the real economy, and this entails extracting more and more value from both people and from the earth. At some point in time perpetual growth will exhaust all available resources and will destroy the material basis for human survival. This growth imperative of capitalism stands in stark contrast to ecological sustainability.

As we pointed out in Chapter Nine, there are other factors contributing to the exhaustion of resources besides capitalist growth. Global population growth and growth in non-capitalist economies have also put heavy strains on resources and have led to much environmental damage. These factors aside, capitalist growth is nonetheless inherently destructive and is voraciously using up resources like never before, particularly in the United States.

Capitalism is also not the only way to organize production and distribution. Around the world people have organized alternative economic systems designed to produce and distribute goods and services for the betterment of the people, not for profit accumulation. If done in a mindful way, alternative economies can thrive without the need for perpetual growth, predatory exploitation, or depletion of resources. But a mindful approach requires people to face the reality that their habitual ways of living are not sustainable. A mindful approach also requires that people understand exactly what it means for an economy to be sustainable.

ENVIRONMENTAL SUSTAINABILITY

A sustainable natural environment is a system that does not deteriorate over time. It is a steady-state system that is not structurally altered and remains basically intact. The natural environment is, of course, the foundation on which economic systems rest. Sustainable economics and sustainable ecology are thus indistinguishable. As ecology is the study of the relation between living organisms and their environment, ecological sustainability means that humans interact with their natural environment in a way that is stable and keeps the natural foundation intact. The words "economy" and "ecology" share the same root prefix "eco," which originates from the ancient Greek word for "household" or "habitat." In a general sense, therefore, a sustainable economy is a steady-state system in which the processes of production, distribution, and consumption are carried out in such a way that they do not structurally alter the natural habitat in which we live.

A more specific definition of sustainability was developed in the early 1980s by the United Nation's World Commission on Environment and Development (WCED). The WCED came to be known as the Brundtland Commission as it was headed by Gro Harlem Brundtland, former Prime Minister of Norway. The Brundtland Commission convened to address critical issues of poverty and economic development as well as concerns about environmental degradation. The goal was to institutionalize, at a global level, certain guiding principles for dealing with world poverty and caring for natural environments.

The commission produced a report titled, "Our Common Future," in 1987. The report contained the first widely accepted and practical definition of sustainability as a guiding principle for economic development. Since then, the "Brundtland Definition" has become the standard definition of sustainable economic development and reads as follows:

> . . . [economic] development that meets the needs of the present without compromising the ability of future generations to meet their own needs.[225]

This definition served as a platform from which researchers and scholars began working to formulate more precise principles for a sustainable society. This led to the development of the "Socio-Ecological Principles for a Sustainable Society" by John Holmburg, Karl Henrik Roberts and Karl Erik Erikkson of the Institute of Physical Resource Theory.[226] These principles are listed below and are also integrated into the values-based core principles of a mindful economy:

1. Substances extracted from the lithosphere must not systematically accumulate in the ecosphere.
2. Society-produced substances must not systematically accumulate in the ecosphere.

3.   The physical conditions for production and diversity within the ecosphere must not be systematically deteriorated.
4.   The use of resources must be effective and just with respect to meeting human needs.

We will explore each of these in more detail, but first a note to clarify some terminology used in these principles. The *ecosphere* is the part of our world that includes our air, water, topsoil, as well as plants and animals that harness energy from the sun and interact with each other. The *lithosphere* is the rest of the planet that includes minerals, fossil fuels, geothermal processes, as well as the radioactive decay of heavy elements. A true model of sustainability is one that achieves ecological balance both within the ecosphere and between the ecosphere and the lithosphere.

PRINCIPLE ONE: SUBSTANCES EXTRACTED FROM THE LITHOSPHERE MUST NOT SYSTEMATICALLY ACCUMULATE IN THE ECOSPHERE

There exists a dynamic interplay between the ecosphere and lithosphere in which all living organisms play a role. Of course the most significant role is played by humans. Humans are actively producing goods and services, and during this process, are extracting substances from the lithosphere such as minerals, ore, fissionable materials, and fossil fuels. Once extracted, these substances will remain in the ecosphere either in their original state or in a transformed state as chemical compounds or even radioactive fallout. In other words, by extracting substances from the lithosphere and allowing those substances to accumulate in the ecosphere, humans are creating pollution. The planet can, however, reabsorb and assimilate these pollutants to minimize the destructive effects. The rate of extraction and accumulation compared to the rate of re-absorption between the ecosphere and the lithosphere is a core ecological concern.

The concern for sustainability arises when extraction takes place at a rate faster than absorption, resulting in the systematic accumulation of polluting substances in the ecosphere. The best example of this is our use of fossil fuels. Substances contained in oil, coal, and natural gas are being extracted and used at a rate much faster than the ecosphere's capacity for absorption. The result, as we saw in Chapter Nine, is the systematic accumulation of chemical compounds such as carbon dioxide and other greenhouse gasses in the ecosphere, which is the leading cause of global warming and other forms of environmental damage. For us to follow this principle of sustainability and achieve balance between the two spheres, we would have to dramatically decrease the flow of substances from the lithosphere into the ecosphere. We would have to dramatically reduce the amount of fossil fuel use, which means a dramatic change in our economic systems away from perpetual growth to steady-state.

PRINCIPLE TWO: SOCIETY-PRODUCED SUBSTANCES MUST NOT SYSTEMATICALLY ACCUMULATE IN THE ECOSPHERE

Similar to the way that our processes of production and distribution give rise to the build-up of substances from the lithosphere, they can also lead to the accumulation of human-made substances. These substances are materials, molecules, and chemical compounds that are newly created and did not previously exist in the ecosphere. One of the most alarming examples of this is the build-up of chlorofluorocarbons that damage the layer of ozone molecules in the earth's atmosphere. By damaging the ozone layer, the earth becomes increasingly vulnerable to damaging solar radiation—particularly ultraviolet radiation. Society-produced substances are all around us and to follow this principle of sustainability would also require a significant change in the way we produce things.

PRINCIPLE THREE: THE PHYSICAL CONDITIONS FOR PRODUCTION AND DIVERSITY WITHIN THE ECOSPHERE MUST NOT BE SYSTEMATICALLY DETERIORATED

In other words, the earth's physical capacity for future production depends in part on the integrity of the natural environment. As we saw in Chapter Nine, deforestation, land and topsoil ruination, fresh water contamination, and the depletion of fuels and other natural resources are just a few examples of such deterioration. Just about every important non-renewable resource, including fossil water, will become increasingly scarce in the future. Moreover, we are currently experiencing a period during which more fauna and flora species are being lost than ever before.[227] Along with this downward spike in the number of species is a systematic loss of biological diversity. In the laws of thermodynamics, such loss of diversity is associated with entropy or heat death. If there is such a thing as the death of a planet, then a significant decline in biological diversity would certainly be one of its signs. Significant systemic change will be necessary to avoid this grim outcome.

PRINCIPLE FOUR: THE USE OF RESOURCES MUST BE EFFECTIVE AND JUST WITH RESPECT TO MEETING HUMAN NEEDS

An effective allocation of resources would be to channel them where they are needed the most. Yet where or for whom resources are needed most is difficult to define. In a mindful economy, this would be determined by where the resources are most needed to serve the basic needs of humans and other living organisms. In a capitalist economy, however, resources are allocated on the basis of purchasing power and profits. The capitalist market system allocates resources according to who is most able to pay. People who have money are not necessarily the ones who need the resources the most, but simply are fortunate to have the money to pay for them. And when the money is paid it is revenue and profits for sellers. Resources in the global economy are also allocated according to the market system and thus will always allow for the wealthier countries or individuals to get a disproportionately large share of available resources. Such a system is neither effective nor just, and to change how resources are allocated would require significant systemic change.

In the Darwinistic model of survival of the fittest of the capitalist market system, those who lack the financial means are selected to do without the resources they need. The rationing function of the price system automatically rations poor people out of the market. As resources become increasingly scarce and expensive, poorer families will automatically be selected as the ones to make sacrifices. And as capitalism continues to grow and the depletion of water, fuels, topsoil, and forests intensifies, scarcity will be expressed as higher market prices. So as we envision these principles of sustainability, we must see that justice and ecological concerns are inseparable. As people began to realize this, a broader and more comprehensive model of sustainability emerged that includes not only ecological concerns, but also equity and economy—the so-called "Three E's" of sustainability.

THE "THREE E'S" OF SUSTAINABLE DEVELOPMENT

The 1987 Brundtland Report brought the problem of global wealth and income inequality out into the open. It highlighted instances of great affluence in some parts of the world and abject poverty in others so that nations could address the problem openly and work toward solutions. Traditionally guided by the "rising tide lifts all boats" principle, policy-makers have been convinced that economic growth and development would solve the problem of poverty. Eventually some economists began to see that economic growth could not alleviate poverty if the benefits of this growth accrued only to the already wealthier segments of the world's population. Increasing the size of the economic pie could help, but changing the way the pie was divided would also be necessary. Scientists and economists also began stressing that the negative side of economic growth is long-term environmental damage, and this damage would offset the efforts to alleviate poverty. It eventually became clear that economic growth, environmental sustainability, and inequality of living standards were inseparable problems. They came to be seen as three dimensions to the same core economic problem, and the paradigm of "The Three E's" emerged: Economy, Ecology, and Equity.

The Three E paradigm attempts to place ecological and environmental protection, economic production, and social equity all on an equal footing. Ideally, no single dimension is held to be more important than the others, and all Three E's have to be addressed simultaneously. Proponents of sustainable economics who also wanted to preserve the institutions of capitalism began looking for business models in which the goal of profit maximization could be achieved alongside social and environmental goals. It became fashionable for businesses to follow the Three E's model as they looked for ways that their bottom lines could be improved without sacrificing environmental sustainability.

As sustainability became fashionable, a myriad of guidelines for sustainable business practices emerged. Governments and nonprofit organizations began developing standards for tracking and assessing business performance records on sustainability, such as Sustainable Profit Appraisal Routine (SPeAR), Life Cycle Assessment (LCA), and many others. Perhaps the most well-known model for guiding businesses toward sustainable practices is the Natural Step, and the most generally accepted system for setting sustainability standards is the ISO 14000.

Karl-Henrik Robert, one of the co-authors of the Brundtland definition of sustainability, also founded The Natural Step in 1989. The Natural Step is an organization that provides information and conducts workshops on how to incorporate the four Brundtland principles of sustainability into business practices. Robert's vision is based on a non-reductionistic, systems-based approach to science. He and others at The Natural Step see environmental problems as systemic. They conclude that solutions must therefore also be systemic and refer to their four principles as "systems conditions." Their aim is to give businesses practical guidelines on how to produce and distribute goods and services, while at the same time keeping with the framework of the systems conditions necessary for sustainability, social equity, and sound economic performance.

The International Standards Organization (ISO) was established in 1947 to provide industrial and commercial standards for over nine thousand product categories (ISO 9000). In the early 1990s, it expanded into environmental management in over fourteen thousand product categories (ISO 14000). Although the ISO 14000 is still in development, its goal is to promote standardized practices and technology in environmental management worldwide. ISO also seeks to measure businesses' performance in following these practices and adopting new technologies.

These and other organizations have made much headway in establishing both guidelines and measuring systems directed at fostering sustainable practices in business. The work of these organizations, as well as the development of environmental consciousness in general, has led to much progress in environmentally friendlier practices and technology. Without question, technology will play a role in the process of development. But up to now, virtually all of the emphasis in public discussion has been on technology and education. There has been very little discussion of institutional change, and virtually no mention of the incompatibility of the growth imperative of capitalism and sustainability. We will return to this point later, however, as real change toward a truly steady-state economy will require much more than education and technology; it will require comprehensive systemic change.

SUSTAINABLE PRACTICES

In a mindful economy, basic economic processes should be guided by the Brundtland's four principles of sustainability such that life on this planet will have a fighting chance to survive into the twenty-second century. In a mindful economy, production and consumption are carried out while directly, purposefully adhering to these principles. As such, sustainability in production and consumption would be practiced in ways that respect both nature and humanity—now and in future generations.

SUSTAINABILITY IN CONSUMPTION

The impact our production and consumption of goods and services has on the planet is often referred to as leaving an "ecological footprint." As consumers, to reduce the size of the ecological footprints we leave on the planet, we must follow two practices: we must consume green and consume less.

Consuming green is to consume organic, natural, recycled products, or products that are produced by sustainable methods. This is a significant step, but not sufficient to achieve a truly sustainable economy. Consuming green is qualitatively better for the environment, but it is not better if people quantitatively over-consume green products. Growing the U.S. economy into $20 trillion worth of organic and recycled products is not sustainable as it will continue to strain the planet's resource base beyond its limits. Sustainability will also require that Americans adopt simpler and less resource-consuming lifestyles.

Opting for a simpler lifestyle is for many people a moral resolution to pursue new and lighter ways of living. Treading more lightly on the planet does not mean that people must retrogress to a primitive existence. It does, however, call into question the consumerist ethos that "more is better." Measured in terms of material consumption, the United States is one of the most affluent countries in the world. Yet there is an abundance of social and health indicators such as teen suicide, divorce, obesity, drug and alcohol abuse, homicide, incarceration rates, domestic violence, and other crimes that clearly suggest that unhappiness is a pervasive epidemic in America. From these indicators it would seem that more is not necessarily better.

Households in America are cluttered with things not because those things have made people happier or more comfortable, but because the capitalist system requires it. The drive for business profits keeps people slavishly running on the consumerist treadmill: following fashion trends and throwing out old clothes in order to buy new ones every season, paying for endless computer hardware and software upgrades, buying new models of cars and trucks every two years, and accumulating mountains of plastic children's toys, vacation property, and swimming pools. The culture of consumerism in America assures that people continue to buy more and not less. It complicates people's lives, fills them with pretension, and is not sustainable.

The scientific realities of scarcity and resource depletion will be imposed on people eventually and simpler lifestyles will be inevitable. If simplicity is something that is imposed on people without thought given to meaningful change, it will most certainly mean poverty. In a mindful economy, living more simply does not mean becoming poor. It means to consume directly and honestly with an ecological purpose. Consuming less could come from consuming products that are more durable, simpler in design, or smaller. It could come from consuming things that are easy to repair and do not have to be replaced, appliances that are more energy-efficient, children's toys that are simple but encourage creativity and intellectual development, and in thousands of other ways that may not necessarily mean a deterioration of people's quality of life.

Living more simply and lightly will also require more self-reliance. People will have to relearn how to do basic repairs and how to share resources within their communities. The typical American household is stocked with power tools, ladders, lawn-mowers, and many other things that get used only a few times out of the year. Cooperatives can be established such that people can collectively and more efficiently share and maintain these resources.

Living more simply and lightly also means living in smaller, more energy-efficient homes. As of this writing, the U.S. has reached what looks like the end of a booming housing construction industry that took place in an over-inflated housing market. Developers were aggressively buying and tearing down perfectly good homes. They turned these homes into debris to be dumped in landfills and replaced them with larger and more energy-consuming homes that yield the developers higher profits. The new and significantly larger homes are most often inhabited by the same number of people (though more in debt) that resided in pre-existing ones. This kind of economic activity contributes to growth and profits, yet is clearly a violation of any concept of sustainable practices. If the process were to continue to its logical conclusion, all the smaller and more sustainable homes would be destroyed and people will have no choice but to live in large, wasteful homes with four-car garages.

Living more simply and lightly on the planet need not mean painful sacrifices for people, but it would mean sacrificing the capitalist drive for profits. By calling the principle of "more is better" into question, people must develop a vision of new institutions that will foster not only sustainability in consumption, but sustainable production technology.

In fact, the most significant contribution that could be made to sustainable consumption is sustainable production. If people were to step off of the treadmill of consumerism, they must have environmentally sustainable products to choose from. In the sections that follow we will explore sustainable production, but to keep within the scope of this book we will focus only on some basic necessities of life: food, clothing, shelter, energy, and transportation.

SUSTAINABLE PRODUCTION, FOOD

In Chapter Nine, we saw that agriculture is practiced today in a way that is not sustainable. What makes it unsustainable is that it is dependent on

processes that result in the systematic buildup of toxic substances in the ecosphere as well as the systematical degradation of topsoil and depletion of
freshwater supplies. Conventional agriculture is largely based on industrial
processes involving vast acreage of monocultures (vast crops of only one
species of plant) of wheat, corn, or cotton. All other plants and wildlife are
mechanically and chemically eliminated. With resulting low costs and high
yields, these farms are more profitable and farmers are compelled into this
practice. Large monocultures also tend to create imbalances in which a single
species of plant will attract a single species of insect—also massive in scale.
These insects must be treated with pesticides that contaminate the water and
soil. As the natural organisms are systematically eliminated, a deeper reliance
on chemical fertilizers is created. These fertilizers are also damaging and
deepen the need for chemicals, and so on in a downward spiral—a perfect
model of unsustainable agricultural production.

In a mindful economy, sustainable food production would need to be
developed such that agricultural production is carried out in order to provide
healthy food for the population, not to generate ongoing profits for investors.
It would also have to be done in ways that do not deplete fresh water supplies,
ruin the topsoil, and jeopardize future generations' ability to feed themselves;
nor should it allow for the use of harmful chemical agents, growth hormones,
antibiotics, and pesticides. In other words, a significant step toward sustainable agriculture is to produce organically.

Attempts to create standards for what would be considered as certifiably
"organic" by the USDA were codified into law by the National Organic Foods
Production Act of 1990.[228] According to Section 2104 of this Act, organic food
is defined as that which was produced according to the following criteria:

> To be sold or labeled as an organically produced agricultural product
> under this title, an agricultural product shall—
> (1) have been produced and handled without the use of synthetic
> chemicals, except as otherwise provided in this title;
> (2) except as otherwise provided in this title and excluding livestock,
> not be produced on land to which any prohibited substances, includ-
> ing synthetic chemicals, have been applied during the three years
> immediately preceding the harvest of the agricultural products; and
> (3) be produced and handled in compliance with an organic plan
> agreed to by the producer and handler of such product and the cer-
> tifying agent.

These standards for organics apply mainly to chemicals and not to soil or water conservation methods and cannot be seen as sufficient criteria for sustainability, although arguably are a step in that direction.

The standards for "organics" set by the USDA are changing largely from the political pressure coming from corporate farms. The USDA is allowing for an increasingly large number of synthetic chemicals to be used and still carry the "USDA Organic" certification. How a synthetic chemical gets on the list is determined by the Natural Organic Standards Board (NOSB). The NOSB consists of mainly agricultural industry insiders—growers, handlers, and retailers. Products can be certified by the USDA as organic if they are produced without "most" synthetic chemicals, pesticides, antibiotics, and other substances. By allowing for a margin outside of the "most" category, a door is open for further deterioration of what is meant as organic. Moreover, what is allowable is determined by the NOSB, and that body currently consists of a majority of industry insiders.

Industry insiders are keen on this issue because the fastest-growing area in the U.S. agricultural sector is organics. Most of the growth in organic food production is found in large corporate farms and marketed in chic, upscale retail stores and within the more expensive organic section of large corporate retail chains. These are all capitalist business enterprises, which are seizing on the opportunity to profit from a multi-billion-dollar organic food industry. Corporate food production and processing giants such as Kraft, General Mills, Con Agra, Archer Daniels Midland, and even Wal-Mart are getting in on the business. What once was a small margin of food commerce is now a $14 billion industry and is growing by about 20 percent annually.[229] The concern of these businesses is profit maximization first and foremost, and the production and distribution of healthy, environmentally sustainable food is of secondary importance.

Large corporate organic farms are often operated by the same businesses that still use poisonous fumigants that are destroying farmland. These large, corporate organic farms are large monocultures employing workers at substandard, non-living wages, and with their political clout they are succeeding in weakening federal standards for what can now be considered certifiably organic. For example, in 2004, the EPA, bending under pressure from corporate giants, now allows for harmful sewage sludge to be used as "organic" fertilizer. On the production side of the organic food market, the distinction between organic and conventionally grown food is becoming increasingly blurred.

Organic farms are also sourcing production globally in order to stay competitive. For example, according to a report by *Business Week*, milk used in organic yogurt production is produced in dairy farms in New Zealand. The milk is processed into powder and shipped nine thousand miles to be processed into yogurt and sold in U.S. markets.[230] The yogurt producers can claim their products to be organic and sell in high-end markets, but the methods used in production are not sustainable.

Another unsustainable aspect of the corporate, organic food industry is that the organic label also carries a higher price tag. Premium prices are, of course, why the large agricultural giants are scrambling to get into the business. Many of the proponents of sustainability advocate that by educating people about the health and environmental benefits of organic food, people will vote with their dollars in the marketplace and buy organic. By doing so, the capitalist market system will automatically respond to consumer demands and eventually organic food will take over the market. On the surface, this appears to be happening given the rapid growth of the organic industry, but a look below the surface reveals that this is not sustainable.

The organic food industry exploded in the 1990s as an expensive corner of the food industry. Consumers pay approximately 50 percent more when they buy organic over conventionally grown food.[231] Organic food stores typically are located in affluent neighborhoods. Low-income and working-class neighborhoods have stores that sell little or no organics because people simply cannot afford them. The pricey organic food market effectively rations away from low-income shoppers and toward those who have the money to spend. It favors the rich over the poor, which implies that only the wealthy will have access to cleaner, healthier food. Organic food production as it is carried out within American capitalism may be taking a step toward the E of ecology, but is moving away from the E of equity in the name of the E of economy, namely the capitalist economy.

A key problem with organic food production is that it is driven by the same growth imperative as any other capitalist enterprise. Organic food production cannot defy the laws of physics and is subject to limits to growth like any other form of production. Once again, referring to the *Business Week* article on organic yogurt:

> Just as mainstream consumers are growing hungry for untainted food . . . it is getting harder and harder to find organic ingredients. There simply aren't enough organic cows in the U.S., never mind the

organic grain to feed them, to go around. Nor are there sufficient organic strawberries, sugar or apple pulp. . . . Now companies from Wal-Mart to General Mills to Kellogg are wading into the organic game, attracted by fat margins that old-fashioned food purveyors can only dream of. What was once a cottage industry of family farms has become Big Business, with all that implies, including pressure from Wall Street to scale up and boost profits.[232]

Growth in organic is more difficult to achieve than conventional agriculture. Producing crops without synthetic chemicals and other non-organic methods yield less per acre of land. In one estimate, corn yields declined by 20 percent after adopting organic methods.[233] Growth in output of organic food would therefore require more land and other inputs. Given the resource limitation, the organic food industry is searching the entire planet for ingredients. Importing organic food from as far away as China, Sierra Leone, and Brazil, and monitoring true organic standards from these areas is next to impossible. Moreover, growth in organic farming means growth in pollution and resource depletion. Growth in organic dairy farms includes growth in manure, methane, and carbon dioxide emissions. It also includes growth in fresh water consumption. Growth is what organic farms are doing because it is what is required of them as capitalist business enterprises. As one CEO of an organic food products company expressed: "I have to answer to shareholders."[234] Shareholders, of course, expect exponential returns and this means everwidening growth in the industry.

Truly sustainable food production and capitalism, with its need for profit maximization and growth, are not compatible. In a mindful economy, food production, as with any other form of production, should be democratically controlled by all the stakeholders: farmers, farm workers, and consumers. More specifically, it is governed by consumers who want healthy and organic food, and by producers whose primary concern is sustainable food production, not the ongoing accumulation of profits. The most direct way to achieve mindful and sustainable food is directly and purposefully through local food cooperatives and farmers' markets; that is, through the same community corporations described in the last chapter.

By forming cooperatives, people can directly control what is or is not provided to the community. As nonprofits, cooperatives can make sustainable organic food more affordable by eliminating the capitalist need for profits. Buying from local farmers' markets also eliminates expensive transportation and storage costs, and profits are paid to the small businesses/producers, not absentee shareholders. Cooperative farms that are on the same mission can produce both for local consumption and export their surpluses to other food cooperatives in other communities through cooperative networks. Organizations like the Environmental Working Group, Food First, Genetic Engineering Action Network, and others provide guides on what foods are marketed through cooperative networks.[235]

These organizations also provide a wealth of information about sustainable food choices. Some make available on their websites a shopper's guide to pesticides in produce and some of the food types that are most likely to be contaminated. They provide updated information about a range of sustainable practices and technology. Their websites also provide information on other consumer products such as pets supplies, baby products, cosmetics, cleaning products, as well as a guide for finding sustainably produced products in one's geographic location.

In a mindful economy, the community corporations that are chartered to produce and distribute food will have the values-based core principles of mindful economics written into their legal documentation. One such principle is respect for all life and natural processes. This would mean that businesses would be governed by principles of sustainability and the Three E's, not profit maximization and the growth imperative. It is a legal requirement to describe the purpose of the corporation in the articles of incorporation. Rather than specifying something vague such as "engaging in lawful activity," a community corporation can legally define its purpose specifically as to produce and distribute food in a manner that is ecologically sustainable and socially just.

SUSTAINABLE PRODUCTION, CLOTHING

There is much overlap between sustainable food and sustainable clothing production. Like conventional food production, conventional cotton and synthetic fiber production are not sustainable. Most cotton is produced in a way that destroys topsoil and relies heavily on a myriad of toxins such as parathion as a pesticide, and synthetically produced fertilizers such as nitrogen, phosphorous, and potash. After cotton is harvested and spun, it is typically treated with highly toxic anti-wrinkle finishing agents such as formaldehyde. The fabric is typically transported to sweatshops in poorer regions where cheap labor is exploited. All of course is done to achieve maximum possible profits. Alternatives to this model of capitalist clothing production are very limited and are usually small Internet-based companies that produce a very limited product line. Organic cotton on the other hand employs more costly systems of composted soil, rather than chemical fertilizers and carefully placed insect species that act as natural pesticides.

Although largely, but unfairly, associated with marijuana, hemp is among the best fibers that can be produced sustainably and with high yields. Hemp has been banned since the 1930s largely as a result of cotton industry lobbyists seeking to eliminate its competition. Hemp plants require very little pesticides or herbicides, and when properly rotated with soy beans and corn, the fertility of topsoil can be sustained indefinitely. This "industrial grade" hemp has virtually no value as a narcotic. However, federal drug enforcement officials argue that controlling marijuana production and distribution would be made more difficult and expensive if legal, industrial hemp farms were allowed to grow and develop. On the other side of the controversy are the advocates for the legalization of marijuana. Although industrial hemp and marijuana are significantly different varieties of the same plant species, it is often the same groups that lobby for the legalization of marijuana and the legalization of hemp. Lawmakers are, therefore, wary of the motives of the hemp legalization activists.

Perhaps the most high-profile mark of unsustainability is the sweatshop conditions under which most clothing is produced. It is difficult to find clothing that is not produced where textile workers are paid poverty wages in dismal working conditions, and are unable to afford to buy the things they produce. Information on working conditions is provided by Sweatshop Watch, a network of dozens of organizations interested in making the apparel industry accountable for earning living wages and decent working conditions.[236]

As with food, the community corporations that are chartered to produce and distribute clothing will have the values-based core principles of mindful economics written into their legal documentation. This would include the principle of respect for humanity as well as the principle of respect for all life and natural processes. This would mean that clothing businesses would also be governed by principles of sustainability and the Three E's, not profit maximization.

Part of the mindful economy therefore would include community corporations chartered to make clothing made with natural, organically produced fibers. These businesses also process fabric without harmful chemical dyes, bleaches, and they finish the clothing in workshops that are owned and operated by stakeholders in the local community.

SUSTAINABLE PRODUCTION, SHELTER

Part of the mindful economy includes community corporations chartered to build residential and commercial buildings using "green building" technology and sustainable practices. Like all other institutions that comprise a mindful economy, the building companies are owned and operated by stakeholders in the local community and are organized for the purposes of building, not profit maximization.

Eco-building or green building is at the forefront of sustainable technology. As with agriculture, rigorous standards for certifying building sustainability have been developed by organizations such as the Forest Stewardship Council (FSC) and the U.S. Green Building Council. These standards apply to forest products or lumber production as well as the buildings themselves.

Homes built with wood products that are certified by the FSC use only sustainably harvested or recycled wood. To be certified, the practice must include protection of watersheds, the prevention of soil erosion, and protection of wildlife from endangerment. In addition, FSC certification will not certify the unsustainable use of chemicals or unfair labor practices. Sustainable harvesting means that the forests' original condition is not compromised or systematically altered in any way. Sustainably harvested wood fiber also means that wood fiber will be extracted at a much slower pace than the conventional and unsustainable clear-cut method. Sustainable wood fiber thus comes at the cost of fewer profits for the timber industry.

The U.S. Green Building Council developed a green building rating system known as Leadership in Energy and Environmental Design (LEED). The core mission of the Council has been to define environmentally sustainable building construction methods and to standardize measurements of environmentally sound and healthy living spaces. The LEED rating system includes a wide array of project standards for building design and construction. LEED specifies standards for efficient design, water and energy use, insulation building materials, appliances, wiring and lighting, and a host of other specifications. A LEED green site provides guidelines and assessment for new construction such that the construction does not encroach on environmentally sensitive area or on farmland, and that the construction can be sustained with the constraints of community resources. LEED certification is based on a scoring or rating system in which the builders get points for following a checklist of eco-friendly design and construction principles.

To be considered a green building, for example, a home should be constructed without composite building materials such as plywood, laminated wood, or particle boards that are made with toxic, volatile organic compounds (VOCs). Such building materials emit toxic gases with natural wear and decay and these gasses pollute both the air inside and outside the home. Home building should also be free of carcinogenic substances such as asbestos and lead. Alternative materials include milled and pressed bamboo—bamboo is actually a kind of grass that grows quickly and can easily be harvested on a sustainable yield basis. Other environmentally safe building materials for the interior include ceramic tile, stone, marble, and slate. The downside of using these materials, however, is that they are expensive and limited in supply with the exception of bamboo which is currently relatively inexpensive to grow and harvest sustainably.

There is some uncertainty, however, about whether what is categorized as "green building" is actually sustainable or just some greener improvements on past practices. FSC and LEED guidelines do not guarantee sustainability any more than certified organic food. LEED guidelines can be considered steps in that direction qualitatively, but quantitatively they cannot assure sustainability if people overconsume. As with organic food or clothing made in non-sweatshop conditions, sustainably harvested timber generally means higher costs. Higher costs can create scarcity and ration many who cannot afford to pay them out of the market for these vital goods and services. Perhaps the biggest challenge in a mindful economy is channeling resources into production systems that assure *both* ecological sustainability and social equity. On the other hand, capitalism assures neither.

SUSTAINABLE PRODUCTION, ENERGY, AND TRANSPORTATION

As we saw in Chapter Nine, perhaps the most dire threat to human civilization is global warming. In late August and Early September of 2005, Hurricane Katrina devastated the entire Gulf Coast region of the southern United States. The hurricane resulted in hundreds of billions of dollars worth of damage and hundreds of deaths, and permanent destruction and deterioration of the lives of thousands of people. Katrina was the worst natural disaster ever to strike the United States. Such extreme weather conditions have been accurately predicted by climatologists who continue to issue warnings about the dangers of global warming stemming from an overuse of fossil fuels. The need for alternative ways of harnessing and using energy is as dire as our need to reduce our use and dependence on fossil fuels. Harnessing solar, wind, and other renewable energy sources and recycling waste are partial steps away from this dependence.

Wind power is technology that dates back hundreds of years. Wind power is typically generated in wind farms where a series of wind turbines are set up to capture the kinetic energy of wind and turn it into electricity. Of course, this energy relies on the availability of adequate wind, and on the availability of financial resources of a community to build wind infrastructure: mills, turbines, transmission lines, etc. However, unlike other sustainable practices we have been exploring, wind is actually less costly than conventional practices. In fact, wind is the lowest-cost renewable energy resource. Whereas environmentally damaging hydroelectric and fossil fuel sources of electricity cost at present between $.10 and $.60 per kilowatt hour, wind costs about $.05 and does little or no harm to the environment. This figure includes the cost of financing the development of a wind plant as well as its costs of operation and maintenance.

Wind power infrastructure can be adapted to the scale of use. Most of the larger, utility-scale wind turbines can generate about 700 kilowatts to 1.8 megawatts (mw). A 1.8 mw turbine, with the right amount of wind, can generate enough electricity to power more than five hundred households. Small micro turbines (1 to 1.5 kilowatt) can also be erected for the use of a single home or village. Although the amount of capital investment has gone down substantially, it is still prohibitively high for most individual homeowners. The start-up costs are about $1,000/kilowatt of electricity, but wind is still an inexpensive way to generate electricity and it does not generate air pollution, water pollution, or hazardous waste. Wind does not contribute to global warming or the depletion of fossil fuels, all of which are high but unmeasured costs of conventional electricity.

Solar or photovoltaic (PV) energy converts sunlight directly into electricity or heat. Comprised of thin sheets or wafers made of crystalline silicon (the same material used to make semiconductors), solar cells are exposed to sunlight and an electrical current is generated. The current can be used to power watches, calculators, radios, other small electronic devices, and even lawn mowers. Solar energy is also harnessed for street lamps in which solar radiation is converted to electricity during the day, stored in a battery, and then used for illumination at night.

The typical PV system is complex and expensive. For now, the most common applications of PV systems are those that are in remote areas and are completely disconnected from conventional power grids. There are also grid-connected PV systems in which households generate their own solar self-sustaining electricity when there is ample sun, or where they use a combination of electricity from conventional grid and PV sources. Most conventional electric utilities automatically deliver electricity when the amount generated from PVs is not sufficient. In some cases, households with efficient and powerful PV systems can sell surplus electricity to the conventional utility by transmitting power back on to the grid.

PV systems generally consist of an array of roof-top solar panels, devices for converting direct current (DC) electricity created by PV cells to the alternating current (AC) electricity on which most households operate, and batteries for storing electricity for use during the hours without sunlight. For those disconnected from a conventional grid, back-up generators can be kept available in case battery-stored electricity is insufficient—typically during dark and cold winter months.

Larger and more complex solar systems can be used for heating and refrigeration systems, and arrays of panels are used to provide power for centralized grid systems. These are more practical in summer and in warmer regions where there is ample sunlight. Solar heating technology runs water through pipes contained within solar panels and the heated water is used to heat interior spaces, hot water tanks, and even swimming pools.

The high initial investment required for fitting a home with photovoltaic solar panels, batteries for storage, and control systems make it an expensive alternative. The initial investment required is high. Although it has decreased substantially in the last twenty years, estimates of start-up costs range from $15,000 to $25,000 for a relatively small house. Governments can encourage households to use PV systems, and can make them more affordable by offering tax breaks as financial incentives. For example, a new federal energy law recently enacted includes a tax credit of as much as $2,000 for the purchase and installation of a residential solar power system. When amortized over the life of the system, PV systems cost about $.25 per kilowatt hour (kwh).[237] For a household using 400-500 kwh/month this would be an electricity cost of $100 to $125 per month. This is substantially more expensive than conventional electricity, and five times greater than wind power.

Some experts in the PV field see the costs of solar power declining with new technology. One example of new PV technology is known as "sliver cell" solar technology. Sliver cell technology uses crystalline silicon but processes it in such a way to create very thin solar cells that promise to be as much as 20 percent more efficient than traditional PV technology in harnessing electricity from sunlight.[238] Moreover, PV is a rapidly growing industry worldwide and has become even more so in recent years—as much as 65 percent in one year—as prices of oil, natural gas, and other energy sources continue to rise.[239]

The development of PV technology as a widespread and affordable energy alternative will require significant institutional change. In a mindful economy, the most direct way to deal with the high cost problem is to create public sector utilities. Solar infrastructure can be developed in the same way that conventional infrastructure projects—hydroelectric dams, interstate freeways, and nuclear power plants—were developed in the past. Even if this infrastructure were developed through a public institution, people will probably have to pay higher prices for electricity generated with PV technology and this will place a greater burden on low-income households. If channeled through the public sector, however, energy subsidies for those at the bottom of the income scale can offset higher costs. Building solar infrastructure at this scale may seem like a daunting task, but so was the task of making education universally accessible, and so was the World War II war effort. Such an effort requires will and a democratic polity made up of active mindful economic citizens.

Biofuels are also alternative energy technologies that can lead toward sustainability. With this technology, agricultural residue such as peanut shells, sugar canes, corn husks, rice hulls, as well as yard debris, wood chips, animal waste, and even sewage can be used to make fuel. Organic crops such as corn or soy beans can be grown specifically to make renewable energy as well. The fuel processed from organic waste and organically grown crops is burned in furnaces that power steam-driven turbines to generate electricity.

Although burning biomass releases carbon dioxide into the atmosphere, it originates from vegetation that absorbs carbon dioxide from the ecosphere. Unlike with fossil fuels that originate in the lithosphere, carbon dioxide from biomass originates in the ecosphere as it is absorbed by plants, and thus can be continually recycled. This renewable and recyclable system would lessen the amount of carbon dioxide that systematically builds up in the ecosphere, particularly if the biomass sources are also developed sustainably and organically. Harnessing these energy sources will not be sustainable if the agricultural processes they are linked to are also sustainable.

Biodiesel is extracted from vegetable oil such as from soybean, canola, or rapeseed and is combined with methanol (a kind of alcohol) to make a fuel that can be used to power diesel-powered engines. Biodiesel is a fully biodegradable motor fuel. According to EPA tests, compared to petroleum-based diesel fuel, biodiesel releases less than half of the air pollutants of petroleum-based diesel. Again, the carbon dioxide originates in the atmosphere and does not contribute to a systematic increase if it comes from sustainable sources. Moreover, biodiesel produces practically none of the acid rain toxins such as sulfur dioxide and sulfates.

Public transportation infrastructure can be erected on a foundation of biofuels as a practical alternative to current gas-powered automobiles. However, it would be impossible to organically and sustainably produce enough vegetable oil to power the 100 million cars on American freeways with biodiesel. Efficient local public transportation systems, however, can be developed and sustained on vegetable oil production. One of the greatest advantages of biodiesel is that it can be raised and processed locally to serve local transportation needs. Thus, the movement toward biodiesel as a principal fuel source will be predicated on dramatic change in transportation systems and infrastructure—significant institutional change.

As with other sustainable practices, direct costs of truly sustainable fuels are likely to be higher than traditional fossil fuels. Higher costs can create scarcity and ration too many people out of these vital goods and services. It should be noted, however, that when comparing costs of renewable or sustainable energy with conventional ones, conventional costs are often incomplete as they do not take into account costs that were externalized into other spheres as a result of environmental damage. If these costs were taken into consideration, it might be possible to prove that, over the long run, sustainable technology is actually less costly. The central problem with making such comparisons is that many of the costs associated with unsustainable practices are qualitative or moral costs. It is difficult, if not impossible, to make comparisons using dollar values of the costs associated with loss of biodiversity, habitat destruction, or the magnitude of destruction caused by global warming. We can factor in the costs of damage done by hurricanes, but these costs are only the immediate and currently knowable ones. There are many costs that are coming with recurring storms, floods, and other damage associated with unsustainable practices. These costs are currently unknowable. Given a broader view, moving to these alternative technologies requires not only institutional change, but also a change in ideology.

Sustainable transportation infrastructure would have to be completely redesigned to reduce Americans' dependence on motor vehicle commutes and their vast consumption of fuel. Consumer choices and habits—which over the last two decades have been leaning toward larger and less energy-efficient vehicles—will have to be redirected. Much can be accomplished with regard to sustainability and energy use by simple conservation habits such as turning off lights, using energy-saving fixtures and appliances, weatherizing homes, taking public transportation, or by voluntarily opting for a simpler lifestyle that treads more lightly on the planet. Again, these practices are inconsistent with the growth-orientation of capitalism, and to develop real alternatives will require deep and thoroughgoing institutional change.

Material technology will, of course, always play a role in efficient resource use. But efficiency is a relative term. In economic terms, efficiency means getting the maximum output for a given amount of inputs. Yet just because resources are efficiently used does not mean that they are not overused. Producing cars that have hybrid—gas, electric, biodiesel, or ethanol—power systems will realize a more efficient mode of transportation than the traditional gasoline-powered internal combustion motor. But continuing with a transportation system in which people commute daily in single-occupancy vehicles, is nonetheless depleting our resources and is not sustainable regardless of the fuel source. And much of what is considered to be renewable resources are harnessed in part by burning fossil fuels. In other words, efficiency is a necessary but not sufficient condition for true sustainability. Consuming green is not enough, people must also consume less. According to a study conducted released in the journal *Science* in early 2008, increasing reliance on biofuels is likely to release more greenhouse gasses than reduce them. The study points to a likelihood that as economies grow, more forests and grasslands will be cleared to make room for ethanol production.[240]

The development of sustainable energy technology over the last few decades has been impressive and will be a key aspect of the evolution to a mindful economy. Material technology is only part of the equation, however, and is often an overemphasized part. Technological developments are mitigating factors but not solutions. What is underemphasized is the much deeper and difficult problem of systemic and institutional change away from the business-as-usual system of capitalist growth and profits.

Under the capitalist mode of production and consumption, the purpose of economic activity is to make and accumulate profits. Respect for nature and humanity—critical elements for any sustainable system—may or may not occur depending on whether it is consistent with profit-making. The current and historical evidence is overwhelmingly clear that these purposes are not consistent, and are in fact opposite. Although there are many sustainable practices which households and businesses can follow that do not require significant institutional change, evolving toward a truly sustainable economy will necessitate deep and thoroughgoing institutional change. Rather than focusing on institutional change, many prefer to turn to blind faith in material technology. Technology can lighten people's ecological footprints, but it cannot solve the core problems associated with capitalism.

Perhaps even more troubling is that, rather than face the need for systemic change, many believe in fallacies that suggest the capitalist system can be preserved and at the same time achieve the Three E's of sustainability. The Three E paradigm became subsumed under a kind of "Three W" paradigm of win-win-win in which it was envisioned that economic growth, environmental sustainability, and equity could all be achieved at once. The win-win-win paradigm has resonated profoundly in the business community and among those who believe that capitalism can be sustainable.

WIN-WIN-WIN FALLACIES

There appears to be a slippery slope that connects the Three E's of ecology, equity, and economy to a belief that the profit-driven capitalist system can prevail. In an attempt to link Ecology and Economy, many have opted to believe that we can achieve ecological sustainability without compromising corporate bottom lines. This is a popular approach to selling the business community on the topic of sustainability. The win-win-win folks rely on a handful of companies as case studies in which business leaders found that by adopting more sustainable practices they became more efficient, reduced production costs, and actually became even more profitable.

To be sure, there are gains to be made by adopting energy and resource conservation practices and reducing waste. In some cases, businesses may have achieved their goal of simultaneously becoming more sustainable and more profitable. But to conclude that this can be true for all businesses and thus for the entire economy is classic reductionistic, non-systems thinking. The fallacy in the win-win-win arguments lies in the mistaken belief that ecological sustainability, social equity, and the capitalist drive for profits can somehow be compatibly stitched together as common objectives. Perhaps under very limited circumstances they have been, but the historical record shows practically no evidence of this. Moreover, the historical record shows overwhelming evidence—clear-cuts, strip mines, sweatshops—that the opposite is true.

The crux of the matter is that a sustainable system is a steady-state system and capitalism cannot operate in a steady-state environment anymore than a polar bear can survive on a vegetarian diet. As we have argued throughout, the issue is not that sustainability is incompatible with business or industry, it is incompatible with capitalism. Capitalism requires exponential growth and no matter how intelligently you design it, is not sustainable. Continuous economic growth, like cancerous cell growth, will eventually kill its habitat.

Never in the two hundred years of American capitalism has it been reported in the business or financial press that a steady-state level of national output was a good thing. This is because ongoing growth is not merely an aspiration of corporations operating with outdated assumptions, it is a systemic requirement.

The systemic requirement of growth would prevail even if capitalism were made greener. If a business adopts more sustainable practices rooted in green friendly technology and consumption habits—organic food, organic clothing, green building, etc.—it will still be required to grow if it is to remain as a capitalist system. Having more and more organic farms, growing articles of hemp clothing, and a spreading number of green buildings is no more sustainable than the conventional practices as they too will deplete resources. And the depletion of resources is a certainty if production is saddled with a requirement of ongoing growth.

Sustainability requires treading more lightly on the planet and consuming less. Yet a decrease in consumption would lead to a decline in business revenues and profits, a decline in the rate of return to investors, and eventually a crisis in the capitalist economy. To deny this fact is to deny the very essence of capitalism. Yet this denial is rampant. Consider this passage from *E* magazine's, *Green Living*:

> . . . most environmentalists know that "doing without" is good for the planet. But they may not realize just how good it is for their savings account . . . After all, money one might spend on an impressive SUV, a large engagement ring, or even a regular habit of junk food snacks, leaves you with less money to invest . . . If, for example, from the ages of twenty-three to sixty-seven you bypassed the popular American habit of buying a new mid-size car every two years and instead . . . invested your savings, you'd end up with an extra $869,638. Manage without a car altogether, invest the savings, and that money alone can make you a millionaire.[241]

E magazine is failing to see the systemic nature of the problem. How can one's financial investment grow to a million dollars if these investments were not put in a fund that experiences exponential or compound growth? And if they are, the compound growth must be anchored to growth in the real economy that is producing the very SUVs, engagement rings, and junk food snacks they are telling people not to buy.

Imagine if all households decided to lighten their ecological footprints. They would buy fewer goods in the stores. Sales revenue would decline, and with declining revenues, profits would fall, and the economy would slide into a recessionary spiral. Stock markets and other aspects of our financial system would begin a downward spiral as well. The end result is systemic collapse. This is only half the story.

Imagine also that all the corporations that dominate the economy of the United States suddenly decided to adopt the Three E's and placed social and environmental concerns on an equal footing with profit-making. Profits would certainly go down. As profits declined, the sources of investment capital would begin to dry up and business investments—what keeps the "drive wheel" of growth moving—would recede. As business investments decline, economic growth turns to recession and the capitalist system begins, once again, its downward spiral into a crisis. Maximized profits or "business as usual" are not merely corporate vices, they are central aspects of the capitalist system.

In the face of this conundrum, businesses will abandon their attempts at sustainability in the name of profits and their own survival. Jeanne and Dick Roy, founders of the Northwest Earth Institute, see this contradiction between the Three E's and capitalism. The Roys assert that there is asymmetry within the Three E's: with too much emphasis placed on the Economy and with the other two E's taking subordinate positions. The result, the Roys write, is "sustainability lite" or a half-hearted approach to sustainability. The Roys quote a typical business-oriented approach to sustainable practice: "I am an advocate of sustainable practices so long as they increase the bottom line. Otherwise, how would I sell this approach to management."[242] This, stated succinctly, is the contradiction inherent in the win-win-win fallacy.

According to *Business Week*, the popular notion of making a business both environmentally friendly and more profitable has been largely a fantasy. It has also led to a multi-billion-dollar public relations frenzy. When faced with priorties and with the reality that sustainability and profitability are at cross-purposes, corporate executives invariably weigh in on the side of investors, "We do have a fiduciary responsibility to our shareholders."[243]

CONCLUSION

Much of what has been recently written on the "sustainability revolution" that is patterned on the Three E's is anchored to this win-win-win fallacy. Without systemic or institutional change and with the growth imperative of capitalism remaining unchallenged, the sustainability revolution will languish in a stunted interpretation of the Three E's and it will be neither sustainable nor revolutionary.

To be lasting and meaningful, sustainability will come about not as a revolutionary force, but as an evolutionary one. Mindful economics is an approach that is based on the idea that institutions and systems evolve over time. It is our hope that people can take charge of the direction that this evolution takes and consciously and purposefully bring about institutional change. Mindful economics is also an approach based on direct action. If sustainability is desirable, then people must mobilize and begin building institutions that will direct economic production, distribution, and consumption in a sustainable way. People can thoughtfully and systematically institutionalize sustainable practices by integrating these practices into their governance of community corporations and other institutions. More importantly, however, is that these institutions must stand outside the capitalist system.

CONCLUSION
Toward a Mindful Economy

All of the elements of a mindful economy exist in the U.S. today. Like so many pieces of a jigsaw puzzle, they are merely waiting to be put together in such a way that they cohere into a big picture. The elements are, of course, institutions. The big picture of a mindful economy is a network of institutions that are compatible, and are compatible because people will have mindfully and purposefully made them so. A mindful economy, therefore, is an economic system comprised of a network of institutions created by people who share a core set of values-based principles: social justice, equity, and democracy; environmental sustainability; and economic stability.

In a mindful economy, people value democracy and take it seriously. They are full-fledged members of their communities and play an active, four-dimensional role in the economy: as employees, consumers, owners, and citizens. As employees, people in a mindful economy earn incomes by working for community-based, non-capitalist businesses. As consumers their incomes are also spent in these same community-based businesses whose operations are guided by core values-based principles. What makes these businesses community-based is the fact they are owned by the people in the community. By becoming owners, people have the constitutionally guaranteed right to sovereignty over their businesses; that is, they govern the actions of the businesses democratically. To govern means to actively participate in the decision-making process as mindful economic citizens. Unlike capitalism where people are separated from ownership, in a mindful economy people are empowered with ownership as well as the rights and responsibilities that go with it.

People's motivations in a mindful economy are significantly different from those of capitalism. Capitalism is a system that is based on the cynical assumptions that people are naturally greedy and self-interested. In a capitalist system it is assumed that people aspire to own businesses because their only interest is to become wealthy. It is also assumed that people consume as a means to indulge self-interest and to elevate their social status. There is certainly plenty of evidence of greed, self-interest, and conspicuous consumption in America, but it is our contention that these human traits have been allowed to grow and have become institutionalized by the capitalist system's need to produce, sell, and expand.

In a mindful economy, other human characteristics and traits can be fostered and developed under a different system. In a mindful economy, people are motivated by certain core values, not greed and self-indulgence. Consumption is not a means to elevated social status, but an integral part of a sustainable healthy life of light ecological footprints and minimal waste through consuming green and consuming less. Ownership is not a path to riches but is local or community-based, and is part of a truly democratic system.

Imagine also the business firms in a mindful economy. The large transnational capitalist enterprises do not exist here. Instead you will find community corporations, small family-owned businesses, and public enterprises—none are capitalist and all fundamentally integrate ownership and work. These businesses are created to achieve specific purposes that are, again, guided by the core values-based principles of mindful economics. Unlike capitalism, in which the purpose is to make profits for investors, businesses in a mindful economy openly and directly work to serve the needs of people by producing and distributing food, clothing, shelter, healthcare, education, transportation, etc.

The community corporations and public enterprises in a mindful economy are chartered to produce and distribute goods and services for the good of the community. In various places throughout this book we have referred to the process of creating a corporation and defining the purpose of these businesses in the legal documentation. This is arguably the single most important step in evolving an economic system toward a mindful economy. It is here that the DNA of the business institutions is defined, and it is from these institutions that the system develops its characteristics. In these legal documents a corporation can be defined to be a predatory transnational company, or it can be defined as a community-based cooperative. It can be made to maximize profits for its shareholders, or it can be made to serve the needs of the community. What makes the distinction is the description of the business, the purpose, its activities, and so on, included in their corporate charters.

Recall that the process of creating a corporation begins with a legal draft of the articles of incorporation. This is the legal description of the corporation including the name, place, description of activities as board members, and so on. From the point of creation the corporation exists as a distinct legal entity that is contractually obligated to follow the rules and guidelines set out in the articles. Corporate bylaws—also part of the legal documentation—provide legal and managerial guidelines directing the day-to-day business activities along the lines set out by the articles. Exactly what a community wants the corporation to do is established in this process. In a mindful economy, therefore, we contend that each business enterprise must have the following elements built into its articles and bylaws:

1. The company is to be guided by the values-based core principles of mindful economics:

A Mindful Economy is Intrinsically Democratic, Equitable, and Just

An intrinsically democratic economic institution is one which is governed directly by all the stakeholders in the community including workers, consumers, suppliers, and any others who are affected in some way by the activities of the business. A mindful economy is based on the fair and equitable value of each individual's contribution, their right to work without harassment or racial or gender discrimination, and the right to a decent livelihood are all important to the overall livability of the community.

A Mindful Economy is Based on Respect for All Life and Natural Processes

In a mindful economy, the natural environment is seen as something to be valued and preserved in its own right, not only on the merits that it provides something useful to people. A mindful economy is also committed to a proper stewardship of the planet and its resources, and is committed to following the "Socio-Ecological Principles for a Sustainable Society."

A Mindful Economy is Stable

Unlike the boom and bust instabilities of capitalism, a mindful economy rests on a secure foundation that is firmly embedded in the local community. It is independent from the Wall Street speculators and other predatory practices that cause the financial system to swing up and down with instability.

2. The company is also to be guided by the principles of governance of cooperatives established by the ICA Commission on Co-operative Principles. The principles could also apply to small businesses and public enterprises.

3. The company is fundamentally non-capitalist as it is not characterized by the profit motive, the social separation of ownership and work, or the growth imperative. The company is driven by the motive to serve

the community, integrates ownership and work, and does not pursue growth for growth's sake.

4. The company extends ownership and control to all stakeholders in the community who are affected by its operations, including employees, consumers, suppliers, and members in the immediate surrounding community.

These elements should be present in all businesses whether they are in manufacturing, agriculture, banking, retail, or any other sector.

In a mindful economy, households are still locked together with these businesses through a network of markets. Unlike capitalism, however, they are not locked together in a mutually antagonistic cash nexus fraught with conflict and opposition. In a mindful economy they are brought together by shared values and a fundamental integration of ownership, work, and consumption.

Imagine further a monetary and banking system that is democratically controlled by local community corporations—financial cooperatives—and citizens. Unlike the non-democratic and centrally controlled system of capitalism, the financial system of a mindful economy serves the true needs of the community by providing financial services for economic development, homes, public works projects, etc., and provides monetary stability. Since the mindful economy is not driven by the profit motive, it is not subject to speculative greed that creates financial market instability. A community-based system of money and finance can achieve independence from Wall Street and to some degree from the Federal Reserve System.

Imagine a mindful economy supported by local government that is firmly rooted in procedural and substantive democracy. Democratically accountable government does not imply accountability to special interests or powerful institutions or money. It implies that it is directly accountable to its citizens, and the citizens are also responsible for participating in the democratic governance of the community. And imagine an economy in which people are living in homes, eating food, and wearing clothes that were all produced using sustainable practices. All these elements of a mindful economy exist in one form or another like the pieces of a puzzle. What is missing is bringing these pieces or anecdotes together into a full-fledged system. The whole of the system is at least as great as the institutional parts.

FROM ANECDOTES TO A MINDFUL ECONOMIC SYSTEM

The process of moving from dispersed anecdotes—a food co-op here, community corporation there, financial cooperative elsewhere—to a networked and unified system will be difficult and will take time. Institutional change is difficult and systemic change is even more difficult. But change is inevitable nonetheless. Recall Daniel Quinn, "If there are still people here in 200 years, they won't be living the way we do. I can make that prediction with confidence, because if people go on living the way we do, there won't be any people here in 200 years" (See Chapter One). The question therefore should not be about whether or not we will change, but how to bring about the right kind of change. Bookshelves are loaded with books that take a critical view of our economic system, but very few venture a suggestion as to how to change it. This is probably because as we make suggestions for change, the suggestions are always met with much resistance. Resistance often comes from what famous sociologist William F. Ogburn dubbed "cultural lag."

William F. Ogburn was among the first sociologists to address cultural lag as a specific problem in social evolution. Taking a systems approach in which economic activity is embedded in a totality of culture, Ogburn noted that change and adaptation can occur at a different pace for different parts of society. For example, he noted that auto-manufacturing technology has evolved at a rate faster than the development of transportation infrastructure necessary to accommodate the newer, larger, and faster vehicles. During the Stone Age, Ogburn noted, non-material or institutional aspects of cultures were evolving much more quickly than stone technology. In the modern period, however, he sees science and technology as the prime movers of culture and social institutions as having lagged behind.[244] Currently we seem to be in a new phase in which the long-term consequences of economic growth are becoming manifest, but social institutions are slow to change in order to accommodate the transformations and adaptations necessary for our survival.

The totality of culture consists of both material (physical property and artifacts) and non-material (institutions), and both must evolve to adapt to our changing world environment. Social institutions need to change and evolve so as to allow new technology to develop and to foster its development. Technology is institutionally engendered and a passively blind faith in technology is tantamount to blind faith in existing social institutions. People must be proactive and actively pursue institutional change and this change will foster new technologies—necessity is, as the saying goes, the mother of invention.

Our concern is that we cannot afford to have cultural lag in the face of a multifaceted crisis of resource depletion, rising instabilities, and crushing inequalities. We must be proactive and actively begin building new institutions despite fierce opposition. Those growing problems all require institutional change and adaptation away from capitalism.

Capitalism began as an anecdotal model and evolved, with institutional change and adaptation, into a full-fledged economic system. We can learn from this historical precedent. In Mindful Economics we see that economies can once again evolve. We see it evolving, step by step, away from the growth-oriented, profit-driven capitalist system to a community-based, sustainable system. This must necessarily involve mindful institutional development and change. And unlike a Utopia, which means "nowhere," the alternatives are everywhere all around us.

NOTES

1. HBS Bulletin Online, http://www.alumni.hbs.edu/bulletin/1997/december/theory.html.
2. David Cassidy, "The Decline of Economics," *New Yorker*, December 1997.
3. Stanford University News Service, February 11, 1997.
4. E. K. Hunt, *Property and Prophets: The Evolution of Economic Institutions and Ideologies* (New York: M.E. Sharpe, 2003), 126.
5. David Korten, *When Corporations Rule the World* (San Francisco: Berrett-Koehler, 2001), 75–76.
6. Daniel Quinn, "The New Renaissance." An address delivered at the University of Texas Health Science Center at Houston, March 2002.
7. Clarence E. Ayres. *The Theory of Economic Progress*, 3rd edition (Kalamazoo, MI: New Issues Press, 1978), 178.
8. John Stuart Mill, *Principles of Political Economy* (New York: Penguin Books, 1970), 349–350.
9. U.S. Const., Fourteenth Amendment, sec. 1.
10. Karl Polanyi, *The Great Transformation: The Political and Economic Origins of Our Time* (Boston: Beacon Press, 1944).
11. Source data for these comparisons came from the Organization for Economic Cooperation and Development.
12. "Laissez Faire," *Chartism* (1839), Chapter IV, http://www.uoguelph.ca/englit/victorian/HTML/laissez.html.
13. "OECD Economic Outlook No. 73," *Economic Report of the President*, June 2003.
14. The Bureau of Labor Statistics makes no distinction between family and household income data.
15. http://www.census.gov/prod/2007pubs/p60-233.pdf, 12, August 2007.
16. Bureau of Labor Statistics, May 7, 2008, http://www.bls.gov/news.release/prod2.t01.htm.
17. "Where Wealth Lives," *Business Week*, April 19, 2004, 37.
18. Glenn B. Canner, Arthur B. Kennickell, and Charles A. Luckett. "Household Sector Borrowing and the Burden of Debt," *Federal Reserve Bulletin*, April 1995, 323-338, http://www.federalreserve.gov/pubs.
19. "Where Wealth Lives," *Business Week*, 36.
20. *Fortune Magazine*'s list of the 500 largest corporations.
21. "Executive Pay," *Business Week*, April 19, 2004, 106–120.
22. Thorstein Veblen. *Absentee Ownership, Business Enterprise in Recent Times: The Case of America* [1923] (New Brunswick, NJ: Transaction Publishers, 1997), 84.
23. *The Constitution of the United States*, Amendment 13, Section 1.
24. Ibid, Amendment 14, Section 1.
25. Joel Bakan, *The Corporation: The Pathological Pursuit of Profit and Power* (New York: Free Press, 2004), 14.
26. William Letwin, "The Past and Future of the American Businessman," *Daedalus*, Winter 1969, 11.
27. Veblen, *Absentee Ownership*, 4.
28. Bakan, *The Corporation*, 46–47.
29. "Drugs: Is Something Rotten?," *Business Week*, April 19, 2004, 24.

30. Although this quote is often attributed to Jefferson, it is not clear where this quote originated. It appears to have been in common use among late-18th-century reformers.

31. Howard Zinn, *A People's History of the United States* (New York: Harper Collins, 2003), 256, and John Tipple, "The Robber Baron in the Gilded Age," in H. Wayne Morgan, ed., *The Gilded Age* (Syracuse, New York: Syracuse University Press, 1963), 26.

32. Zinn, *People's History*, 255–258, and Robert Heilbroner and Aaron Singer, *The Economic Transformation of America: 1600 to the Present*, 2nd ed. (New York: Harcourt Brace Jovanovich, 1984), 156–160, 197–205.

33. David Korten, *When Corporations Rule the World*, 2nd ed. (San Francisco, CA: Berrett Koehler Publishers, 2001), 67.

34. Matthew Josephson, *The Robber Barons [1886]* (New York: Harcourt Brace Jovanovich, 1962), 358.

35. Daniel Fusfeld, *The Age of the Economist* (New York: Addison Wesley, 2002), 81.

36. Josephson, *Robber Barrons*, 187.

37. Ibid.

38. Zinn, *People's History*, 260.

39. *Clayton Act* (1914), Section 6, Title 15, United States Code.

40. J. R. Hollingsworth and Robert Boyer, eds., *Contemporary Capitalism: The Embeddedness of Institutions* (New York: Cambridge University Press, 1997), Chapters 1 and 4.

41. See www.nam.org.

42. See www.uschamber.com.

43. "The U.S. Chamber of Commerce Leads the Campaign to Eviscerate Victim's Rights to Sue," *Multinational Monitor* 6, nos. 3 and 4, March/April 2005.

44. Ibid.

45. Ibid.

46. "Chamber of Commerce Vows to Punish Anti-Business Candidates," *Los Angeles Times*, January 8, 2008.

47. "Corporate Governance-Business Roundtable," Value Based Management.net, March 25, 2008, http://www.valuebasedmanagement.net/organizations_businessroundtablecorporate-governance.html.

48. Zinn, *People's History*, 218.

49. Heilbroner and Singer, *Economic Transformation*, 24.

50. Ibid., 227.

51. Scientific management, also known as Taylorism named after Frederick W. Taylor, was an approach to workplace management that employed time-motion studies to increase workplace efficiency.

52. *National Labor Relations Act*, U.S. Const. art XXIX, sec. 7.

53. Ibid., sec. 8.

54. "Wal-Mart Store Closing Chills Union Drive in 25 Canada Outlets," *Bloomberg.com*, April 29, 2005.

55. Ibid.

56. Polanyi, *The Great Transformation*, 72.

57. Ibid., 140–141.

58. Ibid., 102.

59. Ibid., 69.

60. Ibid., 133.

61. George Soros, *The Crisis of Global Capitalism: Open Society Endangered* (New York: Public Affairs, 1998), xx-xxii.

62. All modern coins have reeded edges so as to prevent debasement. This practice was invented by Sir Isaac Newton, who was England's Master of the Royal Mint in the late 17th and early 18th centuries.

63. Gary Walton and Hugh Rockoff, *The History of the American Economy*, 6th ed. (New York: Harcourt, Brace Jovanovich, 1990), 240.

64. For a complete list of Fed regulations see the website: http://www.federalreserve.gov/pf/pdf/frspfap.pdf.

65. "Any Dividend from the Microsoft Dividend?," *Business Week*, August 2, 2004, 47.

66. Doug Henwood, *Wall Street* (New York: Verso, 1997), 3–4.

67. The unequal pattern of wealth and income distribution will be explored in detail in Chapter 10.

68. Nomi Prins, *Left Business Observer*, no. 107, April 2004, 4–5, and *Other People's Money* (New York: The New Press, 2004).

69. Ibid, 1–2.

70. Ibid.

71. Henwood, *Wall Street*, 4.

72. Andrew Terborgh, "The Post-War Rise of World Trade: Does the Bretton Woods System Deserve Credit?" (working paper no. 78/03, London School of Economics, September 2003), http://www.lse.ac.uk/collections/economicHistory/pdf/wp7803.pdf.

73. Korten, *When Corporations*, 125.

74. Ibid, 126.

75. Ibid.

76. Under the Marshall Plan, named after Secretary of State George Marshall, the U.S. provided about $13 billion in aid to European countries for rebuilding their economies from 1947 to the early 1950s. Much of the aid came back to the U.S. as these countries used the borrowed dollars to buy U.S. goods needed for their reconstruction efforts.

77. Thom Hartmann, "When Americans No Longer Own America," February 2006, www.thomhartmann.com.

78. Geoff Dyer and Andrew Balls, "China Signals Reserves Switch Away From Dollar," *The Financial Times*, January 5, 2006.

79. Jabier Blas, "IMF Warns High Prices Risk Global Crisis," *Financial Times*, April 6, 2006.

80. This figure is measured in "real" terms meaning that price inflation is factored out by measuring GDP using 2000 prices. If it were measured in "nominal" terms, meaning using current prices, then the figure would be higher.

81. "Economic Report of the President," 1969. See Federal Reserve Archival System for Economic Research (Fraser), htttp://fraser.stlouisfed.org/publications/ERP/issue/1141/.

82. Ibid.

83. The "GI Bill of Rights" or "GI Bill" is officially known as the Servicemen's Readjustment Act of 1944.

84. "Economic Report of the President," 1976.

85. Ibid.

86. Ibid.

87. Ibid.

88. Ibid. See also, Gary M. Walton and Hugh Rockoff, *History of American Economy* (New York: Harcourt, Brace & Jovanovich, 1990), 543.

89. Ibid.

90. Richard Douthwaite, *The Growth Illusion* (Tulsa, OK: Council Oak Books, 1993), 9–10.

91. *Holy Bible* (King James) Proverbs 28:19, 30:8.

92. William Leach, *Land of Desire: Merchants, Power and the Rise of a New American Culture* (New York: Random House, 1993), 15.

93. Ibid, 9.

94. Mary E. Clark, *Ariadne's Thread: The Search for New Modes of Thinking* (New York: St. Martin's Press, 1989), 99.

95. See www.hubbertpeak.com/bartlett/flatearth.htm.

96. Donella Meadows, Jorgen Randers, and Dennis Meadows, *Limits to Growth: The 30-year Update* (White River Junction, VT: Chelsea Green Publishing Company, 2004), 89.

97. Richard C. Duncan and Walter Youngquist, "The World Petroleum Life-Cycle," Petroleum Technology Transfer Council Workshop, University of Southern California, October 22, 1998, www.dieoff.com/page133.pdf.

98. Meadows, et al., *Limits to Growth*, 89.

99. "The End of Cheap Oil," *National Geographic*, June 2004, 85.

100. Ibid.

101. Ibid.

102. Bill McKibben, "Crossing the Red Line," *New York Review of Books* LI, no. 10, June 2004, 34.

103. Ibid.

104. See http://ipcc-wg1.ucar.edu/wg1/docs/WG1AR4_SPM_PlenaryApproved.pdf.

105. Ibid.

106. Ben Elgin, "Little Green Lies," *Business Week*, October 29, 2007, 47.

107. Ibid.

108. Fritjof Capra, *The Turning Point* (New York: Bantam Books, 1982), 247.

109. Bob Edward, "How Many More Lives Will Chernobyl Claim?," *New Scientist* 190, no. 2546 (April 8, 2006), 11.

110. Steve Wing, et al., "A Reevaluation of Cancer Incidence Near the Three Mile Island Nuclear Plant: The Collision of Evidence and Assumptions,"*Environmental Health Perspectives* 105, no. 1 (January 1997): 52–57.

111. This and other examples of nuclear accidents are reported by the Institute for Energy and Environmental Research (IEER) based in Takoma Park, Maryland.

112. Capra, *The Turning Point*, 247.

113. "Farming Systems Principles for Improved Food Production and the Control of Soil degradation in the Arid, Semi-Arid, and Humid Tropics," Published for the United Nations Environment Programme, by the International Crops Research Institute for the Semi-Arid Tropics, 1986.

114. Thomas Prugh, *Natural Capital and Human Economic Survival* (Solomons, MD: International Society for Ecological Economics, 1995), 75.

115. B. L. Turner, et al., "The Earth as Transformed by Human Action: Global and Regional Changes in the Biosphere over the Past 30 Years," in B.G. Rosanov, V. Targulian, and D.S. Orlov, eds. *Soils* (Cambridge, UK: Cambridge University Press, 1990): 203-214.

116. Clark, *Ariadne's Thread*, 109.

117. Bill McKibben, "Our Thirsty Future," *New York Review of Books,* June 2004, 58.

118. Ibid.

119. Ibid., 59.

120. Clark, *Ariadne's Thread*, 107.

121. Ibid.

122. For statistics on Ogallala see http://enterprise.cc.uakron.edu/geology.

123. "Comprehensive Assessment of the Freshwater Resources of the World," 1997, Preparation coordinated by Stockholm Environment Institute (SEI) for UN/UNDP/UNEP/FAO/ UNESCO/WMO/WorldBank/WHO/UNIDO, http://www.un.org/earthwatch/freshwater/.

124. Chris Maser, *The Redesigned Forest* (San Pedro, CA: R & E Miles, 1988), 17.

125. Meadows, et al., *Limits to Growth*, 65.

126. Ibid., 36.

127. Elliot Norse, *Ancient Forests of the Pacific Northwest* (Washington, DC: Island Press, 1990), 6.

128. Vandana Shiva, *Staying Alive:Women, Ecology and* Development (London: Zed, 1989), 108.

129. Edward O. Wilson, "Threats to Biodiversity," *Scientific American*, September 1989, 108.

130. Norse, *Ancient Forests*, 218.

131. Ibid., 219.

132. Karl Marx and Frederick Engels, *The Manifesto of the Communist Party* [1848] (New York: Verso Press, 1998), 40–41.

133. Korten, *When Corporations*, 27.

134. The concept of the circular and cumulative nature of income polarization was conceived by Swedish economist and Nobel Prize winner, Gunnar Myrdal.

135. William Blake, *Selected Poems* (New York: St. Martins Press, 1995), 76.

136. "National Income and Product Accounts," *Statistical Abstract of the United States,* Table 680, Bureau of Economic Analysis, 2006.

137. *Income,* U.S. Census Data 2003, Table RDI-5.

138. Data is from UN Human Development Report, *World Bank Development Indicators 2003*; and *Income,* U.S. Census Data 2003, Table RDI-5.

139. Doug Henwood, *After the New Economy* (New York: The New Press, 2003), 134–138.

140. "Issues 2000," *The Economist,* September 2000.

141. "Spreading the Way of Yankee Pay," *Business Week,* April 19, 2001.

142. Henwood, *After,* 86.

143. Directly held means that it is not indirectly held through managed funds like 401Ks or mutual funds.

144. Henwood, *After,* 123.

145. "UN Human Development Report," *Monthly Labor Review,* January 2006, 45, Table 3; World Bank Development Indicators, 2003; and U.S. Census Data, 2003, Table RDI-5.

146. Pete Engardio, et al., "Is Your Job Next?," *Business Week,* February 3, 2003.

147. Ronald Grover and Tom Lowry, "Rupert's World," *Business Week,* January 19, 2004

148. Ibid.

149. Timothy Mullaney and Ronald Grover, "The Web Mogul," *Business Week,* October 13, 2003, 64.

150. Ibid.

151. "The Wal-Mart of Meat," *Business Week,* September 20, 2004, 92.

152. Dylan Rivera, "Timber Giant Faces Challenge Today," *Oregonian,* March 9, 2004, B1.

153. "The China Price" *Business Week* (special report), December 6, 2004, 105.

154. This and other information on campaign finance data and political influence can be found in two books: Charles Lewis, *The Buying of the President, 2004* (New York: Harper Collins, 2004) and Mark Green, *Selling Out: How Big Corporate Money Buys Elections, Rams Through Legislation, and Betrays our Democracy* (New York: Harper Collins, 2002).

155. Thom Hartmann, *Unequal Protection: The Rise of Corporate Dominance and the Theft of Human Rights* (New York: Rodale 2002), 204.

156. Green, *Selling Out,* 2.

157. Ibid.

158. The Federal Election Campaign Act (1971) requires disclosure of contributions for federal campaigns and was amended in 1974 placing legal limits on the campaign contributions.

159. Bakan, *The Corporation,* 104.

160. Green, *Selling Out,* 162.

161. Ibid, 169.

162. Bakan, *The Corporation,* 105.

163. Green, *Selling Out,* 184–191.

164. Ibid., 171–172.

165. Citizens for Tax Justice, Should Big Corporations Be Exempt from Helping the War On Terrorism?" September 25, 2001, "http://www.ctj.org/html/amt0901.htm.

166. Bakan, *The Corporation,* 105.

167. Robert McChesney, *The Problem of the Media: U.S. Communication Politics in the 21st Century* (New York: Monthly Review Press, 2004), 22–23.

168. Hartmann, *Unequal Protection,* 223; see also a letter to George Logan, 1816 in "Favorite Jefferson Quotes" compiled by Eyler Robert Coates, 1996 at http://etext.virginia.edu/jefferson/quotations/jeff5.htm.

169. McChesney, *The Problem,* 29.

170. Ibid., 79.

171. Ibid., 85.

172. Ibid., 83.

173. Russ Lewis, "The Press's Business . . . ," *Washington Post,* January 30, 2002, A23, http://www.washingtonpost.com/ac2/wp-dyn?pagename=article&contentId=A58605-2002Jan29&notFound=true.

174. Hyman P. Minsky, *Can 'It' happen again? Essays on Instability and Finance* (Armonk, New York: M.E. Sharpe, 1982), and "The Financial Instability Hypothesis," in M. Feldstein, ed., *The Risk of Economic Crisis* (Chicago, IL: University of Chicago Press, 1991).

175. Charles Kindelberger, *Mania, Panics and Crashes: A History of Financial Crises* (New York: John Wiley and Sons, 1978), 13.

176. *Holy Bible* (King James) St. Matthew, Chr 21: 12–13.

177. Edward Chancellor, *Devil Get the Hindmost: A History of Financial Speculation* (New York: Farrar, Strauss and Giroux, 1999) 5.

178. Joseph Penso de al Vega, Confusion de Confusiones, Quoted in Edward Chancellor, *Devil*, 11.

179. Chancellor, *Devil*, 69.

180. Harry N. Scheiber, Harold G. Vatter, and Harold U. Faulkner, *American Economic History* (New York: Harper and Row, 1976), 223.

181. Ibid; E.K. Hunt, *Property and Prophets* (New York: M.E. Sharpe, 2003), 191; John K. Galbraith, *The Great Crash* (Boston, MA: Houghton Mifflin, 1988), 2–3; and US Department of Commerce, *Statistical Abstract of the United States*, 1944–1945.

182. Scheiber et al., *American*, 224-225 , 230; Heilbroner and Singer, *Economic Transformation*, 260-261.

183. Heilbroner and Singer, *Economic Transformation*, 262.

184. Chancellor, *Devil*, 206.

185. Heilbroner, *Economic Transformation*, 262.

186. Ibid., 266.

187. Ibid., 266.

188. John Kenneth Galbraith, *The Great Crash 1929* (Boston MA: Houghton Mifflin, 1988) 20-21.

189. Ibid., 31.

190. *The Crash of 1929*, PBS Documentary, 2005.

191. Galbraith, *The Great Crash*, 52.

192. Ibid., 107.

193. "Stocks Collapse In 16,410,030-share Day, But Rally At Close Cheers Brokers; Bankers Optimistic, To Continue Aid," *New York Times*, October 29, 1929, http://www.nytimes.com/learning/general/onthisday/big/1029.html#article.

194. Ibid.

195. Gary Walton and Hugh Rockoff, *History of the American Economy* (New York: Harcourt Brace, 1990), 485.

196. *New York Review of Books* "Globalization: Stiglitz Case" by Benjamin Friedman, August 15, 2002, Vol. 49, Issue 13, 89-90.

197. See http://en.wikipedia.org/wiki/Asian_financial_crisis#Thailand for more details on these events.

198. Ibid., 97.

199. Friedman, "Globalization," 2002, 89–90.

200. Ibid., 95.

201. Ibid.

202. See transcripts from the PBS documentary *Commanding Heights*, Fall 2002.

203. Ibid.

204. John K. Galbraith, *A Short History of Financial Euphoria* (New York: Penguin Books, 1990), 4.

205. James Glassman and Kevin Hassett, *DOW 36,000: The New Strategy for Profiting from the Coming Rise in the Stock Market* (New York: Times Books, 1999), 22.

206. Doug Henwood, *Left Business Observer*, "Whose Bubble Was It?" no. 102, 2.

207. "Too Much Money," *BusinessWeek*, July 11, 2005, 62.

208. "In come the waves," The Economist.com, June 16, 2005.

209. "Housing Meltdown," *BusinessWeek*, February 11, 2008, 41.

210. "In come the waves," The Economist.com.

211. "Greenspan Heightens Warning on Risky Mortgages," *Washington Post*, July 21, 2005, D1.

212. "In come the waves," The Economist.com.

213. "Too Much Money," *Business Week*, 66.

214. *Washington Post*, July 21, 2005, D01.

215. "In come the waves," The Economist.com.

216. Javier Blas, "IMF Warns High Prices Risk Global Crisis," *Financial Times*, April 6, 2006.

217. Ibid.

218. Mary Gregor, ed. *Foundations of the Metaphysics of Morals* (London: Cambridge University Press, 1991), 429.

219. John Locke, *The Second Treatise on Civil Government* [1690] (New York: Prometheus Books, 1986), 8–9, 20.

220. Polanyi, *The Great Transformation*, 160, 178.

221. Marx and Engels, *The Communist Manifesto*, 38–40.

222. Ibid.

223. Michael Mandel, "The Real Cost of Offshoring," *Business Week*, June 18, 2007, 31.

224. See "The Global Campaign Against Poverty: Cooperating Out of Poverty," 2005, www.ica.coop/outofpoverty/documents/campaign.pdf.

225. The World Commission on Environment and Development, *Our Common Future* (Oxford University Press, 1987), ix.

226. John Holmberg, Karl-Henrik Robert, and Karl-Erik Eriksson, "Socio-Ecological Principles For A Sustainable Society," in Robert Costanza, Olman Segura, and Juan Martinez-Alier, eds., *Getting Down To Earth: Practical Applications of Ecological Economics* (Washington, D.C.: Island Press, 1994), 17.

227. Edward O. Wilson, "Threats to Biodiversity," *Scientific American*, September 1989, 108-116.

228. See http://www.ams.usda.gov/nop/archive/OFPA.html.

229. Diane Brady, "The Organic Myth," *Business Week*, October 16, 2006, 51–56.

230. Ibid.

231. Ibid.

232. Ibid.

233. Ibid.

234. Ibid.

235. See www.ewg.org, www.foodfirst.org, and www.geaction.org.

236. See www.sweatshopwatch.org.

237. The relative costs of PV, wind, and conventional electricity cost data comes from the U.S. Department of Energy website: www.nrel.gov/docs/fyosti/35297.pdf.

238. See Andrew Blakers, Klaus Weber, and Vernie Everett "SOLAR ELECTRICITY," Centre for Sustainable Energy Systems Australian National University, *Outlook*, 2006, Canberra, 0200 at http://www.abareconomics.com/outlook/speeches/papers/Blakers,A-ClimateII.doc.

239. Ibid.

240. Elizabeth Rosenthal, "Biofuels Deemed a Greenhouse Threat," *New York Times*, February 8, 2008.

241. Editors of *E/Environmental Magazine*, *Green Living: The E Magazine Handbook for Living Lightly on the Earth* (New York: Plume, 2005), 109.

242. Jeanne and Dick Roy, "Deep Sustainability" in *Earth Matters: The Newsletter of the Northwest Earth Institute* 12, no. 1, 1–2.

243. Elgin, "Little Green Lies," 45-52.

244. William F. Ogburn, *On Culture and Social Change* (Chicago, IL: University of Chicago Press, 1964), 86–95

INDEX